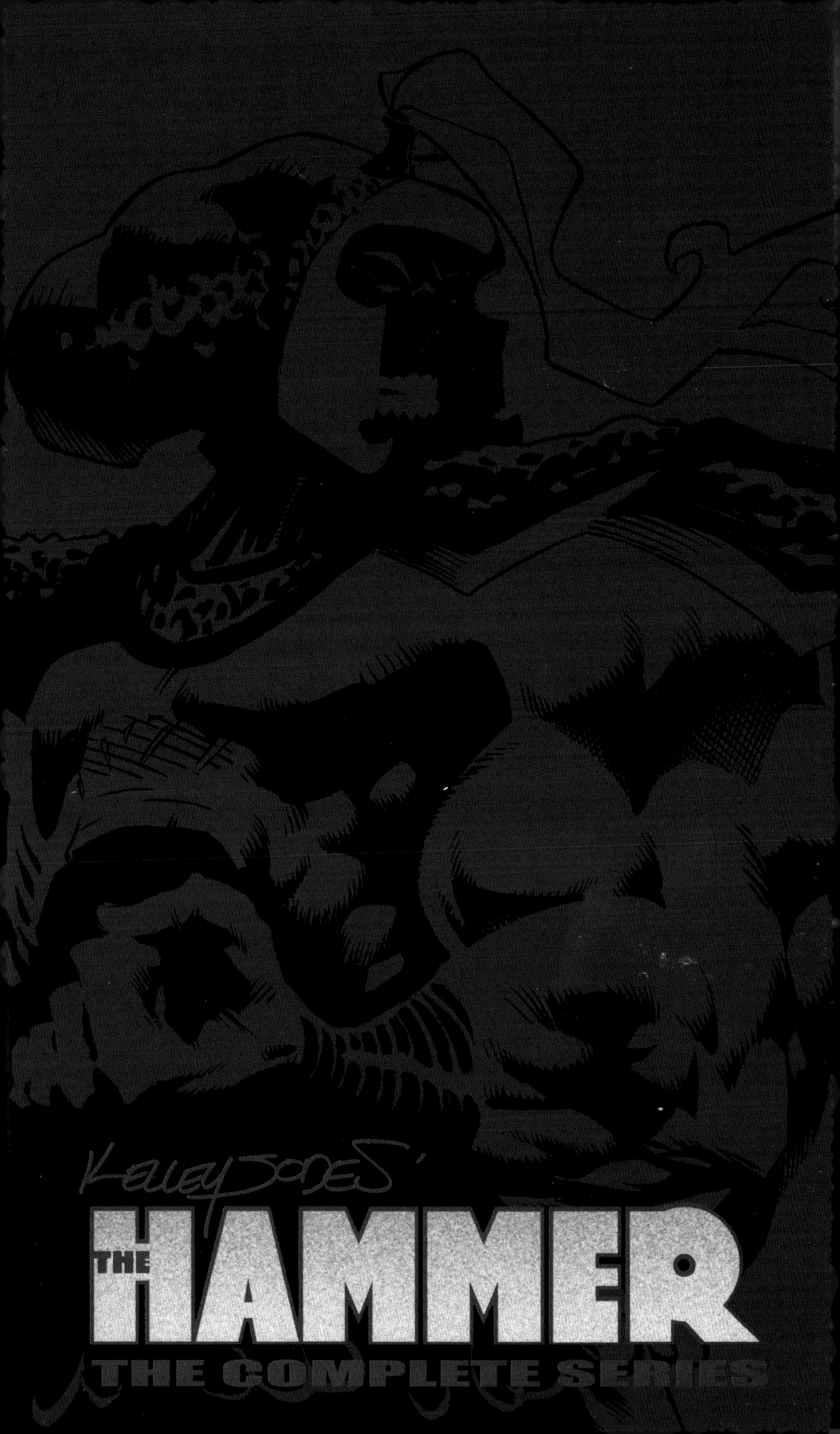
Kelley Jones'
THE HAMMER
THE COMPLETE SERIES

Story and Art by Kelley Jones
Colors by Les Dorscheid
Letters by Ken Bruzenak
Original Series Edits by Scott Allie
and Barbara Randall Kesel

Collection Edits by Justin Eisinger & Alonzo Simon
Cover Colors by Michelle Madsen
Collection Design by Clyde Grapa

The Hammer created by Kelley Jones

ISBN: 978-1-63140-125-1

17 16 15 14   1 2 3 4

Ted Adams, CEO & Publisher
Greg Goldstein, President & COO
Robbie Robbins, EVP/Sr. Graphic Artist
Chris Ryall, Chief Creative Officer/Editor-in-Chief
Matthew Ruzicka, CPA, Chief Financial Officer
Alan Payne, VP of Sales
Dirk Wood, VP of Marketing
Lorelei Bunjes, VP of Digital Services
Jeff Webber, VP of Digital Publishing & Business Development

www.IDWPUBLISHING.com
IDW founded by Ted Adams, Alex Garner, Kris Oprisko, and Robbie Robbins

Facebook: facebook.com/idwpublishing
Twitter: @idwpublishing
YouTube: youtube.com/idwpublishing
Instagram: instagram.com/idwpublishing
deviantART: idwpublishing.deviantart.com
Pinterest: pinterest.com/idwpublishing/idw-staff-faves

The Thing at the Drawing Board

Anyone who enjoys Kelley Jones' work enough to read the introduction to such a bizarre collection of his comics knows that he is a singular talent. And I doubt he'll mind me saying that he is also not the most popular artist in comics. In fact, lots of people hate his work. Hate it! His linework is certainly unmistakable—deeply saturated with atmosphere and black inkiness, especially when he inks his own work, as he does on *The Hammer*.

But where other people (let's be honest, they're stupid) see grotesque lines and unrealistic distortions, fans like you and I see nothing but expressive genius. Soaking in the abundance of deeply deformed ideas that are packed into these pages—that's what we're here for. The bulging weirdness of Conan's musculature. Freaky Batman and the too-long ears of his mask. The giant walking vagina monster/succubus from Steve Niles' *Last Train to Deadsville*. (I edited that script—never was there any mention of the succubus turning into a giant vagina. Not even a hint. That was all Kelley!). I was also his editor on the only other entirely creator-owned comic Kelley has done—the absurdly terrifying *The 13th Son*. The titular character of that book is one of the most God-awful creations you'd ever want to meet—a 10 foot-tall creature with one glowing red eye who rummages through graves for bone-meat pickins after savagely raping the village maidens in an attempt to impregnate them with seeds that will turn into the most powerful monster ever. And that character is the protagonist!

This is why we love Kelley Jones. Because his ideas just don't know when to stop—the more ludicrous and horrific and cartoonish, the better. Especially when it's a horror story he's telling. And he can draw the hell out of whatever he imagines, so why not see these ridiculously monstrous ideas through to the end?

If you are an editor working on his books, talking on the phone is The Thing with Kelley. Have you ever heard the trope about the pent-up artist working in solitary conditions while he draws deranged scenarios of bloodlust and depravity? That's not a trope. That artist is Kelley! So when it comes time for an editor to give Kelley a call to discuss deadlines, or to choose a colorist for a new project, one quickly realizes those calls are the only human contact Kelley has had outside of his immediate family in weeks. Months, maybe! By the time that phone finally rings, and Kelley's gnarled, black-stained hands reach out for the receiver, you know he's been salivating alone in the dark just waiting to hear a human voice that's not emanating from the TV screen. Or from the hole cut into the door of his pen—I mean office!—through which his family feeds him bowls of fetid gruel to keep the unhinged aberration slaving away for endless hours.

All this considered, it's no wonder Kelley draws at least a smidge of inspiration from that other beloved and hermetic horror icon, H.P. Lovecraft. In fact, it's not hard to picture Kelley—if one can indeed picture something as unknowably miscreant as that face!—living the life of Charles Dexter Ward, or more probably, a character like Erich Zann, who plays his cursed viol in solitude for insanely nefarious purposes. Picture Kelley in a scene like that, all lumps and pustules, composing his vile and forbidden works in tribute to something far more terrible than his own putrid self. There might be a decomposing body on ice in a vat somewhere in the room. There are most certainly brains in jars lining every shelf. And dare you enter that malodorous chamber, or dial up that northern California area code, who knows what raving abominations will be unleashed?

This is what Kelley would have you believe, anyway. But the truth is, he is almost not completely abnormal. And he does truly flourish during those occasional breaks to converse with other humans after untold hours spent hunched at the drawing board. Those calls reveal everything, and they are bonkers!

It's during these hours-long, utterly ridiculous conversations with Kelley that you'll learn everything that matters about his art; what he thinks is funny, what he thinks is gross, what he thinks is brilliant. He'll tell you why he wants his comics to be colored like Mario Bava films, and why he thinks the female body is the best, ickiest thing around. He will spare no details. He will recommend 15 horror movies you've never heard of. He will tell you all about his unusual affection for *Star Trek* Christmas tree ornaments. And somewhere in the midst of all of this, his very essence will be revealed, and you will know him. This is my long-winded way of saying that it takes weird people to create weird stories, and you won't find a more bizarre story on any bookshelf than *The Hammer*. I would try to explain a bit more about the story here, but I truly believe it's better to go into this a little cold. Not keep-your-undead-self-alive-in-a-tub-of-ice cold, but almost. Gird your eyeballs, and your sanity, for a cosmic trip through koo-koo land horror fans, because you are about to embark on an adventure that even H.P. Lovecraft would have a hard time describing.

Shawna Gore
Portland, Oregon

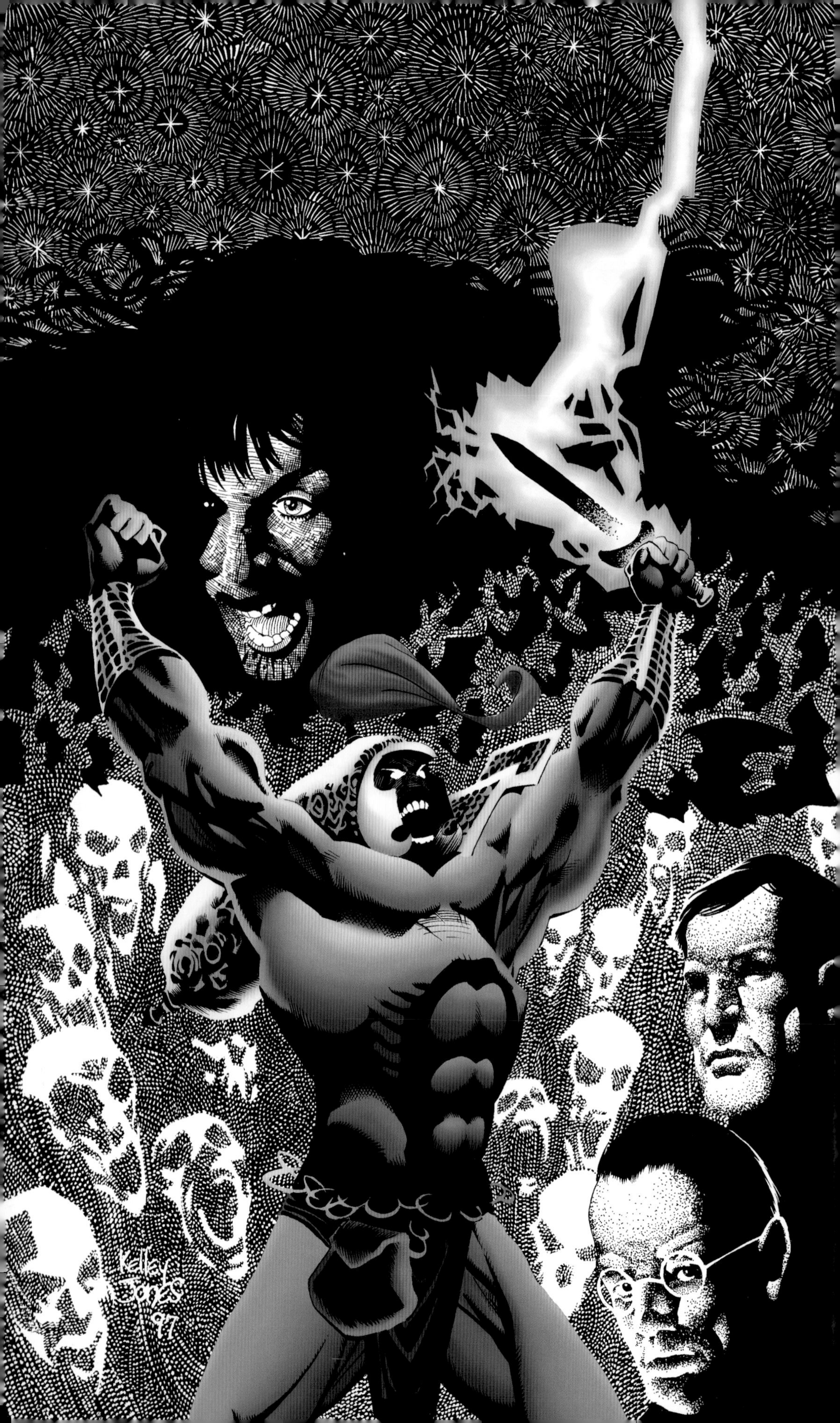
Kelley Jones '97

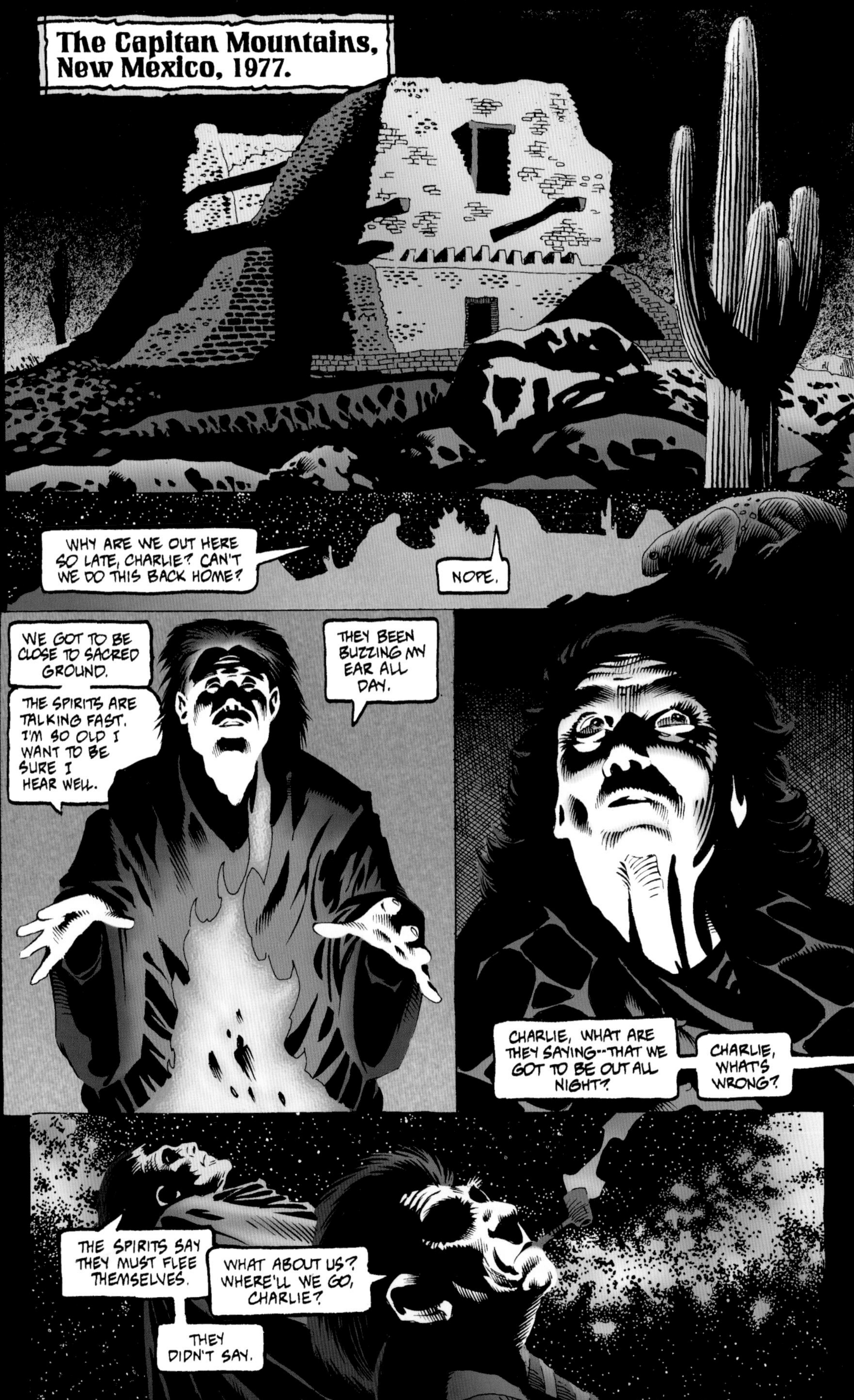
The Capitan Mountains, New Mexico, 1977.
WHY ARE WE OUT HERE SO LATE, CHARLIE? CAN'T WE DO THIS BACK HOME?
NOPE.
WE GOT TO BE CLOSE TO SACRED GROUND.
THE SPIRITS ARE TALKING FAST. I'M SO OLD I WANT TO BE SURE I HEAR WELL.
THEY BEEN BUZZING MY EAR ALL DAY.
CHARLIE, WHAT ARE THEY SAYING--THAT WE GOT TO BE OUT ALL NIGHT?
CHARLIE, WHAT'S WRONG?
THE SPIRITS SAY THEY MUST FLEE THEMSELVES.
WHAT ABOUT US? WHERE'LL WE GO, CHARLIE?
THEY DIDN'T SAY.

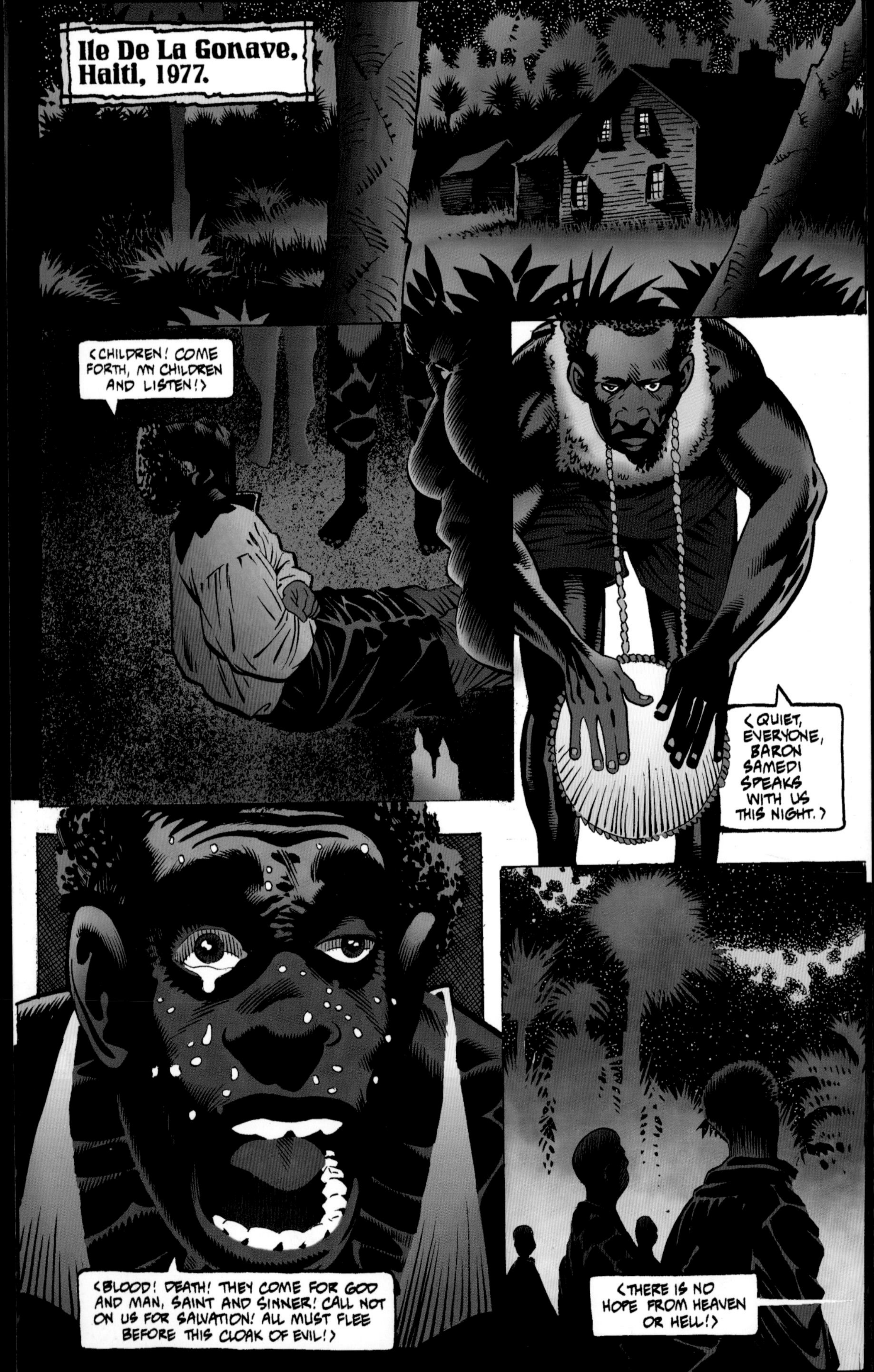
Ile De La Gonave, Haiti, 1977.
<CHILDREN! COME FORTH, MY CHILDREN AND LISTEN!>
<QUIET, EVERYONE, BARON SAMEDI SPEAKS WITH US THIS NIGHT.>
<BLOOD! DEATH! THEY COME FOR GOD AND MAN, SAINT AND SINNER! CALL NOT ON US FOR SALVATION! ALL MUST FLEE BEFORE THIS CLOAK OF EVIL!>
<THERE IS NO HOPE FROM HEAVEN OR HELL!>

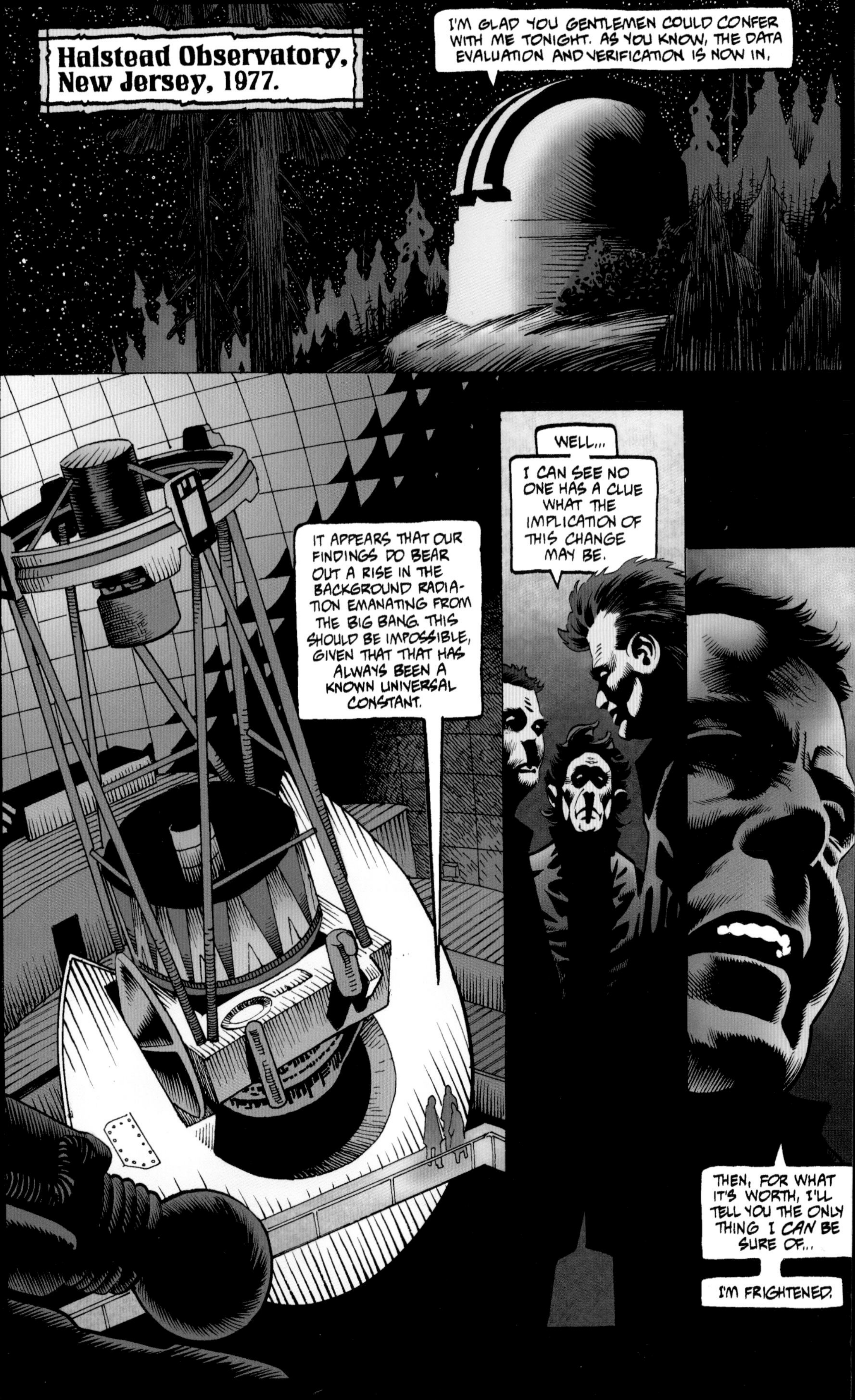
Halstead Observatory, New Jersey, 1977.
I'M GLAD YOU GENTLEMEN COULD CONFER WITH ME TONIGHT. AS YOU KNOW, THE DATA EVALUATION AND VERIFICATION IS NOW IN.
IT APPEARS THAT OUR FINDINGS DO BEAR OUT A RISE IN THE BACKGROUND RADIATION EMANATING FROM THE BIG BANG. THIS SHOULD BE IMPOSSIBLE, GIVEN THAT THAT HAS ALWAYS BEEN A KNOWN UNIVERSAL CONSTANT.
WELL...
I CAN SEE NO ONE HAS A CLUE WHAT THE IMPLICATION OF THIS CHANGE MAY BE.
THEN, FOR WHAT IT'S WORTH, I'LL TELL YOU THE ONLY THING I *CAN* BE SURE OF...
I'M FRIGHTENED.

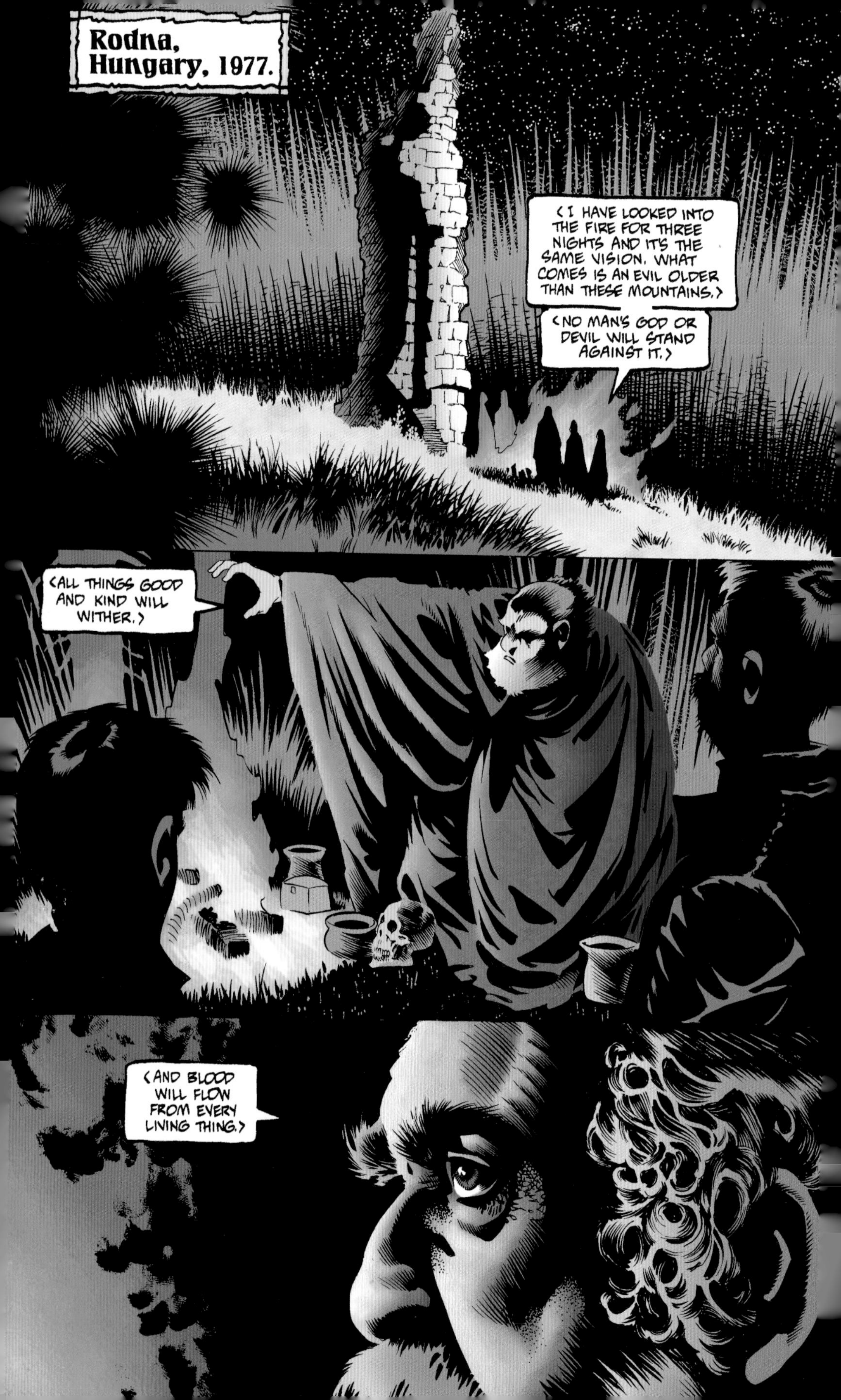
Rodna, Hungary, 1977.
<I HAVE LOOKED INTO THE FIRE FOR THREE NIGHTS AND IT'S THE SAME VISION. WHAT COMES IS AN EVIL OLDER THAN THESE MOUNTAINS.>
<NO MAN'S GOD OR DEVIL WILL STAND AGAINST IT.>
<ALL THINGS GOOD AND KIND WILL WITHER.>
<AND BLOOD WILL FLOW FROM EVERY LIVING THING.>

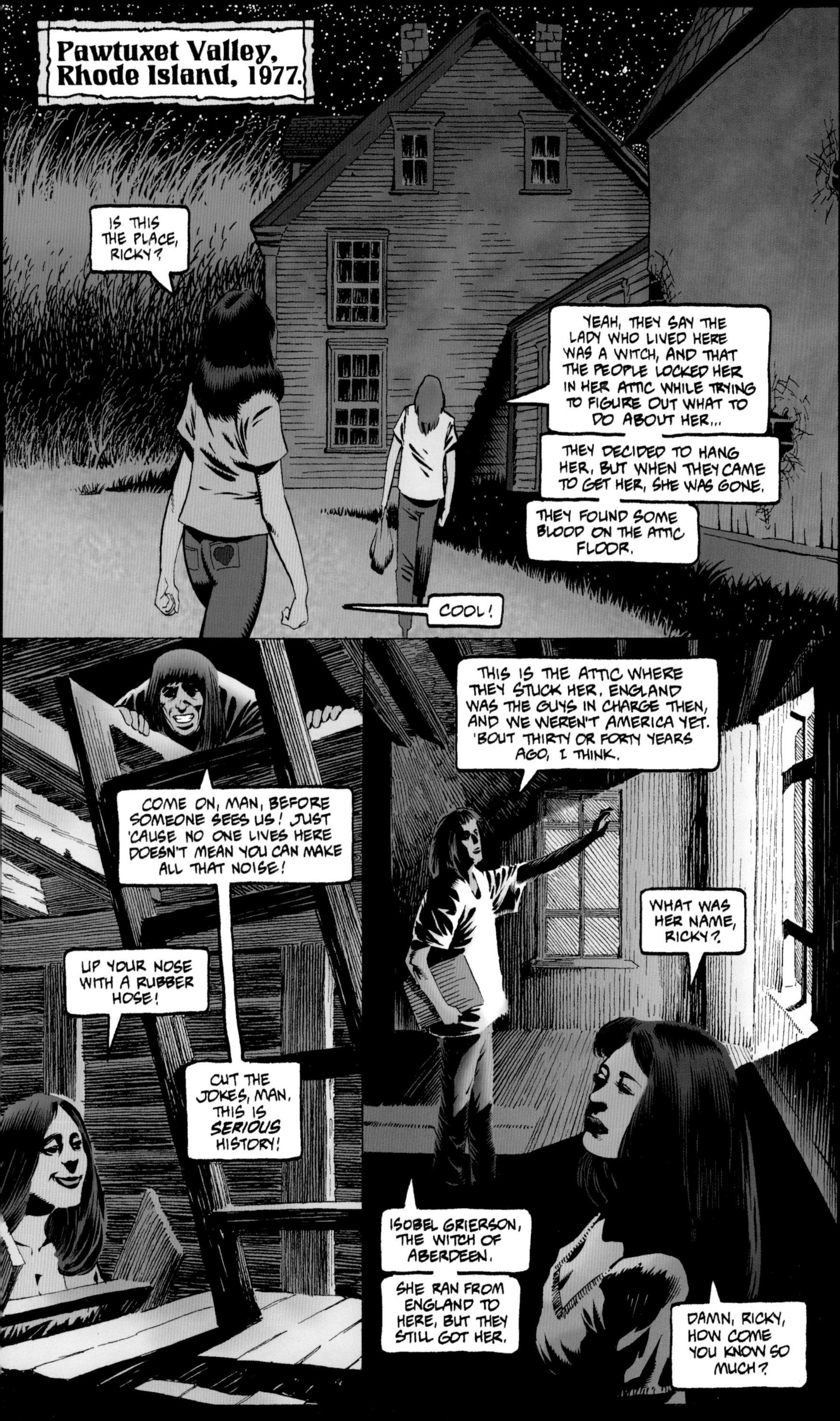

Pawtuxet Valley, Rhode Island, 1977.
IS THIS THE PLACE, RICKY?
YEAH, THEY SAY THE LADY WHO LIVED HERE WAS A WITCH, AND THAT THE PEOPLE LOCKED HER IN HER ATTIC WHILE TRYING TO FIGURE OUT WHAT TO DO ABOUT HER...
THEY DECIDED TO HANG HER, BUT WHEN THEY CAME TO GET HER, SHE WAS GONE.
THEY FOUND SOME BLOOD ON THE ATTIC FLOOR.
COOL!
COME ON, MAN, BEFORE SOMEONE SEES US! JUST 'CAUSE NO ONE LIVES HERE DOESN'T MEAN YOU CAN MAKE ALL THAT NOISE!
UP YOUR NOSE WITH A RUBBER HOSE!
CUT THE JOKES, MAN. THIS IS SERIOUS HISTORY!
THIS IS THE ATTIC WHERE THEY STUCK HER. ENGLAND WAS THE GUYS IN CHARGE THEN, AND WE WEREN'T AMERICA YET. 'BOUT THIRTY OR FORTY YEARS AGO, I THINK.
WHAT WAS HER NAME, RICKY?
ISOBEL GRIERSON, THE WITCH OF ABERDEEN.
SHE RAN FROM ENGLAND TO HERE, BUT THEY STILL GOT HER.
DAMN, RICKY, HOW COME YOU KNOW SO MUCH?

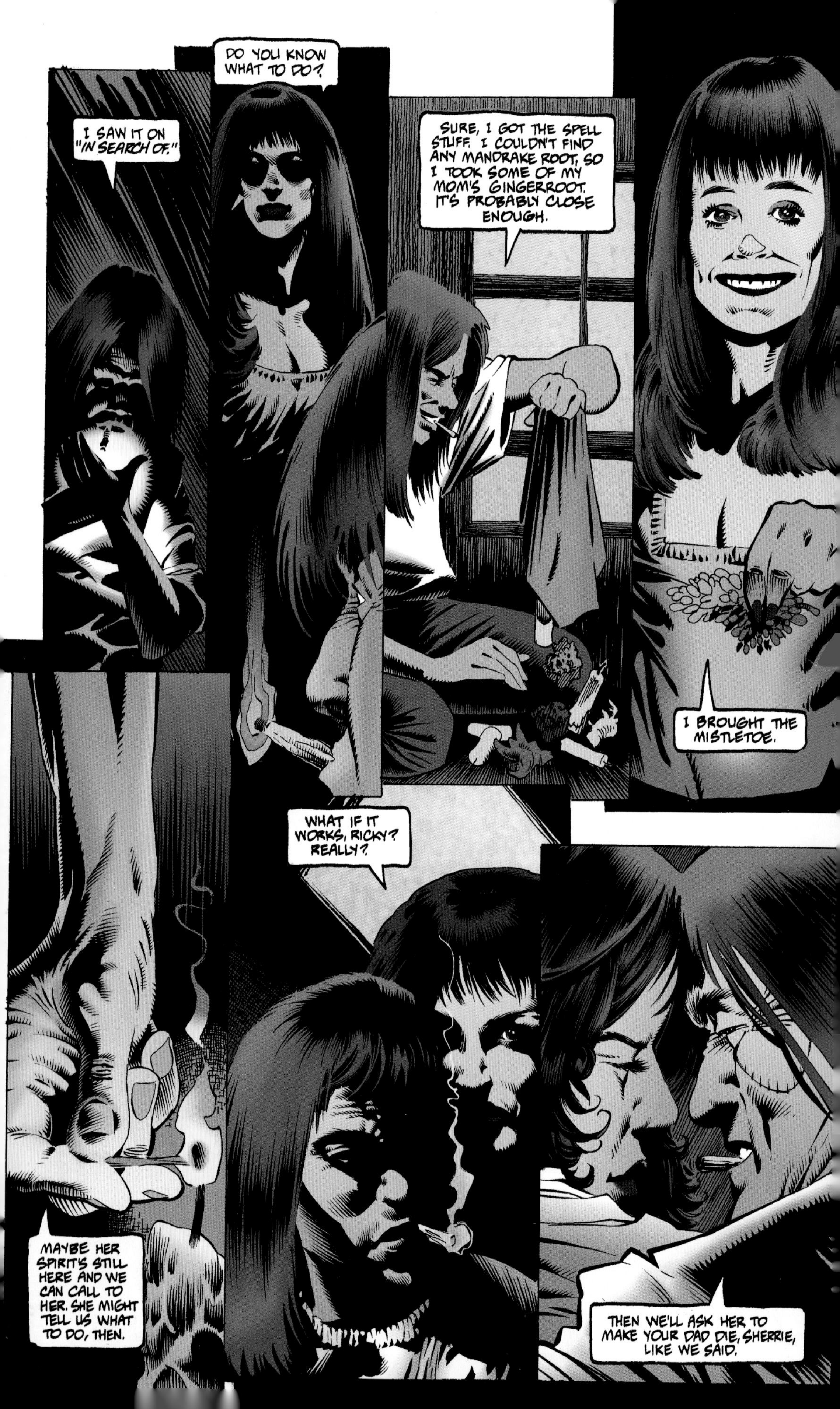
I SAW IT ON "IN SEARCH OF."
DO YOU KNOW WHAT TO DO?
SURE, I GOT THE SPELL STUFF. I COULDN'T FIND ANY MANDRAKE ROOT, SO I TOOK SOME OF MY MOM'S GINGERROOT. IT'S PROBABLY CLOSE ENOUGH.
I BROUGHT THE MISTLETOE.
MAYBE HER SPIRIT'S STILL HERE AND WE CAN CALL TO HER. SHE MIGHT TELL US WHAT TO DO, THEN.
WHAT IF IT WORKS, RICKY? REALLY?
THEN WE'LL ASK HER TO MAKE YOUR DAD DIE, SHERRIE, LIKE WE SAID.

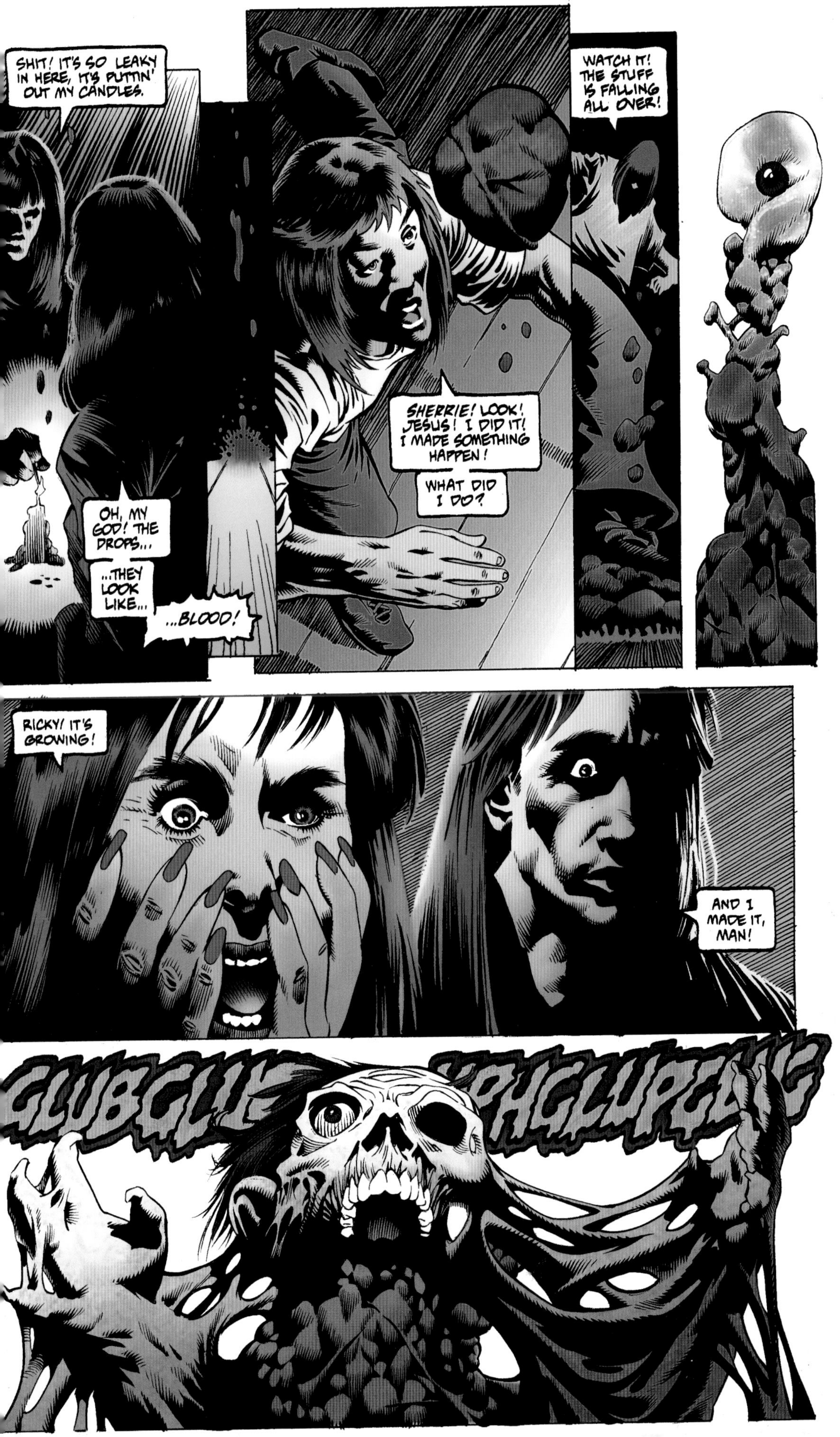
SHIT! IT'S SO LEAKY IN HERE, IT'S PUTTIN' OUT MY CANDLES.
OH, MY GOD! THE DROPS...
...THEY LOOK LIKE...
...BLOOD!
SHERRIE! LOOK! JESUS! I DID IT! I MADE SOMETHING HAPPEN!
WHAT DID I DO?
WATCH IT! THE STUFF IS FALLING ALL OVER!
RICKY! IT'S GROWING!
AND I MADE IT, MAN!

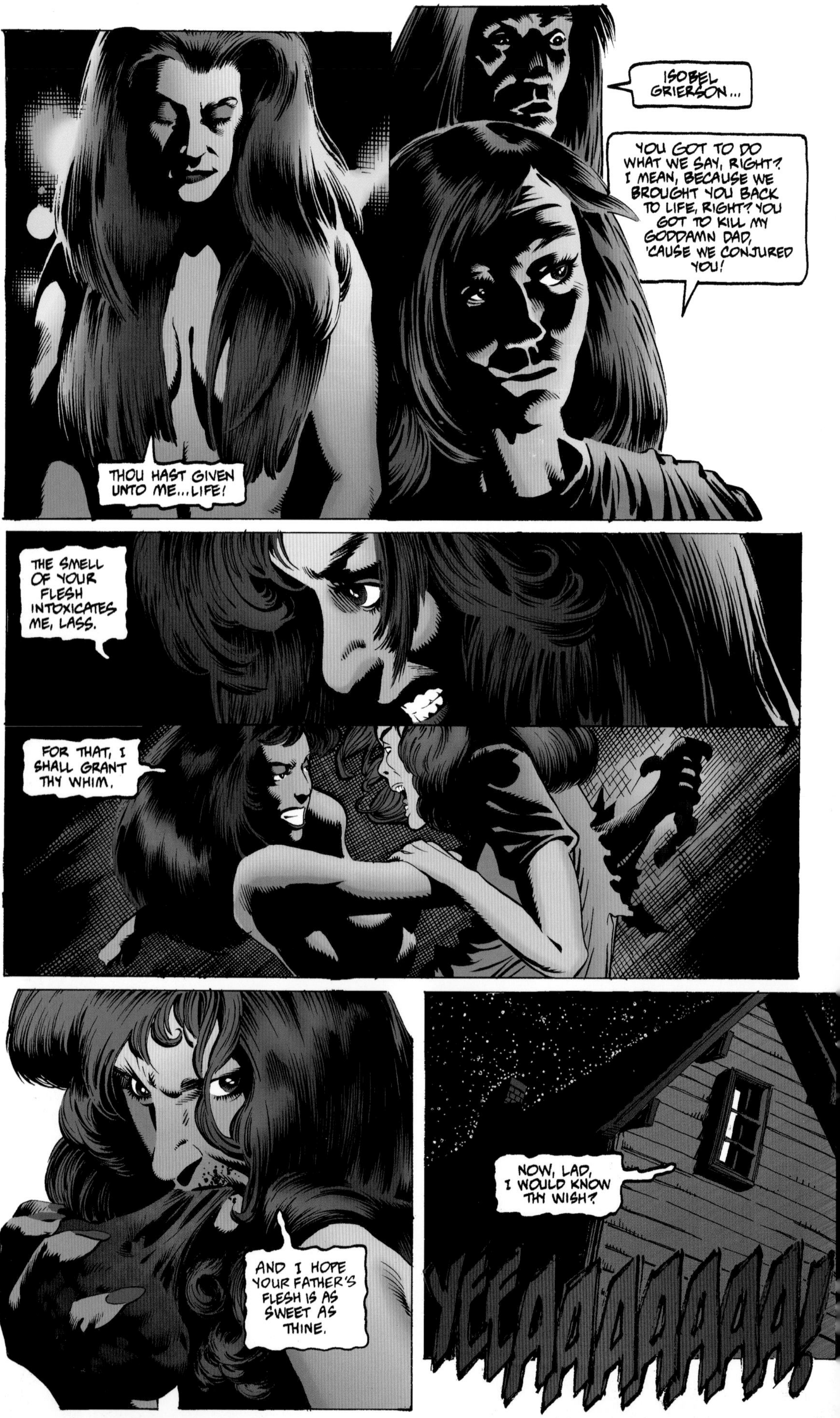
THOU HAST GIVEN UNTO ME...LIFE!
ISOBEL GRIERSON...
YOU GOT TO DO WHAT WE SAY, RIGHT? I MEAN, BECAUSE WE BROUGHT YOU BACK TO LIFE, RIGHT? YOU GOT TO KILL MY GODDAMN DAD, 'CAUSE WE CONJURED YOU!
THE SMELL OF YOUR FLESH INTOXICATES ME, LASS.
FOR THAT, I SHALL GRANT THY WHIM.
AND I HOPE YOUR FATHER'S FLESH IS AS SWEET AS THINE.
NOW, LAD, I WOULD KNOW THY WISH?
YEEAAAAAAAA!

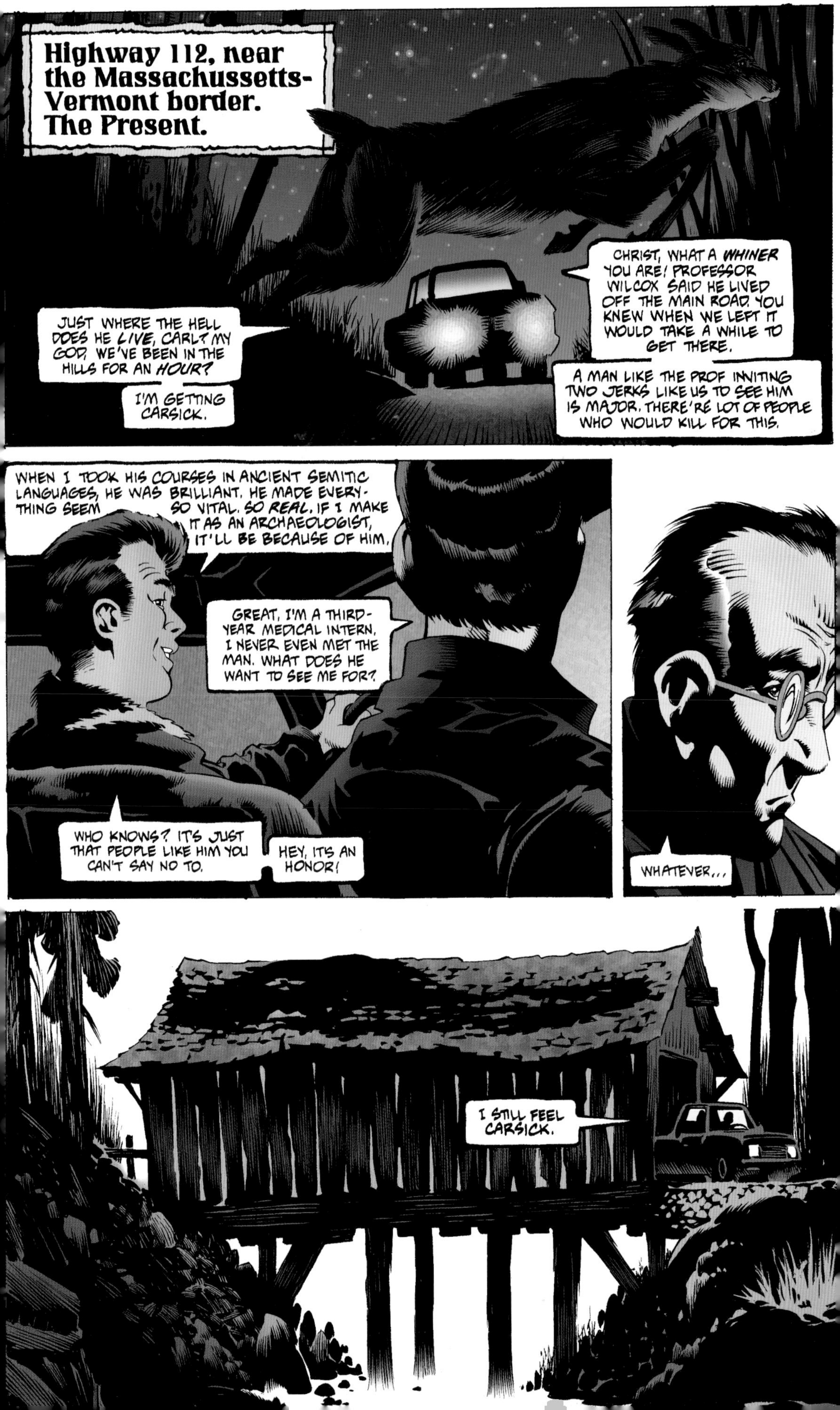

Highway 112, near the Massachussetts-Vermont border. The Present.
JUST WHERE THE HELL DOES HE LIVE, CARL? MY GOD, WE'VE BEEN IN THE HILLS FOR AN HOUR?
I'M GETTING CARSICK.
CHRIST, WHAT A WHINER YOU ARE! PROFESSOR WILCOX SAID HE LIVED OFF THE MAIN ROAD. YOU KNEW WHEN WE LEFT IT WOULD TAKE A WHILE TO GET THERE.
A MAN LIKE THE PROF INVITING TWO JERKS LIKE US TO SEE HIM IS MAJOR. THERE'RE LOT OF PEOPLE WHO WOULD KILL FOR THIS.
WHEN I TOOK HIS COURSES IN ANCIENT SEMITIC LANGUAGES, HE WAS BRILLIANT. HE MADE EVERY-THING SEEM SO VITAL. SO REAL. IF I MAKE IT AS AN ARCHAEOLOGIST, IT'LL BE BECAUSE OF HIM.
GREAT, I'M A THIRD-YEAR MEDICAL INTERN. I NEVER EVEN MET THE MAN. WHAT DOES HE WANT TO SEE ME FOR?
WHO KNOWS? IT'S JUST THAT PEOPLE LIKE HIM YOU CAN'T SAY NO TO.
HEY, IT'S AN HONOR!
WHATEVER...
I STILL FEEL CARSICK.

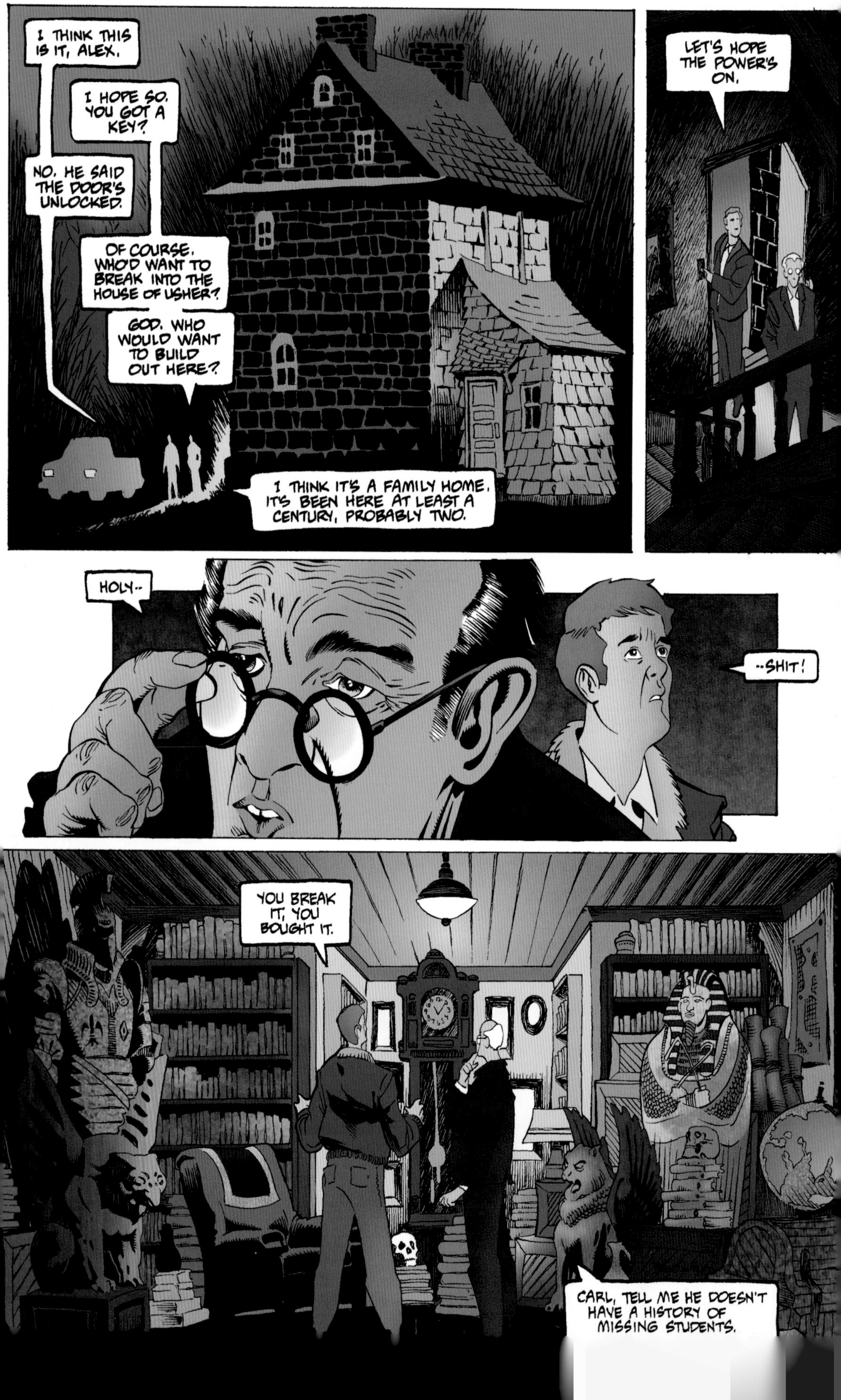
I THINK THIS IS IT, ALEX.
I HOPE SO. YOU GOT A KEY?
NO. HE SAID THE DOOR'S UNLOCKED.
OF COURSE. WHO'D WANT TO BREAK INTO THE HOUSE OF USHER?
GOD. WHO WOULD WANT TO BUILD OUT HERE?
I THINK IT'S A FAMILY HOME. IT'S BEEN HERE AT LEAST A CENTURY, PROBABLY TWO.
LET'S HOPE THE POWER'S ON.
HOLY--
--SHIT!
YOU BREAK IT, YOU BOUGHT IT.
CARL, TELL ME HE DOESN'T HAVE A HISTORY OF MISSING STUDENTS.

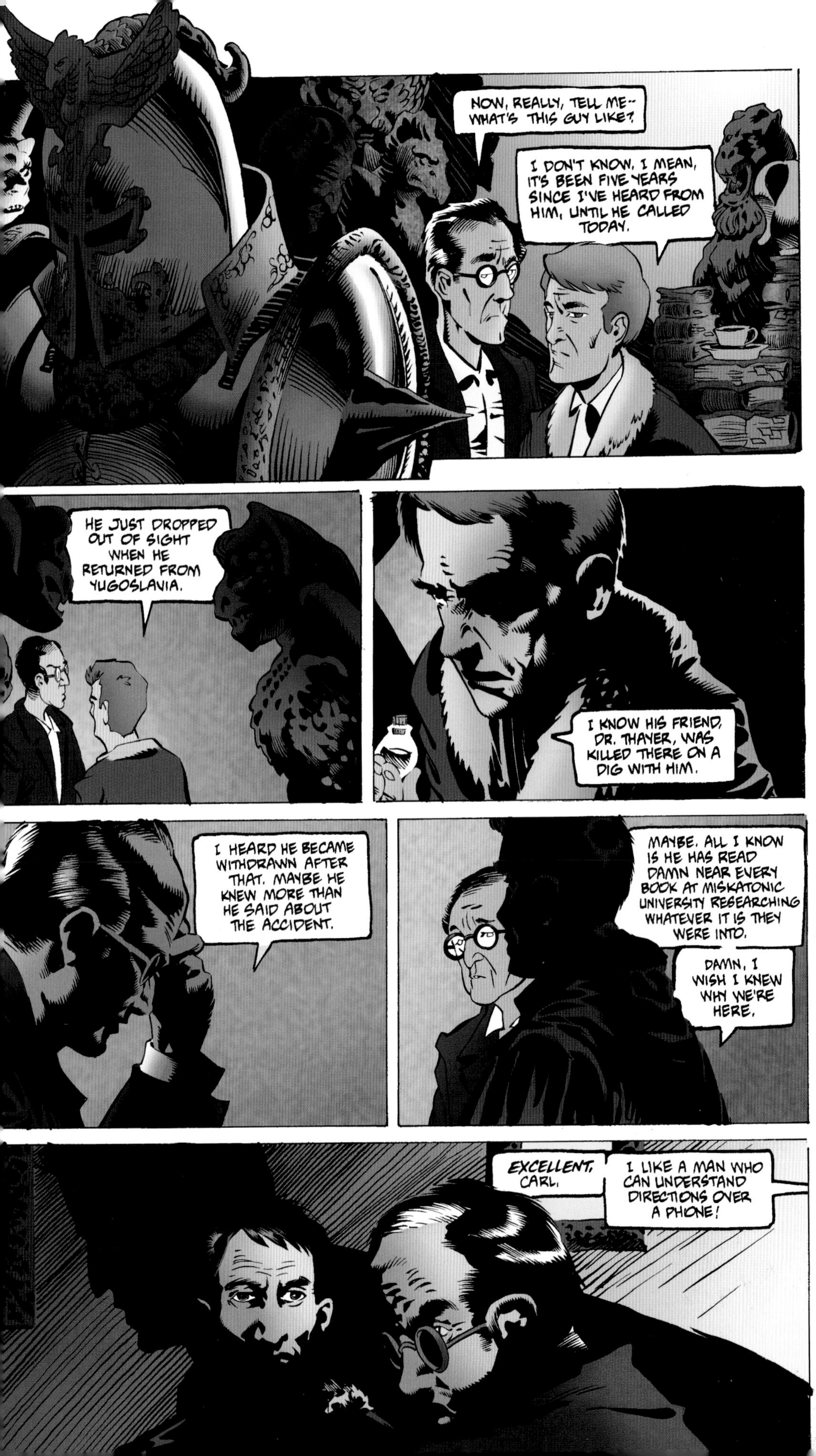
NOW, REALLY, TELL ME-- WHAT'S THIS GUY LIKE?
I DON'T KNOW. I MEAN, IT'S BEEN FIVE YEARS SINCE I'VE HEARD FROM HIM, UNTIL HE CALLED TODAY.
HE JUST DROPPED OUT OF SIGHT WHEN HE RETURNED FROM YUGOSLAVIA.
I KNOW HIS FRIEND, DR. THAYER, WAS KILLED THERE ON A DIG WITH HIM.
I HEARD HE BECAME WITHDRAWN AFTER THAT. MAYBE HE KNEW MORE THAN HE SAID ABOUT THE ACCIDENT.
MAYBE. ALL I KNOW IS HE HAS READ DAMN NEAR EVERY BOOK AT MISKATONIC UNIVERSITY RESEARCHING WHATEVER IT IS THEY WERE INTO.
DAMN, I WISH I KNEW WHY WE'RE HERE.
EXCELLENT, CARL.
I LIKE A MAN WHO CAN UNDERSTAND DIRECTIONS OVER A PHONE!

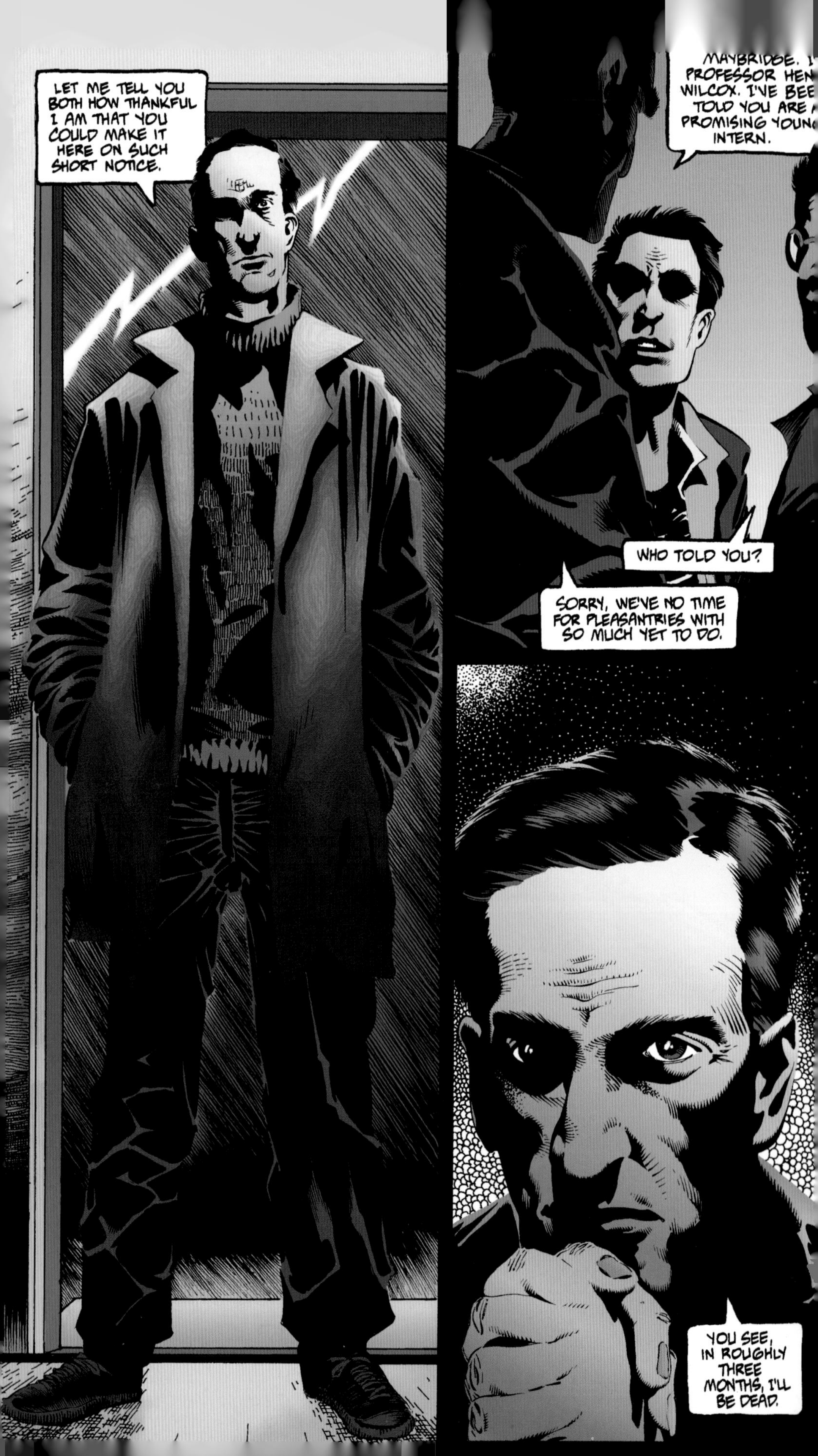
LET ME TELL YOU BOTH HOW THANKFUL I AM THAT YOU COULD MAKE IT HERE ON SUCH SHORT NOTICE.
MAYBRIDGE. I' PROFESSOR HEN WILCOX. I'VE BEE TOLD YOU ARE PROMISING YOUN INTERN.
WHO TOLD YOU?
SORRY, WE'VE NO TIME FOR PLEASANTRIES WITH SO MUCH YET TO DO.
YOU SEE, IN ROUGHLY THREE MONTHS, I'LL BE DEAD.

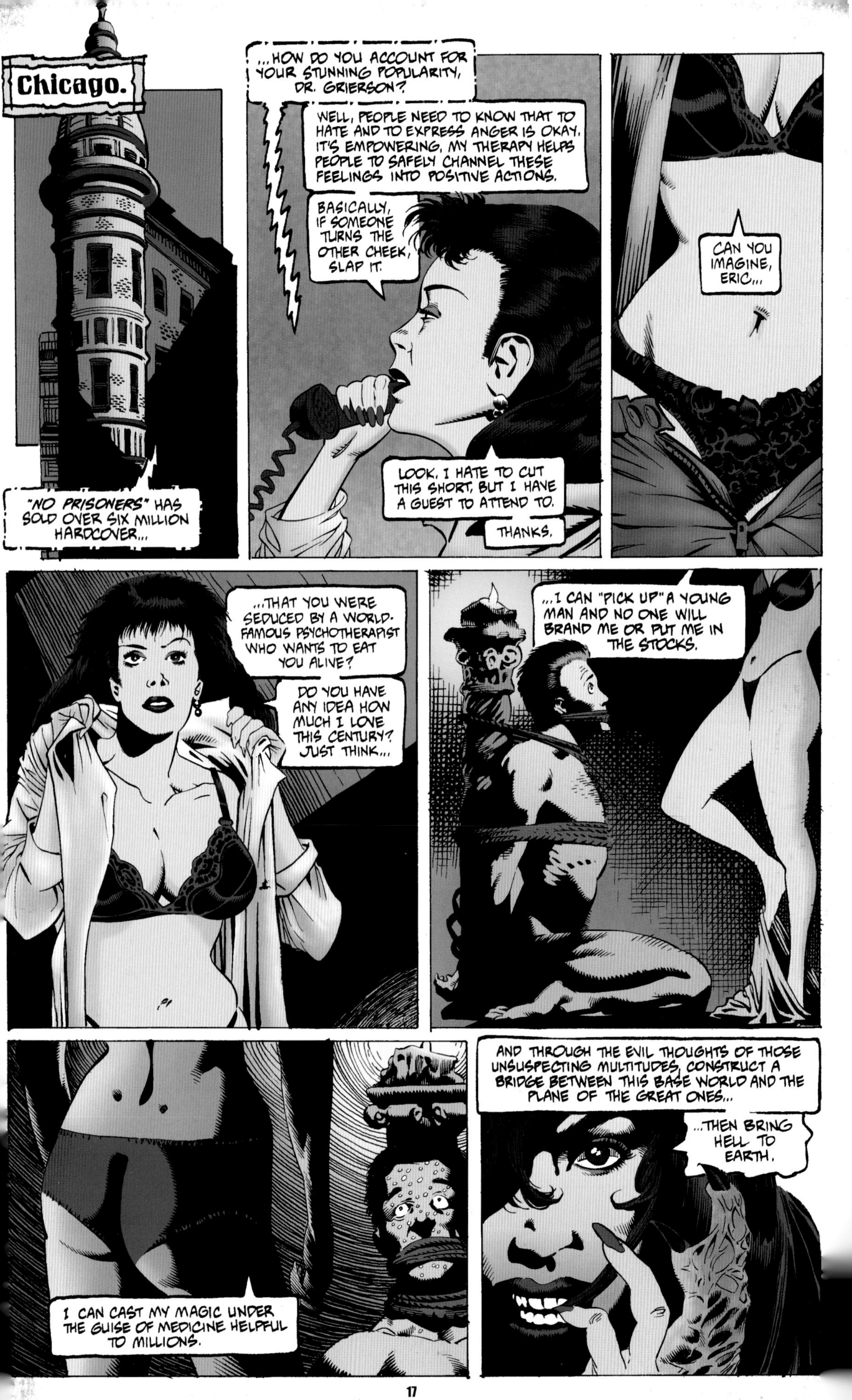
Chicago.
"NO PRISONERS" HAS SOLD OVER SIX MILLION HARDCOVER...
...HOW DO YOU ACCOUNT FOR YOUR STUNNING POPULARITY, DR. GRIERSON?
WELL, PEOPLE NEED TO KNOW THAT TO HATE AND TO EXPRESS ANGER IS OKAY. IT'S EMPOWERING. MY THERAPY HELPS PEOPLE TO SAFELY CHANNEL THESE FEELINGS INTO POSITIVE ACTIONS.
BASICALLY, IF SOMEONE TURNS THE OTHER CHEEK, SLAP IT.
LOOK, I HATE TO CUT THIS SHORT, BUT I HAVE A GUEST TO ATTEND TO.
THANKS.
CAN YOU IMAGINE, ERIC...
...THAT YOU WERE SEDUCED BY A WORLD-FAMOUS PSYCHOTHERAPIST WHO WANTS TO EAT YOU ALIVE?
DO YOU HAVE ANY IDEA HOW MUCH I LOVE THIS CENTURY? JUST THINK...
...I CAN "PICK UP" A YOUNG MAN AND NO ONE WILL BRAND ME OR PUT ME IN THE STOCKS.
I CAN CAST MY MAGIC UNDER THE GUISE OF MEDICINE HELPFUL TO MILLIONS.
AND THROUGH THE EVIL THOUGHTS OF THOSE UNSUSPECTING MULTITUDES, CONSTRUCT A BRIDGE BETWEEN THIS BASE WORLD AND THE PLANE OF THE GREAT ONES...
...THEN BRING HELL TO EARTH.

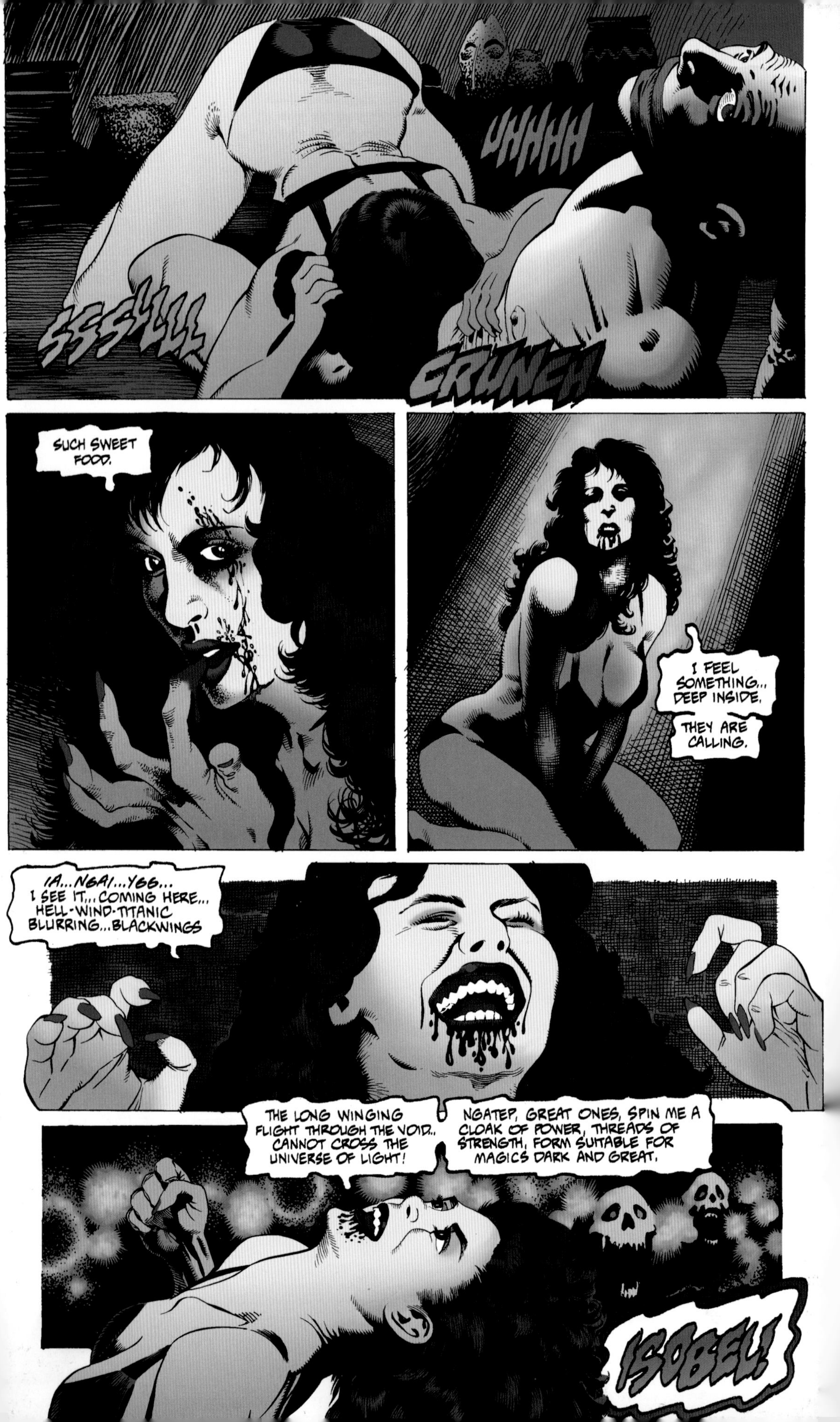
UHHHH
SSSHLLL
CRUNCH
SUCH SWEET FOOD.
I FEEL SOMETHING... DEEP INSIDE.
THEY ARE CALLING.
IA... NGAI... YGG... I SEE IT... COMING HERE... HELL-WIND-TITANIC BLURRING... BLACKWINGS
THE LONG WINGING FLIGHT THROUGH THE VOID.. CANNOT CROSS THE UNIVERSE OF LIGHT!
NGATEP, GREAT ONES, SPIN ME A CLOAK OF POWER, THREADS OF STRENGTH, FORM SUITABLE FOR MAGICS DARK AND GREAT.
ISOBEL!

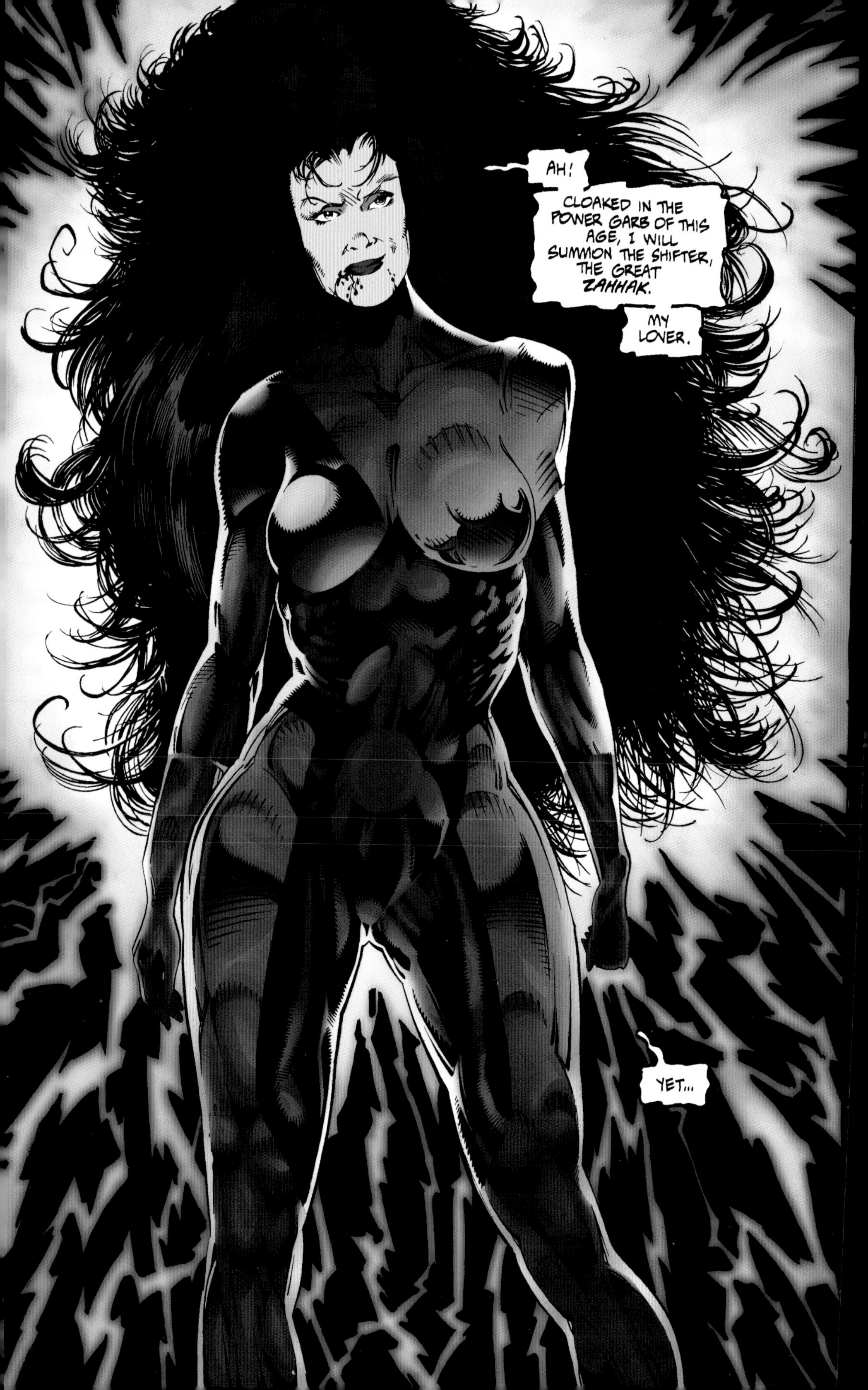
AH!
CLOAKED IN THE POWER GARB OF THIS AGE, I WILL SUMMON THE SHIFTER, THE GREAT ZAHHAK.
MY LOVER.
YET...

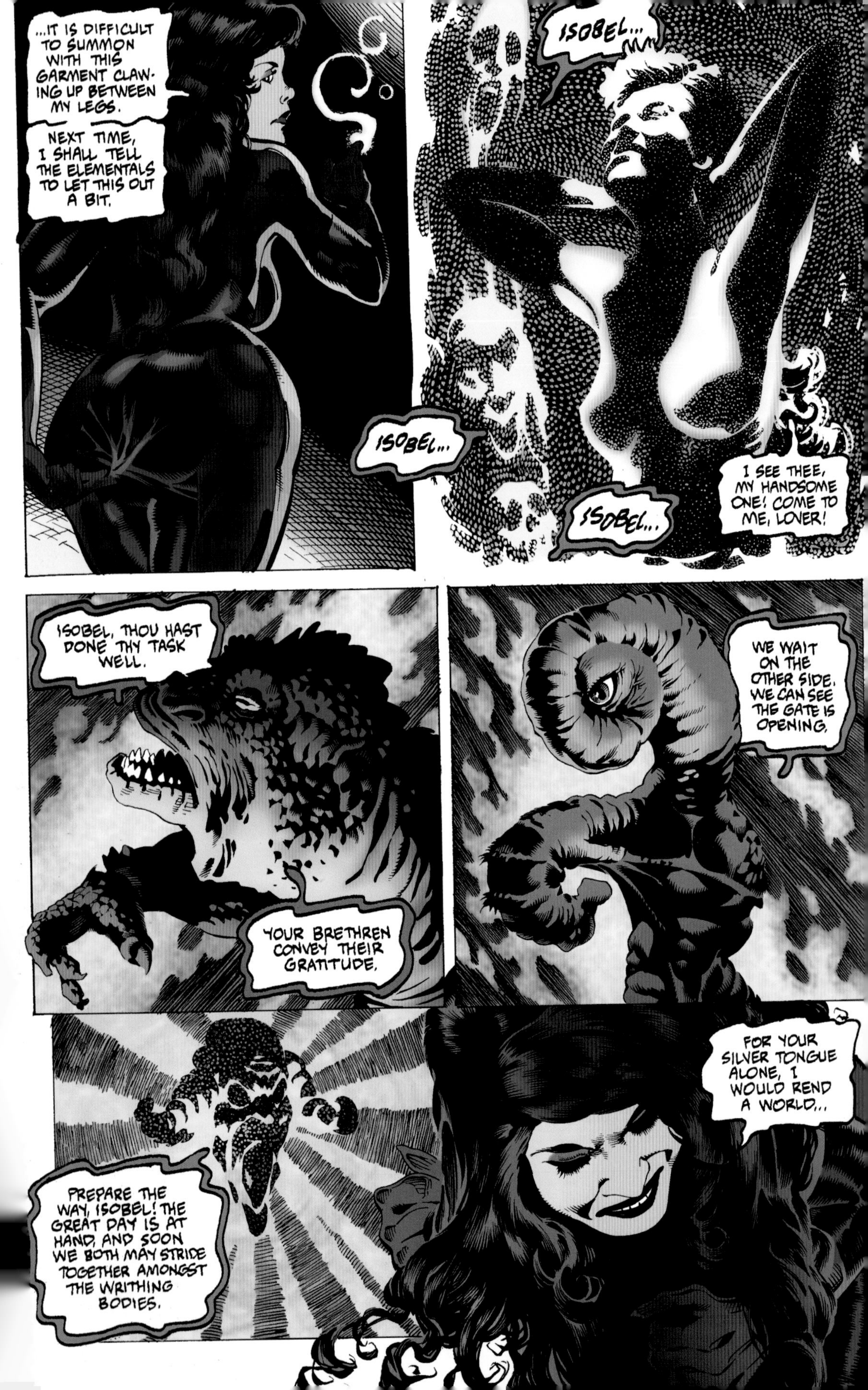
...IT IS DIFFICULT TO SUMMON WITH THIS GARMENT CLAWING UP BETWEEN MY LEGS.
NEXT TIME, I SHALL TELL THE ELEMENTALS TO LET THIS OUT A BIT.
ISOBEL...
ISOBEL...
ISOBEL...
I SEE THEE, MY HANDSOME ONE! COME TO ME, LOVER!
ISOBEL, THOU HAST DONE THY TASK WELL.
YOUR BRETHREN CONVEY THEIR GRATITUDE.
WE WAIT ON THE OTHER SIDE. WE CAN SEE THE GATE IS OPENING.
PREPARE THE WAY, ISOBEL! THE GREAT DAY IS AT HAND, AND SOON WE BOTH MAY STRIDE TOGETHER AMONGST THE WRITHING BODIES.
FOR YOUR SILVER TONGUE ALONE, I WOULD REND A WORLD...

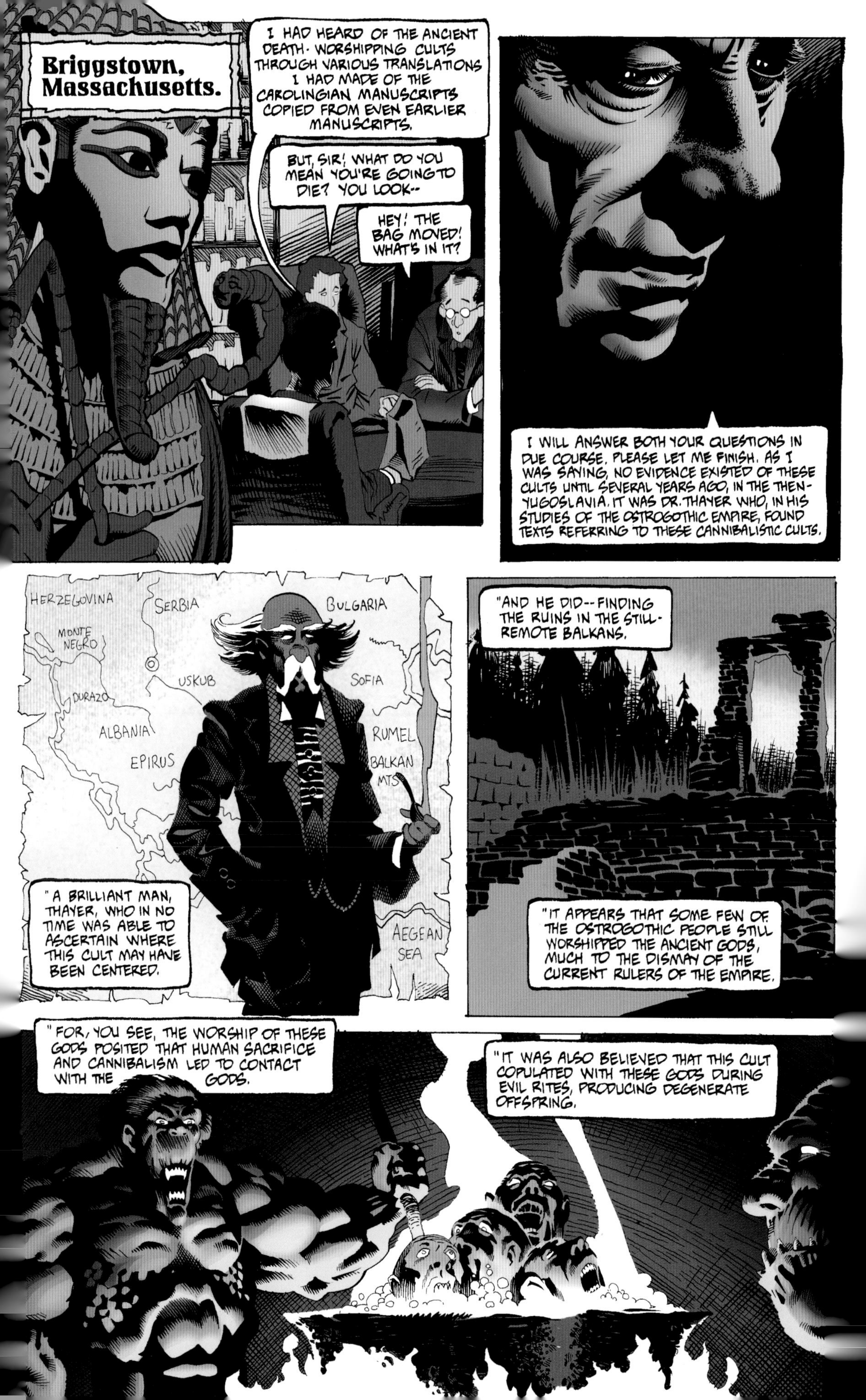
Briggstown, Massachusetts.
I HAD HEARD OF THE ANCIENT DEATH-WORSHIPPING CULTS THROUGH VARIOUS TRANSLATIONS I HAD MADE OF THE CAROLINGIAN MANUSCRIPTS COPIED FROM EVEN EARLIER MANUSCRIPTS.
BUT, SIR! WHAT DO YOU MEAN YOU'RE GOING TO DIE? YOU LOOK--
HEY! THE BAG MOVED! WHAT'S IN IT?
I WILL ANSWER BOTH YOUR QUESTIONS IN DUE COURSE. PLEASE LET ME FINISH. AS I WAS SAYING, NO EVIDENCE EXISTED OF THESE CULTS UNTIL SEVERAL YEARS AGO, IN THE THEN-YUGOSLAVIA. IT WAS DR. THAYER WHO, IN HIS STUDIES OF THE OSTROGOTHIC EMPIRE, FOUND TEXTS REFERRING TO THESE CANNIBALISTIC CULTS.
HERZEGOVINA
SERBIA
BULGARIA
MONTE NEGRO
USKUB
SOFIA
DURAZO
ALBANIA
RUMEL
EPIRUS
BALKAN MTS
AEGEAN SEA
"A BRILLIANT MAN, THAYER, WHO IN NO TIME WAS ABLE TO ASCERTAIN WHERE THIS CULT MAY HAVE BEEN CENTERED.
"AND HE DID--FINDING THE RUINS IN THE STILL-REMOTE BALKANS.
"IT APPEARS THAT SOME FEW OF THE OSTROGOTHIC PEOPLE STILL WORSHIPPED THE ANCIENT GODS, MUCH TO THE DISMAY OF THE CURRENT RULERS OF THE EMPIRE.
"FOR, YOU SEE, THE WORSHIP OF THESE GODS POSITED THAT HUMAN SACRIFICE AND CANNIBALISM LED TO CONTACT WITH THE GODS.
"IT WAS ALSO BELIEVED THAT THIS CULT COPULATED WITH THESE GODS DURING EVIL RITES, PRODUCING DEGENERATE OFFSPRING.

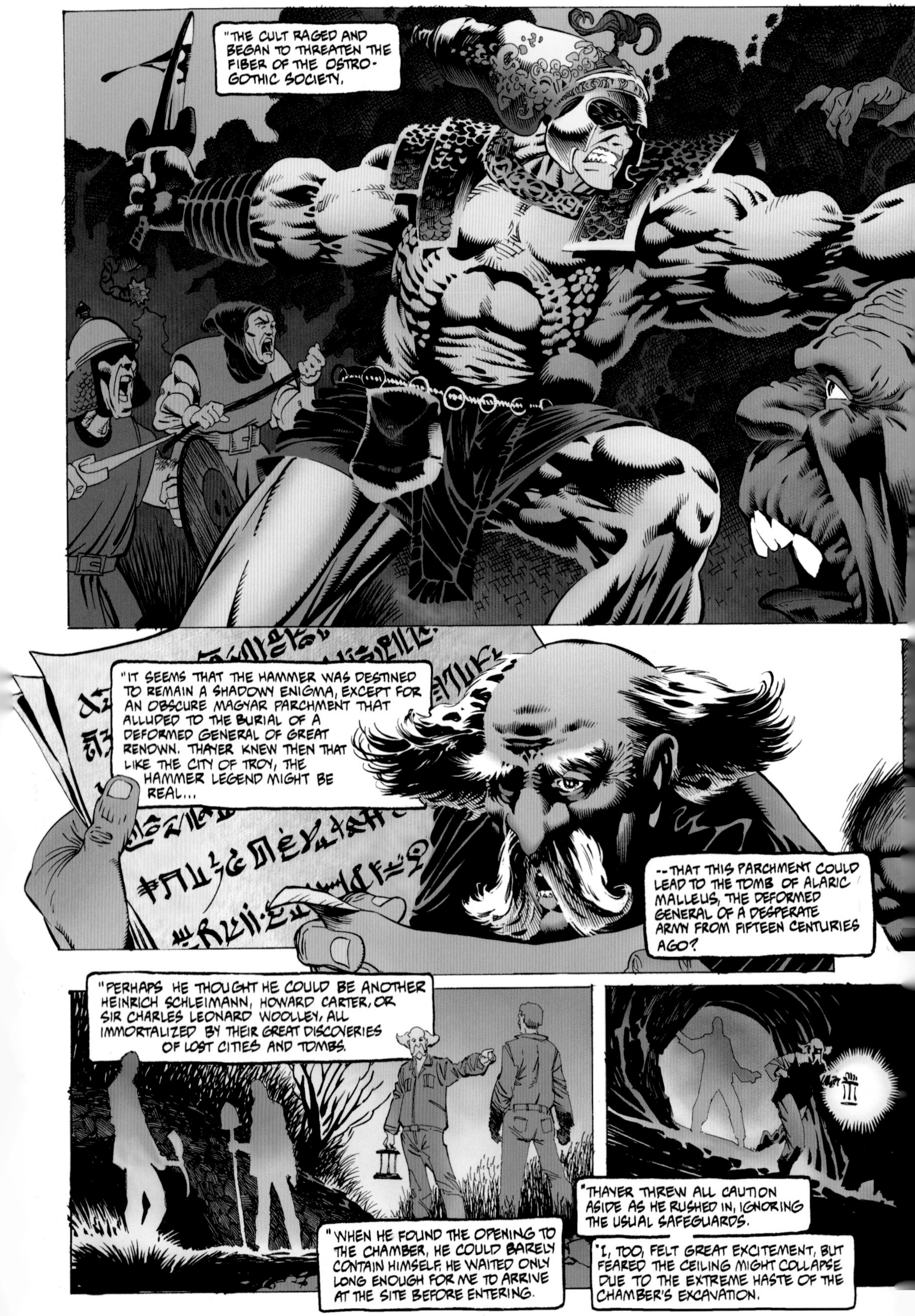
"THE CULT RAGED AND BEGAN TO THREATEN THE FIBER OF THE OSTRO-GOTHIC SOCIETY.
"IT SEEMS THAT THE HAMMER WAS DESTINED TO REMAIN A SHADOWY ENIGMA, EXCEPT FOR AN OBSCURE MAGYAR PARCHMENT THAT ALLUDED TO THE BURIAL OF A DEFORMED GENERAL OF GREAT RENOWN. THAYER KNEW THEN THAT LIKE THE CITY OF TROY, THE HAMMER LEGEND MIGHT BE REAL...
--THAT THIS PARCHMENT COULD LEAD TO THE TOMB OF ALARIC MALLEUS, THE DEFORMED GENERAL OF A DESPERATE ARMY FROM FIFTEEN CENTURIES AGO?
"PERHAPS HE THOUGHT HE COULD BE ANOTHER HEINRICH SCHLEIMANN, HOWARD CARTER, OR SIR CHARLES LEONARD WOOLLEY, ALL IMMORTALIZED BY THEIR GREAT DISCOVERIES OF LOST CITIES AND TOMBS.
"WHEN HE FOUND THE OPENING TO THE CHAMBER, HE COULD BARELY CONTAIN HIMSELF. HE WAITED ONLY LONG ENOUGH FOR ME TO ARRIVE AT THE SITE BEFORE ENTERING.
"THAYER THREW ALL CAUTION ASIDE AS HE RUSHED IN, IGNORING THE USUAL SAFEGUARDS.
"I, TOO, FELT GREAT EXCITEMENT, BUT FEARED THE CEILING MIGHT COLLAPSE DUE TO THE EXTREME HASTE OF THE CHAMBER'S EXCAVATION.

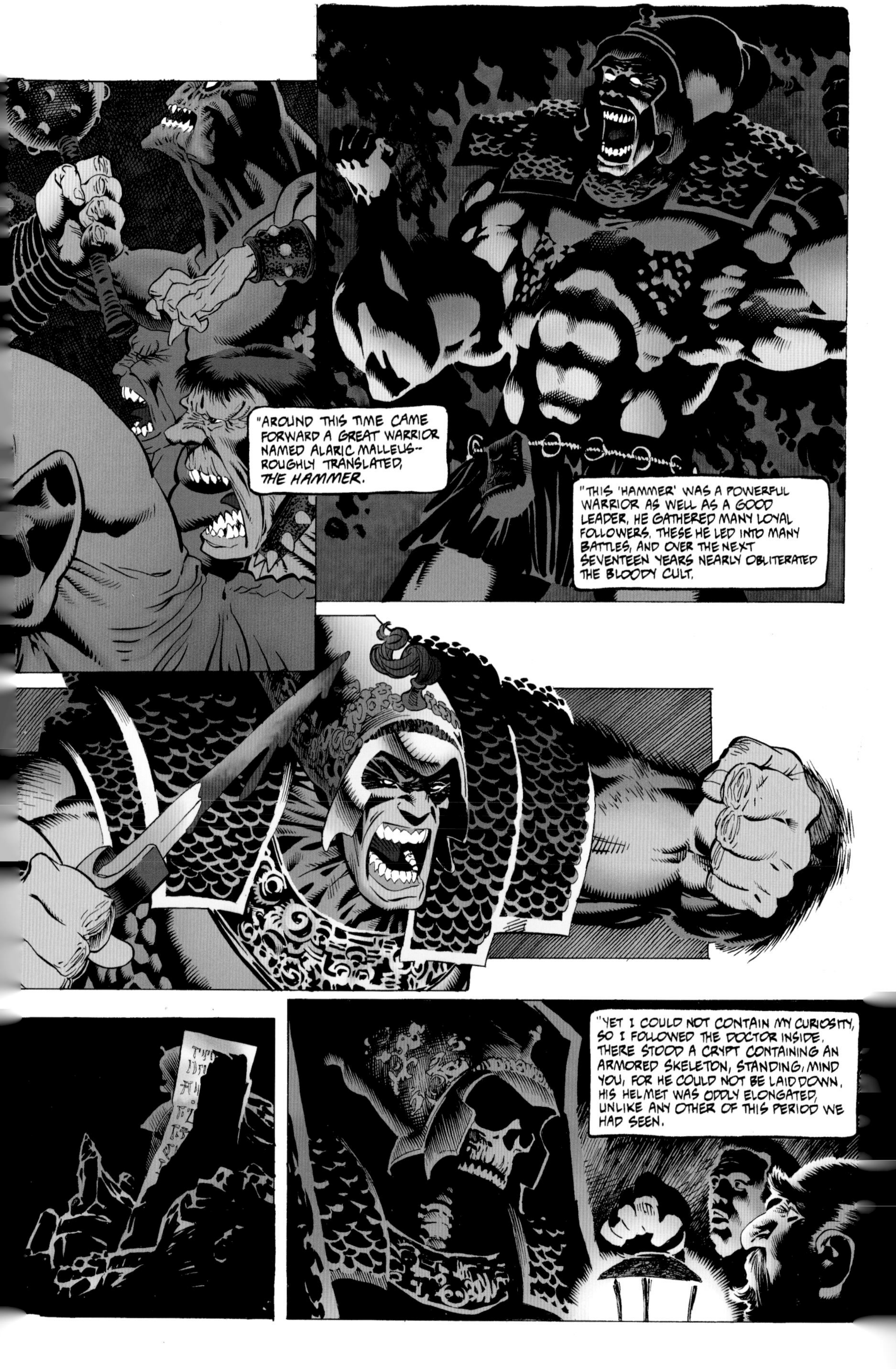
"AROUND THIS TIME CAME FORWARD A GREAT WARRIOR NAMED ALARIC MALLEUS-- ROUGHLY TRANSLATED, *THE HAMMER*.
"THIS 'HAMMER' WAS A POWERFUL WARRIOR AS WELL AS A GOOD LEADER. HE GATHERED MANY LOYAL FOLLOWERS. THESE HE LED INTO MANY BATTLES, AND OVER THE NEXT SEVENTEEN YEARS NEARLY OBLITERATED THE BLOODY CULT.
"YET I COULD NOT CONTAIN MY CURIOSITY, SO I FOLLOWED THE DOCTOR INSIDE. THERE STOOD A CRYPT CONTAINING AN ARMORED SKELETON, STANDING, MIND YOU, FOR HE COULD NOT BE LAID DOWN. HIS HELMET WAS ODDLY ELONGATED, UNLIKE ANY OTHER OF THIS PERIOD WE HAD SEEN.

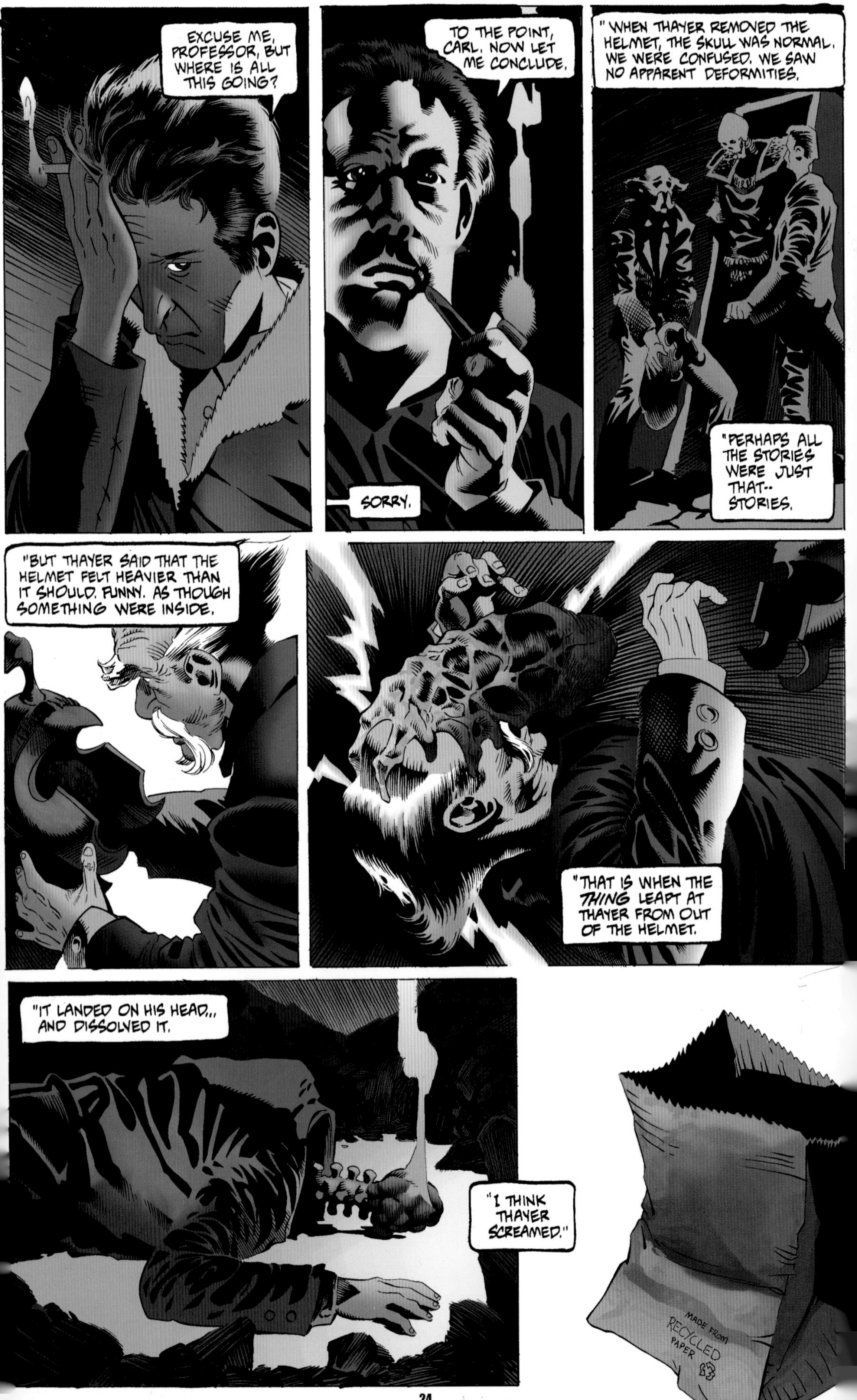

EXCUSE ME, PROFESSOR, BUT WHERE IS ALL THIS GOING?
TO THE POINT, CARL. NOW LET ME CONCLUDE.
SORRY.
"WHEN THAYER REMOVED THE HELMET, THE SKULL WAS NORMAL. WE WERE CONFUSED. WE SAW NO APPARENT DEFORMITIES.
"PERHAPS ALL THE STORIES WERE JUST THAT-- STORIES.
"BUT THAYER SAID THAT THE HELMET FELT HEAVIER THAN IT SHOULD. FUNNY. AS THOUGH SOMETHING WERE INSIDE.
"THAT IS WHEN THE THING LEAPT AT THAYER FROM OUT OF THE HELMET.
"IT LANDED ON HIS HEAD... AND DISSOLVED IT.
"I THINK THAYER SCREAMED."
MADE FROM RECYCLED PAPER

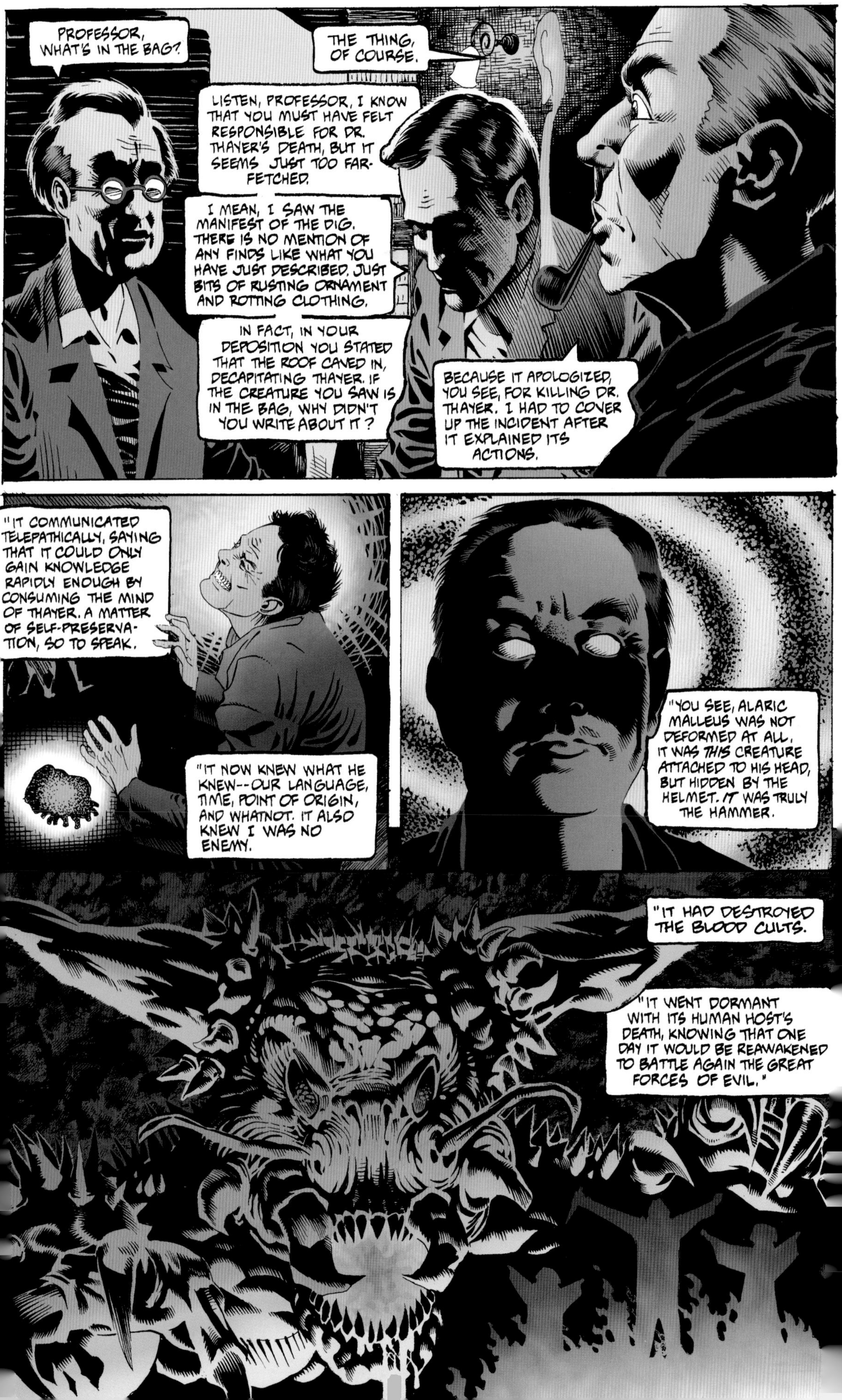
PROFESSOR, WHAT'S IN THE BAG?
THE THING, OF COURSE.
LISTEN, PROFESSOR, I KNOW THAT YOU MUST HAVE FELT RESPONSIBLE FOR DR. THAYER'S DEATH, BUT IT SEEMS JUST TOO FAR-FETCHED.
I MEAN, I SAW THE MANIFEST OF THE DIG. THERE IS NO MENTION OF ANY FINDS LIKE WHAT YOU HAVE JUST DESCRIBED. JUST BITS OF RUSTING ORNAMENT AND ROTTING CLOTHING.
IN FACT, IN YOUR DEPOSITION YOU STATED THAT THE ROOF CAVED IN, DECAPITATING THAYER. IF THE CREATURE YOU SAW IS IN THE BAG, WHY DIDN'T YOU WRITE ABOUT IT?
BECAUSE IT APOLOGIZED, YOU SEE, FOR KILLING DR. THAYER. I HAD TO COVER UP THE INCIDENT AFTER IT EXPLAINED ITS ACTIONS.
"IT COMMUNICATED TELEPATHICALLY, SAYING THAT IT COULD ONLY GAIN KNOWLEDGE RAPIDLY ENOUGH BY CONSUMING THE MIND OF THAYER. A MATTER OF SELF-PRESERVATION, SO TO SPEAK.
"IT NOW KNEW WHAT HE KNEW--OUR LANGUAGE, TIME, POINT OF ORIGIN, AND WHATNOT. IT ALSO KNEW I WAS NO ENEMY.
"YOU SEE, ALARIC MALLEUS WAS NOT DEFORMED AT ALL. IT WAS *THIS* CREATURE ATTACHED TO HIS HEAD, BUT HIDDEN BY THE HELMET. *IT* WAS TRULY THE HAMMER.
"IT HAD DESTROYED THE BLOOD CULTS.
"IT WENT DORMANT WITH ITS HUMAN HOST'S DEATH, KNOWING THAT ONE DAY IT WOULD BE REAWAKENED TO BATTLE AGAIN THE GREAT FORCES OF EVIL."

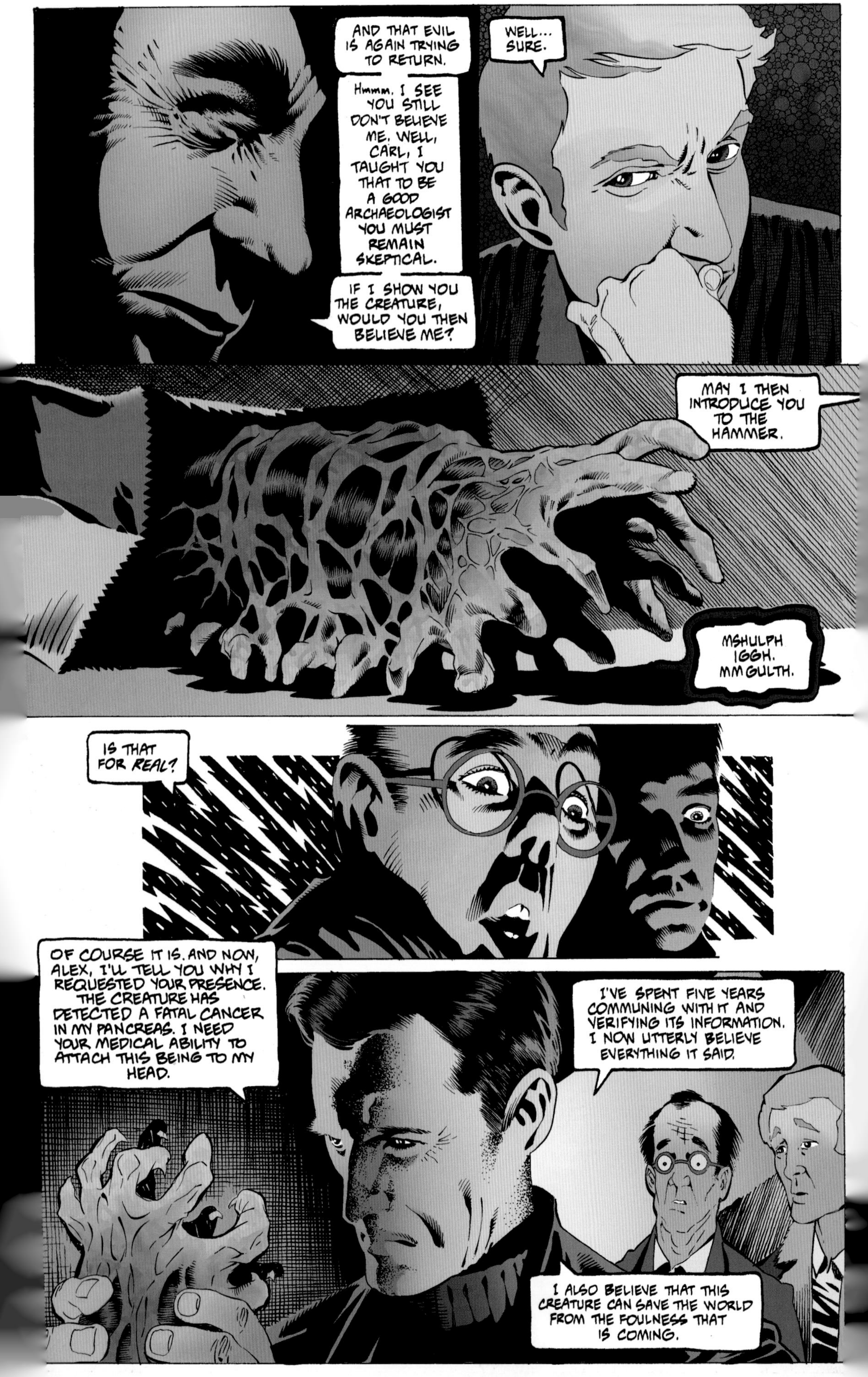
AND THAT EVIL IS AGAIN TRYING TO RETURN.
Hmmm. I SEE YOU STILL DON'T BELIEVE ME. WELL, CARL, I TAUGHT YOU THAT TO BE A GOOD ARCHAEOLOGIST YOU MUST REMAIN SKEPTICAL.
IF I SHOW YOU THE CREATURE, WOULD YOU THEN BELIEVE ME?
WELL... SURE.
MAY I THEN INTRODUCE YOU TO THE HAMMER.
MSHULPH IGGH. MMGULTH.
IS THAT FOR REAL?
OF COURSE IT IS. AND NOW, ALEX, I'LL TELL YOU WHY I REQUESTED YOUR PRESENCE. THE CREATURE HAS DETECTED A FATAL CANCER IN MY PANCREAS. I NEED YOUR MEDICAL ABILITY TO ATTACH THIS BEING TO MY HEAD.
I'VE SPENT FIVE YEARS COMMUNING WITH IT AND VERIFYING ITS INFORMATION. I NOW UTTERLY BELIEVE EVERYTHING IT SAID.
I ALSO BELIEVE THAT THIS CREATURE CAN SAVE THE WORLD FROM THE FOULNESS THAT IS COMING.

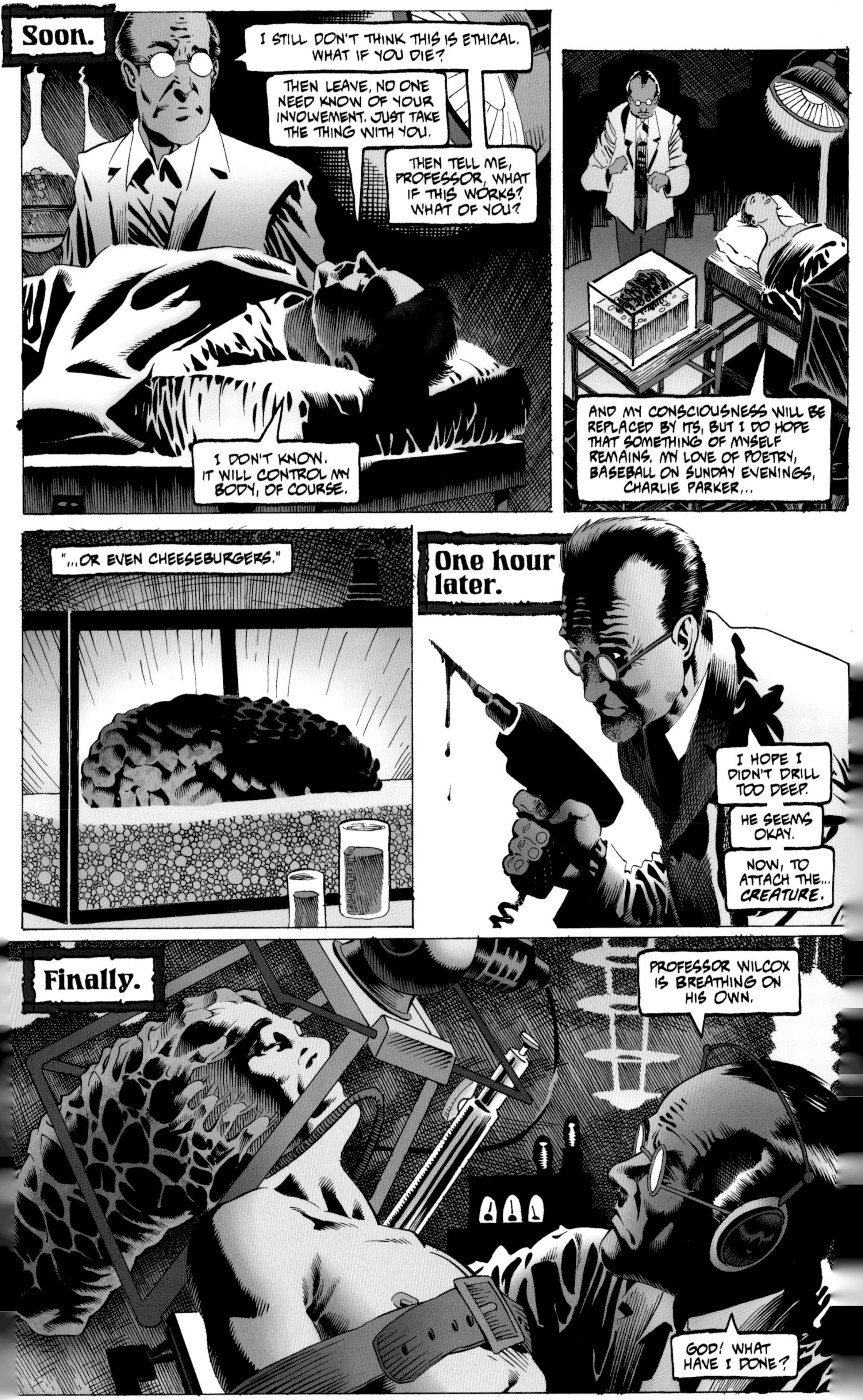
Soon.
I STILL DON'T THINK THIS IS ETHICAL. WHAT IF YOU DIE?
THEN LEAVE, NO ONE NEED KNOW OF YOUR INVOLVEMENT. JUST TAKE THE THING WITH YOU.
THEN TELL ME, PROFESSOR, WHAT IF THIS WORKS? WHAT OF YOU?
I DON'T KNOW. IT WILL CONTROL MY BODY, OF COURSE.
AND MY CONSCIOUSNESS WILL BE REPLACED BY ITS, BUT I DO HOPE THAT SOMETHING OF MYSELF REMAINS. MY LOVE OF POETRY, BASEBALL ON SUNDAY EVENINGS, CHARLIE PARKER,...
"...OR EVEN CHEESEBURGERS."
One hour later.
I HOPE I DIDN'T DRILL TOO DEEP.
HE SEEMS OKAY.
NOW, TO ATTACH THE... CREATURE.
Finally.
PROFESSOR WILCOX IS BREATHING ON HIS OWN.
GOD! WHAT HAVE I DONE?

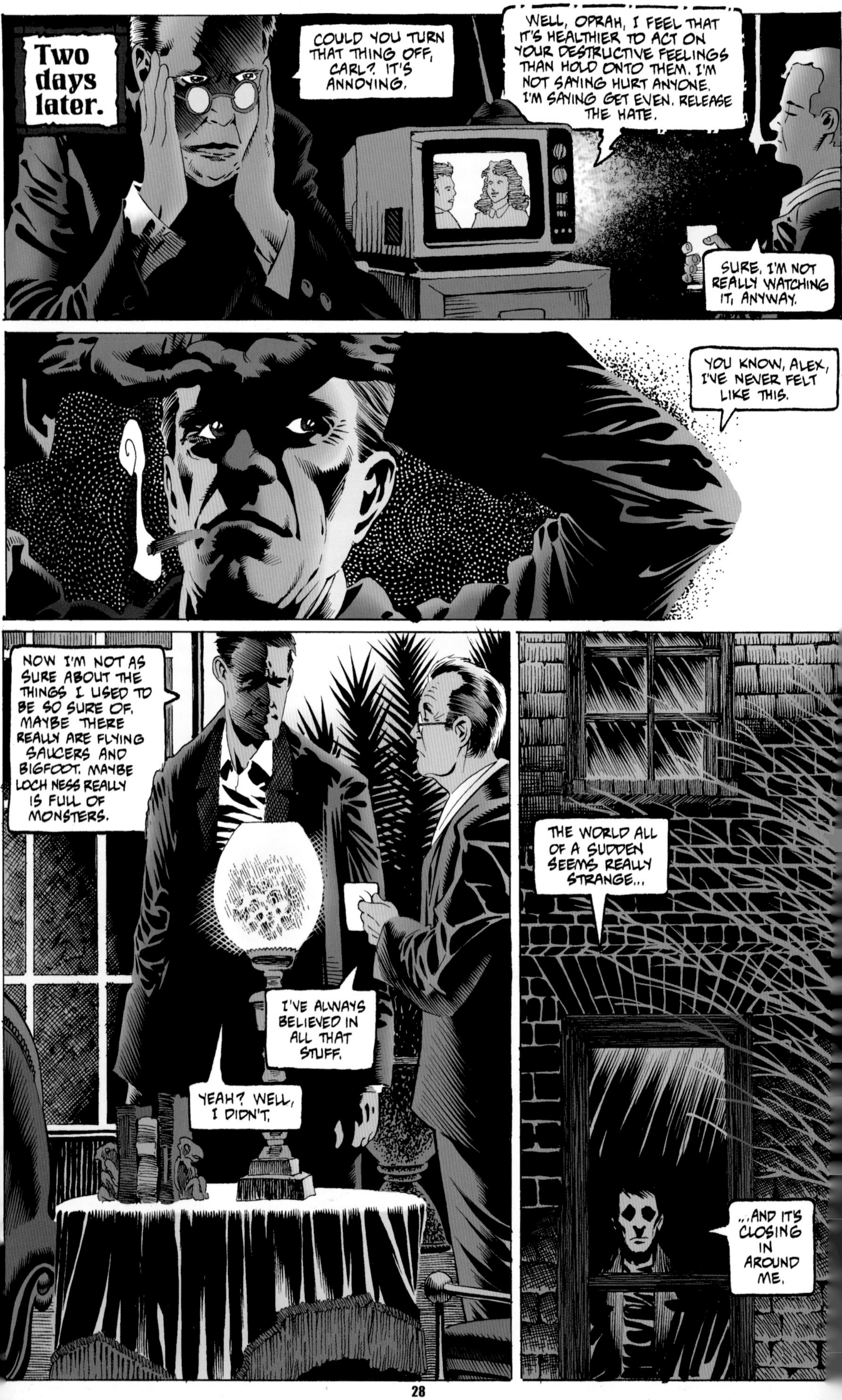
Two days later.
COULD YOU TURN THAT THING OFF, CARL? IT'S ANNOYING.
WELL, OPRAH, I FEEL THAT IT'S HEALTHIER TO ACT ON YOUR DESTRUCTIVE FEELINGS THAN HOLD ONTO THEM. I'M NOT SAYING HURT ANYONE. I'M SAYING GET EVEN. RELEASE THE HATE.
SURE. I'M NOT REALLY WATCHING IT, ANYWAY.
YOU KNOW, ALEX, I'VE NEVER FELT LIKE THIS.
NOW I'M NOT AS SURE ABOUT THE THINGS I USED TO BE SO SURE OF. MAYBE THERE REALLY ARE FLYING SAUCERS AND BIGFOOT. MAYBE LOCH NESS REALLY IS FULL OF MONSTERS.
I'VE ALWAYS BELIEVED IN ALL THAT STUFF.
YEAH? WELL, I DIDN'T.
THE WORLD ALL OF A SUDDEN SEEMS REALLY STRANGE...
...AND IT'S CLOSING IN AROUND ME.

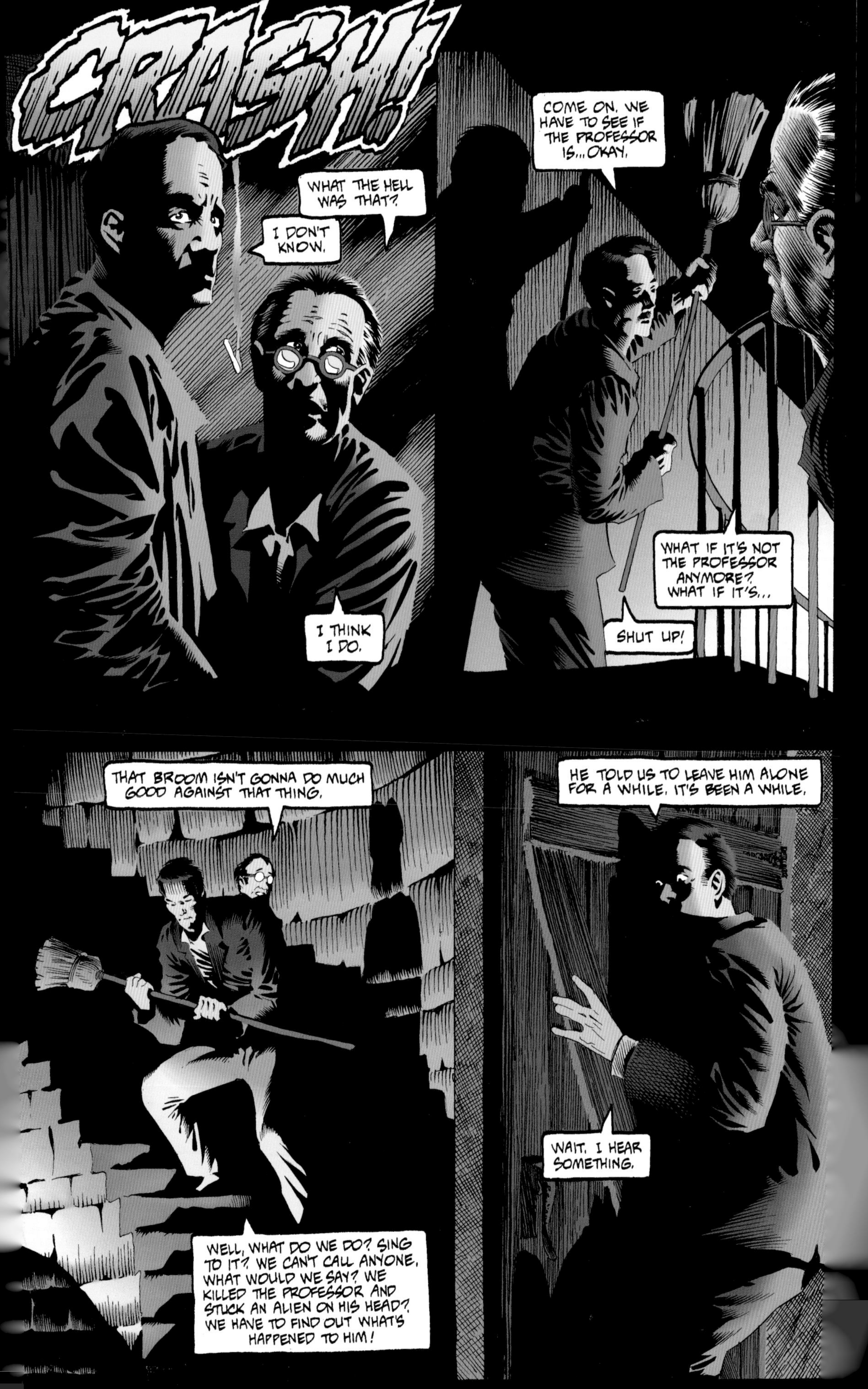
CRASH!
WHAT THE HELL WAS THAT?
I DON'T KNOW.
I THINK I DO.
COME ON. WE HAVE TO SEE IF THE PROFESSOR IS...OKAY.
WHAT IF IT'S NOT THE PROFESSOR ANYMORE? WHAT IF IT'S...
SHUT UP!
THAT BROOM ISN'T GONNA DO MUCH GOOD AGAINST THAT THING.
WELL, WHAT DO WE DO? SING TO IT? WE CAN'T CALL ANYONE. WHAT WOULD WE SAY? WE KILLED THE PROFESSOR AND STUCK AN ALIEN ON HIS HEAD? WE HAVE TO FIND OUT WHAT'S HAPPENED TO HIM!
HE TOLD US TO LEAVE HIM ALONE FOR A WHILE. IT'S BEEN A WHILE.
WAIT. I HEAR SOMETHING.

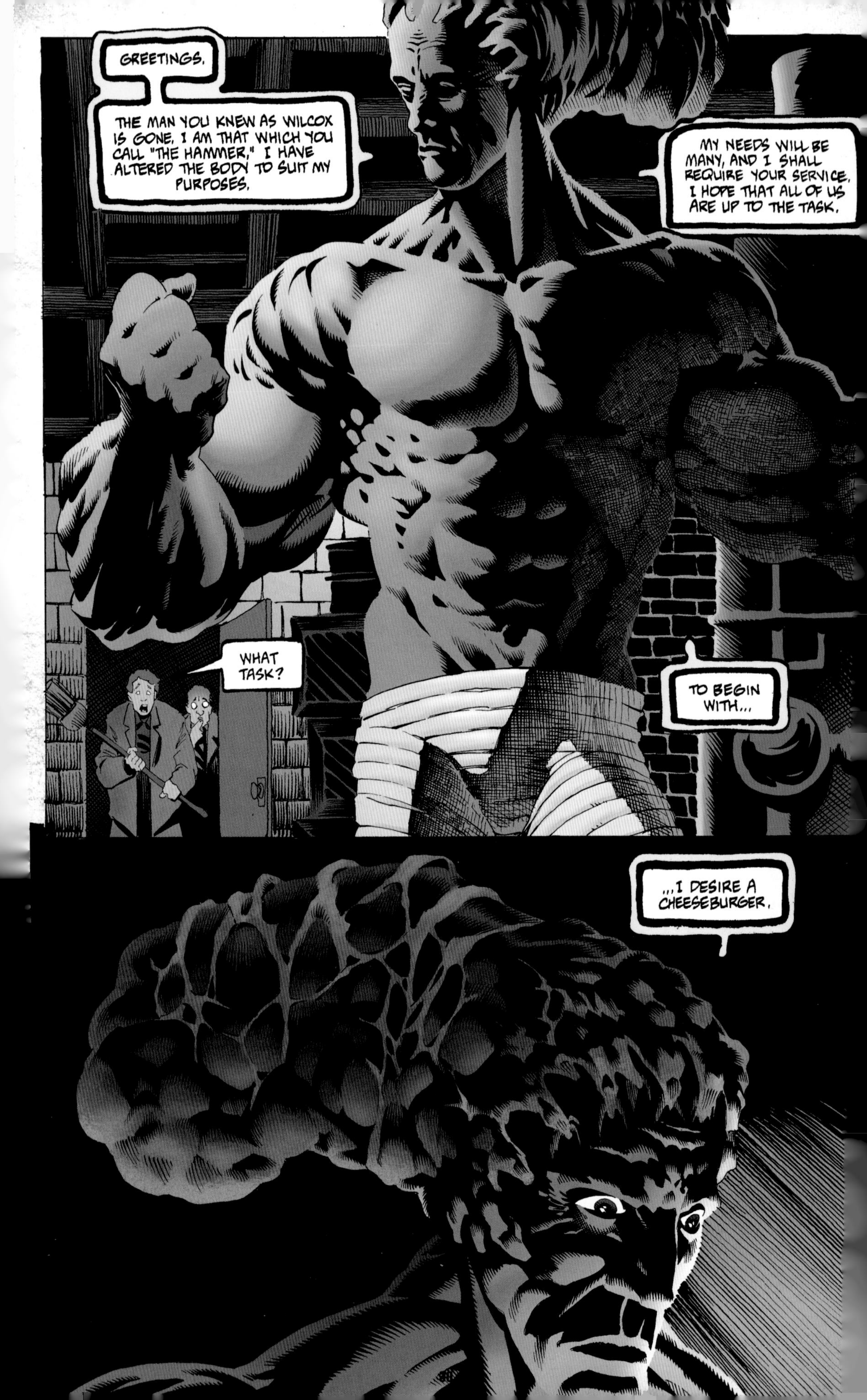
GREETINGS.
THE MAN YOU KNEW AS WILCOX IS GONE. I AM THAT WHICH YOU CALL "THE HAMMER." I HAVE ALTERED THE BODY TO SUIT MY PURPOSES.
MY NEEDS WILL BE MANY, AND I SHALL REQUIRE YOUR SERVICE. I HOPE THAT ALL OF US ARE UP TO THE TASK.
WHAT TASK?
TO BEGIN WITH...
...I DESIRE A CHEESEBURGER.

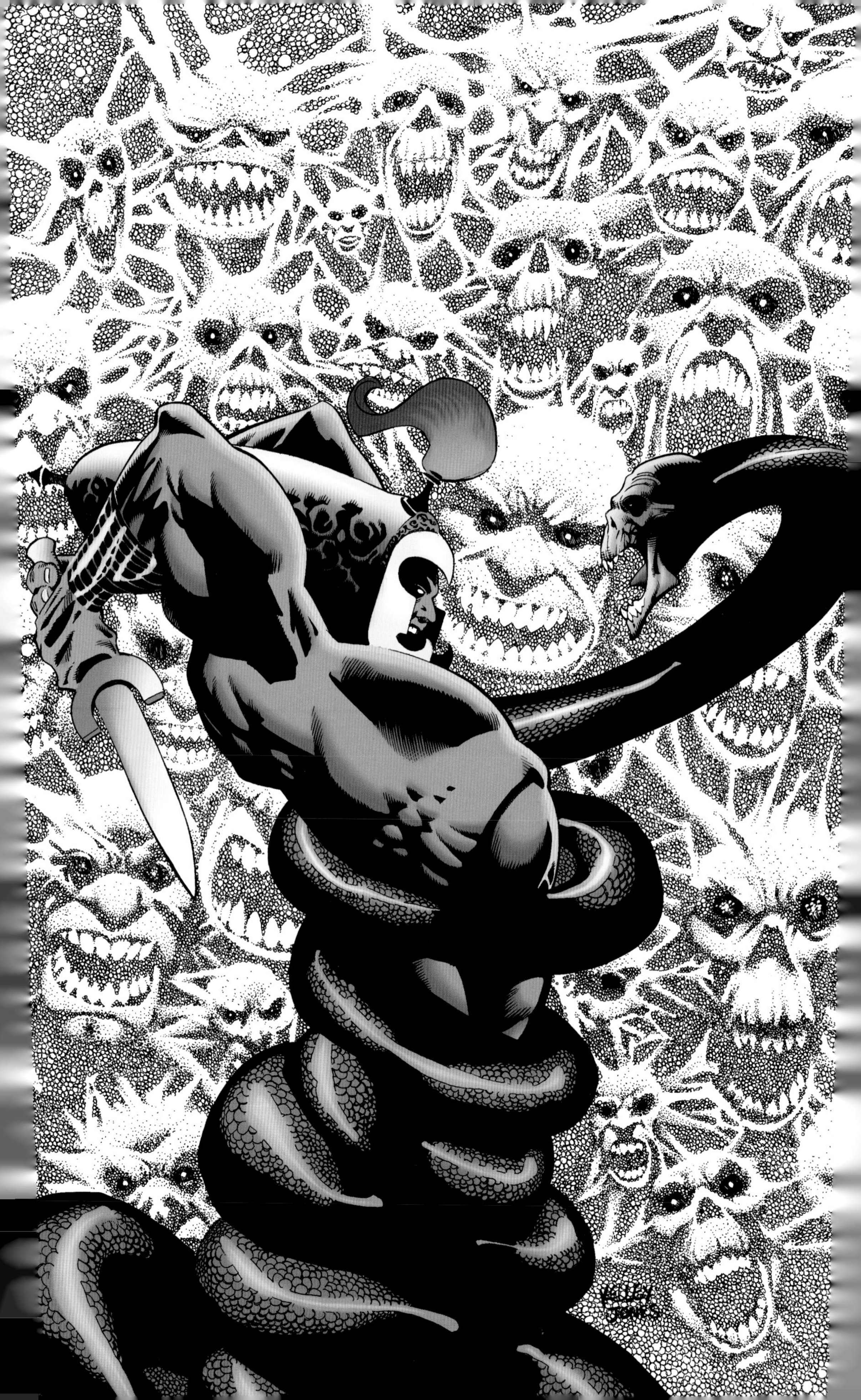

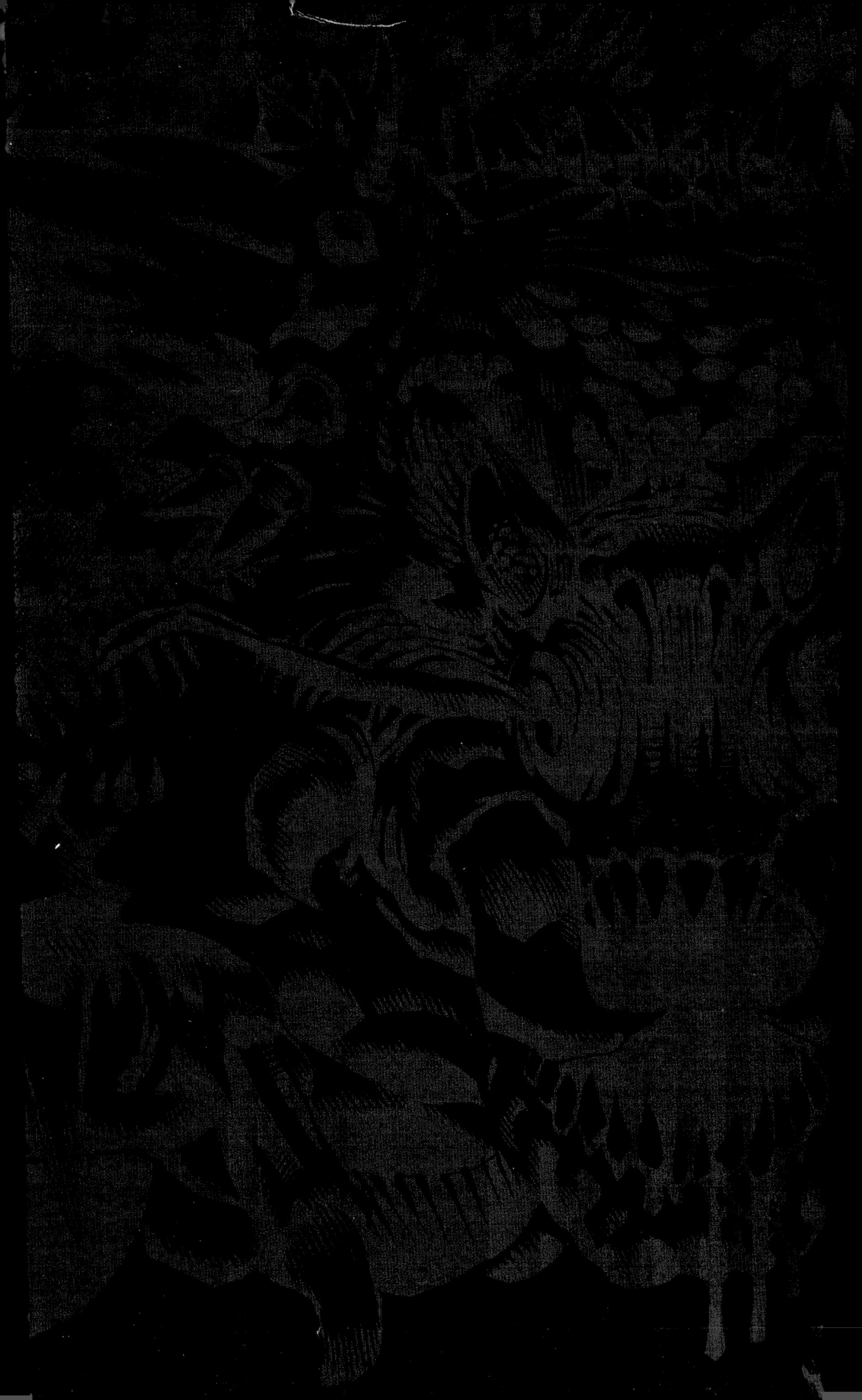

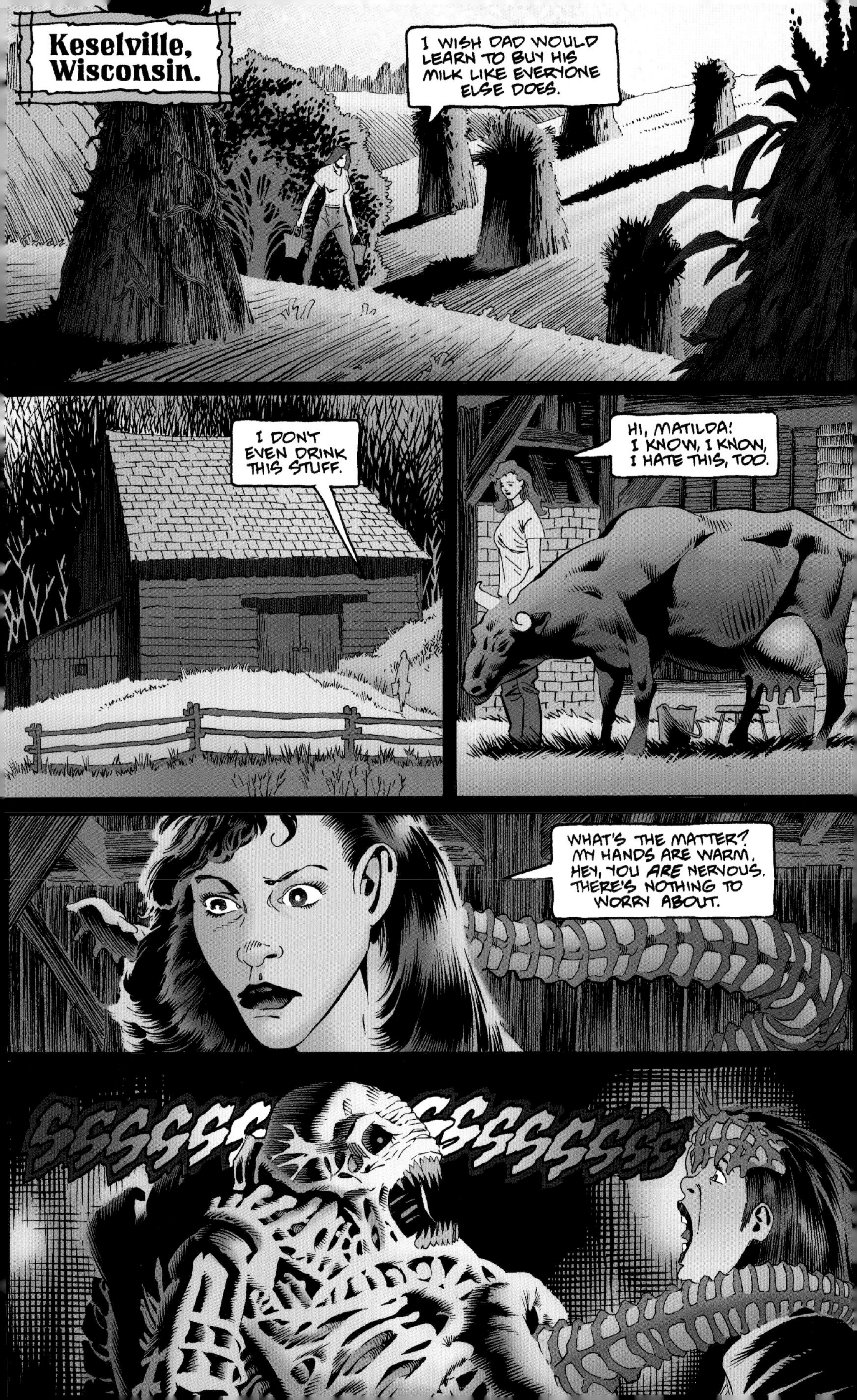
Keselville, Wisconsin.
I WISH DAD WOULD LEARN TO BUY HIS MILK LIKE EVERYONE ELSE DOES.
I DON'T EVEN DRINK THIS STUFF.
HI, MATILDA! I KNOW, I KNOW, I HATE THIS, TOO.
WHAT'S THE MATTER? MY HANDS ARE WARM. HEY, YOU ARE NERVOUS. THERE'S NOTHING TO WORRY ABOUT.
SSSSSSSSSSSSSSSSSS

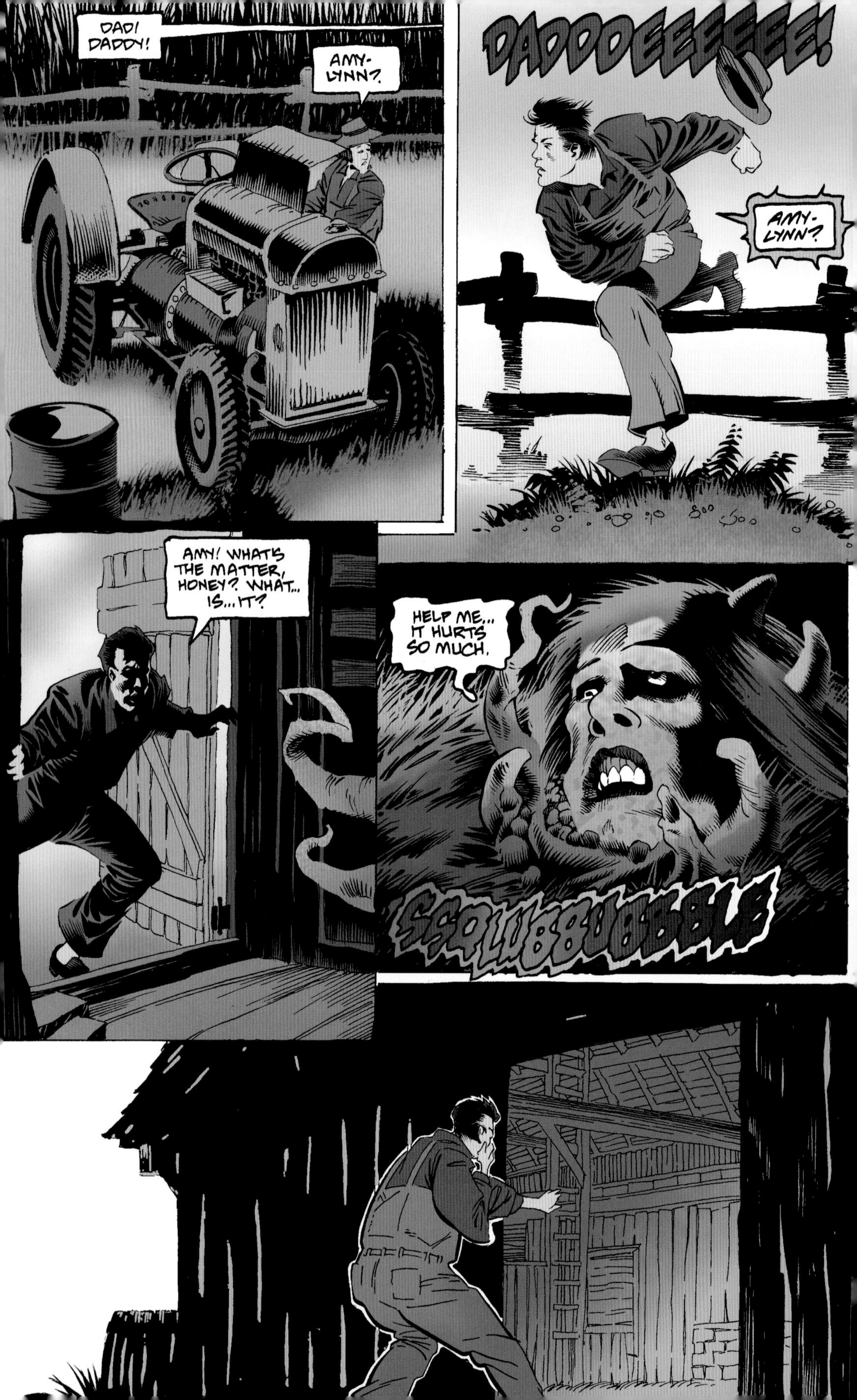
DAD! DADDY!
AMY-LYNN?
DADDOEEEEEEE!
AMY-LYNN?
AMY! WHAT'S THE MATTER, HONEY? WHAT... IS... IT?
HELP ME... IT HURTS SO MUCH.
SSQLUBBUBBBLB

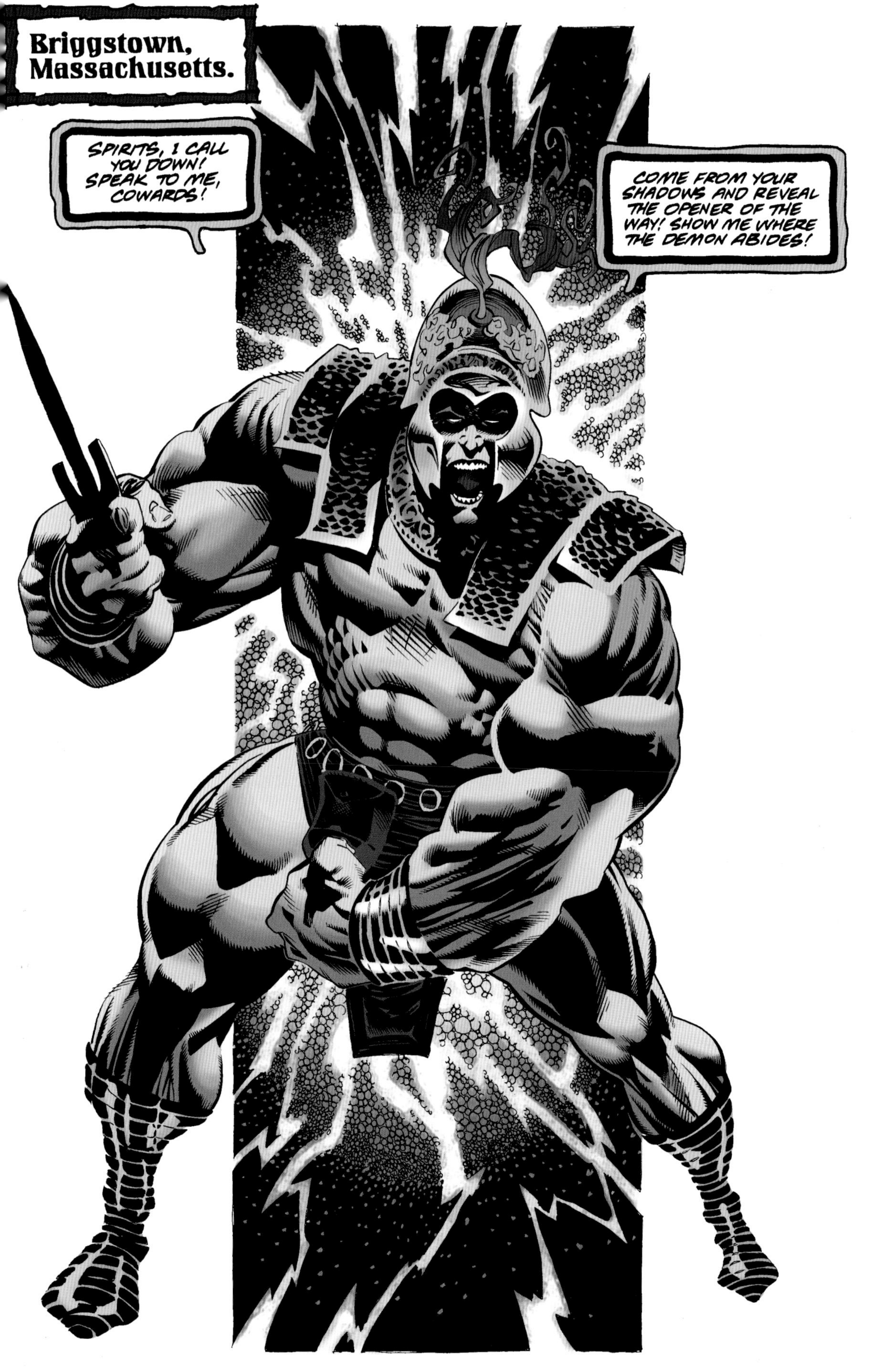
Briggstown, Massachusetts.
SPIRITS, I CALL YOU DOWN! SPEAK TO ME, COWARDS!
COME FROM YOUR SHADOWS AND REVEAL THE OPENER OF THE WAY! SHOW ME WHERE THE DEMON ABIDES!

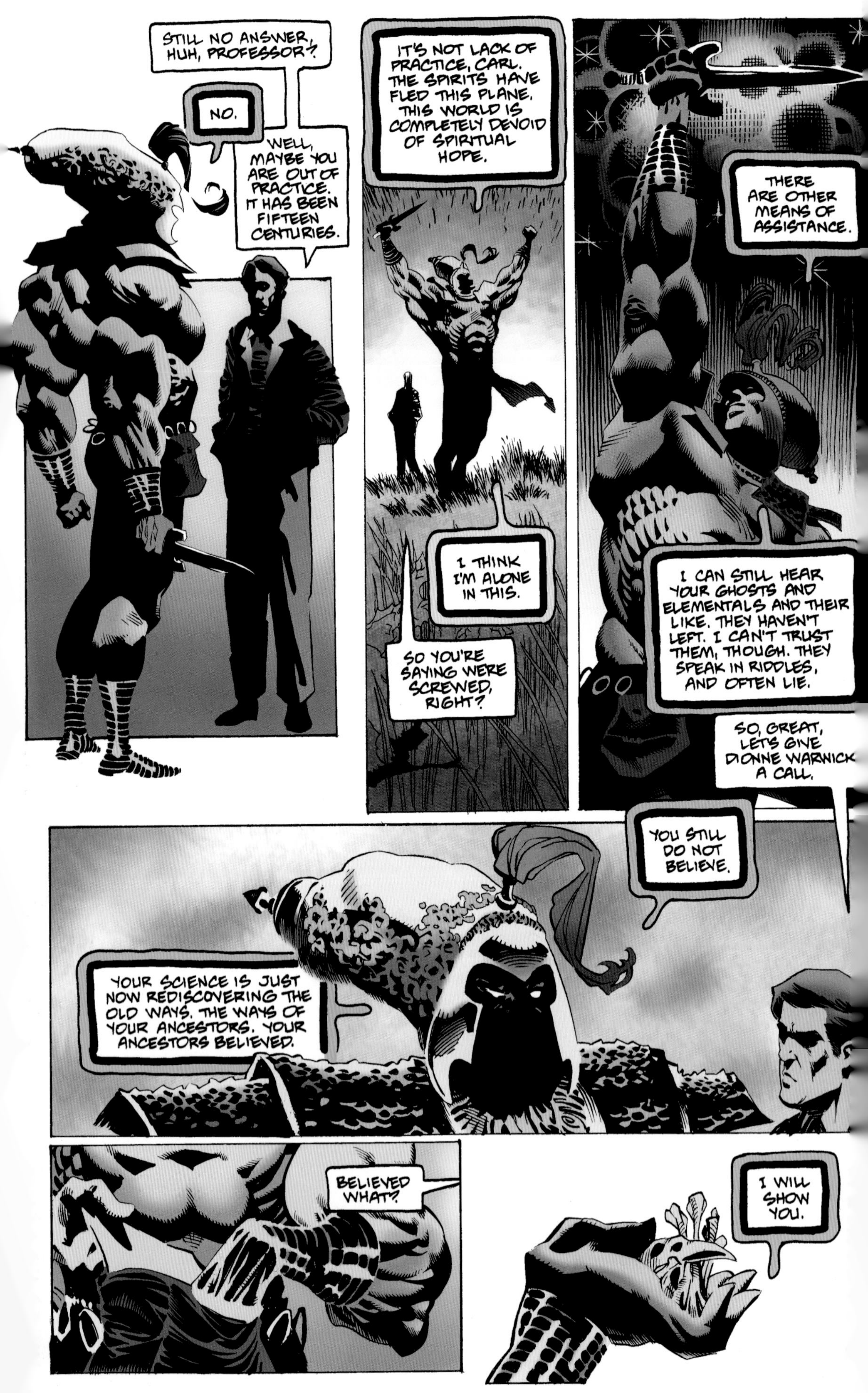
STILL NO ANSWER, HUH, PROFESSOR?
NO.
WELL, MAYBE YOU ARE OUT OF PRACTICE. IT HAS BEEN FIFTEEN CENTURIES.
IT'S NOT LACK OF PRACTICE, CARL. THE SPIRITS HAVE FLED THIS PLANE. THIS WORLD IS COMPLETELY DEVOID OF SPIRITUAL HOPE.
I THINK I'M ALONE IN THIS.
SO YOU'RE SAYING WERE SCREWED, RIGHT?
THERE ARE OTHER MEANS OF ASSISTANCE.
I CAN STILL HEAR YOUR GHOSTS AND ELEMENTALS AND THEIR LIKE. THEY HAVEN'T LEFT. I CAN'T TRUST THEM, THOUGH. THEY SPEAK IN RIDDLES, AND OFTEN LIE.
SO, GREAT, LET'S GIVE DIONNE WARWICK A CALL.
YOU STILL DO NOT BELIEVE.
YOUR SCIENCE IS JUST NOW REDISCOVERING THE OLD WAYS. THE WAYS OF YOUR ANCESTORS. YOUR ANCESTORS BELIEVED.
BELIEVED WHAT?
I WILL SHOW YOU.

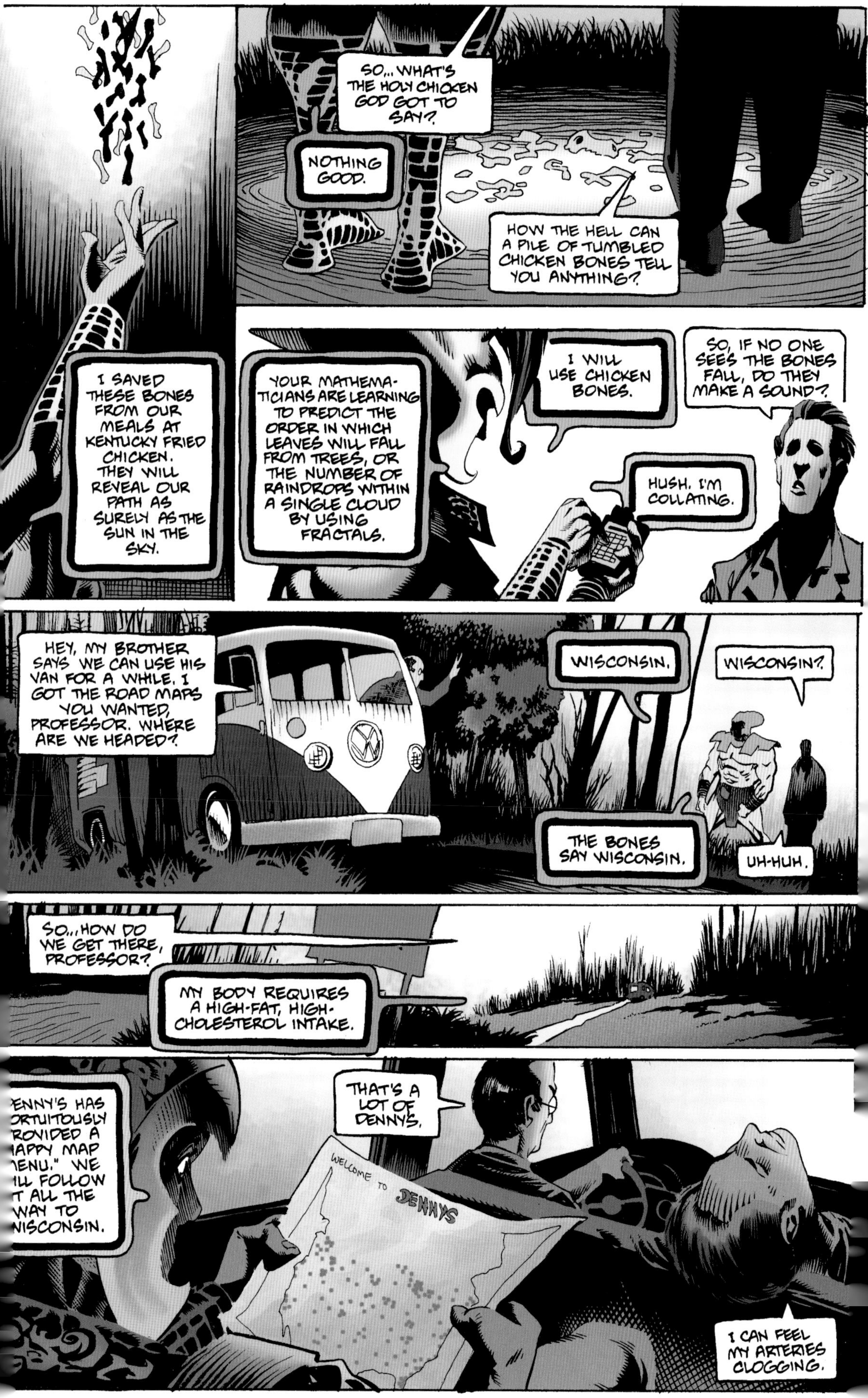
SO... WHAT'S THE HOLY CHICKEN GOD GOT TO SAY?
NOTHING GOOD.
HOW THE HELL CAN A PILE OF TUMBLED CHICKEN BONES TELL YOU ANYTHING?
I SAVED THESE BONES FROM OUR MEALS AT KENTUCKY FRIED CHICKEN. THEY WILL REVEAL OUR PATH AS SURELY AS THE SUN IN THE SKY.
YOUR MATHEMATICIANS ARE LEARNING TO PREDICT THE ORDER IN WHICH LEAVES WILL FALL FROM TREES, OR THE NUMBER OF RAINDROPS WITHIN A SINGLE CLOUD BY USING FRACTALS.
I WILL USE CHICKEN BONES.
SO, IF NO ONE SEES THE BONES FALL, DO THEY MAKE A SOUND?
HUSH. I'M COLLATING.
HEY, MY BROTHER SAYS WE CAN USE HIS VAN FOR A WHILE. I GOT THE ROAD MAPS YOU WANTED, PROFESSOR. WHERE ARE WE HEADED?
WISCONSIN.
WISCONSIN?
THE BONES SAY WISCONSIN.
UH-HUH.
SO... HOW DO WE GET THERE, PROFESSOR?
MY BODY REQUIRES A HIGH-FAT, HIGH-CHOLESTEROL INTAKE.
ENNY'S HAS ORTUITOUSLY ROVIDED A APPY MAP ENU." WE ILL FOLLOW T ALL THE WAY TO ISCONSIN.
THAT'S A LOT OF DENNYS.
WELCOME TO DENNYS
I CAN FEEL MY ARTERIES CLOGGING.

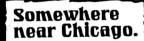

Somewhere near Chicago.

-- MY PAMPHLET, 'BEING GOOD AT BEING BAD', FREE. I'VE SOLD OVER 22 MILLION COPIES OF 'NO PRISONERS', MY BOOK ABOUT POSITIVE, HEALTHY REVENGE. ATHLETES, CELEBRITIES, HAVE ALL SUCCESSFULLY EMPLOY- ED MY PATENTED TECH- NIQUES IN THEIR OWN CAREERS.

THEY'VE ALL READ MY BOOK. AND I'LL BET YOUR NEIGHBOR HAS, TOO.

I REACH MORE PEOPLE WITH THAT INFOMERCIAL THAN WITH ANY SPELL.

STILL, THE OLD WAYS HAVE THEIR MERITS.

IT'S ALMOST TIME NOW.

MY FAVORITE SHOW.

--SEAS WILL BOIL WITH THE BLOOD OF THE SINNERS!

ONE DAY, I WILL MAKE HIM DRINK FROM THAT SEA.

HELLO? YES, I WOULD LIKE TO DONATE $10,000 TO THE REVEREND TRAVIS FOR ALL OF HIS MIGHTY AND GOOD WORKS.

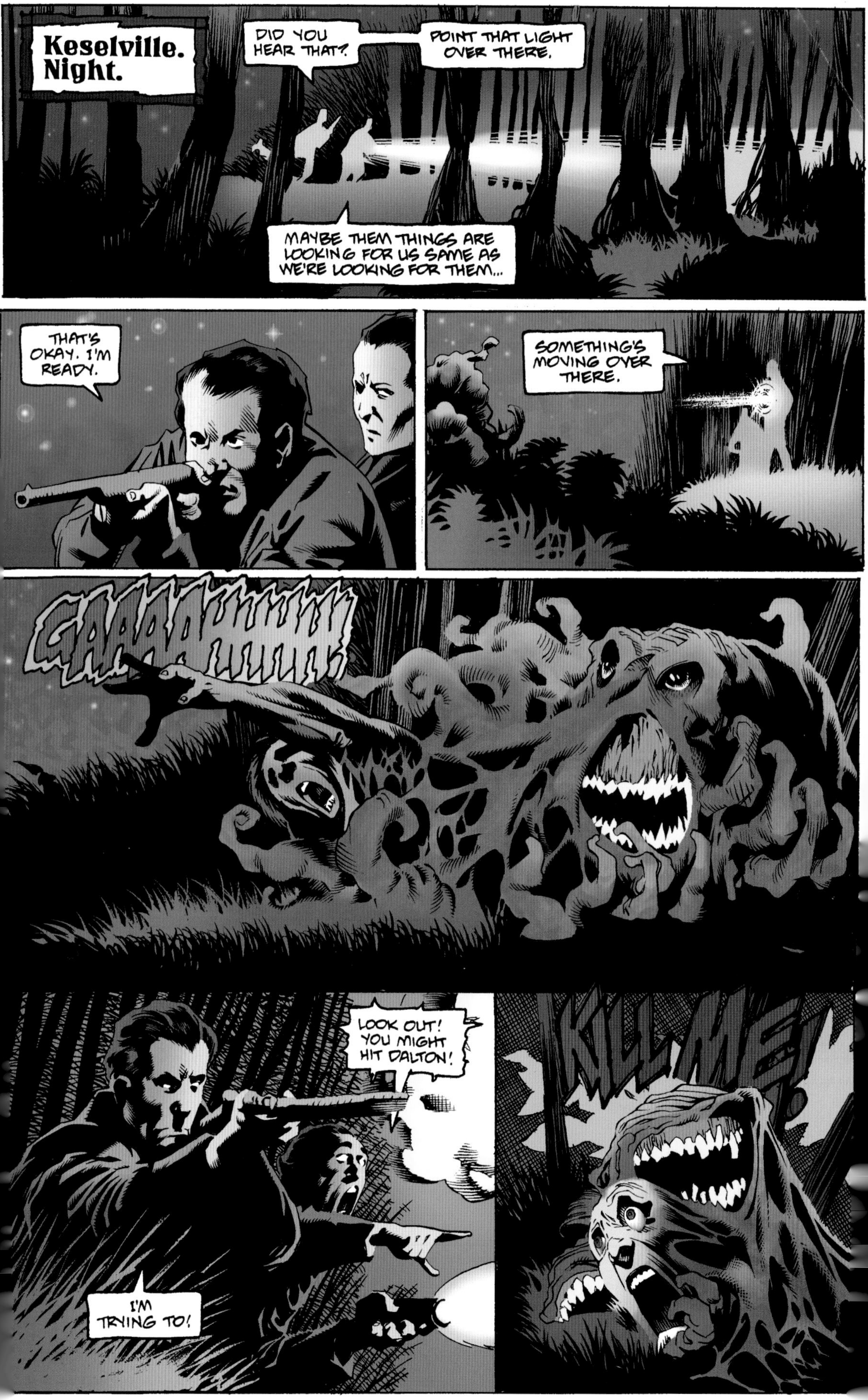
Keselville. Night.
DID YOU HEAR THAT?
POINT THAT LIGHT OVER THERE.
MAYBE THEM THINGS ARE LOOKING FOR US SAME AS WE'RE LOOKING FOR THEM...
THAT'S OKAY. I'M READY.
SOMETHING'S MOVING OVER THERE.
GAAAHHHH!
LOOK OUT! YOU MIGHT HIT DALTON!
I'M TRYING TO!
KILL ME!

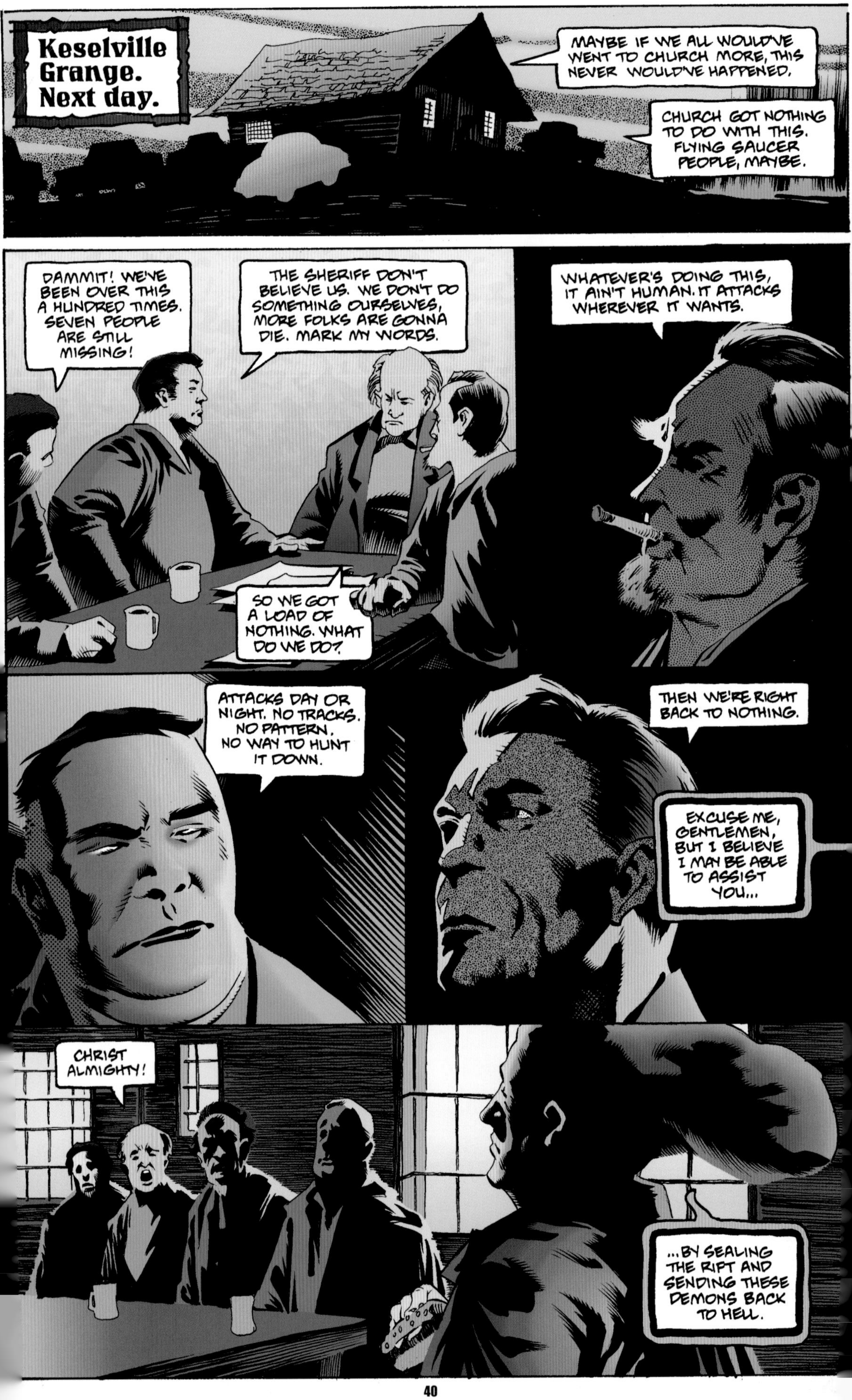
Keselville Grange. Next day.
MAYBE IF WE ALL WOULD'VE WENT TO CHURCH MORE, THIS NEVER WOULD'VE HAPPENED.
CHURCH GOT NOTHING TO DO WITH THIS. FLYING SAUCER PEOPLE, MAYBE.
DAMMIT! WE'VE BEEN OVER THIS A HUNDRED TIMES. SEVEN PEOPLE ARE STILL MISSING!
THE SHERIFF DON'T BELIEVE US. WE DON'T DO SOMETHING OURSELVES, MORE FOLKS ARE GONNA DIE. MARK MY WORDS.
SO WE GOT A LOAD OF NOTHING. WHAT DO WE DO?
WHATEVER'S DOING THIS, IT AIN'T HUMAN. IT ATTACKS WHEREVER IT WANTS.
ATTACKS DAY OR NIGHT. NO TRACKS. NO PATTERN. NO WAY TO HUNT IT DOWN.
THEN WE'RE RIGHT BACK TO NOTHING.
EXCUSE ME, GENTLEMEN, BUT I BELIEVE I MAY BE ABLE TO ASSIST YOU...
CHRIST ALMIGHTY!
...BY SEALING THE RIFT AND SENDING THESE DEMONS BACK TO HELL.

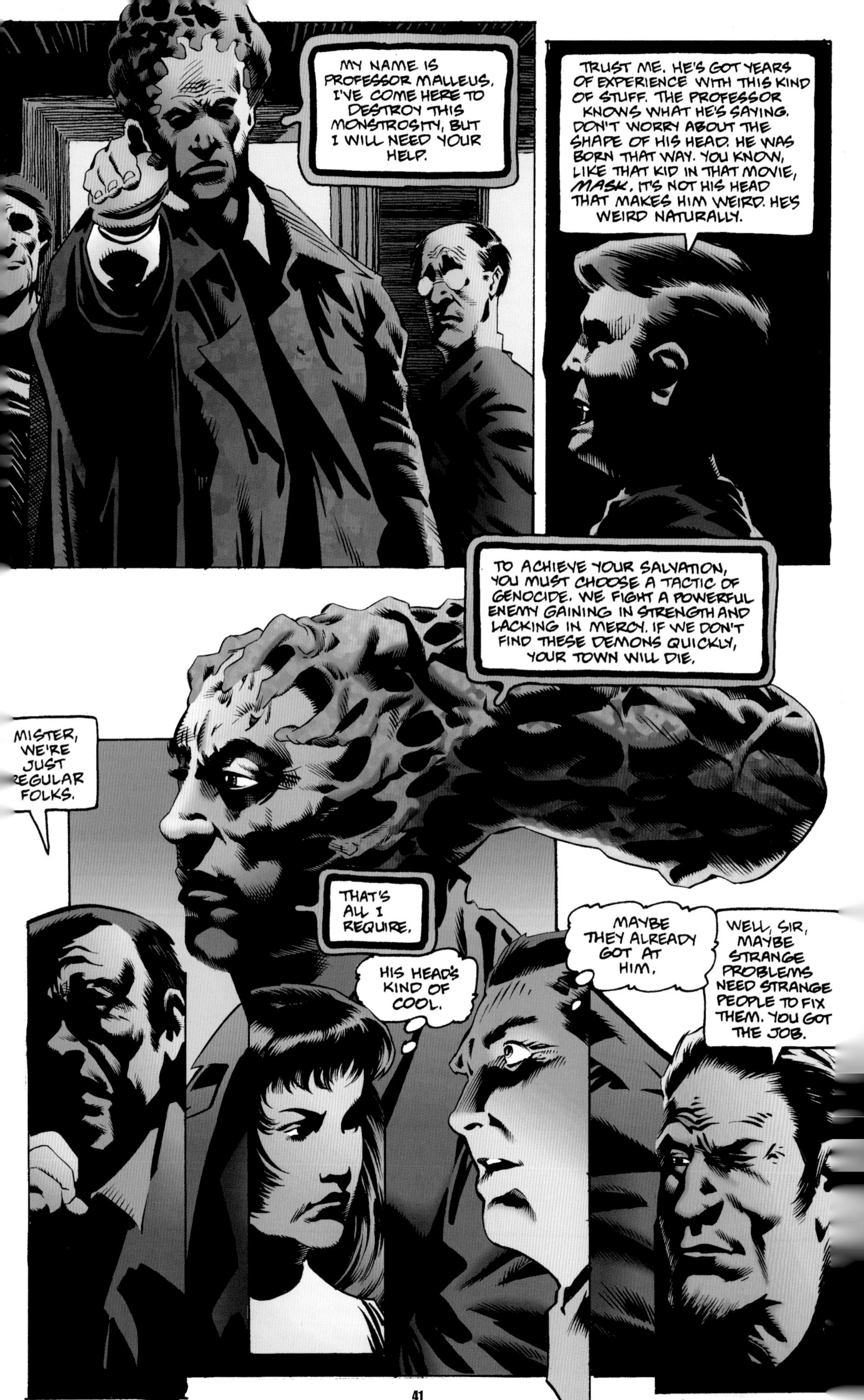
MY NAME IS PROFESSOR MALLEUS. I'VE COME HERE TO DESTROY THIS MONSTROSITY, BUT I WILL NEED YOUR HELP.
TRUST ME. HE'S GOT YEARS OF EXPERIENCE WITH THIS KIND OF STUFF. THE PROFESSOR KNOWS WHAT HE'S SAYING. DON'T WORRY ABOUT THE SHAPE OF HIS HEAD. HE WAS BORN THAT WAY. YOU KNOW, LIKE THAT KID IN THAT MOVIE, MASK. IT'S NOT HIS HEAD THAT MAKES HIM WEIRD. HE'S WEIRD NATURALLY.
TO ACHIEVE YOUR SALVATION, YOU MUST CHOOSE A TACTIC OF GENOCIDE. WE FIGHT A POWERFUL ENEMY GAINING IN STRENGTH AND LACKING IN MERCY. IF WE DON'T FIND THESE DEMONS QUICKLY, YOUR TOWN WILL DIE.
MISTER, WE'RE JUST REGULAR FOLKS.
THAT'S ALL I REQUIRE.
HIS HEAD'S KIND OF COOL.
MAYBE THEY ALREADY GOT AT HIM.
WELL, SIR, MAYBE STRANGE PROBLEMS NEED STRANGE PEOPLE TO FIX THEM. YOU GOT THE JOB.

Later.

EVERYONE STAY IN YOUR HOMES. WE WILL ACT IN THE MORNING. IF I AM CORRECT, THIS WILL ALL BE OVER TOMORROW.

SO, THIS IS WHAT YOU GUYS DO?

WELL, YES. WE RISK OUR LIVES ALL THE TIME WITH PROFESSOR MALLEUS.

MR. MALLEUS, I WANT TO APOLOGIZE FOR US STARING AT YOU SO RUDELY. CAN I GET YOU A CUP OF COFFEE?

YES, THANK YOU.

SALLY, COULD YOU GET THAT?

NO PROBLEM, DAD.

YOU SURE YOU WANT THIS MUCH SUGAR?

YES, THANK YOU.

CAN I ASK YOU SOMETHING-- OUT ON THE BACK PORCH?

SURE.

WHAT DID YOU WANT TO SAY, SALLY?

DO PEOPLE MAKE FUN OF YOU? BECAUSE OF YOUR HEAD, I MEAN?

THEY MOSTLY STARE. I'M DIFFERENT TO THEM. WHY DO YOU ASK?

WELL, I GOT SIX TOES ON ONE FOOT. THE OTHER KIDS MAKE FUN.

THAT MEANS YOU'VE BEEN MARKED, SALLY, YOU'RE A WARRIOR, LIKE ME.

COOL.

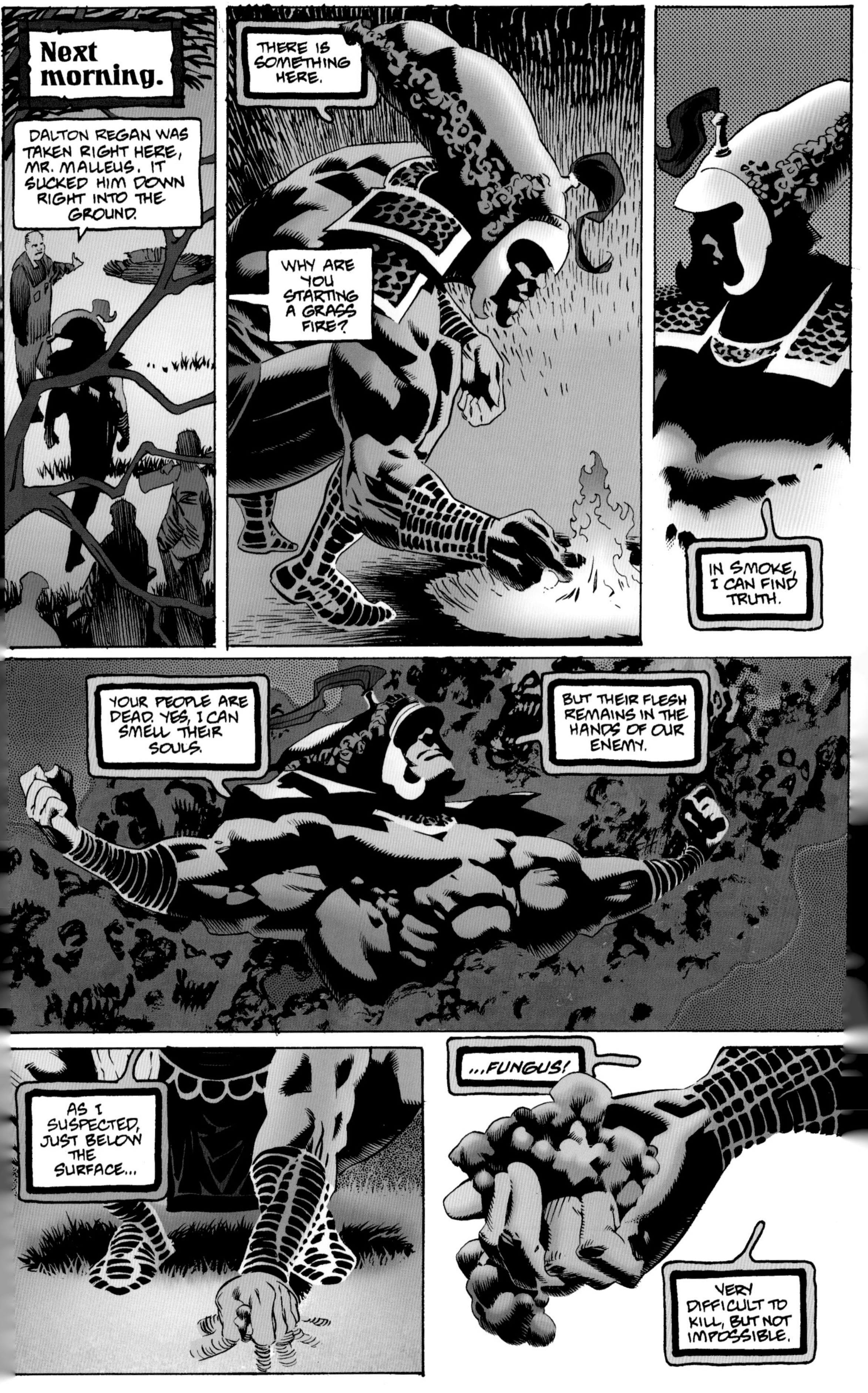
Next morning.
DALTON REGAN WAS TAKEN RIGHT HERE, MR. MALLEUS. IT SUCKED HIM DOWN RIGHT INTO THE GROUND.
THERE IS SOMETHING HERE.
WHY ARE YOU STARTING A GRASS FIRE?
IN SMOKE, I CAN FIND TRUTH.
YOUR PEOPLE ARE DEAD. YES, I CAN SMELL THEIR SOULS.
BUT THEIR FLESH REMAINS IN THE HANDS OF OUR ENEMY.
AS I SUSPECTED, JUST BELOW THE SURFACE...
...FUNGUS!
VERY DIFFICULT TO KILL, BUT NOT IMPOSSIBLE.

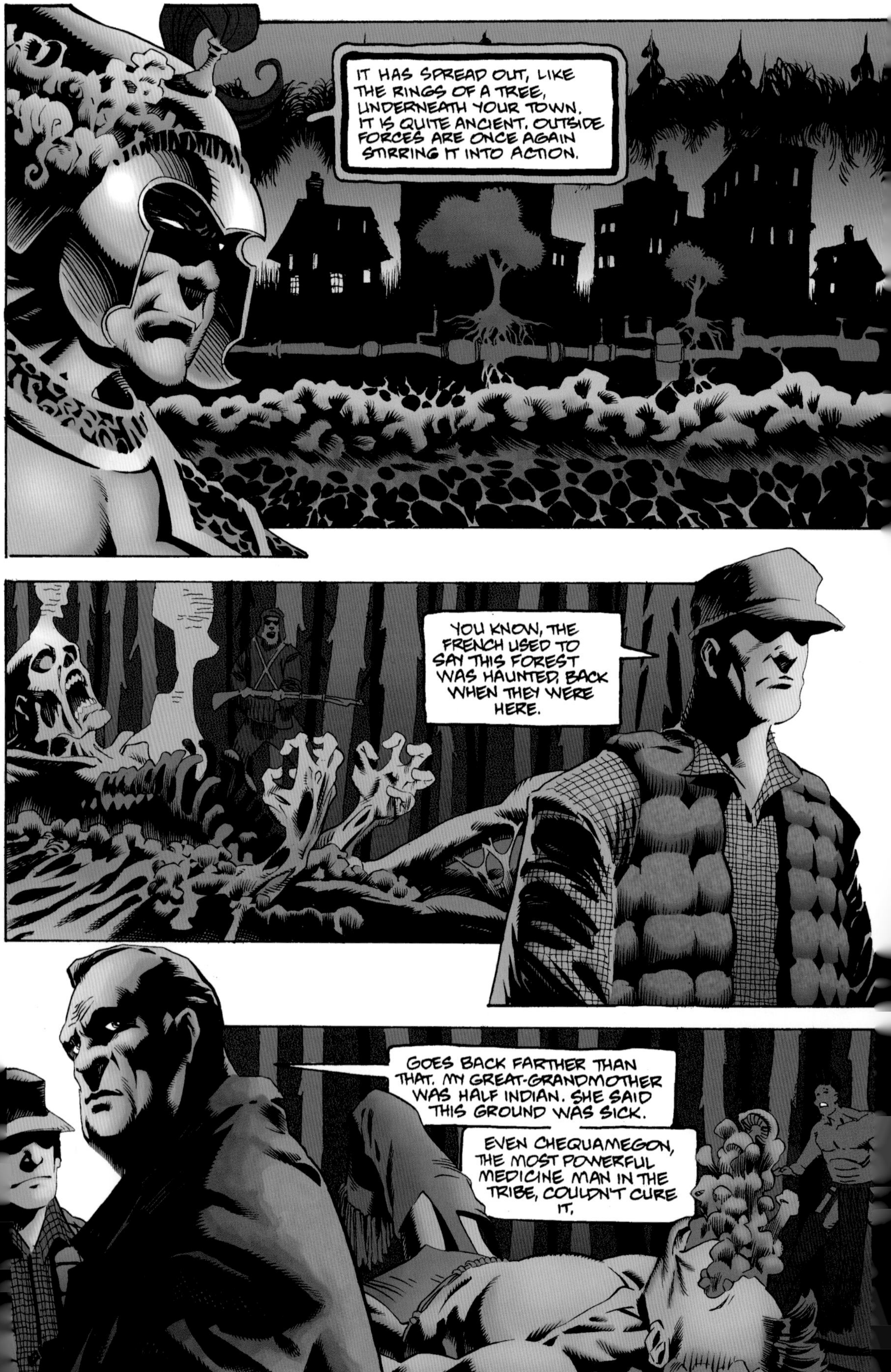
IT HAS SPREAD OUT, LIKE THE RINGS OF A TREE, UNDERNEATH YOUR TOWN. IT IS QUITE ANCIENT. OUTSIDE FORCES ARE ONCE AGAIN STIRRING IT INTO ACTION.
YOU KNOW, THE FRENCH USED TO SAY THIS FOREST WAS HAUNTED, BACK WHEN THEY WERE HERE.
GOES BACK FARTHER THAN THAT. MY GREAT-GRANDMOTHER WAS HALF INDIAN. SHE SAID THIS GROUND WAS SICK.
EVEN CHEQUAMEGON, THE MOST POWERFUL MEDICINE MAN IN THE TRIBE, COULDN'T CURE IT.

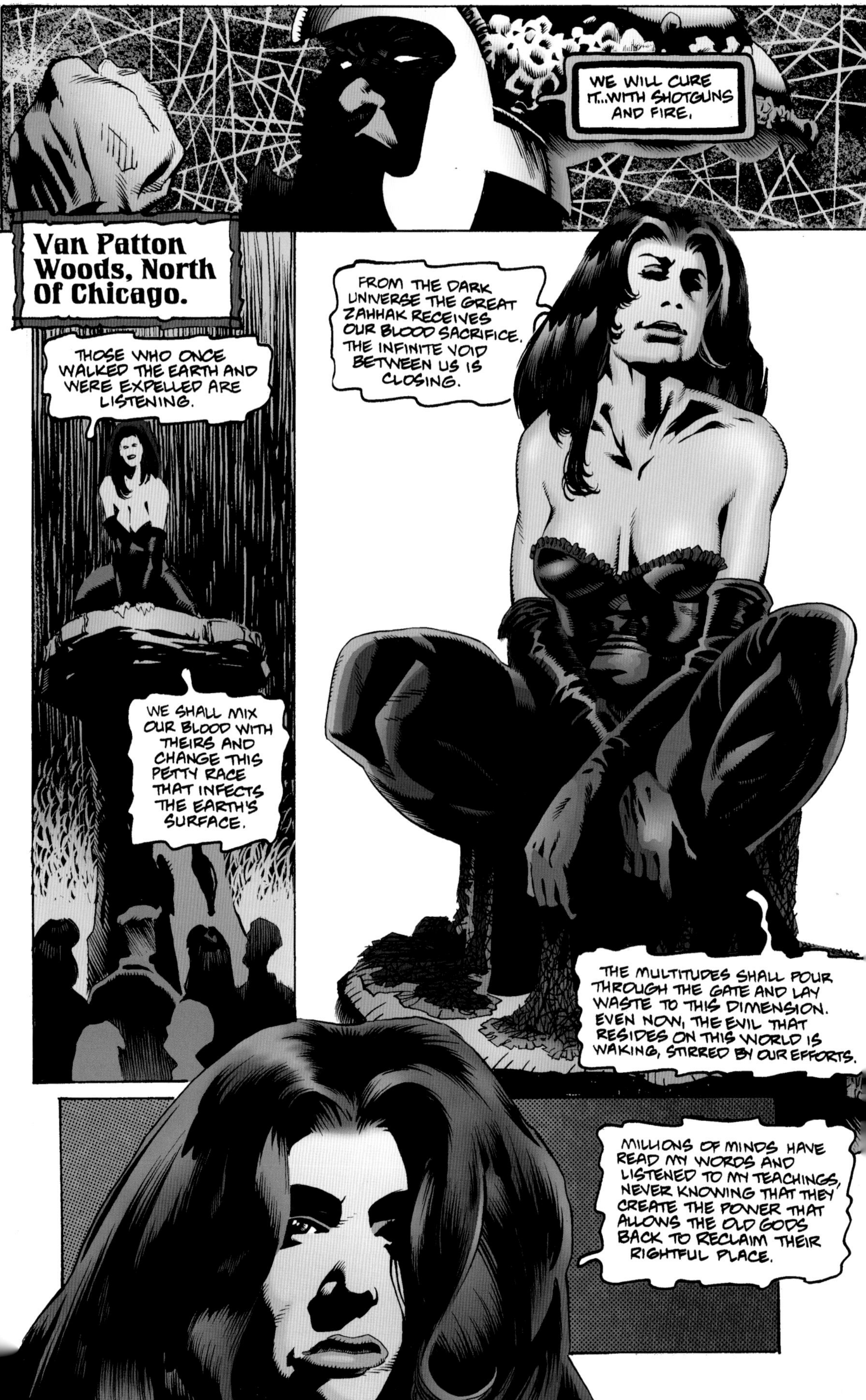

WE WILL CURE IT...WITH SHOTGUNS AND FIRE.
Van Patton Woods, North Of Chicago.
THOSE WHO ONCE WALKED THE EARTH AND WERE EXPELLED ARE LISTENING.
FROM THE DARK UNIVERSE THE GREAT ZAHHAK RECEIVES OUR BLOOD SACRIFICE. THE INFINITE VOID BETWEEN US IS CLOSING.
WE SHALL MIX OUR BLOOD WITH THEIRS AND CHANGE THIS PETTY RACE THAT INFECTS THE EARTH'S SURFACE.
THE MULTITUDES SHALL POUR THROUGH THE GATE AND LAY WASTE TO THIS DIMENSION. EVEN NOW, THE EVIL THAT RESIDES ON THIS WORLD IS WAKING, STIRRED BY OUR EFFORTS.
MILLIONS OF MINDS HAVE READ MY WORDS AND LISTENED TO MY TEACHINGS, NEVER KNOWING THAT THEY CREATE THE POWER THAT ALLOWS THE OLD GODS BACK TO RECLAIM THEIR RIGHTFUL PLACE.

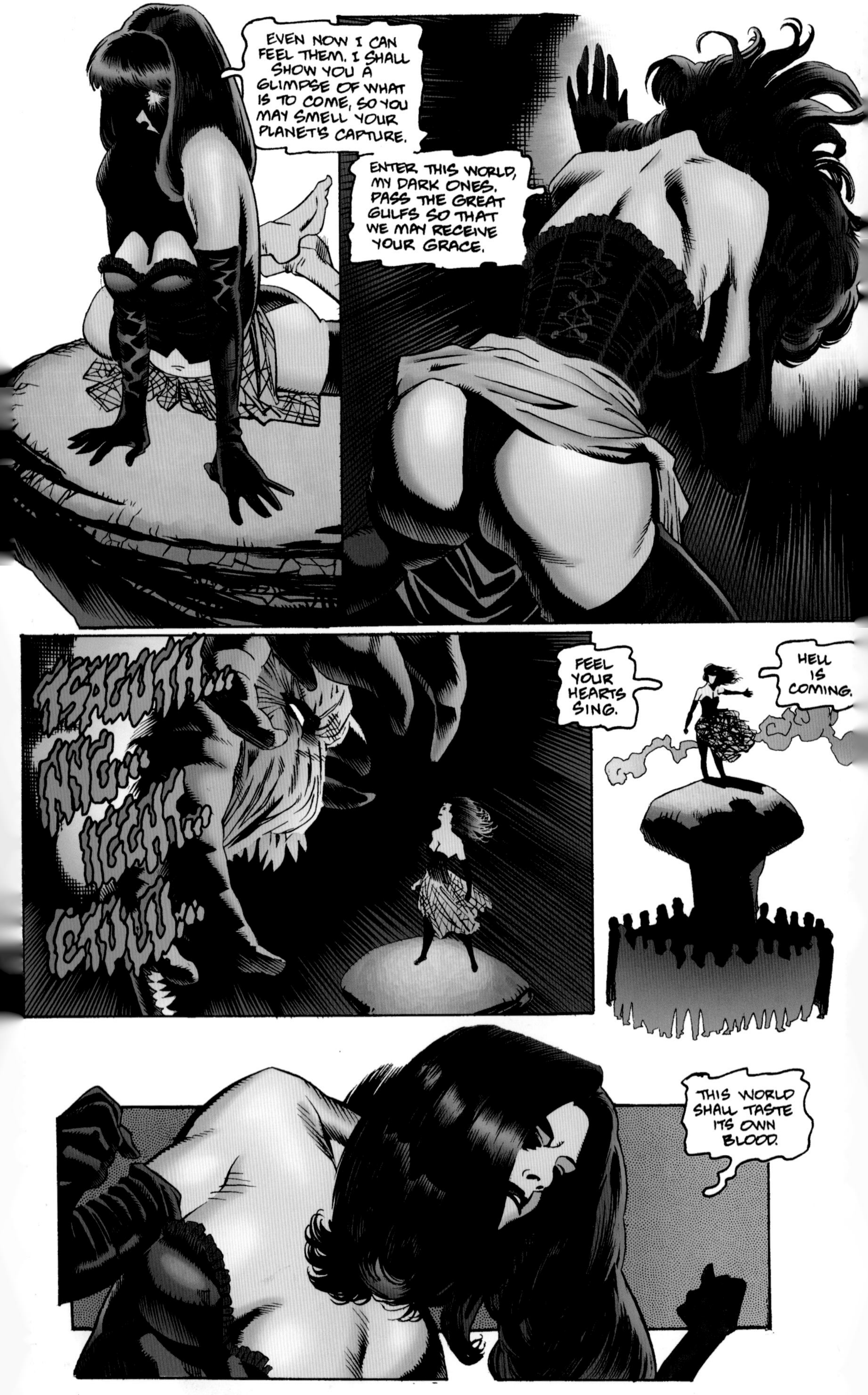
EVEN NOW I CAN FEEL THEM. I SHALL SHOW YOU A GLIMPSE OF WHAT IS TO COME, SO YOU MAY SMELL YOUR PLANET'S CAPTURE.
ENTER THIS WORLD, MY DARK ONES. PASS THE GREAT GULFS SO THAT WE MAY RECEIVE YOUR GRACE.
FEEL YOUR HEARTS SING.
HELL IS COMING.
THIS WORLD SHALL TASTE ITS OWN BLOOD.

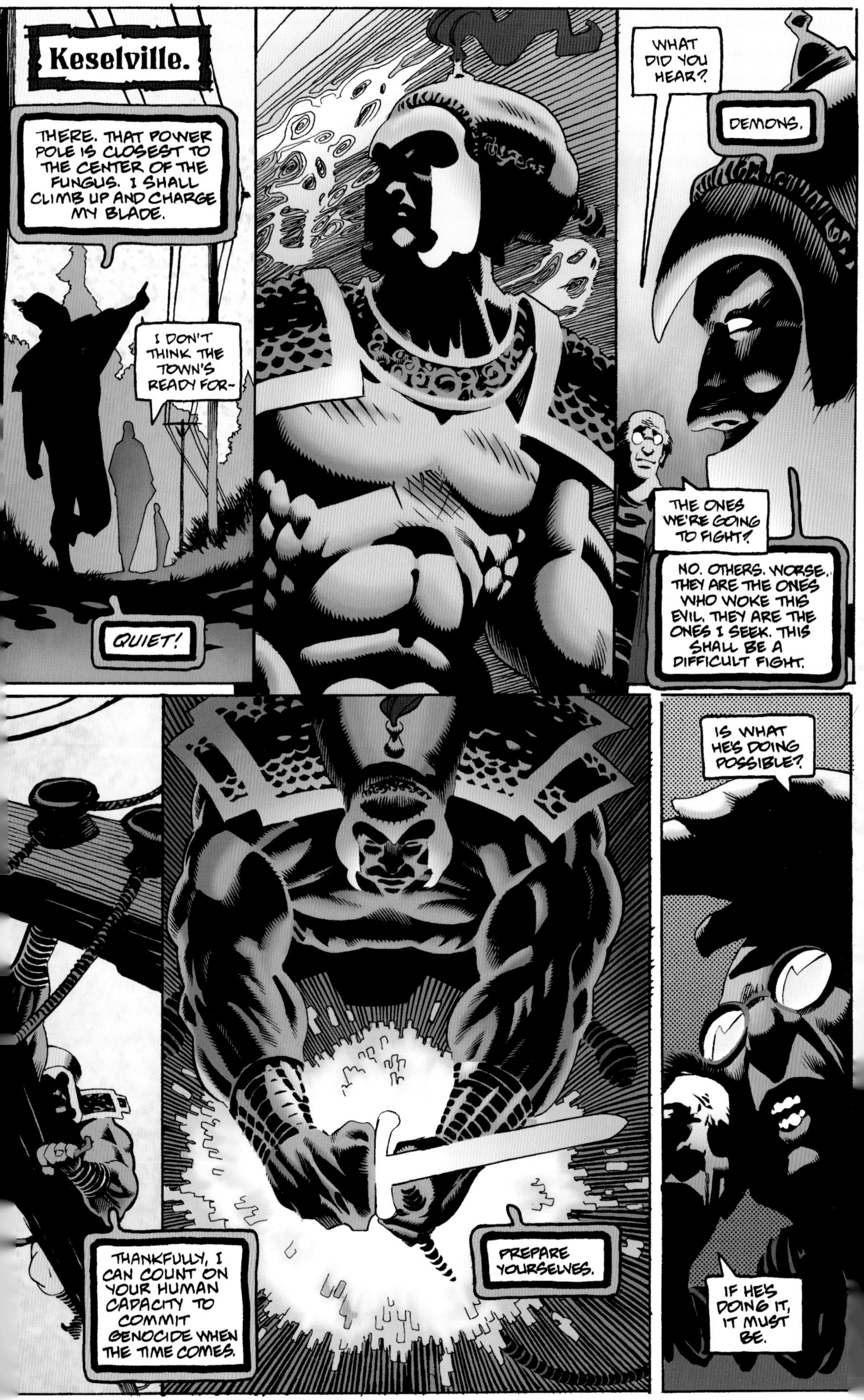
Keselville.
THERE. THAT POWER POLE IS CLOSEST TO THE CENTER OF THE FUNGUS. I SHALL CLIMB UP AND CHARGE MY BLADE.
I DON'T THINK THE TOWN'S READY FOR-
QUIET!
WHAT DID YOU HEAR?
DEMONS.
THE ONES WE'RE GOING TO FIGHT?
NO. OTHERS. WORSE. THEY ARE THE ONES WHO WOKE THIS EVIL. THEY ARE THE ONES I SEEK. THIS SHALL BE A DIFFICULT FIGHT.
THANKFULLY, I CAN COUNT ON YOUR HUMAN CAPACITY TO COMMIT GENOCIDE WHEN THE TIME COMES.
PREPARE YOURSELVES.
IS WHAT HE'S DOING POSSIBLE?
IF HE'S DOING IT, IT MUST BE.

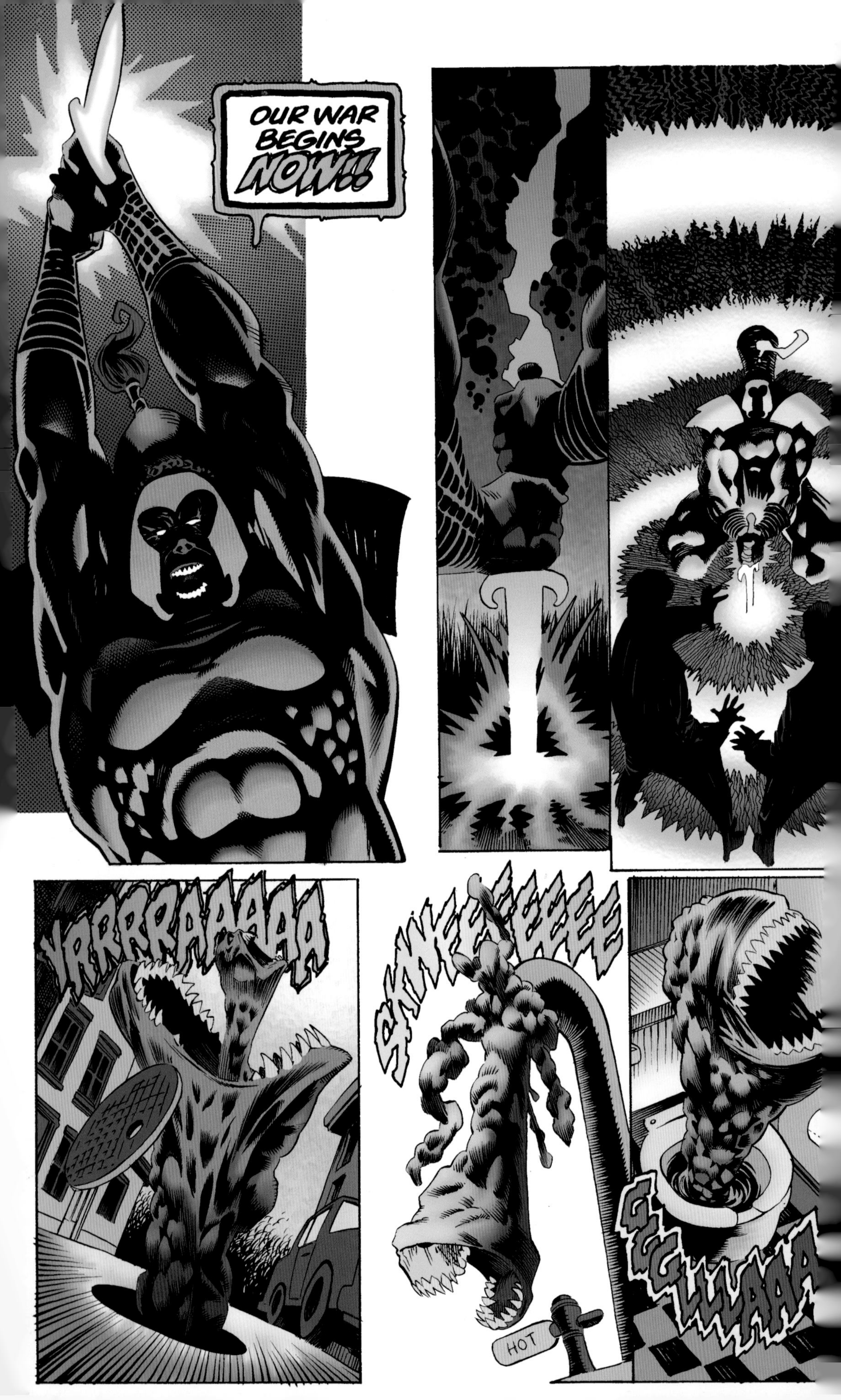
OUR WAR BEGINS NOW!!
HOT

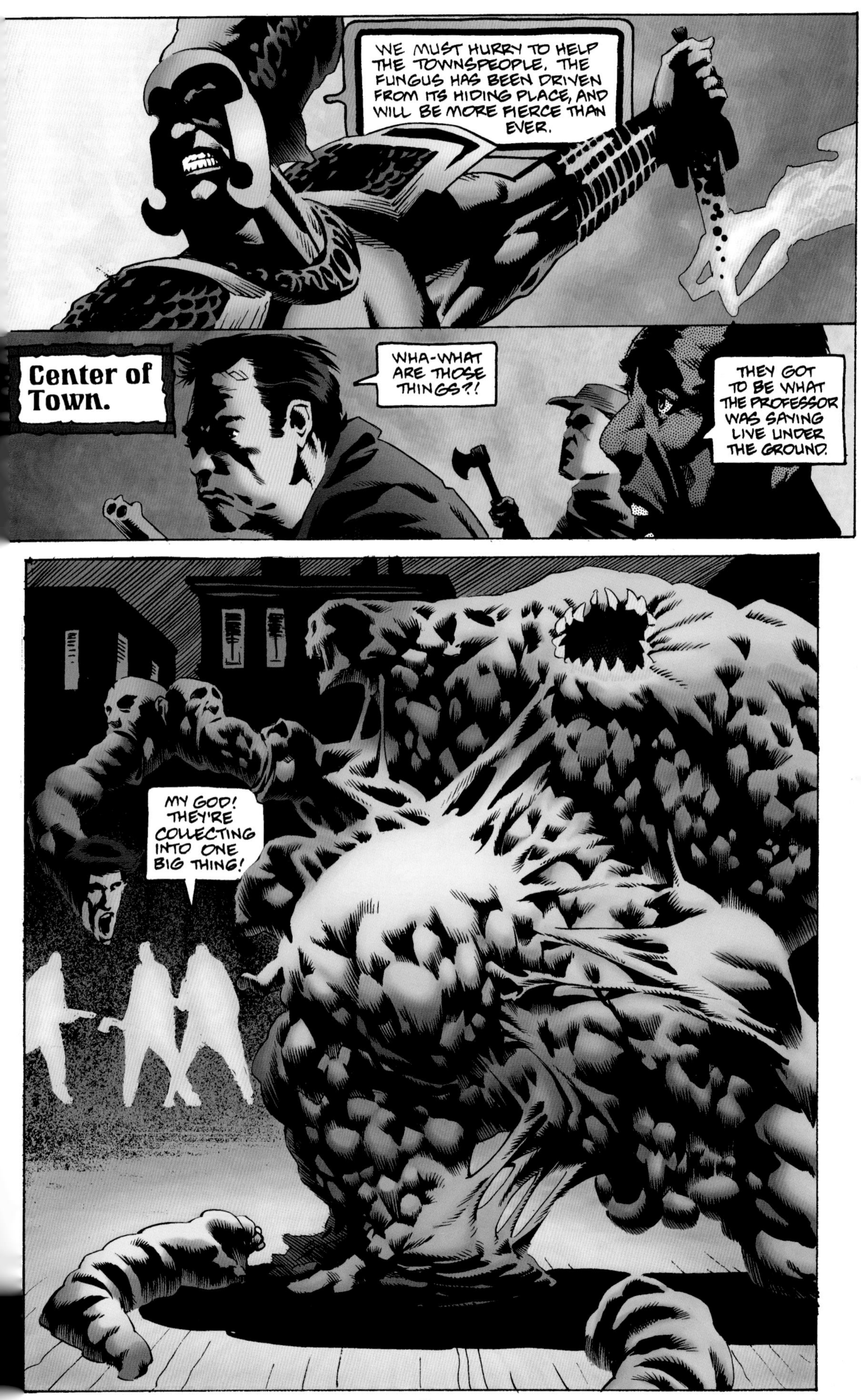
WE MUST HURRY TO HELP THE TOWNSPEOPLE. THE FUNGUS HAS BEEN DRIVEN FROM ITS HIDING PLACE, AND WILL BE MORE FIERCE THAN EVER.
Center of Town.
WHA-WHAT ARE THOSE THINGS?!
THEY GOT TO BE WHAT THE PROFESSOR WAS SAYING LIVE UNDER THE GROUND.
MY GOD! THEY'RE COLLECTING INTO ONE BIG THING!

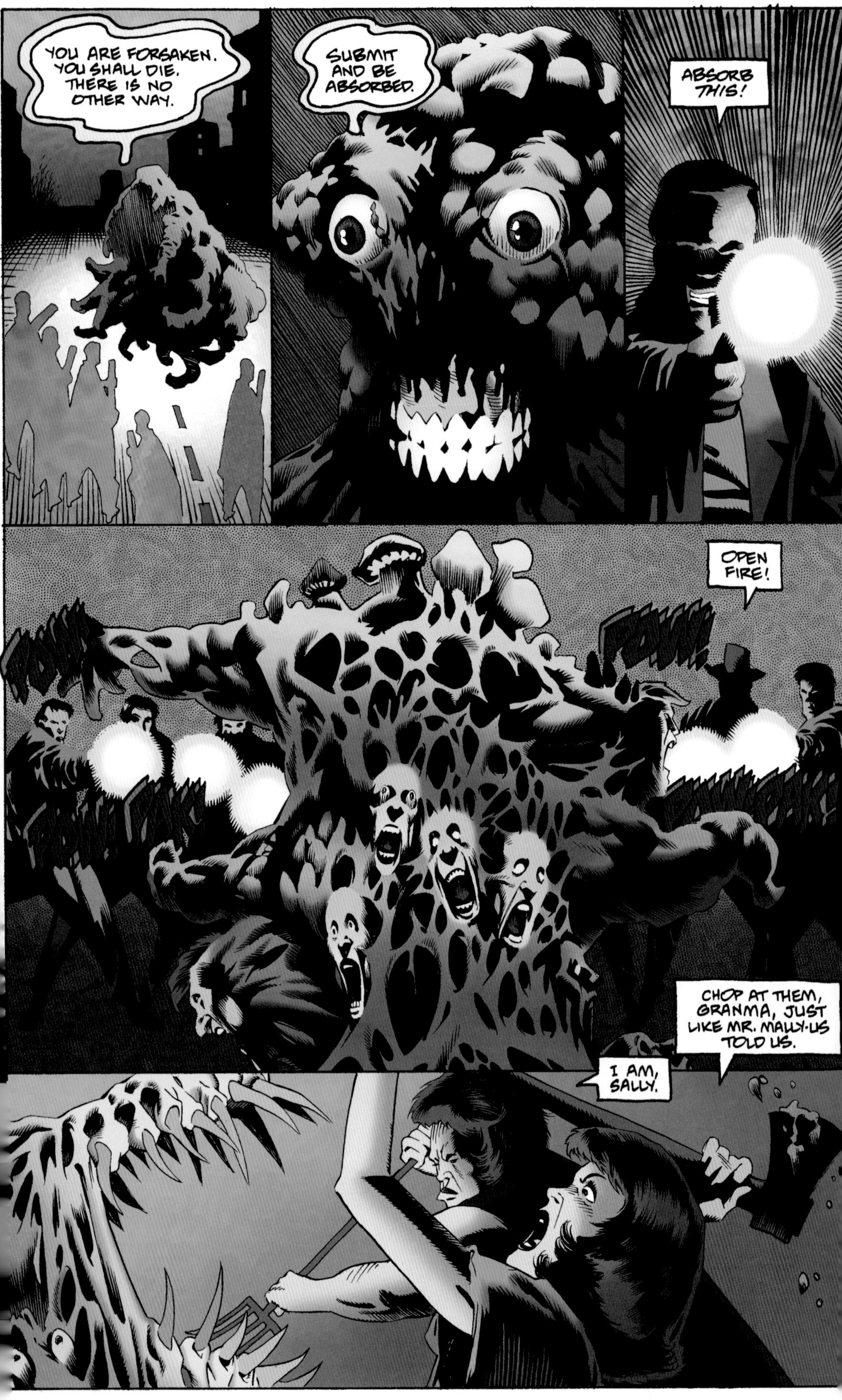
YOU ARE FORSAKEN. YOU SHALL DIE. THERE IS NO OTHER WAY.
SUBMIT AND BE ABSORBED.
ABSORB THIS!
OPEN FIRE!
POW!
POW!
POW! PAK!
PAK! PAK!
CHOP AT THEM, GRANMA, JUST LIKE MR. MALLY-US TOLD US.
I AM, SALLY.

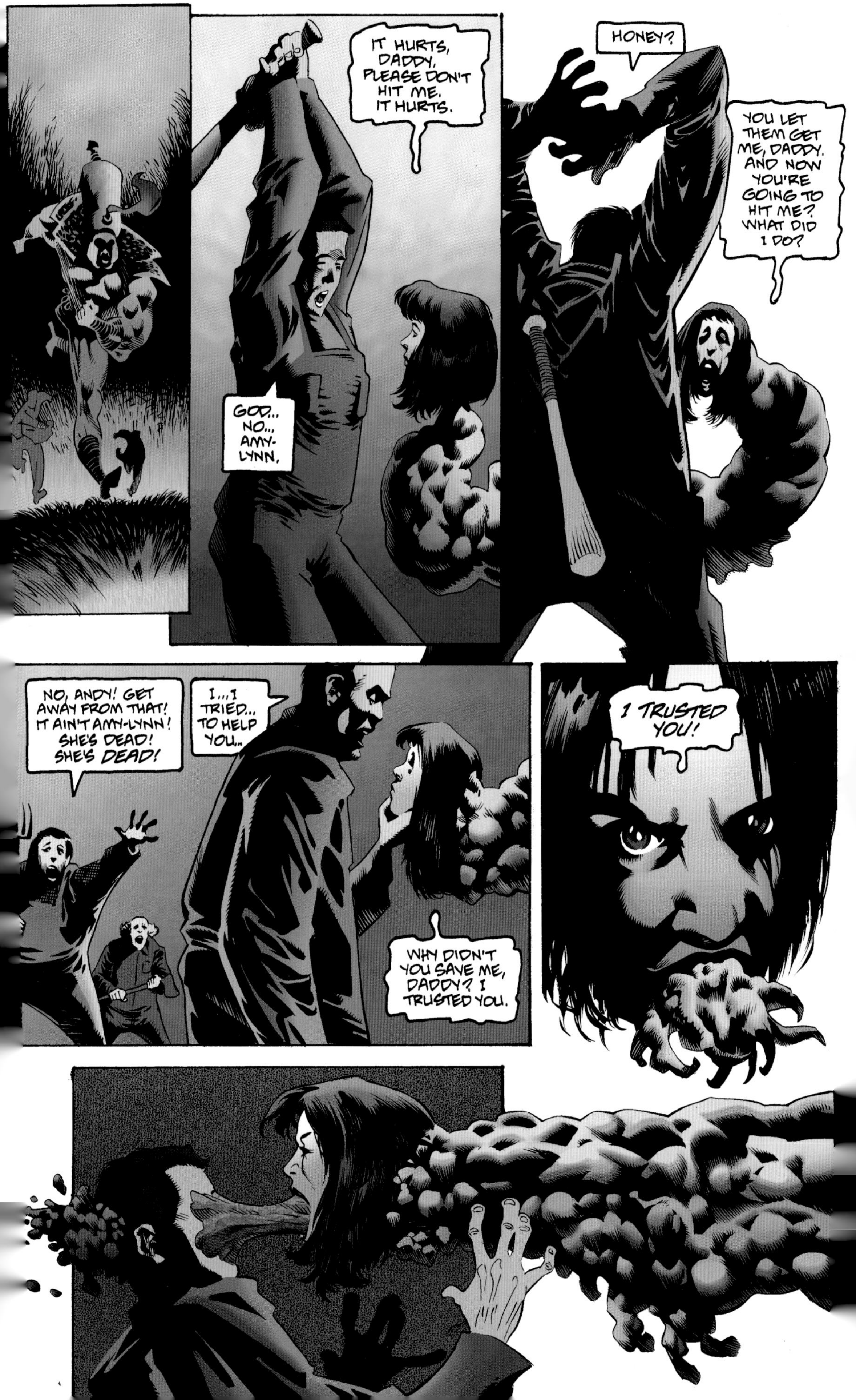

IT HURTS, DADDY, PLEASE DON'T HIT ME. IT HURTS.
GOD... NO... AMY-LYNN.
HONEY?
YOU LET THEM GET ME, DADDY. AND NOW YOU'RE GOING TO HIT ME? WHAT DID I DO?
NO, ANDY! GET AWAY FROM THAT! IT AIN'T AMY-LYNN! SHE'S DEAD! SHE'S DEAD!
I...I TRIED... TO HELP YOU...
WHY DIDN'T YOU SAVE ME, DADDY? I TRUSTED YOU.
I TRUSTED YOU!

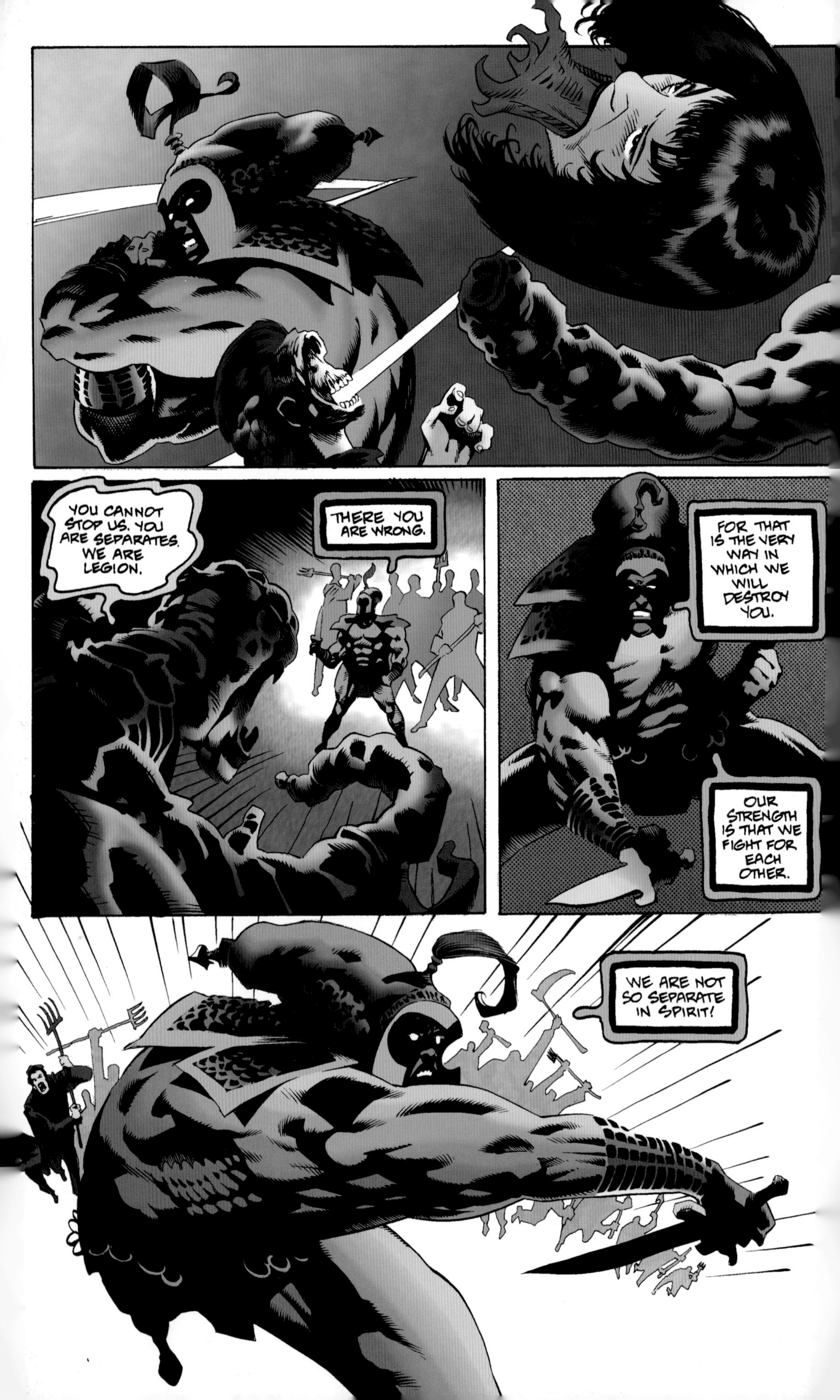

YOU CANNOT STOP US. YOU ARE SEPARATES. WE ARE LEGION.
THERE YOU ARE WRONG.
FOR THAT IS THE VERY WAY IN WHICH WE WILL DESTROY YOU.
OUR STRENGTH IS THAT WE FIGHT FOR EACH OTHER.
WE ARE NOT SO SEPARATE IN SPIRIT!

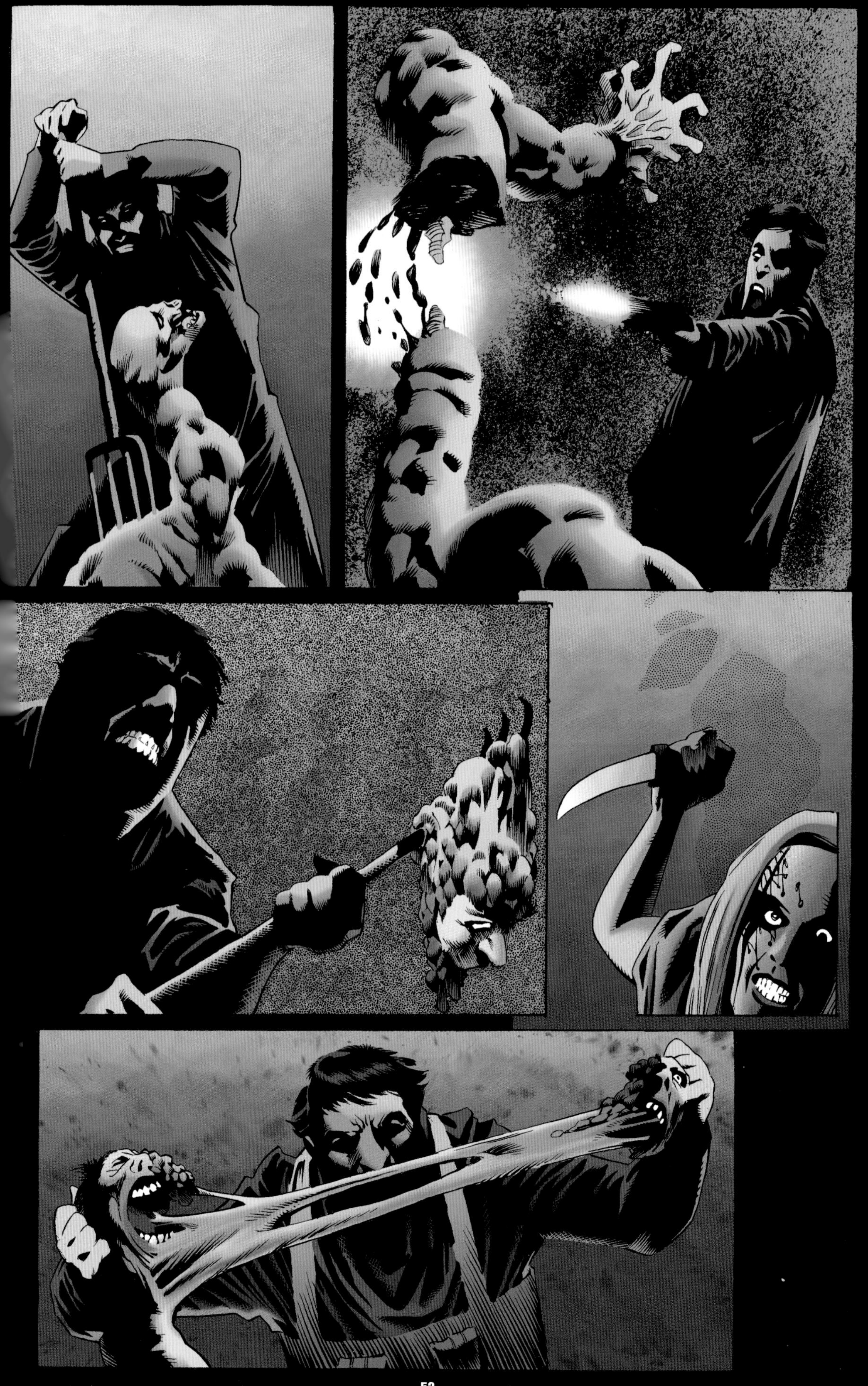

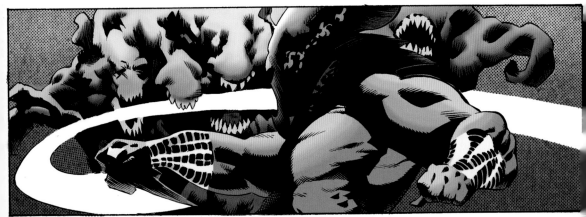

ALL OF YOU—STAND BACK!

I SHALL BRING THIS TO AN END.

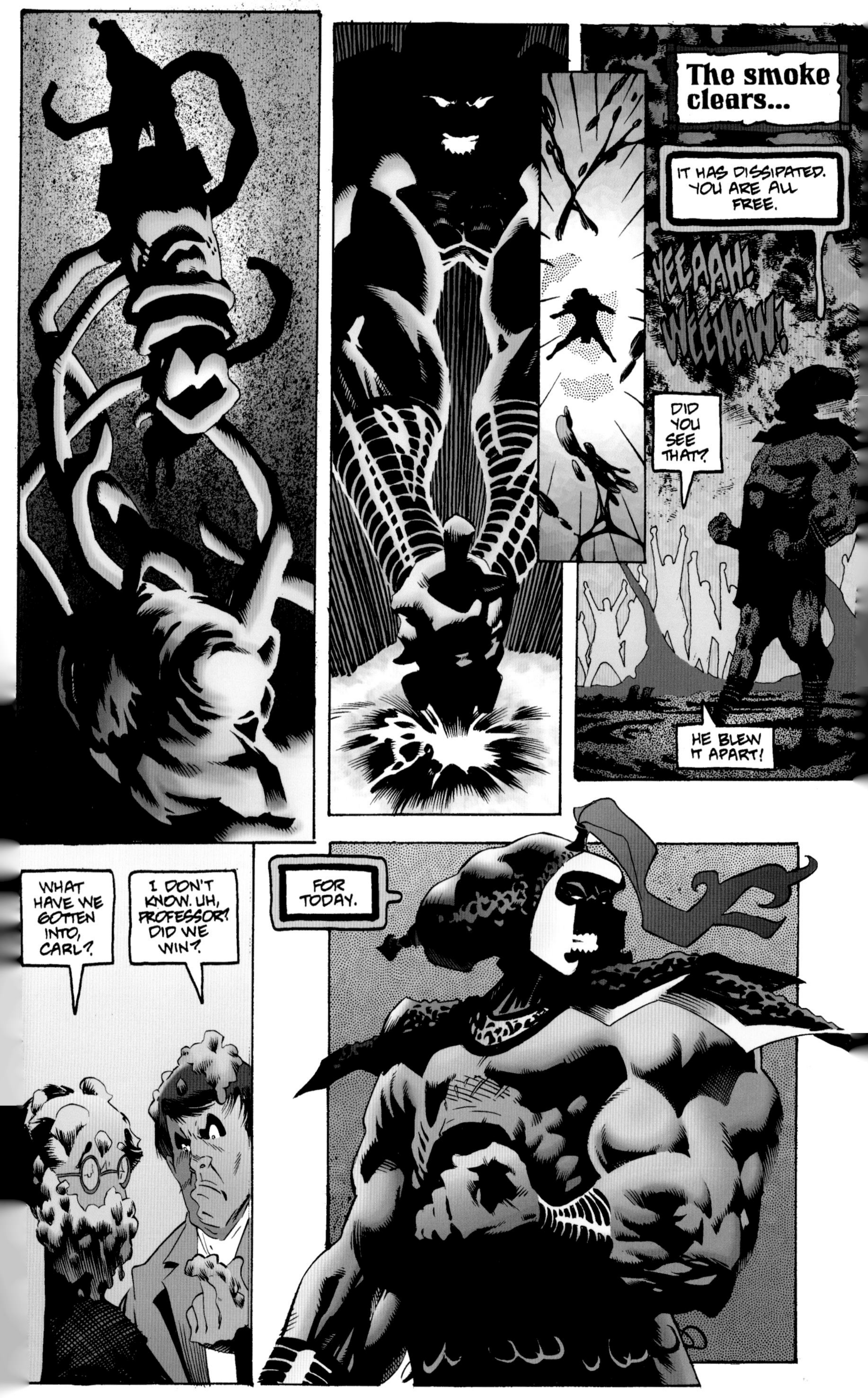
The smoke clears...
IT HAS DISSIPATED. YOU ARE ALL FREE.
YEEAAH! WEEHAW!
DID YOU SEE THAT?
HE BLEW IT APART!
WHAT HAVE WE GOTTEN INTO, CARL?
I DON'T KNOW. UH, PROFESSOR? DID WE WIN?
FOR TODAY.

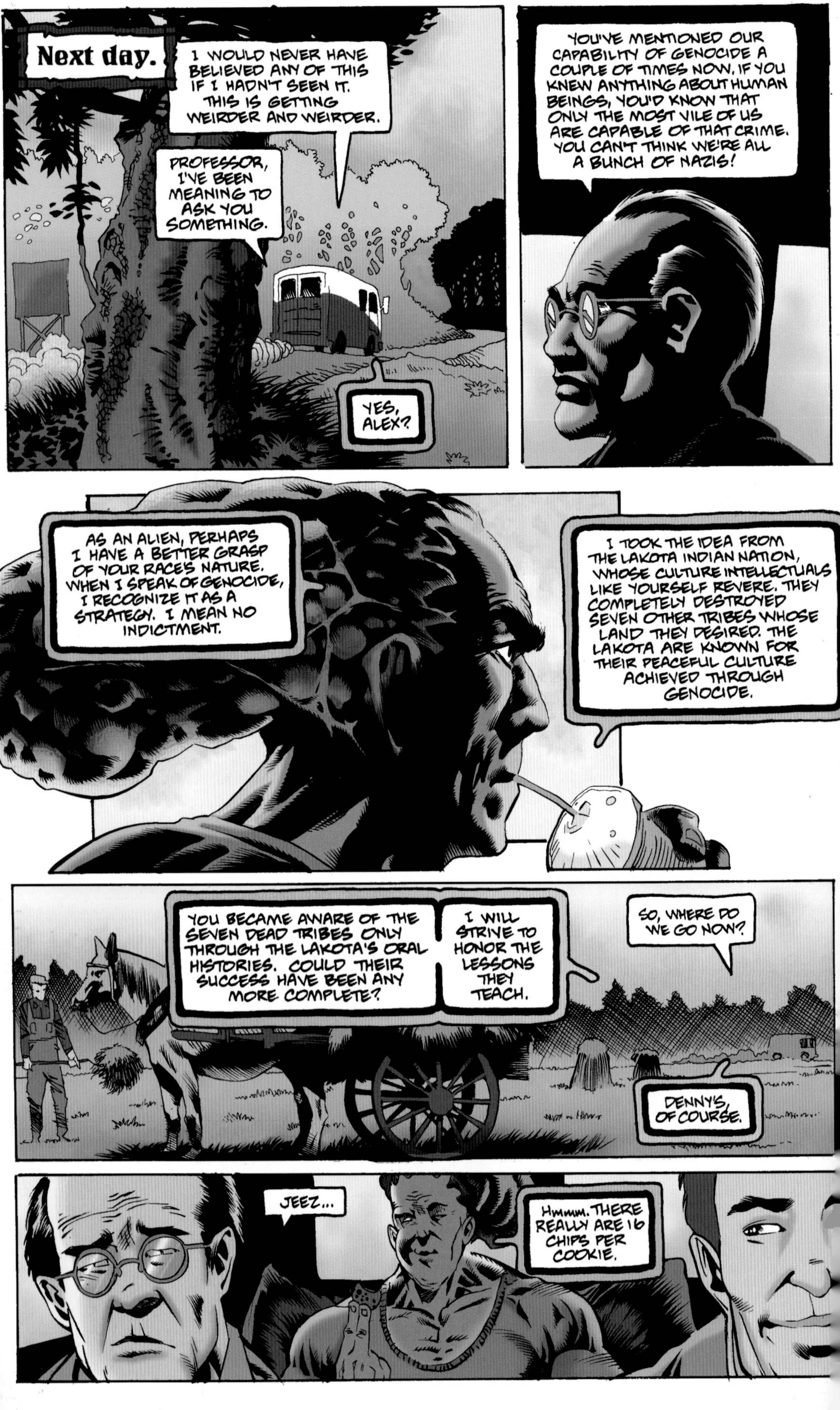
Next day.
I WOULD NEVER HAVE BELIEVED ANY OF THIS IF I HADN'T SEEN IT. THIS IS GETTING WEIRDER AND WEIRDER.
PROFESSOR, I'VE BEEN MEANING TO ASK YOU SOMETHING.
YES, ALEX?
YOU'VE MENTIONED OUR CAPABILITY OF GENOCIDE A COUPLE OF TIMES NOW. IF YOU KNEW ANYTHING ABOUT HUMAN BEINGS, YOU'D KNOW THAT ONLY THE MOST VILE OF US ARE CAPABLE OF THAT CRIME. YOU CAN'T THINK WE'RE ALL A BUNCH OF NAZIS!
AS AN ALIEN, PERHAPS I HAVE A BETTER GRASP OF YOUR RACE'S NATURE. WHEN I SPEAK OF GENOCIDE, I RECOGNIZE IT AS A STRATEGY. I MEAN NO INDICTMENT.
I TOOK THE IDEA FROM THE LAKOTA INDIAN NATION, WHOSE CULTURE INTELLECTUALS LIKE YOURSELF REVERE. THEY COMPLETELY DESTROYED SEVEN OTHER TRIBES WHOSE LAND THEY DESIRED. THE LAKOTA ARE KNOWN FOR THEIR PEACEFUL CULTURE ACHIEVED THROUGH GENOCIDE.
YOU BECAME AWARE OF THE SEVEN DEAD TRIBES ONLY THROUGH THE LAKOTA'S ORAL HISTORIES. COULD THEIR SUCCESS HAVE BEEN ANY MORE COMPLETE?
I WILL STRIVE TO HONOR THE LESSONS THEY TEACH.
SO, WHERE DO WE GO NOW?
DENNY'S, OF COURSE.
JEEZ...
Hmmm. THERE REALLY ARE 16 CHIPS PER COOKIE.

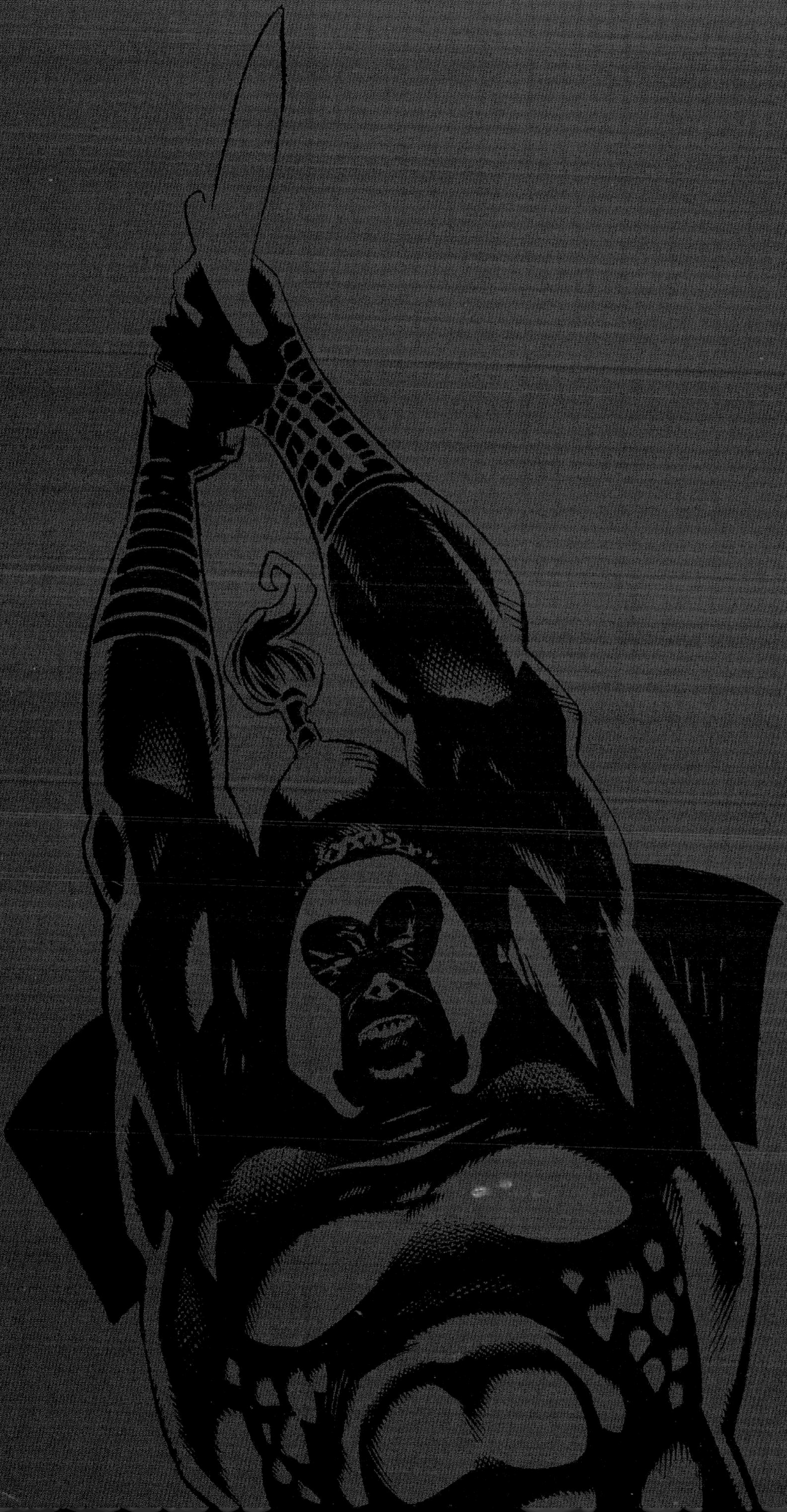

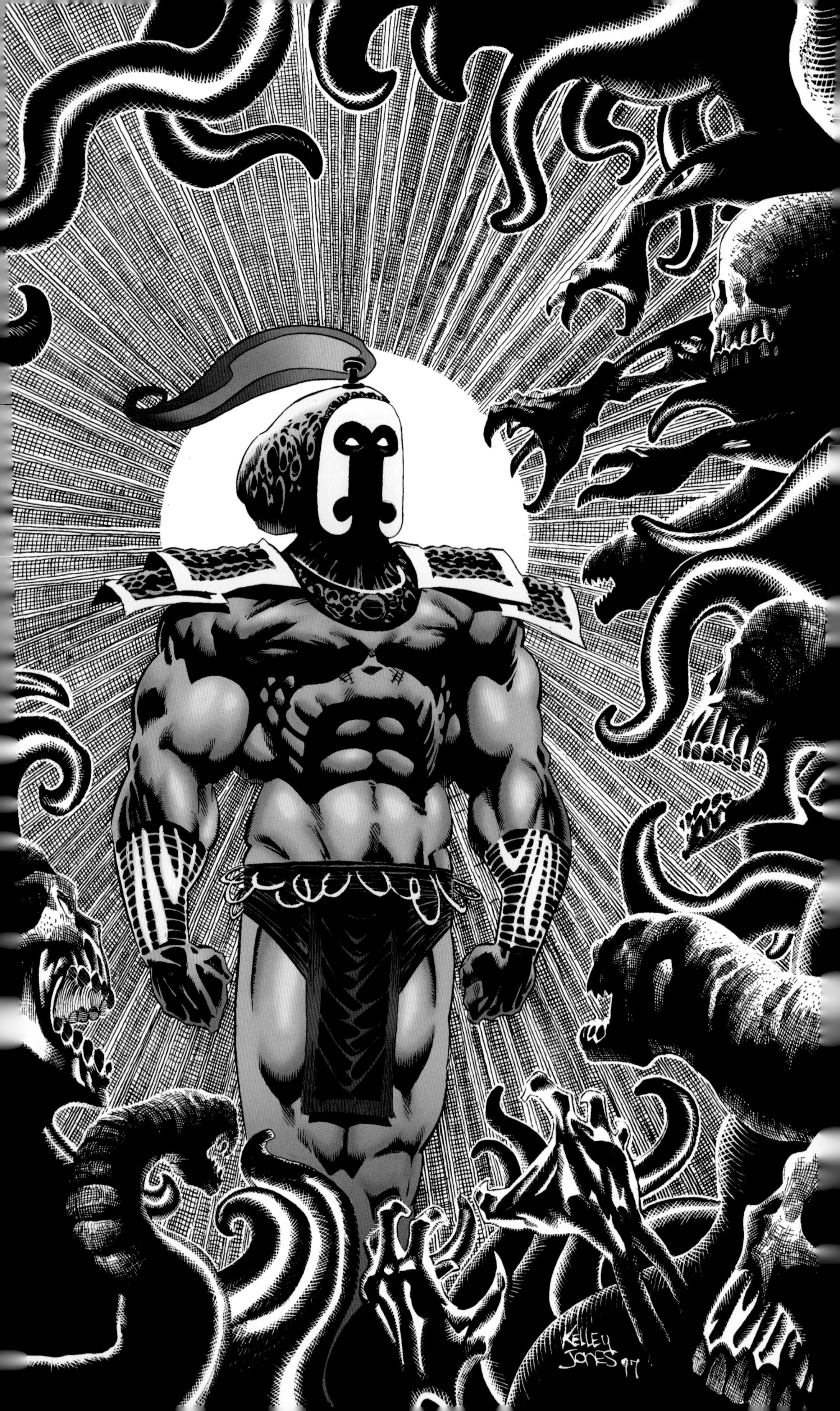
KELLEY JONES '97

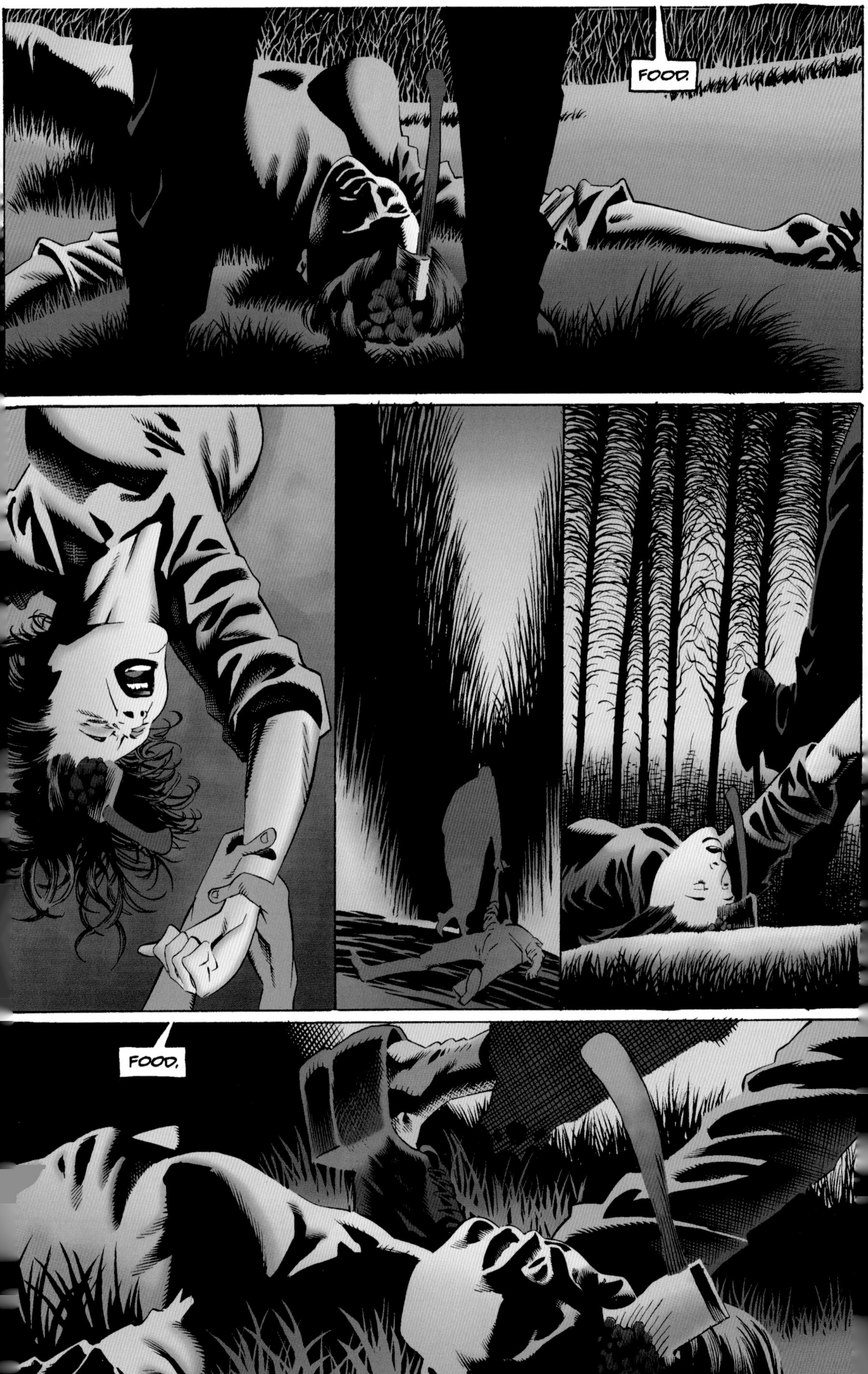
FOOD.
FOOD,

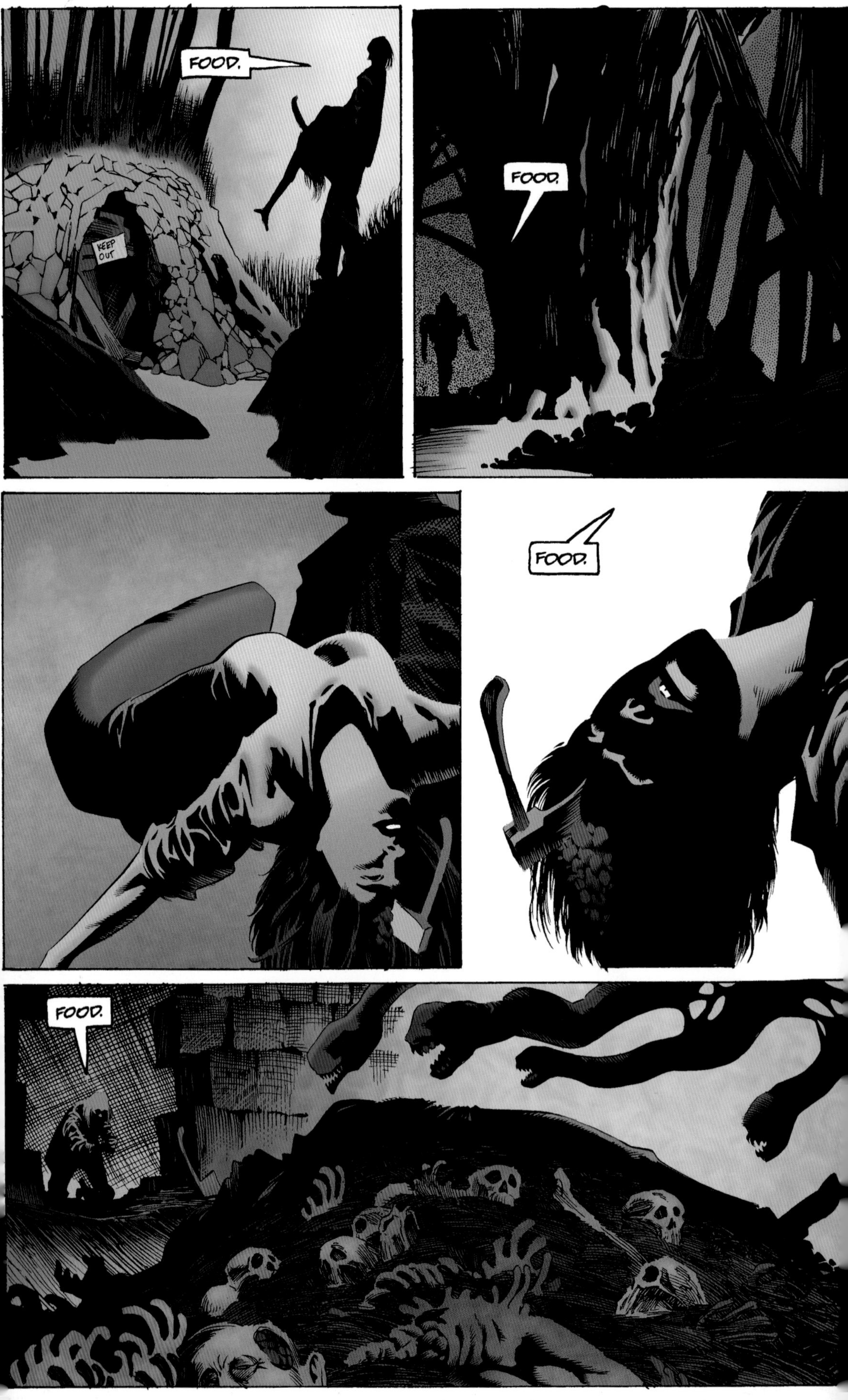
FOOD.
KEEP OUT
FOOD.
FOOD.
FOOD.

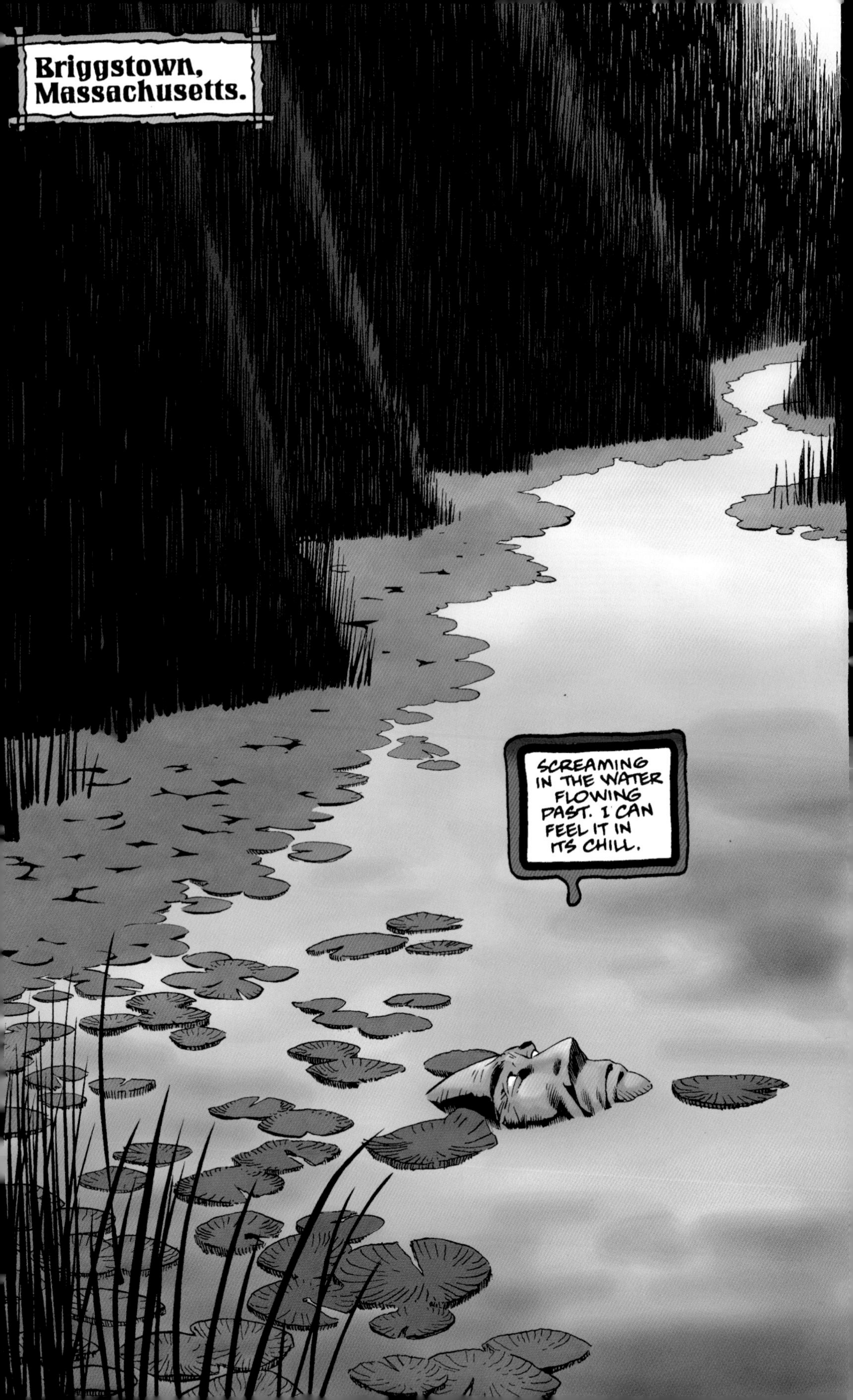
Briggstown, Massachusetts.
SCREAMING IN THE WATER FLOWING PAST. I CAN FEEL IT IN ITS CHILL.

HOW CAN YOU TELL IF IT'S WHAT WE'RE LOOKING FOR?

THE EVIL I SEEK IS IN THE FABRIC OF THE VERY EARTH ITSELF.

I AM ATTEMPTING TO DETERMINE FROM WHERE THIS TERROR EMANATES.

PROFESSOR, THE PAPERS ARE FULL OF SENSELESS VIOLENCE. BY THE TIME YOU TRACK DOWN THE SOURCE OF ONE LONE SCREAM IN THE MIDST OF ALL THOSE OTHERS--

WELL, YOU'RE GOING TO BE A WALKING PRUNE. THERE WAS A BOMBING IN BOSTON, A SNIPER IN PORTLAND, A MISSING GIRL IN NASHVILLE--

CARL, THE PROFESSOR IS DEAD. THAT ALIEN ATTACHED TO HIS SKULL HASN'T BEEN TOO GOOD AT ANSWERING OUR QUESTIONS, BUT I THINK HE'S PROVEN HIMSELF AT FINDING THE BAD GUYS.

SO, MALLEUS, WERE YOU A HERO ON YOUR OWN WORLD? WHY DID THEY EVER LET YOU LEAVE?

THEY DIDN'T. I ESCAPED.

I WAS LABELED CRIMINALLY INSANE.

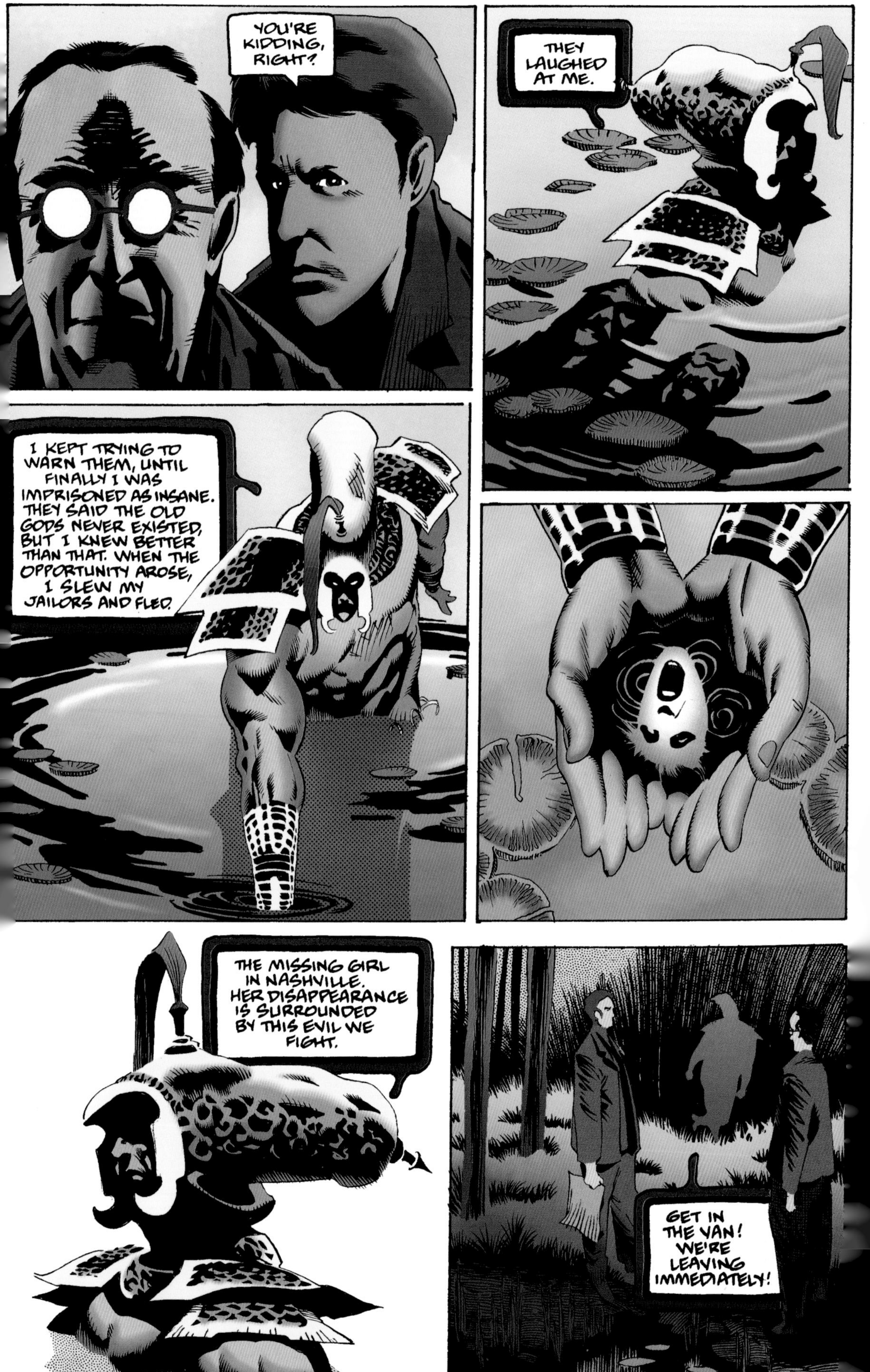
YOU'RE KIDDING, RIGHT?
THEY LAUGHED AT ME.
I KEPT TRYING TO WARN THEM, UNTIL FINALLY I WAS IMPRISONED AS INSANE. THEY SAID THE OLD GODS NEVER EXISTED, BUT I KNEW BETTER THAN THAT. WHEN THE OPPORTUNITY AROSE, I SLEW MY JAILORS AND FLED.
THE MISSING GIRL IN NASHVILLE. HER DISAPPEARANCE IS SURROUNDED BY THIS EVIL WE FIGHT.
GET IN THE VAN! WE'RE LEAVING IMMEDIATELY!

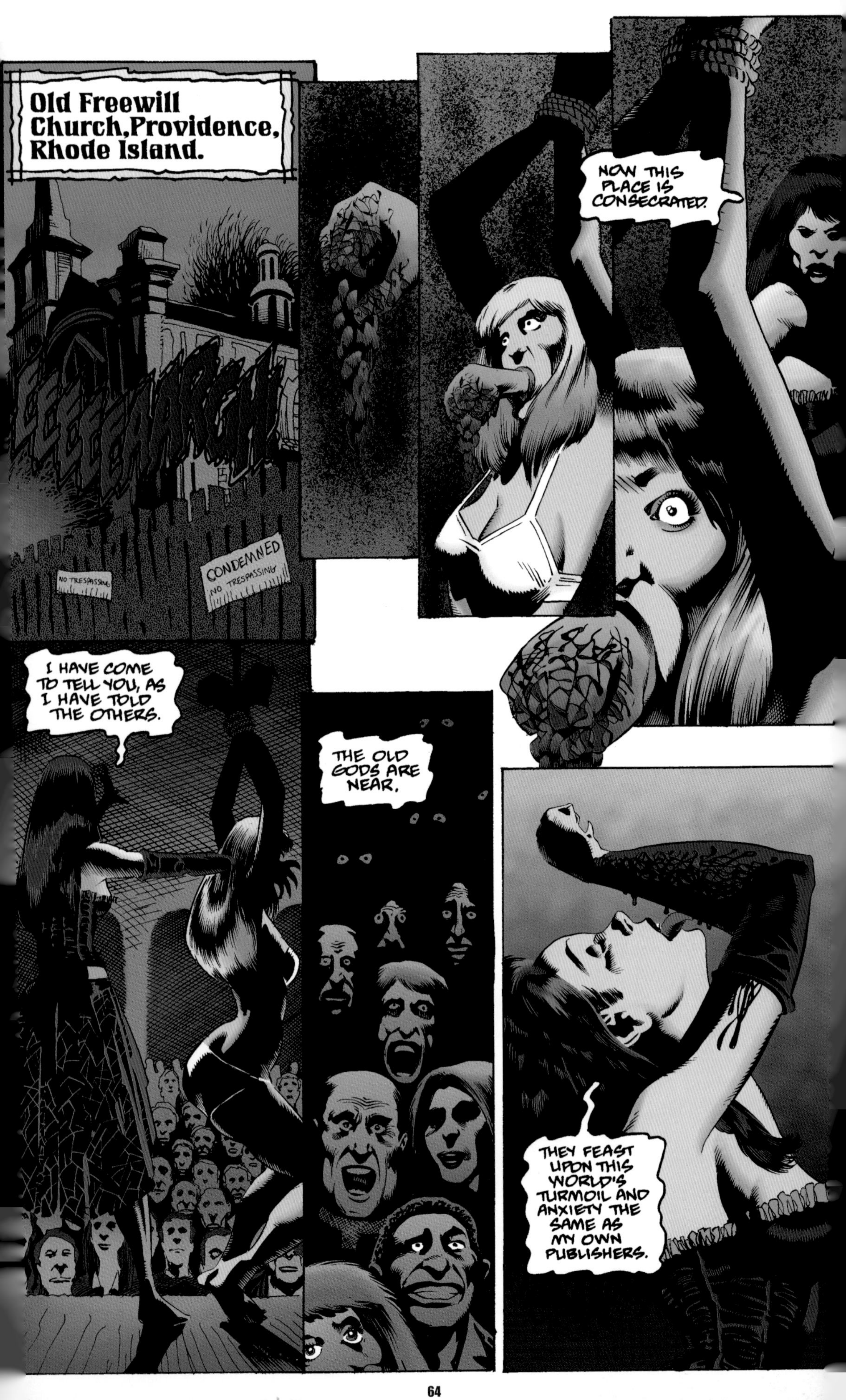
Old Freewill Church, Providence, Rhode Island.
CHURCH
NO TRESPASSING
CONDEMNED NO TRESPASSING
NOW THIS PLACE IS CONSECRATED.
I HAVE COME TO TELL YOU, AS I HAVE TOLD THE OTHERS.
THE OLD GODS ARE NEAR.
THEY FEAST UPON THIS WORLD'S TURMOIL AND ANXIETY THE SAME AS MY OWN PUBLISHERS.

I RETURNED TO PREPARE THE WAY FOR THE OLD ONES, AND TO SPREAD WORD OF THE GRIEVOUS FATE OF THE DEMONS THAT STILL LIE DORMANT ON THIS WORLD, SUFFERING.

" FOR OVER A CENTURY NOW, DREDGING PLATFORMS HAVE PLUNGED GREEDY SPIKES INTO THIS EARTH."

DRILLING DEEP, DOWN BELOW TO PLACES MAN HAS NEVER BEEN...

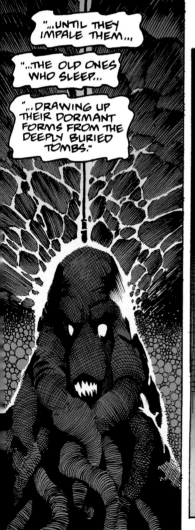

"...UNTIL THEY IMPALE THEM...

"...THE OLD ONES WHO SLEEP...

"...DRAWING UP THEIR DORMANT FORMS FROM THE DEEPLY BURIED TOMBS."

THEN PROCESSING, REFINING, AND BURNING THEIR HOLY FORMS AS FUEL.

"EACH TIME AN ENGINE STARTS, THE OLD ONES ARE CREMATED FURTHER. DEAD FOREVER."

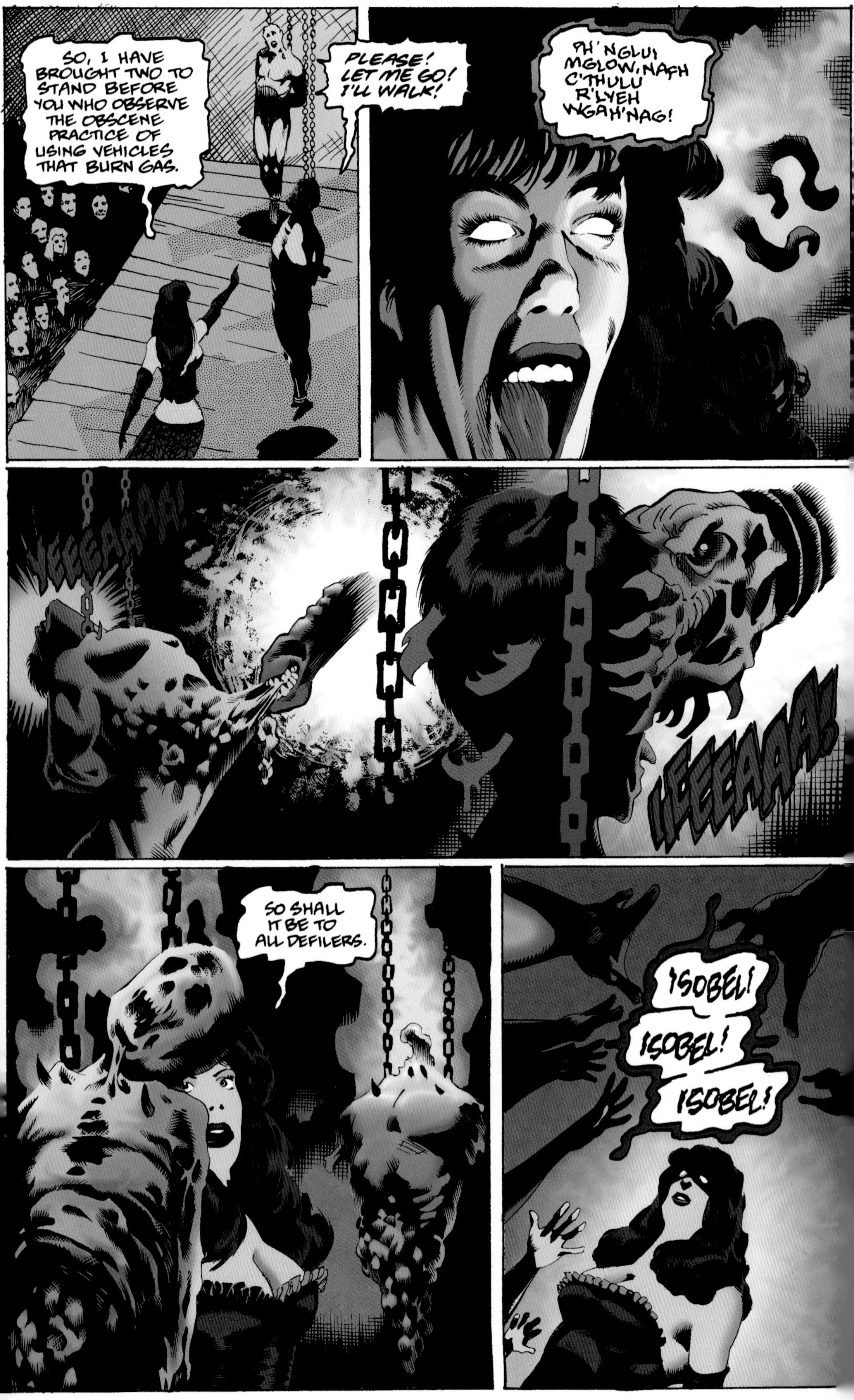
SO, I HAVE BROUGHT TWO TO STAND BEFORE YOU WHO OBSERVE THE OBSCENE PRACTICE OF USING VEHICLES THAT BURN GAS.
PLEASE! LET ME GO! I'LL WALK!
PH'NGLUI MGLOW, NAFH C'THULU R'LYEH WGAH'NAG!
YEEEAAAA!
IEEEAAA!
SO SHALL IT BE TO ALL DEFILERS.
ISOBEL!
ISOBEL!
ISOBEL!

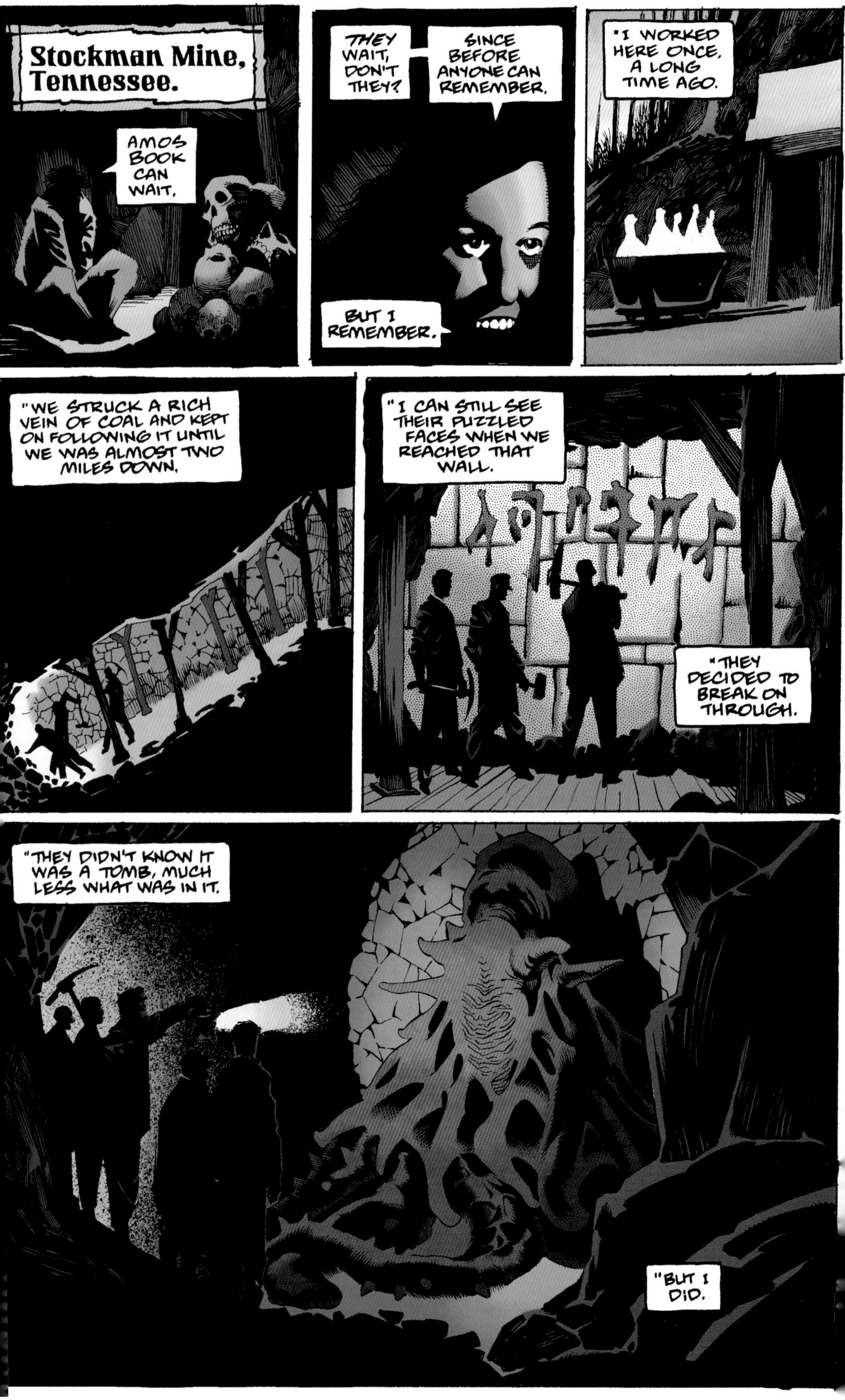
Stockman Mine, Tennessee.
AMOS BOOK CAN WAIT.
THEY WAIT, DON'T THEY?
SINCE BEFORE ANYONE CAN REMEMBER.
BUT I REMEMBER.
"I WORKED HERE ONCE, A LONG TIME AGO.
"WE STRUCK A RICH VEIN OF COAL AND KEPT ON FOLLOWING IT UNTIL WE WAS ALMOST TWO MILES DOWN.
"I CAN STILL SEE THEIR PUZZLED FACES WHEN WE REACHED THAT WALL.
"THEY DECIDED TO BREAK ON THROUGH.
"THEY DIDN'T KNOW IT WAS A TOMB, MUCH LESS WHAT WAS IN IT.
"BUT I DID.

"I KNEW 'CAUSE IT TOLD ME.

"I THOUGHT THEY COULD HEAR IT TELLING ME TO KILL THEM...

"...BUT THEY STOOD STOCK-STILL WHILE I KNOCKED THEIR BRAINS OUT.

" THEN IT TOLD ME WHAT IT'D DO FOR ME IF I BRUNG IT FOOD.

"IT WASN'T DEAD, OR ALIVE. JUST WAITING 'TIL THE STARS WAS RIGHT, AND NEEDING PEACE AND QUIET.

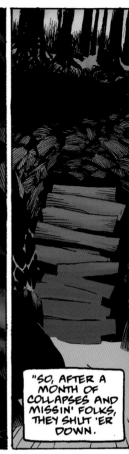

"SO, AFTER A MONTH OF COLLAPSES AND MISSIN' FOLKS, THEY SHUT 'ER DOWN.

"THEN I HAD TO GO OUT LOOKIN' FOR ITS FOOD. AND HAVE BEEN LOOKIN' ALL THESE YEARS.

"AND, AS REWARD, IT LETS ME EAT ITS DROPPINGS. I'M GONNA LIVE FOREVER. WHEN IT WAKES UP, IT'LL MAKE ME A BOSS FOR HELPIN' OUT."

EVEN NOW, I CAN TELL SOMETHIN' ELSE IS OUT THERE STIRRIN' IT UP. SOMETHIN' AS CURSED AS IT IS.

MAYBE MY WORK'S ALMOST DONE.

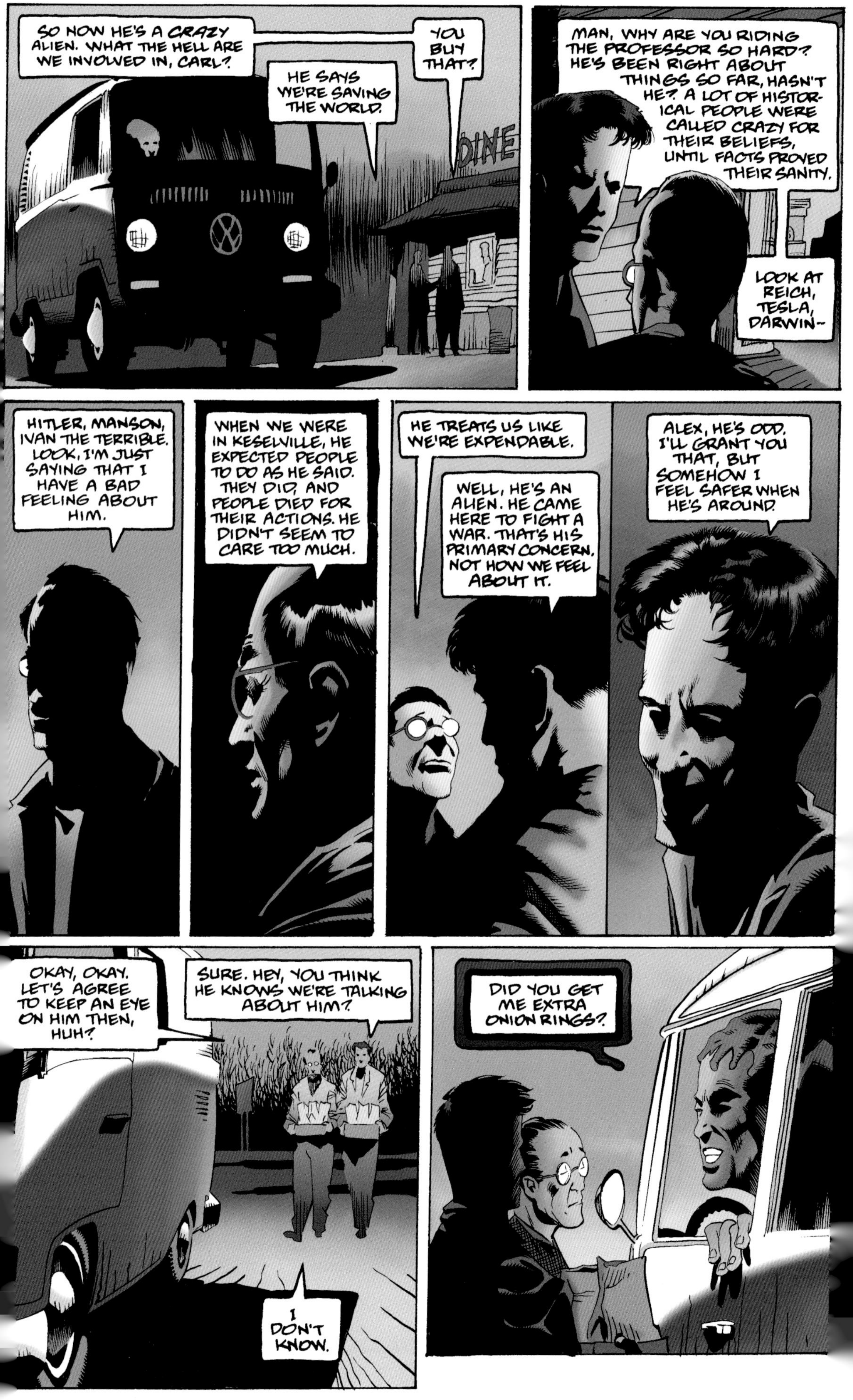
SO NOW HE'S A CRAZY ALIEN. WHAT THE HELL ARE WE INVOLVED IN, CARL?
HE SAYS WE'RE SAVING THE WORLD.
YOU BUY THAT?
DINE
MAN, WHY ARE YOU RIDING THE PROFESSOR SO HARD? HE'S BEEN RIGHT ABOUT THINGS SO FAR, HASN'T HE? A LOT OF HISTORICAL PEOPLE WERE CALLED CRAZY FOR THEIR BELIEFS, UNTIL FACTS PROVED THEIR SANITY.
LOOK AT REICH, TESLA, DARWIN--
HITLER, MANSON, IVAN THE TERRIBLE. LOOK, I'M JUST SAYING THAT I HAVE A BAD FEELING ABOUT HIM.
WHEN WE WERE IN KESELVILLE, HE EXPECTED PEOPLE TO DO AS HE SAID. THEY DID, AND PEOPLE DIED FOR THEIR ACTIONS. HE DIDN'T SEEM TO CARE TOO MUCH.
HE TREATS US LIKE WE'RE EXPENDABLE.
WELL, HE'S AN ALIEN. HE CAME HERE TO FIGHT A WAR. THAT'S HIS PRIMARY CONCERN, NOT HOW WE FEEL ABOUT IT.
ALEX, HE'S ODD, I'LL GRANT YOU THAT, BUT SOMEHOW I FEEL SAFER WHEN HE'S AROUND.
OKAY, OKAY. LET'S AGREE TO KEEP AN EYE ON HIM THEN, HUH?
SURE. HEY, YOU THINK HE KNOWS WE'RE TALKING ABOUT HIM?
I DON'T KNOW.
DID YOU GET ME EXTRA ONION RINGS?

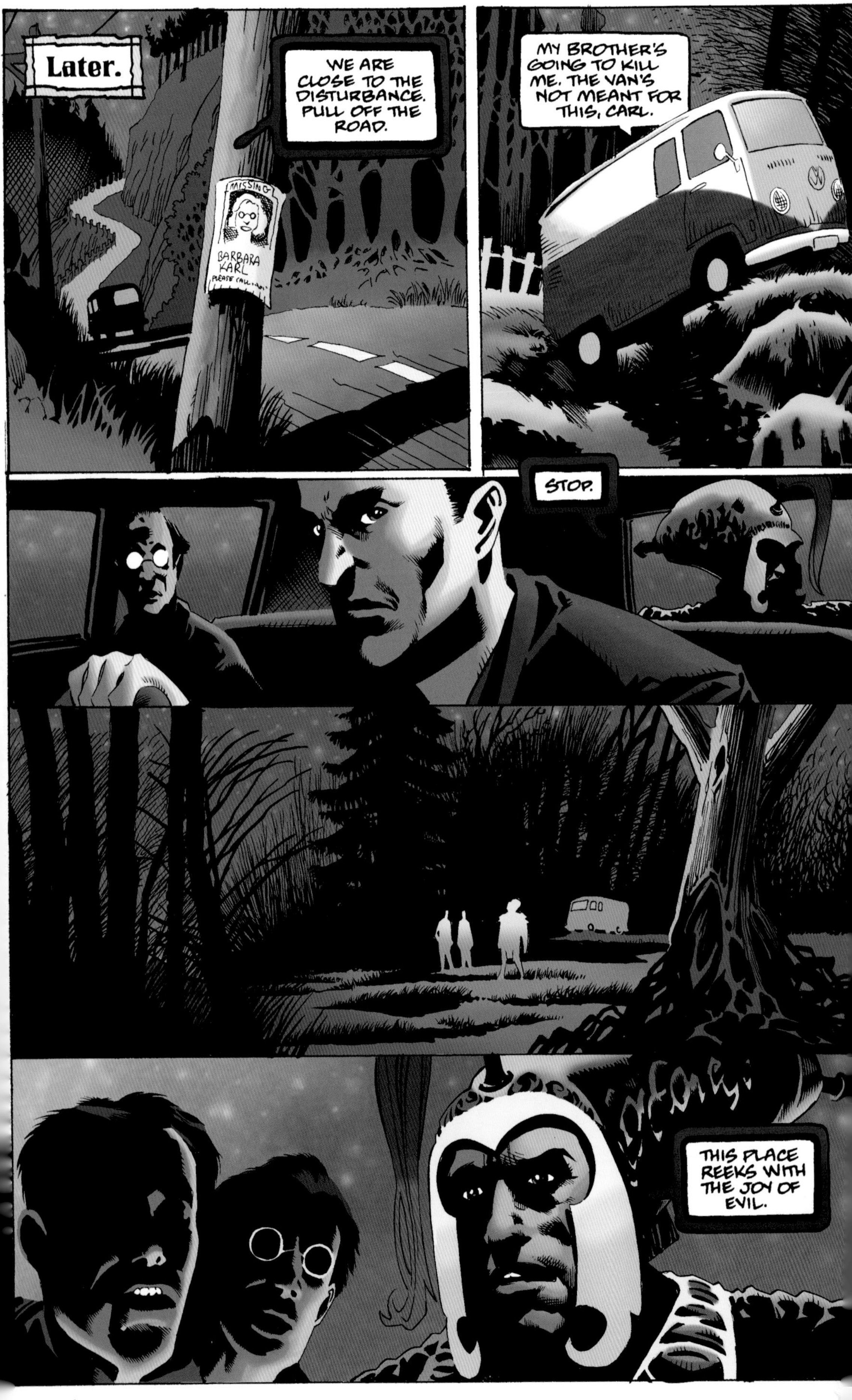

Later.
WE ARE CLOSE TO THE DISTURBANCE. PULL OFF THE ROAD.
MISSING
BARBARA KARL
MY BROTHER'S GOING TO KILL ME. THE VAN'S NOT MEANT FOR THIS, CARL.
STOP.
THIS PLACE REEKS WITH THE JOY OF EVIL.

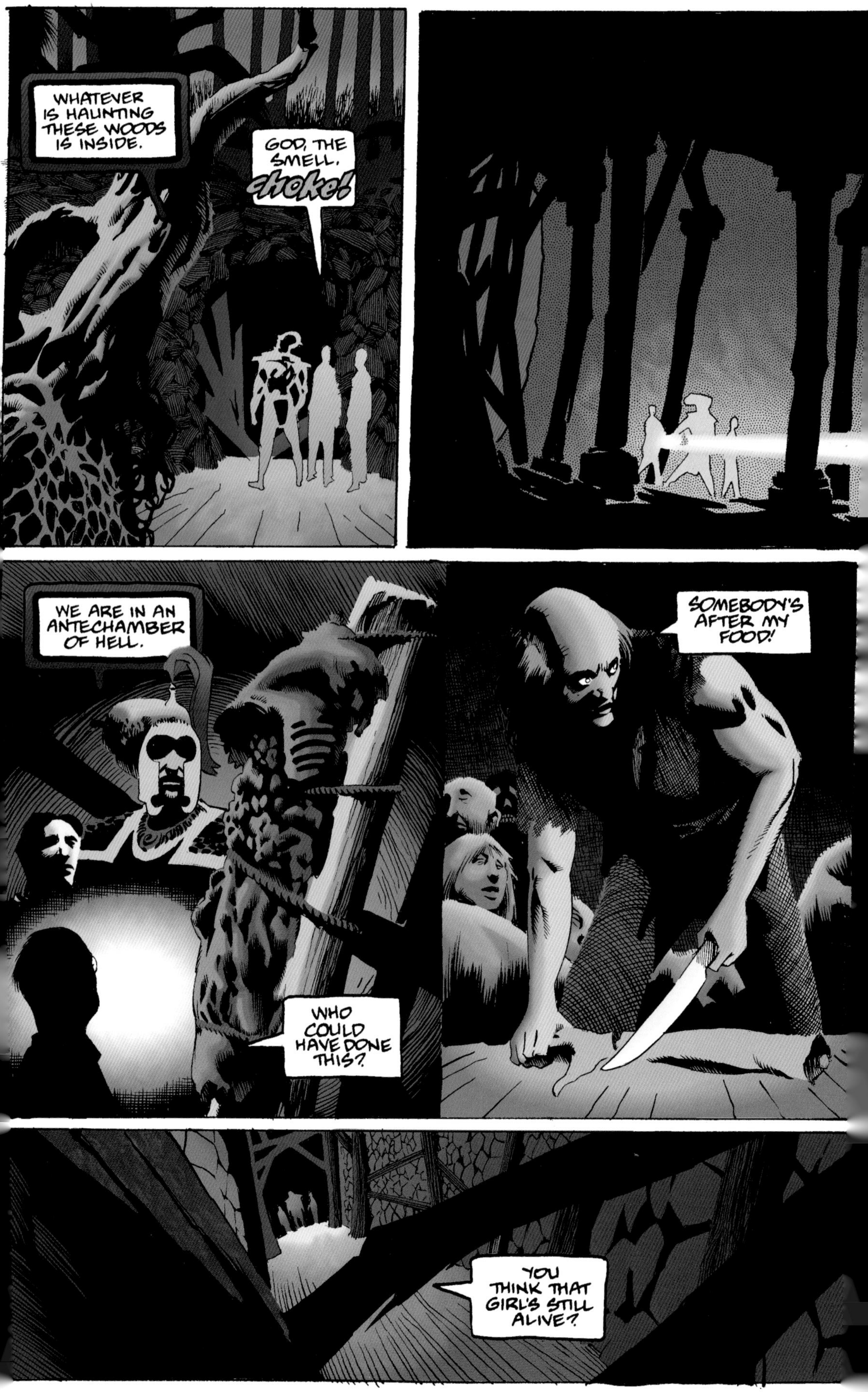
WHATEVER IS HAUNTING THESE WOODS IS INSIDE.
GOD, THE SMELL. choke!
WE ARE IN AN ANTECHAMBER OF HELL.
WHO COULD HAVE DONE THIS?
SOMEBODY'S AFTER MY FOOD!
YOU THINK THAT GIRL'S STILL ALIVE?

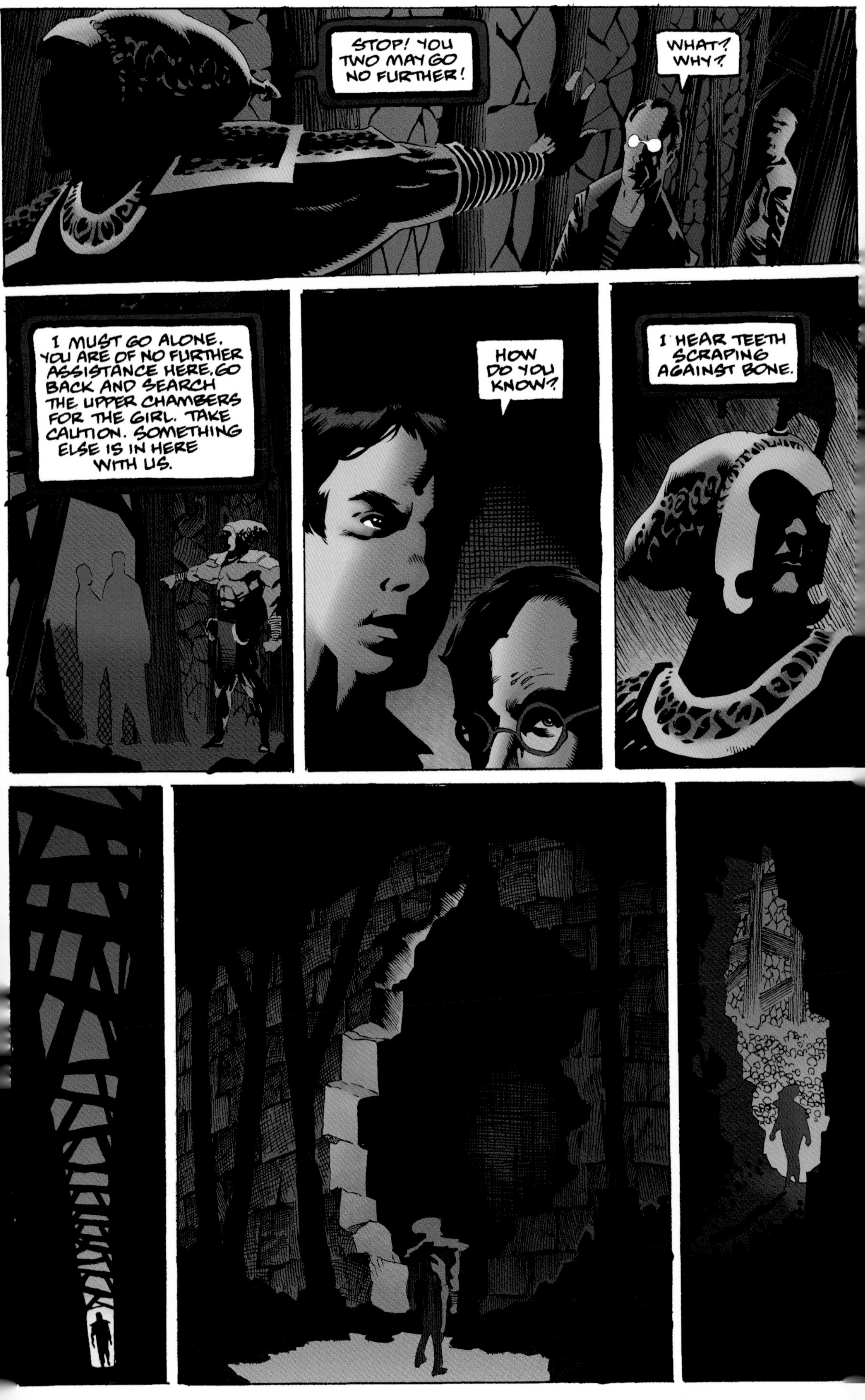
STOP! YOU TWO MAY GO NO FURTHER!
WHAT? WHY?
I MUST GO ALONE. YOU ARE OF NO FURTHER ASSISTANCE HERE, GO BACK AND SEARCH THE UPPER CHAMBERS FOR THE GIRL. TAKE CAUTION. SOMETHING ELSE IS IN HERE WITH US.
HOW DO YOU KNOW?
I HEAR TEETH SCRAPING AGAINST BONE.

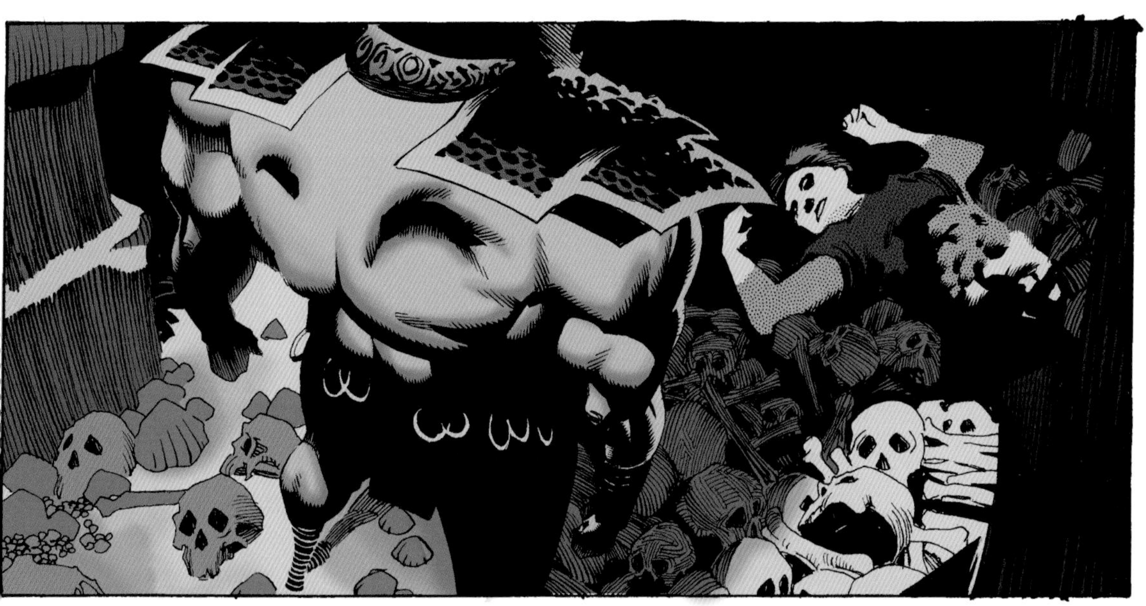

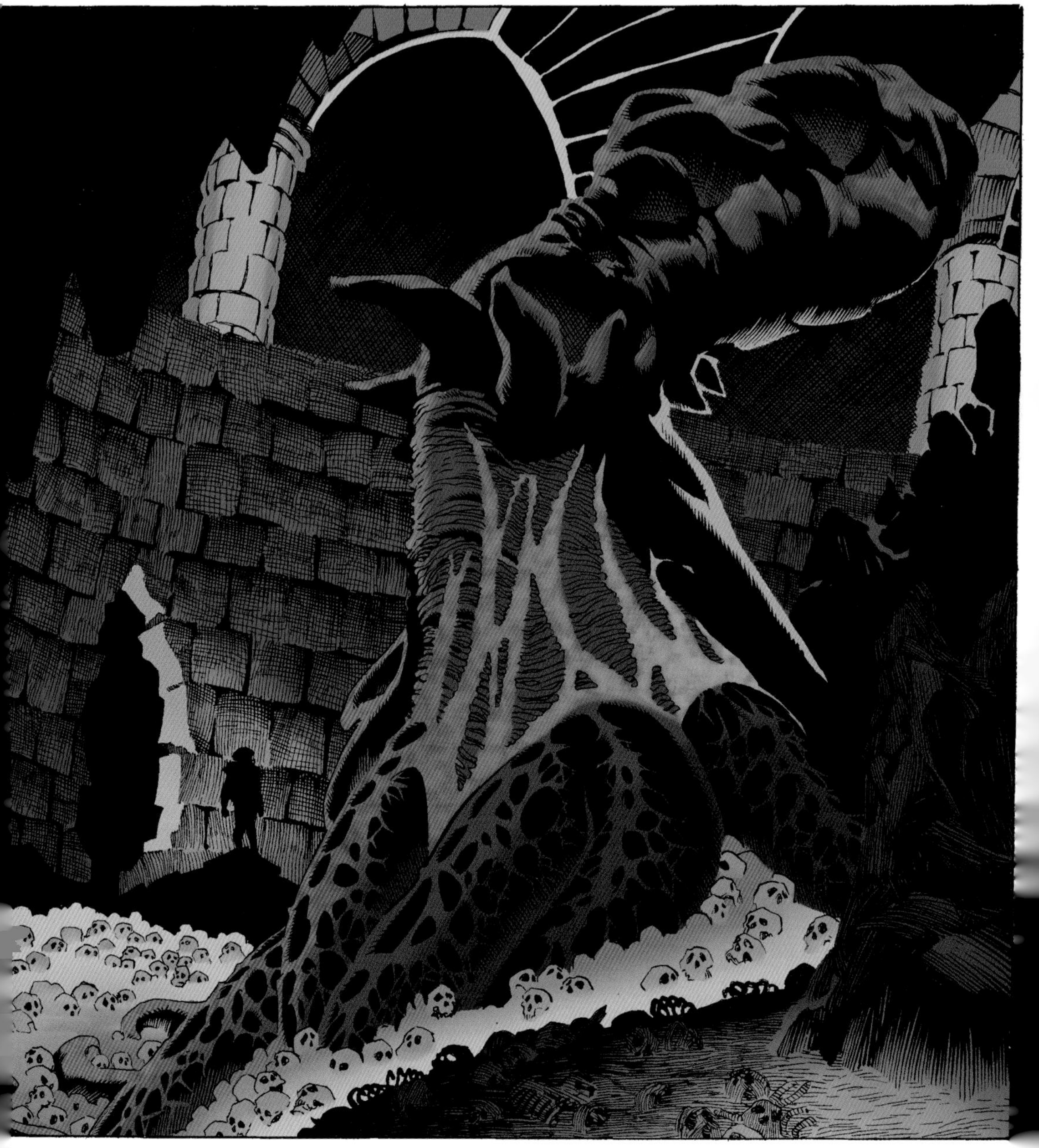

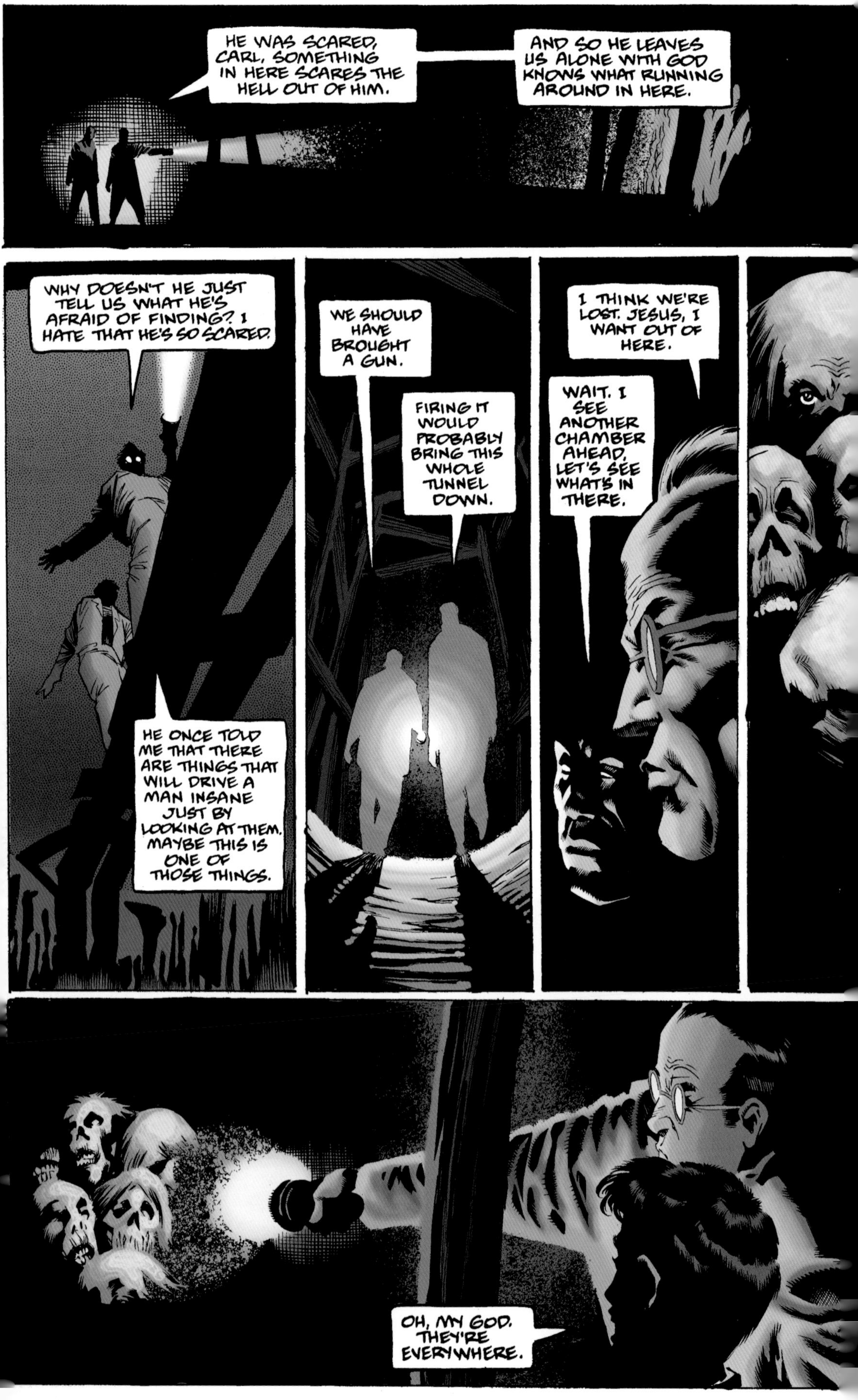
HE WAS SCARED, CARL, SOMETHING IN HERE SCARES THE HELL OUT OF HIM.
AND SO HE LEAVES US ALONE WITH GOD KNOWS WHAT RUNNING AROUND IN HERE.
WHY DOESN'T HE JUST TELL US WHAT HE'S AFRAID OF FINDING? I HATE THAT HE'S SO SCARED.
HE ONCE TOLD ME THAT THERE ARE THINGS THAT WILL DRIVE A MAN INSANE JUST BY LOOKING AT THEM. MAYBE THIS IS ONE OF THOSE THINGS.
WE SHOULD HAVE BROUGHT A GUN.
FIRING IT WOULD PROBABLY BRING THIS WHOLE TUNNEL DOWN.
I THINK WE'RE LOST. JESUS, I WANT OUT OF HERE.
WAIT. I SEE ANOTHER CHAMBER AHEAD, LET'S SEE WHAT'S IN THERE.
OH, MY GOD. THEY'RE EVERYWHERE.

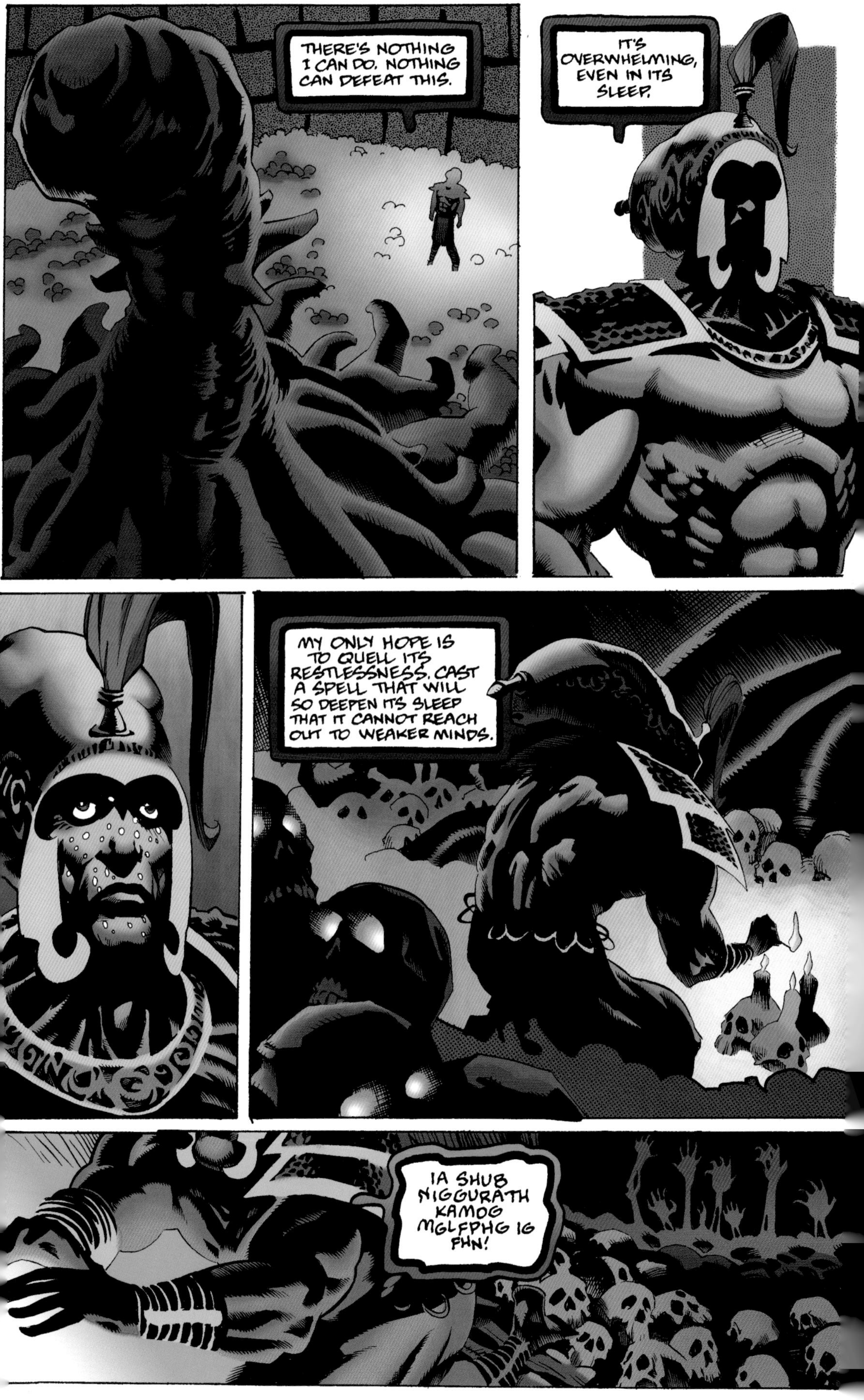
THERE'S NOTHING I CAN DO. NOTHING CAN DEFEAT THIS.
IT'S OVERWHELMING, EVEN IN ITS SLEEP.
MY ONLY HOPE IS TO QUELL ITS RESTLESSNESS. CAST A SPELL THAT WILL SO DEEPEN ITS SLEEP THAT IT CANNOT REACH OUT TO WEAKER MINDS.
IA SHUB NIGGURATH KAMOG MGLFPHG IG FHN!

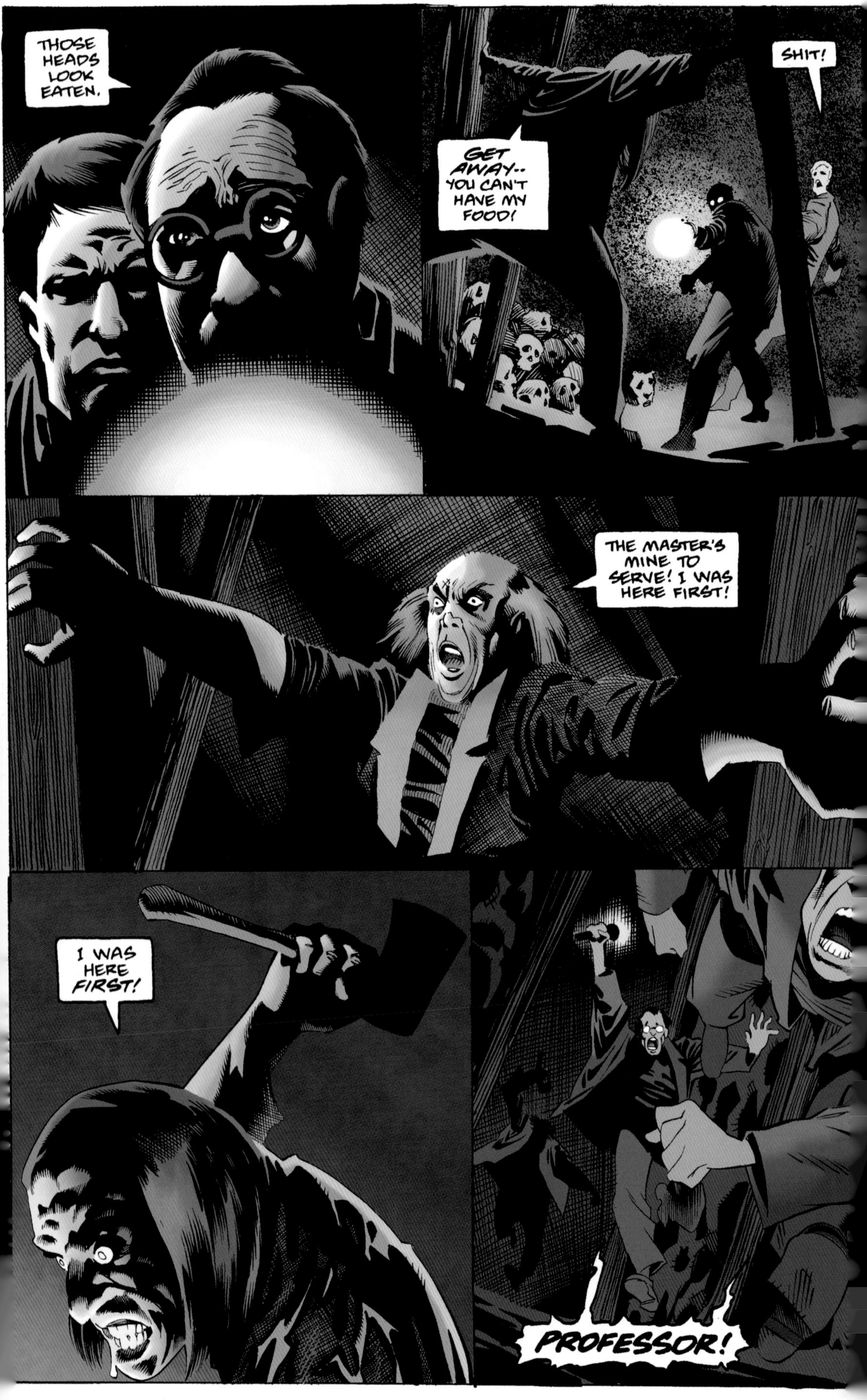
THOSE HEADS LOOK EATEN.
SHIT!
GET AWAY.. YOU CAN'T HAVE MY FOOD!
THE MASTER'S MINE TO SERVE! I WAS HERE FIRST!
I WAS HERE FIRST!
PROFESSOR!

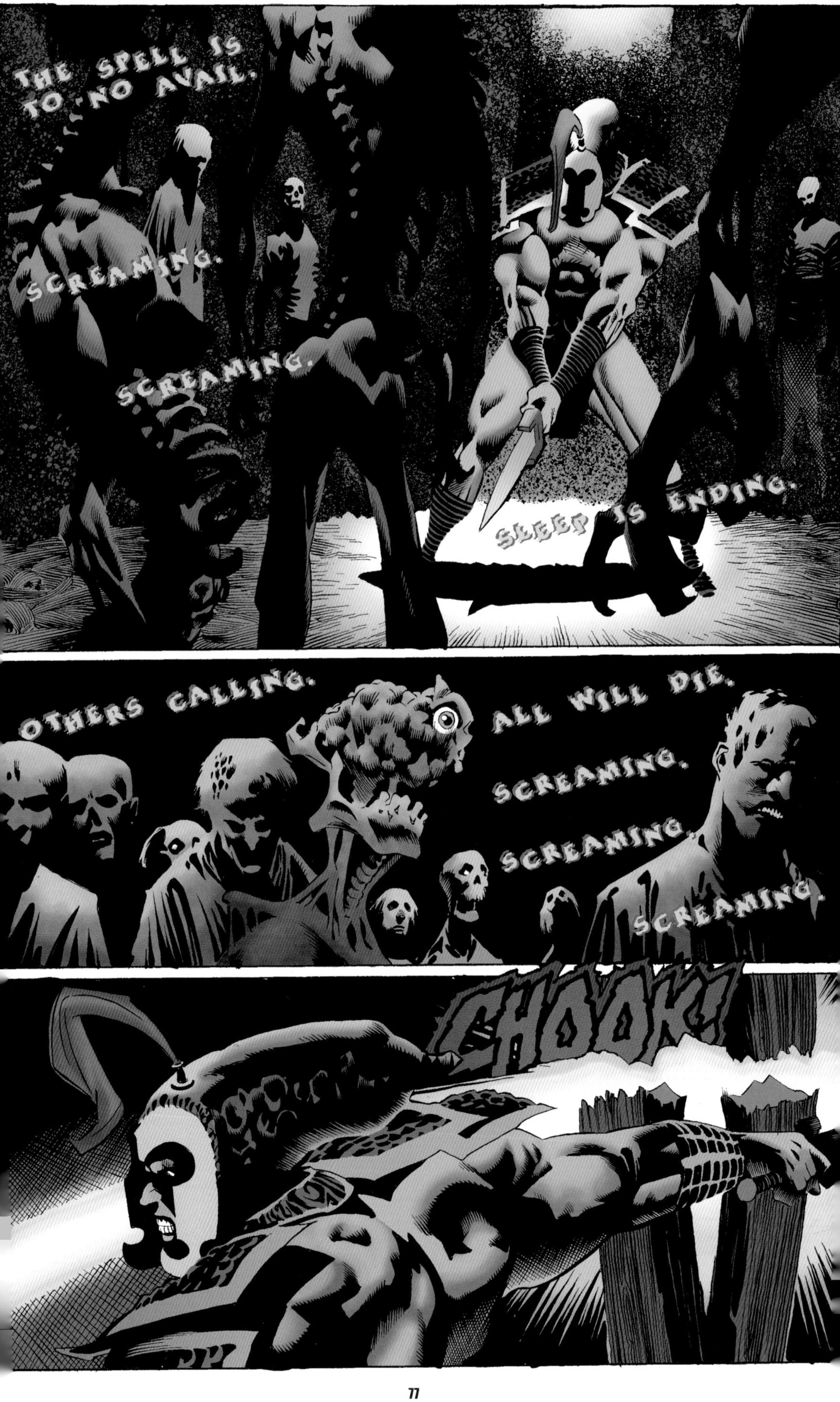
THE SPELL IS TO NO AVAIL.
SCREAMING.
SCREAMING.
SLEEP IS ENDING.
OTHERS CALLING.
ALL WILL DIE.
SCREAMING.
SCREAMING.
SCREAMING.
CHOOK!

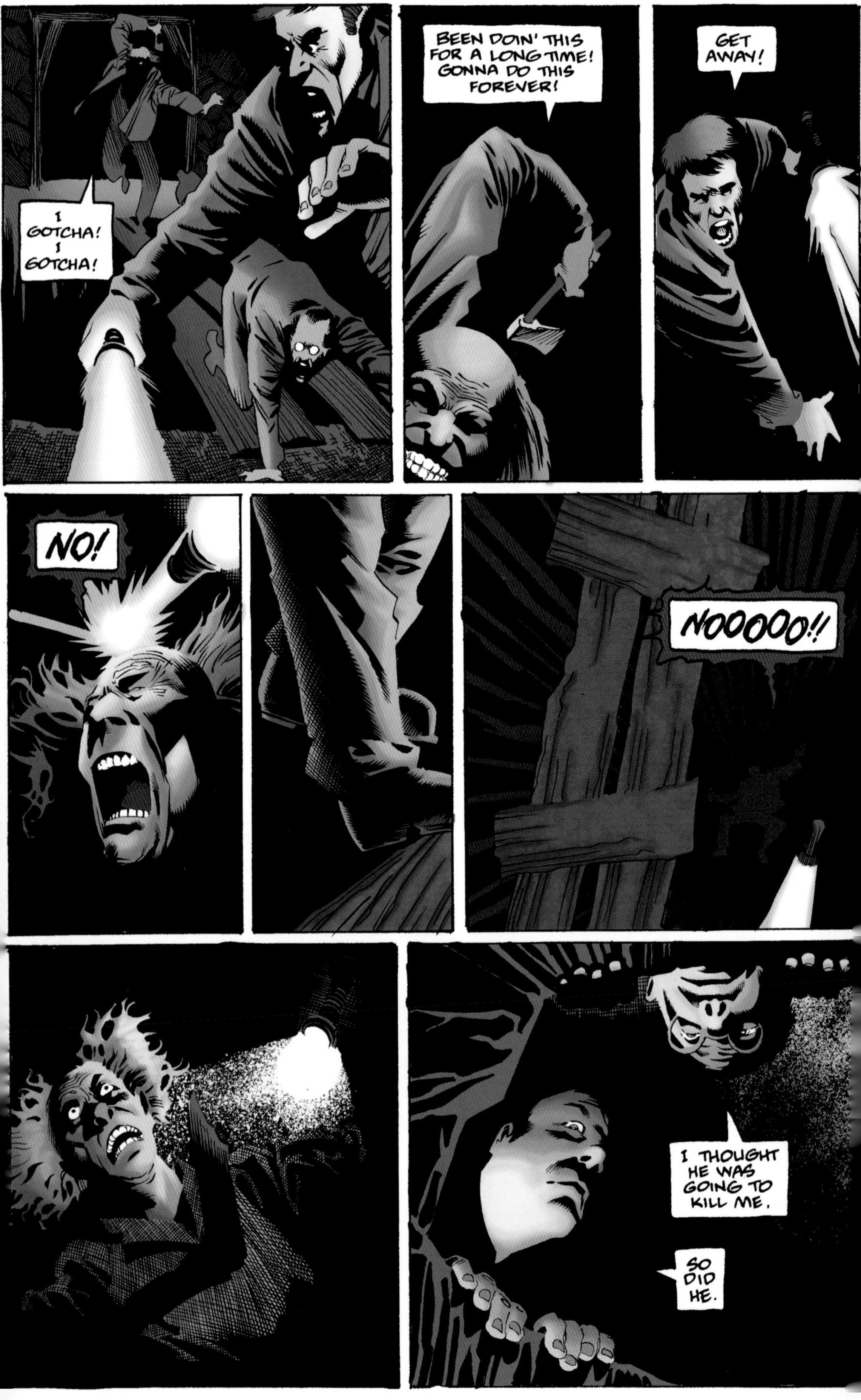

I GOTCHA! I GOTCHA!
BEEN DOIN' THIS FOR A LONG TIME! GONNA DO THIS FOREVER!
GET AWAY!
NO!
NOOOOO!!
I THOUGHT HE WAS GOING TO KILL ME.
SO DID HE.

THIS WILL HAVE TO DO.

I SEE YOU FOUND YOUR WAY OUT.

WITH NO HELP FROM YOU.

WE CAME ACROSS A LUNATIC IN THERE, BUT WE'VE GOT TO GO BACK. WE DIDN'T FIND THE GIRL.

I FOUND HER, SHE'S DEAD.

THEN WE HAVE TO TELL THE POLICE. HER FAMILY'S GOT TO BE TOLD. THERE'S A LOT OF OTHER PEOPLE IN THERE, TOO. LOTS OF THEM. WE HAVE A RESPONSIBILITY TO TELL ABOUT WHAT'S IN THERE.

LOOK, THESE MURDERS WEREN'T COMMITTED BY "OTHERS," JUST SOME NUTCASE. NO HELL'S ANTECHAMBER! NO SPOOKS! NO NOTHING!

THE POLICE WILL NOT BE TOLD. THE FAMILIES OF THE DEAD WILL REMAIN IGNORANT. I WILL NOT REVEAL TO YOU WHAT IS REALLY IN THERE. SUFFICE TO SAY I COULD DO NOTHING BUT TEMPORARILY HALT THE EVENTUAL AWAKENING.

AS FOR THIS "RUNNING AROUND," IT WILL SOON END.

THOUGH I COULD NOT ENGAGE THE EVIL PRESENT, I HAVE LOCATED THE HEART OF THE GREATER DISTURBANCE.

WHAT DO YOU MEAN?

I KNOW WHO IS OPENING THE PORTAL.

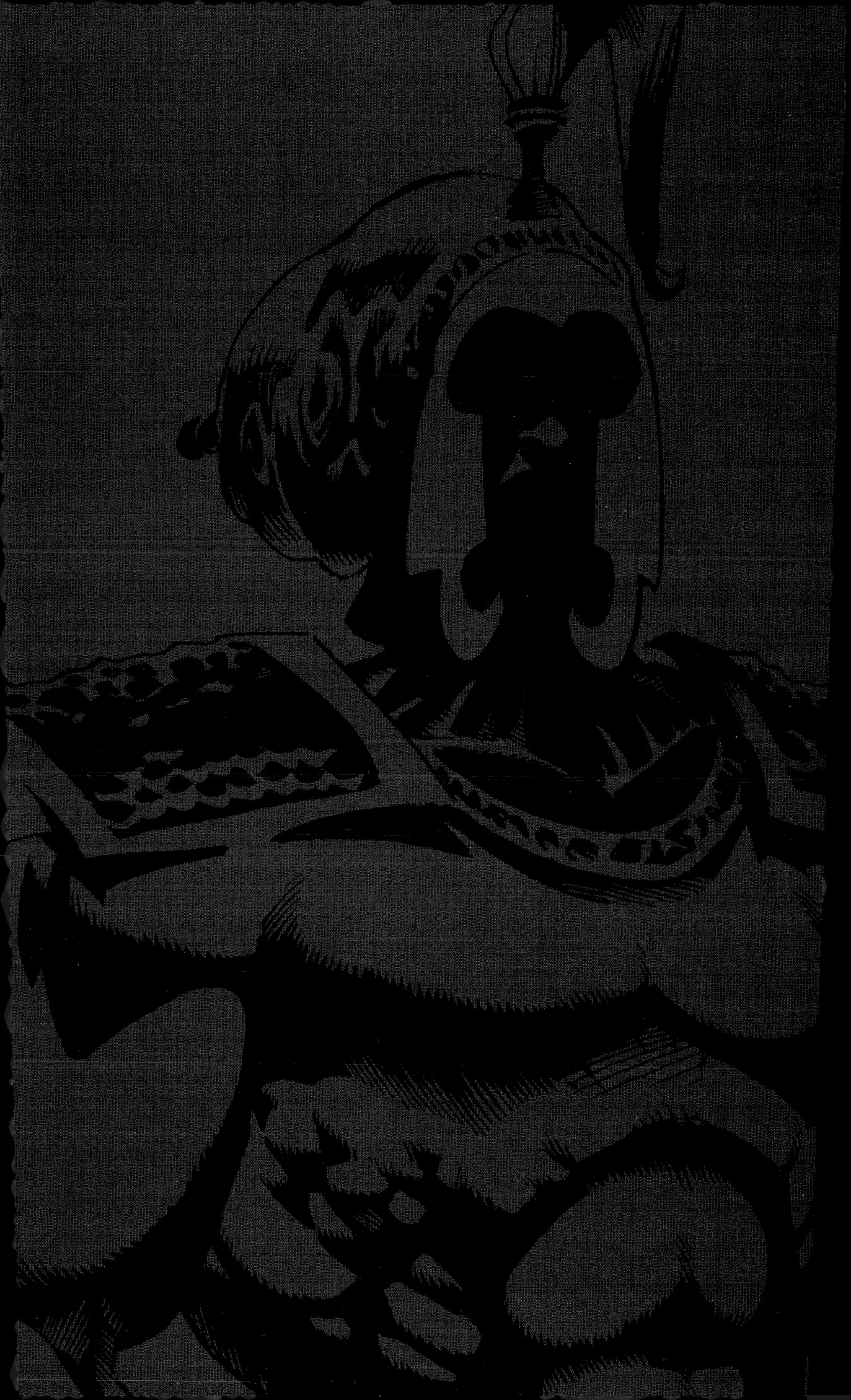

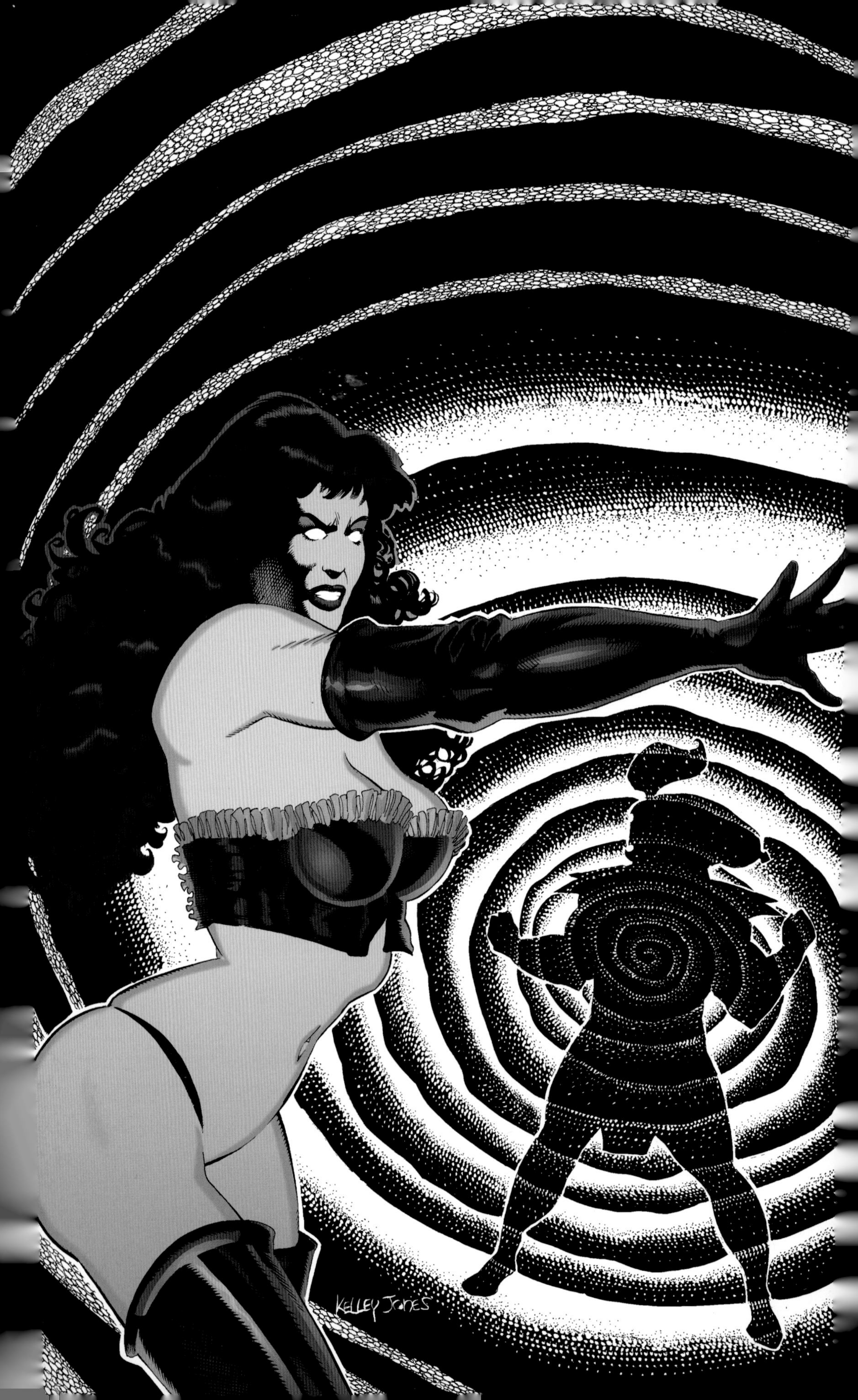
KELLEY JONES

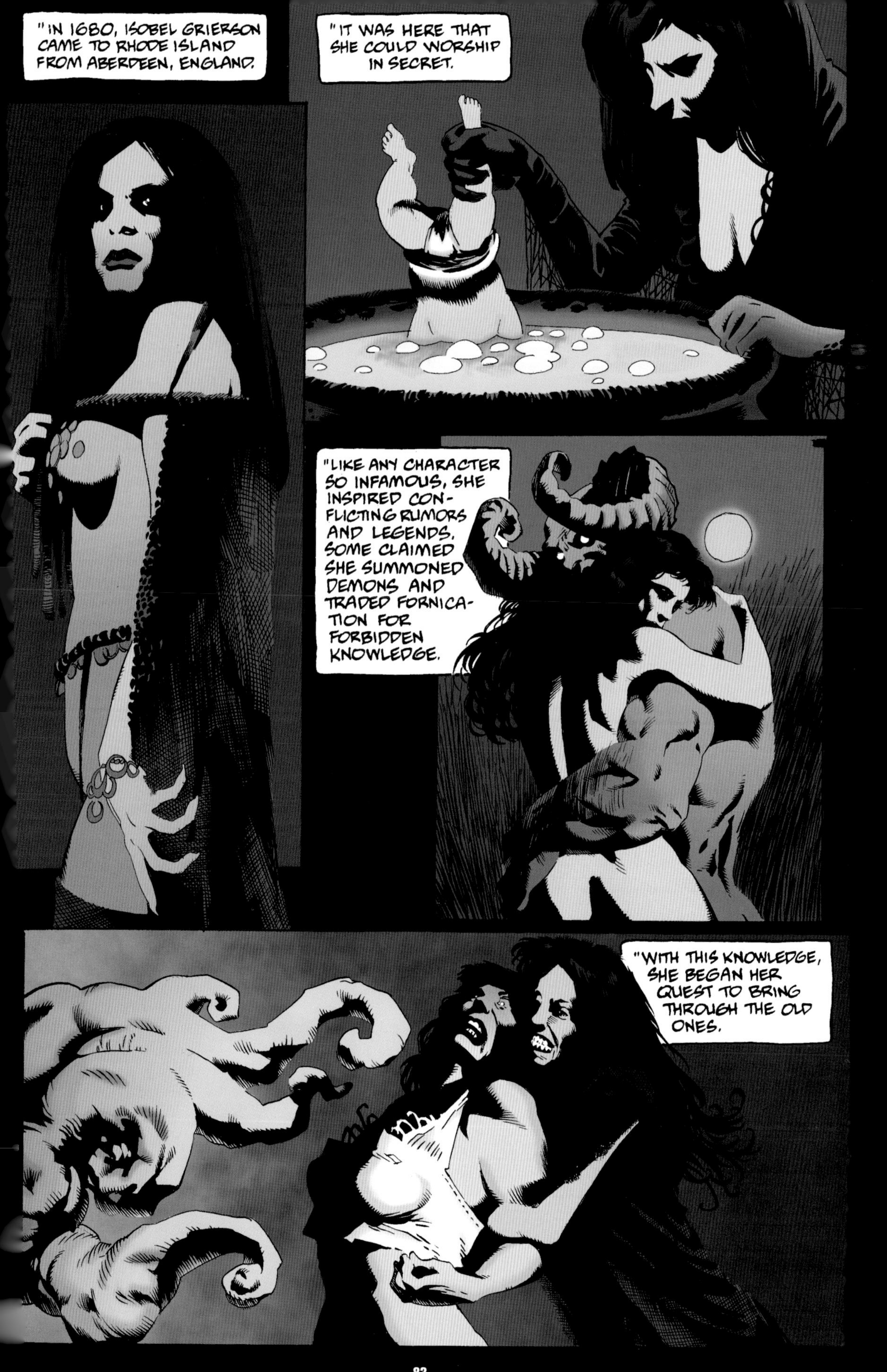

"IN 1680, ISOBEL GRIERSON CAME TO RHODE ISLAND FROM ABERDEEN, ENGLAND.
"IT WAS HERE THAT SHE COULD WORSHIP IN SECRET.
"LIKE ANY CHARACTER SO INFAMOUS, SHE INSPIRED CONFLICTING RUMORS AND LEGENDS. SOME CLAIMED SHE SUMMONED DEMONS AND TRADED FORNICATION FOR FORBIDDEN KNOWLEDGE.
"WITH THIS KNOWLEDGE, SHE BEGAN HER QUEST TO BRING THROUGH THE OLD ONES.

"SHE BECAME CARELESS IN HER ZEAL AND WAS ACCUSED BY JUDGE HAWTHORNE. A NEWSPAPER REPORT FROM 1865 SAYS SHE ESCAPED RHODE ISLAND, WHILE HAWTHORNE'S OWN MEMOIRS TELL OF HER CAPTURE.

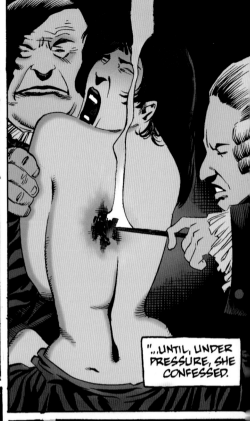

"FOR MANY MONTHS SHE ADMITTED NOTHING...

"...UNTIL, UNDER PRESSURE, SHE CONFESSED.

"SHE SPOKE OF HER MIDNIGHT MEETINGS ON SENTINEL HILL BETWEEN THE TWO STANDING STONES.

"SHE SCREAMED HER SECRET NAME,

"ON THE MORNING OF HER EXECUTION, THEY FOUND ODDLY DRAWN FIGURES ON THE WALL. ISOBEL WAS NOWHERE TO BE FOUND. IT'S HARD TO SAY IF THIS EVER HAPPENED, OR IF IT'S THE RAVINGS OF A SEPTUAGENARIAN PURITAN."

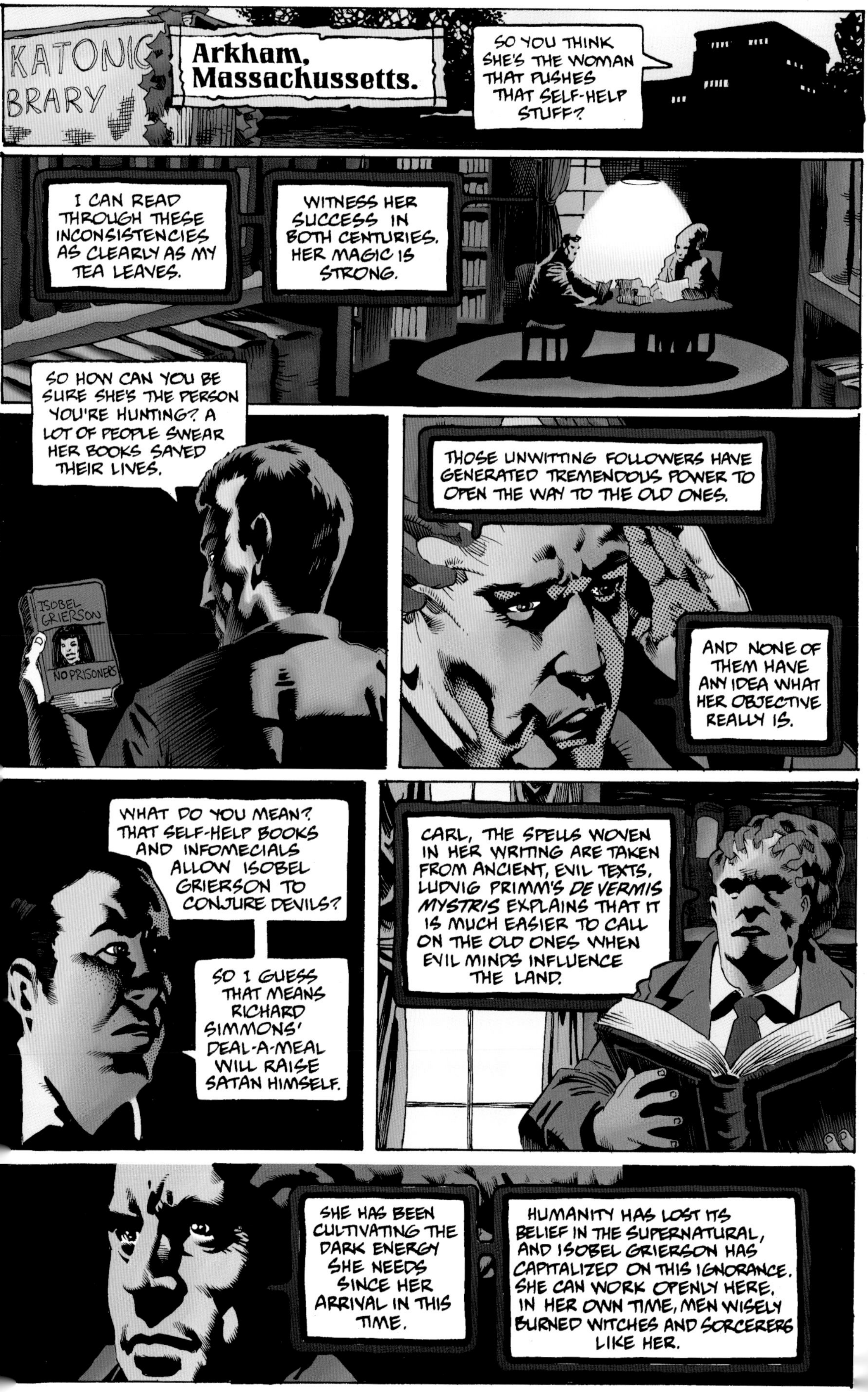
KATONIC
BRARY
Arkham, Massachussetts.
SO YOU THINK SHE'S THE WOMAN THAT PUSHES THAT SELF-HELP STUFF?
I CAN READ THROUGH THESE INCONSISTENCIES AS CLEARLY AS MY TEA LEAVES.
WITNESS HER SUCCESS IN BOTH CENTURIES. HER MAGIC IS STRONG.
SO HOW CAN YOU BE SURE SHE'S THE PERSON YOU'RE HUNTING? A LOT OF PEOPLE SWEAR HER BOOKS SAVED THEIR LIVES.
ISOBEL GRIERSON
NO PRISONERS
THOSE UNWITTING FOLLOWERS HAVE GENERATED TREMENDOUS POWER TO OPEN THE WAY TO THE OLD ONES.
AND NONE OF THEM HAVE ANY IDEA WHAT HER OBJECTIVE REALLY IS.
WHAT DO YOU MEAN? THAT SELF-HELP BOOKS AND INFOMECIALS ALLOW ISOBEL GRIERSON TO CONJURE DEVILS?
SO I GUESS THAT MEANS RICHARD SIMMONS' DEAL-A-MEAL WILL RAISE SATAN HIMSELF.
CARL, THE SPELLS WOVEN IN HER WRITING ARE TAKEN FROM ANCIENT, EVIL TEXTS. LUDVIG PRIMM'S *DE VERMIS MYSTRIS* EXPLAINS THAT IT IS MUCH EASIER TO CALL ON THE OLD ONES WHEN EVIL MINDS INFLUENCE THE LAND.
SHE HAS BEEN CULTIVATING THE DARK ENERGY SHE NEEDS SINCE HER ARRIVAL IN THIS TIME.
HUMANITY HAS LOST ITS BELIEF IN THE SUPERNATURAL, AND ISOBEL GRIERSON HAS CAPITALIZED ON THIS IGNORANCE. SHE CAN WORK OPENLY HERE. IN HER OWN TIME, MEN WISELY BURNED WITCHES AND SORCERERS LIKE HER.

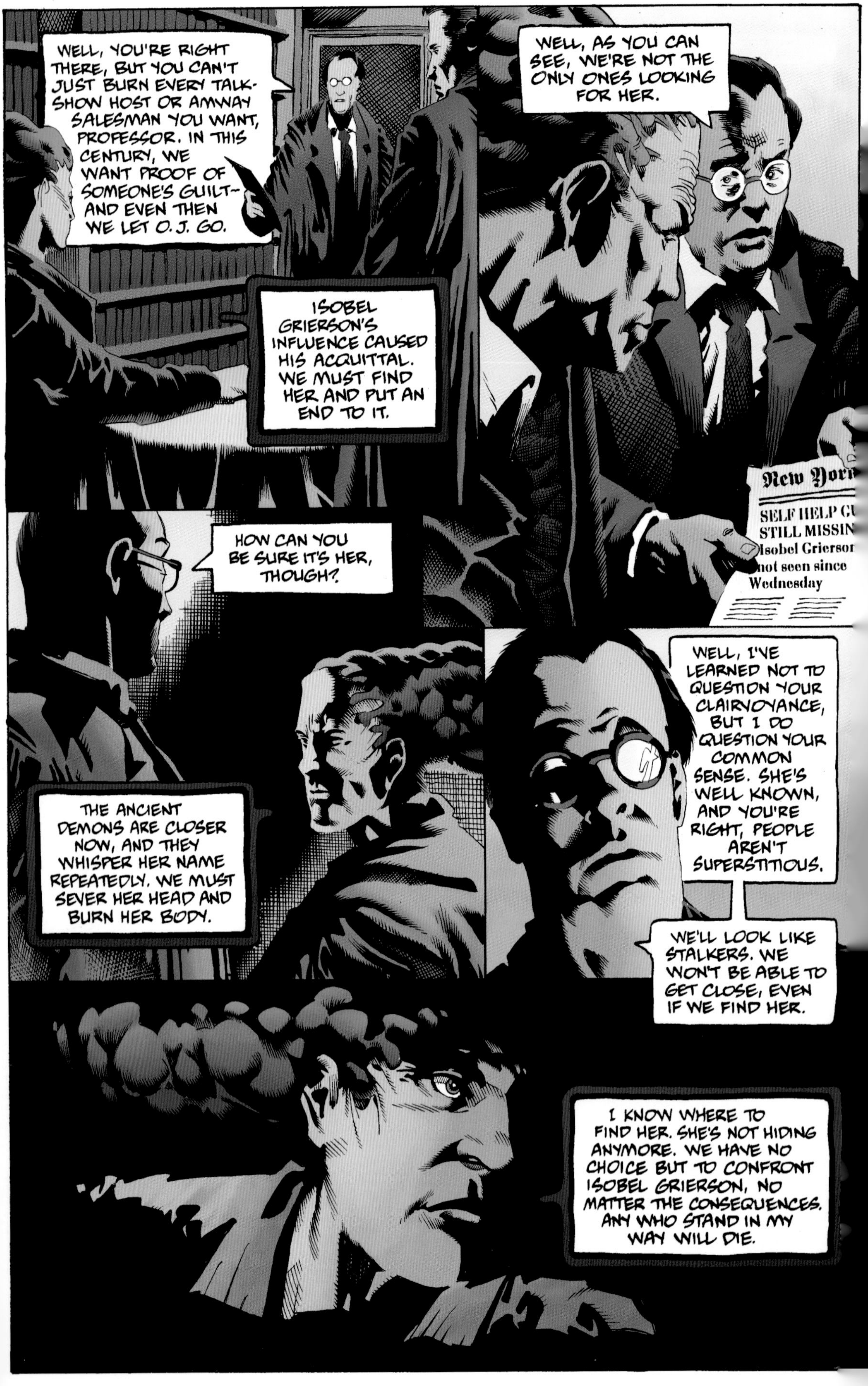

WELL, YOU'RE RIGHT THERE, BUT YOU CAN'T JUST BURN EVERY TALK-SHOW HOST OR AMWAY SALESMAN YOU WANT, PROFESSOR. IN THIS CENTURY, WE WANT PROOF OF SOMEONE'S GUILT-AND EVEN THEN WE LET O. J. GO.
ISOBEL GRIERSON'S INFLUENCE CAUSED HIS ACQUITTAL. WE MUST FIND HER AND PUT AN END TO IT.
WELL, AS YOU CAN SEE, WE'RE NOT THE ONLY ONES LOOKING FOR HER.
SELF HELP GU
STILL MISSIN
Isobel Grierson
not seen since
Wednesday
HOW CAN YOU BE SURE IT'S HER, THOUGH?
THE ANCIENT DEMONS ARE CLOSER NOW, AND THEY WHISPER HER NAME REPEATEDLY. WE MUST SEVER HER HEAD AND BURN HER BODY.
WELL, I'VE LEARNED NOT TO QUESTION YOUR CLAIRVOYANCE, BUT I DO QUESTION YOUR COMMON SENSE. SHE'S WELL KNOWN, AND YOU'RE RIGHT, PEOPLE AREN'T SUPERSTITIOUS.
WE'LL LOOK LIKE STALKERS. WE WON'T BE ABLE TO GET CLOSE, EVEN IF WE FIND HER.
I KNOW WHERE TO FIND HER. SHE'S NOT HIDING ANYMORE. WE HAVE NO CHOICE BUT TO CONFRONT ISOBEL GRIERSON, NO MATTER THE CONSEQUENCES. ANY WHO STAND IN MY WAY WILL DIE.

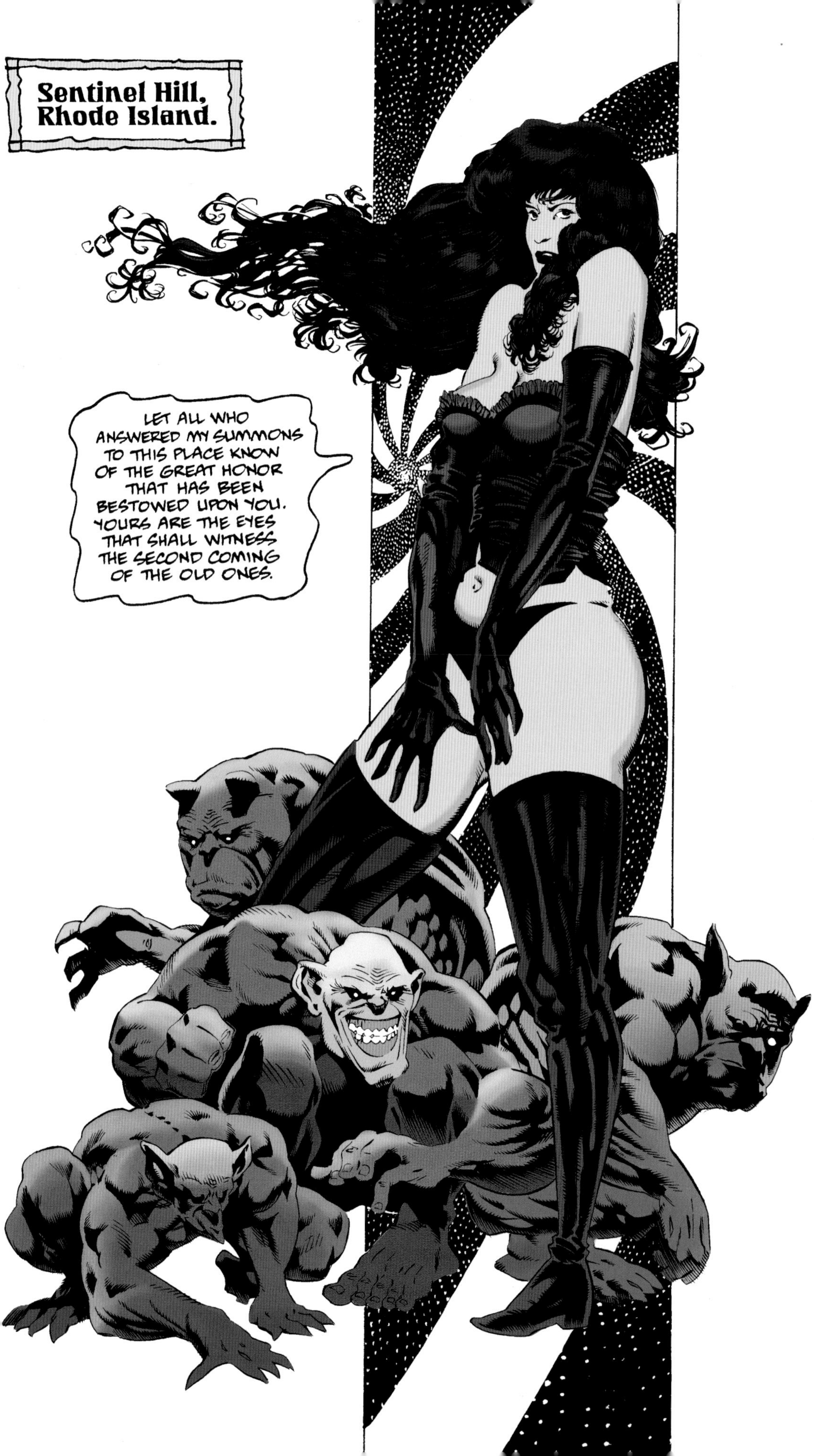
Sentinel Hill, Rhode Island.
LET ALL WHO ANSWERED MY SUMMONS TO THIS PLACE KNOW OF THE GREAT HONOR THAT HAS BEEN BESTOWED UPON YOU. YOURS ARE THE EYES THAT SHALL WITNESS THE SECOND COMING OF THE OLD ONES.

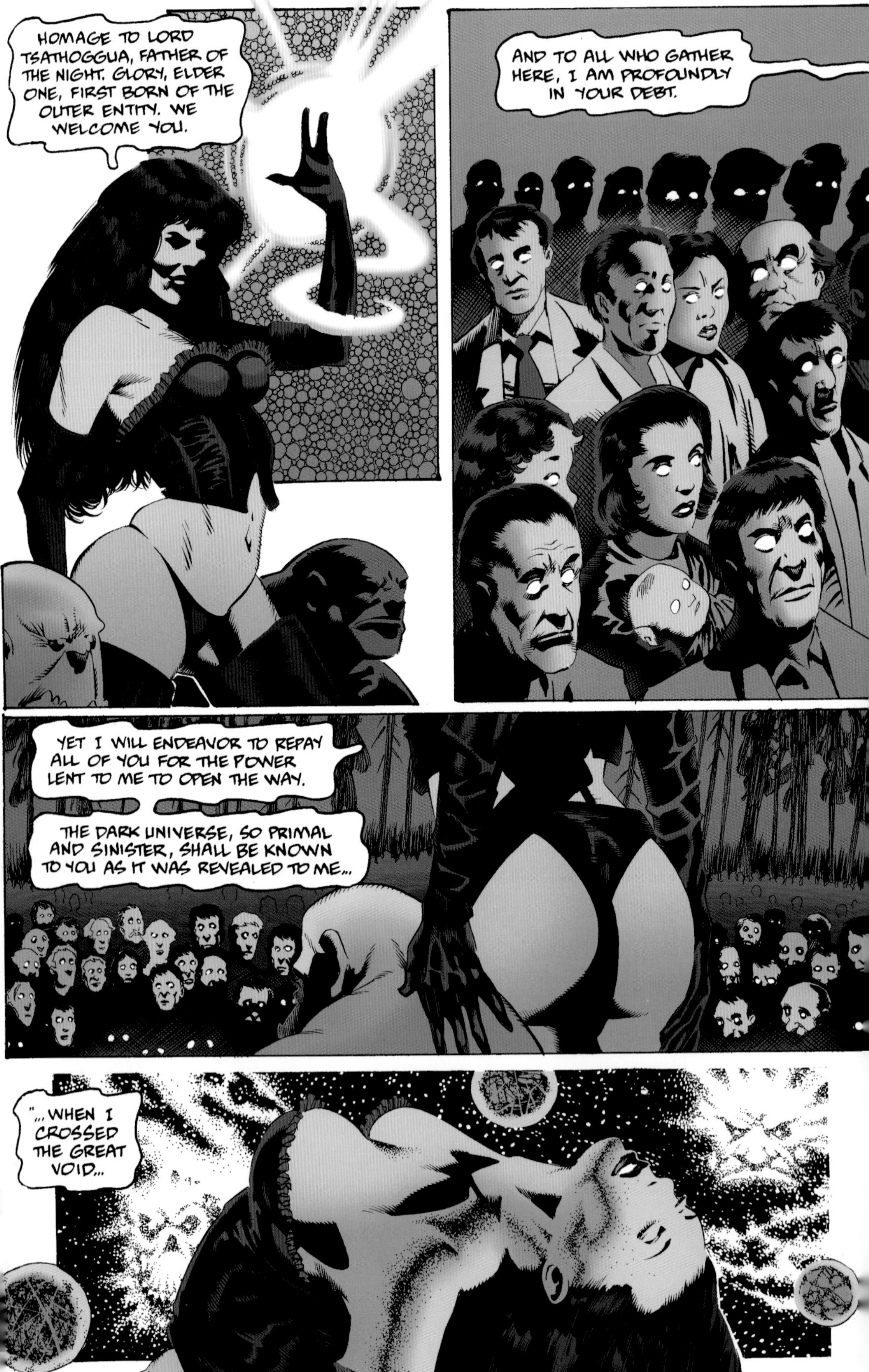
HOMAGE TO LORD TSATHOGGUA, FATHER OF THE NIGHT. GLORY, ELDER ONE, FIRST BORN OF THE OUTER ENTITY. WE WELCOME YOU.
AND TO ALL WHO GATHER HERE, I AM PROFOUNDLY IN YOUR DEBT.
YET I WILL ENDEAVOR TO REPAY ALL OF YOU FOR THE POWER LENT TO ME TO OPEN THE WAY.
THE DARK UNIVERSE, SO PRIMAL AND SINISTER, SHALL BE KNOWN TO YOU AS IT WAS REVEALED TO ME...
"...WHEN I CROSSED THE GREAT VOID...

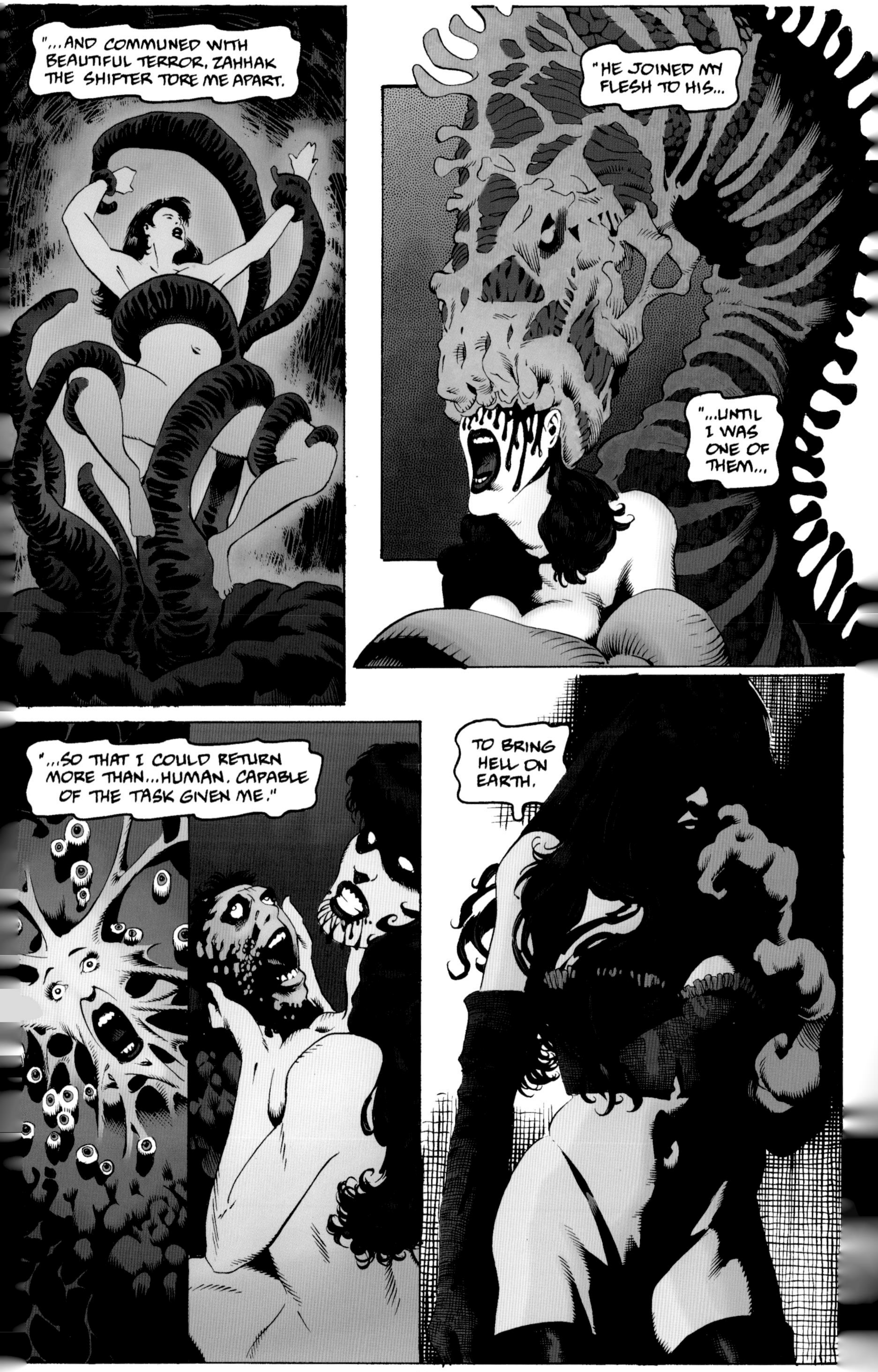
"...AND COMMUNED WITH BEAUTIFUL TERROR, ZAHHAK THE SHIFTER TORE ME APART.
"HE JOINED MY FLESH TO HIS...
"...UNTIL I WAS ONE OF THEM...
"...SO THAT I COULD RETURN MORE THAN...HUMAN. CAPABLE OF THE TASK GIVEN ME."
TO BRING HELL ON EARTH.

MAN, THIS THING IS SURE SPEWING A LOT OF SMOKE. I DON'T THINK IT WILL GO MUCH FURTHER.

SENTINEL HILL IS NOT FAR.

IT'S NOT ON THE MAP.

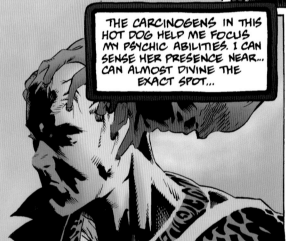

THE CARCINOGENS IN THIS HOT DOG HELP ME FOCUS MY PSYCHIC ABILITIES. I CAN SENSE HER PRESENCE NEAR... CAN ALMOST DIVINE THE EXACT SPOT...

DON'T BOTHER. YOU CAN USE YOUR EYES INSTEAD.

WELL, IT'S EITHER OUR SATANIC HOMECOMING, OR THE PREMIER TO THE LATEST *BATMAN* MOVIE.

WHATEVER IT IS, IT'S A SELLOUT CROWD.

THESE PARTICIPANTS HAVE NO CHOICE BUT TO ATTEND.

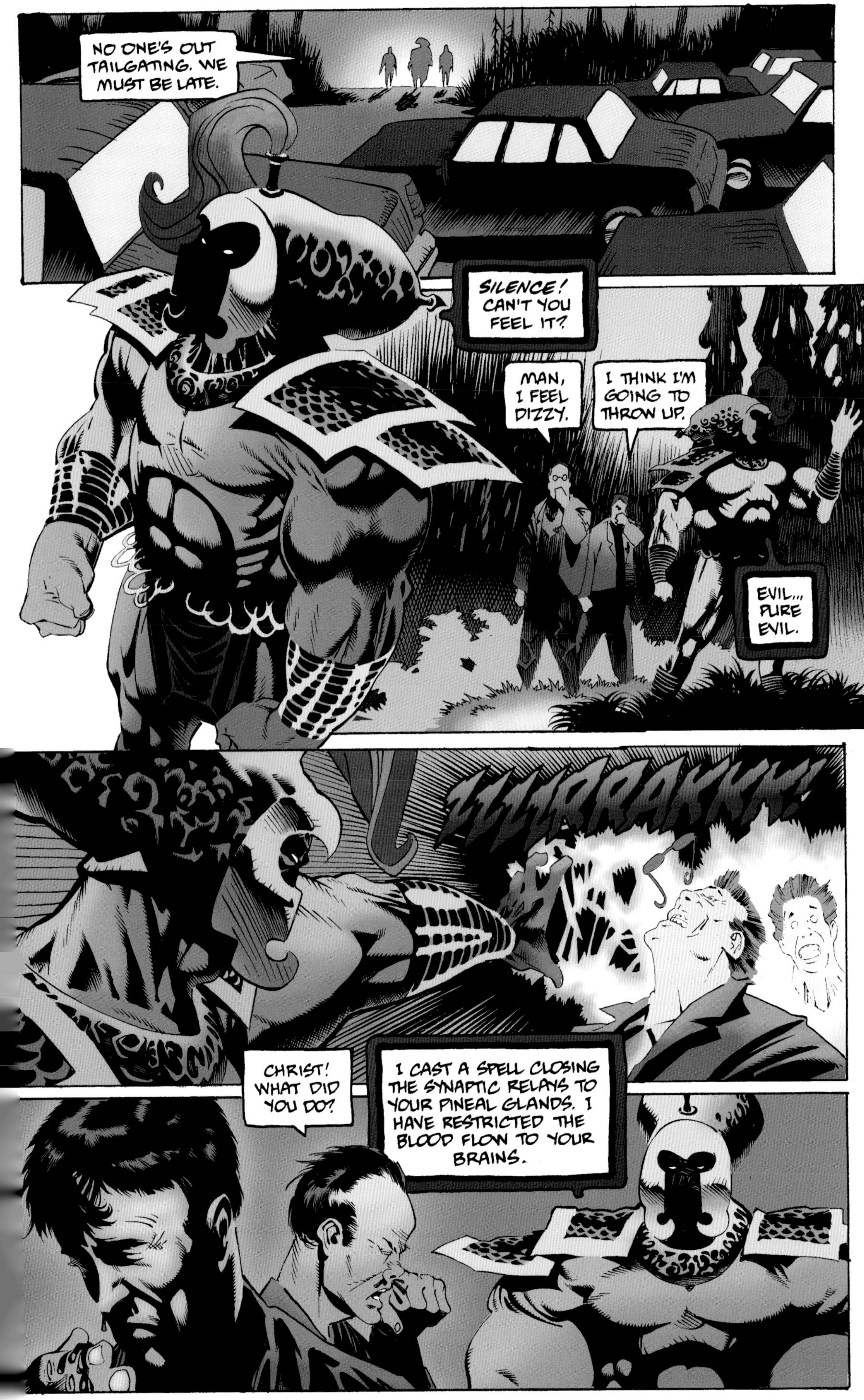
NO ONE'S OUT TAILGATING. WE MUST BE LATE.
SILENCE! CAN'T YOU FEEL IT?
MAN, I FEEL DIZZY.
I THINK I'M GOING TO THROW UP.
EVIL... PURE EVIL.
CHRIST! WHAT DID YOU DO?
I CAST A SPELL CLOSING THE SYNAPTIC RELAYS TO YOUR PINEAL GLANDS. I HAVE RESTRICTED THE BLOOD FLOW TO YOUR BRAINS.

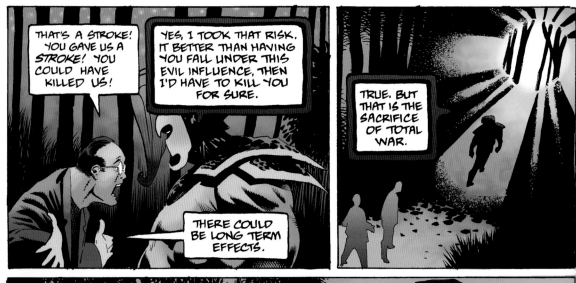

THAT'S A STROKE! YOU GAVE US A STROKE! YOU COULD HAVE KILLED US!

YES, I TOOK THAT RISK. IT BETTER THAN HAVING YOU FALL UNDER THIS EVIL INFLUENCE, THEN I'D HAVE TO KILL YOU FOR SURE.

THERE COULD BE LONG TERM EFFECTS.

TRUE. BUT THAT IS THE SACRIFICE OF TOTAL WAR.

HAIL, GREAT C'THULU, ANCIENT BEYOND MEMORY.

IT IS BEGUN. SHE HAS ALREADY SUMMONED LESSER DEMONS.

YOU TWO WILL HAVE TO DISTRACT THEM SO I CAN GO TO WORK.

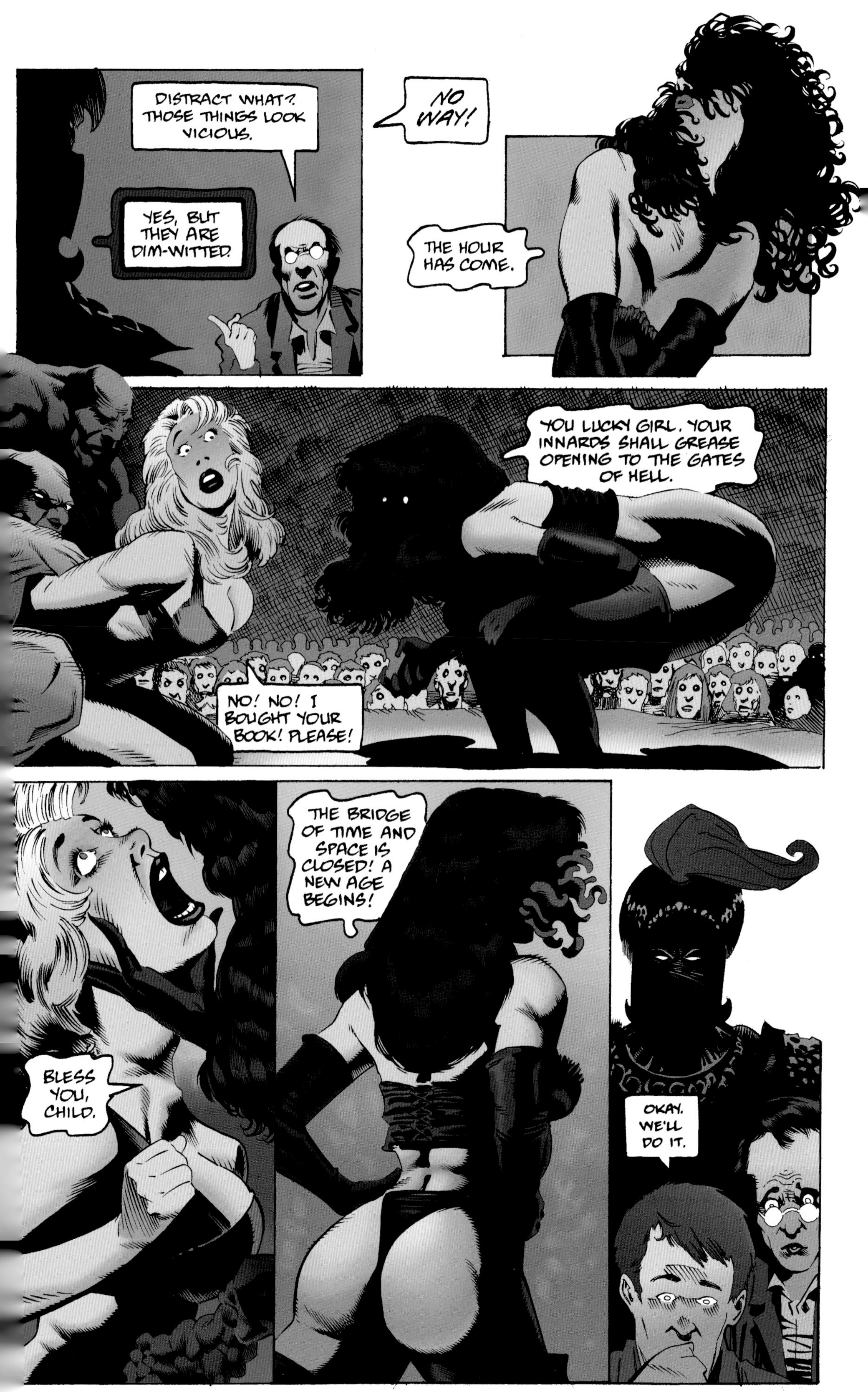
DISTRACT WHAT? THOSE THINGS LOOK VICIOUS.
YES, BUT THEY ARE DIM-WITTED.
NO WAY!
THE HOUR HAS COME.
YOU LUCKY GIRL. YOUR INNARDS SHALL GREASE OPENING TO THE GATES OF HELL.
NO! NO! I BOUGHT YOUR BOOK! PLEASE!
BLESS YOU, CHILD.
THE BRIDGE OF TIME AND SPACE IS CLOSED! A NEW AGE BEGINS!
OKAY. WE'LL DO IT.

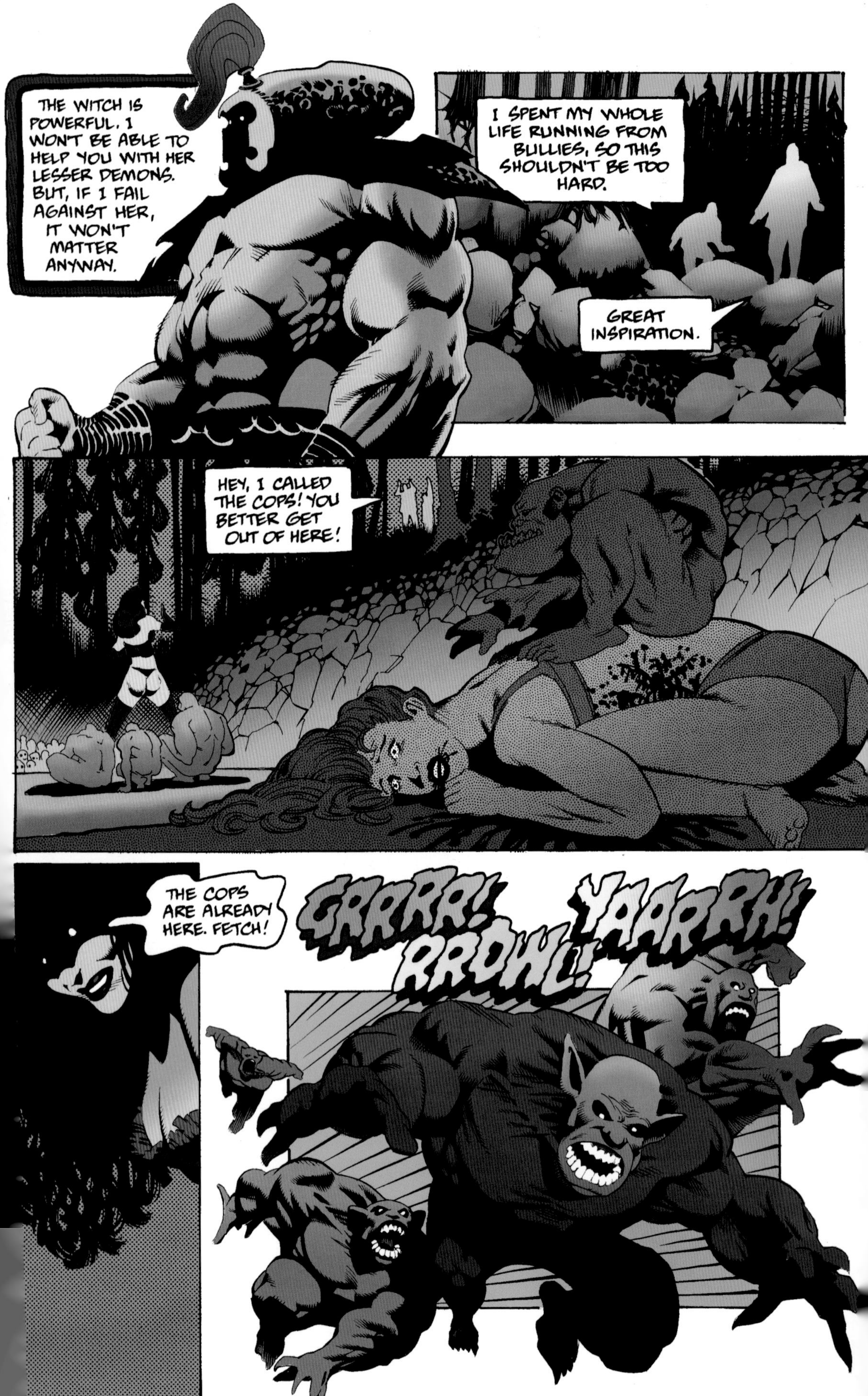
THE WITCH IS POWERFUL. I WON'T BE ABLE TO HELP YOU WITH HER LESSER DEMONS. BUT, IF I FAIL AGAINST HER, IT WON'T MATTER ANYWAY.
I SPENT MY WHOLE LIFE RUNNING FROM BULLIES, SO THIS SHOULDN'T BE TOO HARD.
GREAT INSPIRATION.
HEY, I CALLED THE COPS! YOU BETTER GET OUT OF HERE!
THE COPS ARE ALREADY HERE. FETCH!
GRRRR!
RROWL!
YAARRH!

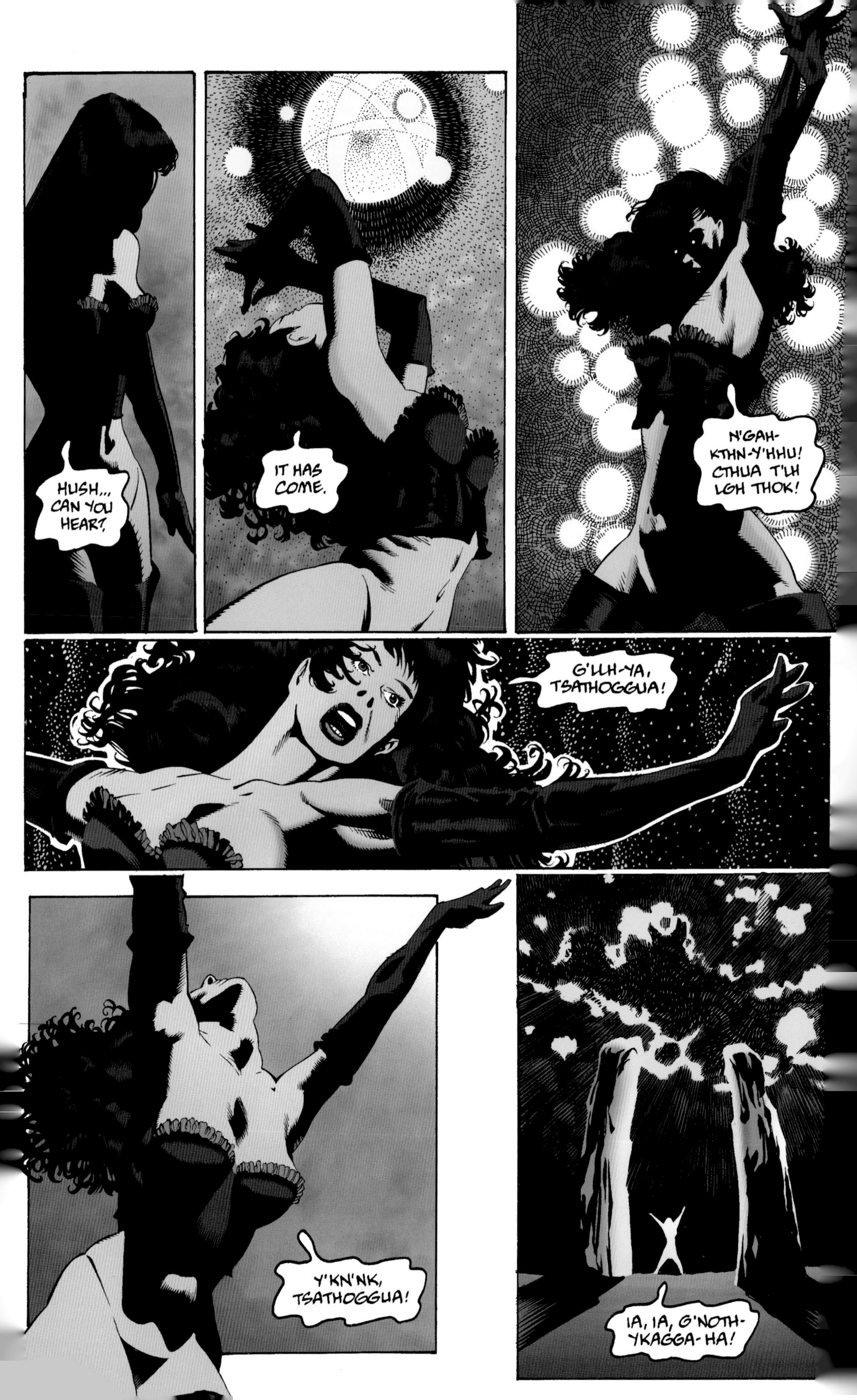
HUSH... CAN YOU HEAR?
IT HAS COME.
N'GAH-KTHN-Y'HHU! CTHUA T'LH LGH THOK!
G'LLH-YA, TSATHOGGUA!
Y'KN'NK, TSATHOGGUA!
IA, IA, G'NOTH-YKAGGA-HA!

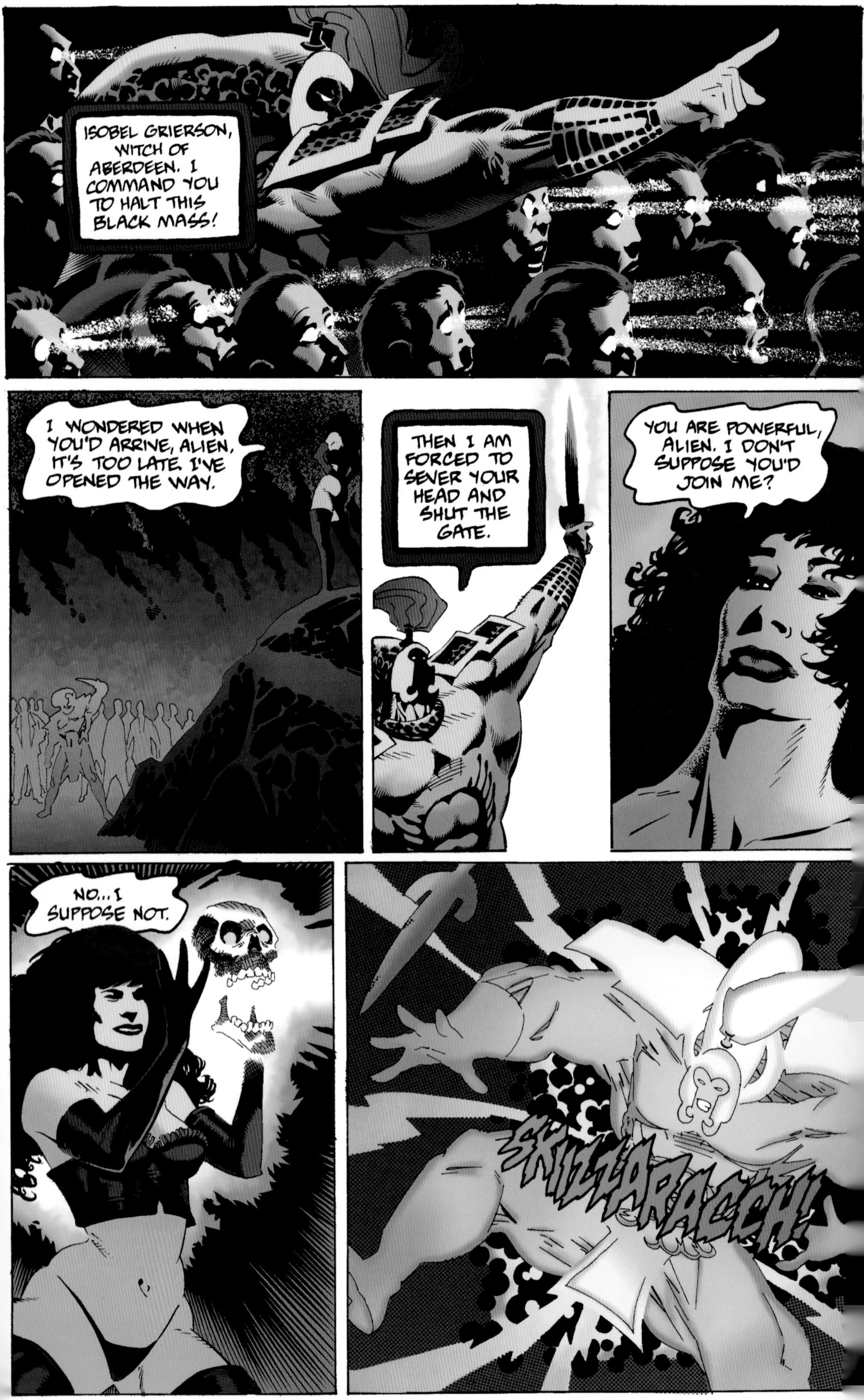
ISOBEL GRIERSON, WITCH OF ABERDEEN. I COMMAND YOU TO HALT THIS BLACK MASS!
I WONDERED WHEN YOU'D ARRIVE, ALIEN. IT'S TOO LATE. I'VE OPENED THE WAY.
THEN I AM FORCED TO SEVER YOUR HEAD AND SHUT THE GATE.
YOU ARE POWERFUL, ALIEN. I DON'T SUPPOSE YOU'D JOIN ME?
NO...I SUPPOSE NOT.
SKIZZARACCH!

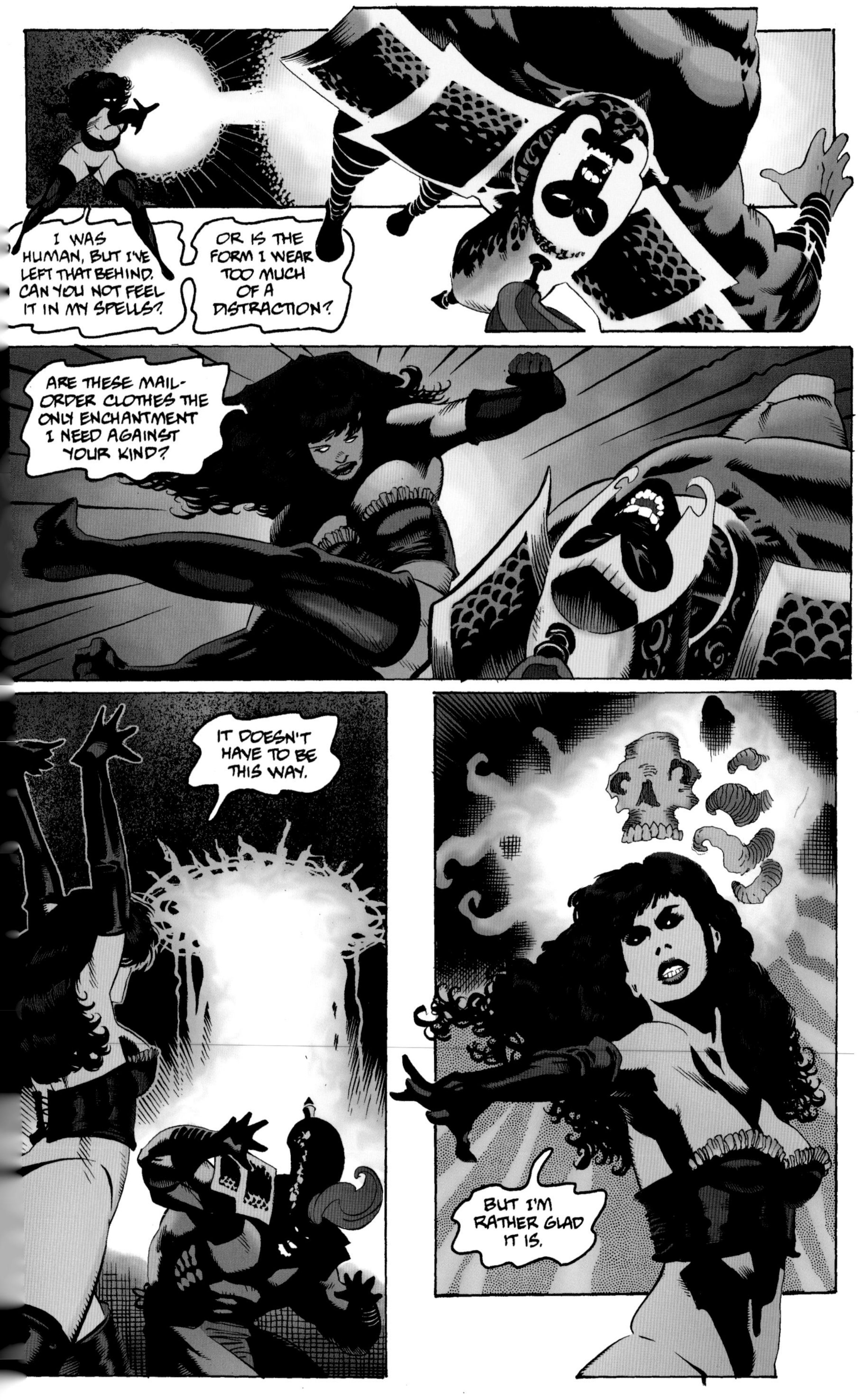
I WAS HUMAN, BUT I'VE LEFT THAT BEHIND. CAN YOU NOT FEEL IT IN MY SPELLS?
OR IS THE FORM I WEAR TOO MUCH OF A DISTRACTION?
ARE THESE MAIL-ORDER CLOTHES THE ONLY ENCHANTMENT I NEED AGAINST YOUR KIND?
IT DOESN'T HAVE TO BE THIS WAY.
BUT I'M RATHER GLAD IT IS.

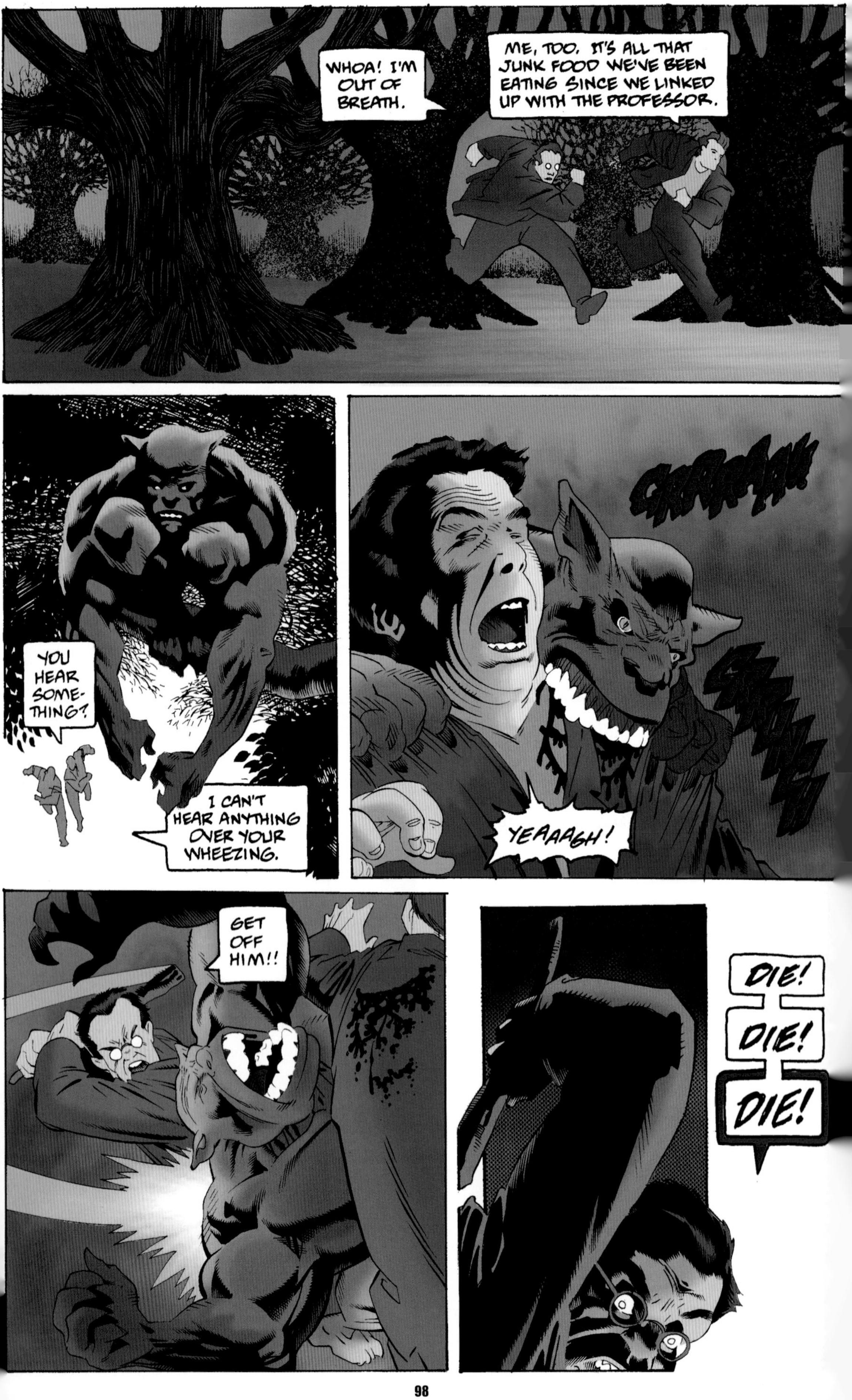

WHOA! I'M OUT OF BREATH.
ME, TOO. IT'S ALL THAT JUNK FOOD WE'VE BEEN EATING SINCE WE LINKED UP WITH THE PROFESSOR.
YOU HEAR SOME-THING?
I CAN'T HEAR ANYTHING OVER YOUR WHEEZING.
YEAAAGH!
GET OFF HIM!!
DIE!
DIE!
DIE!

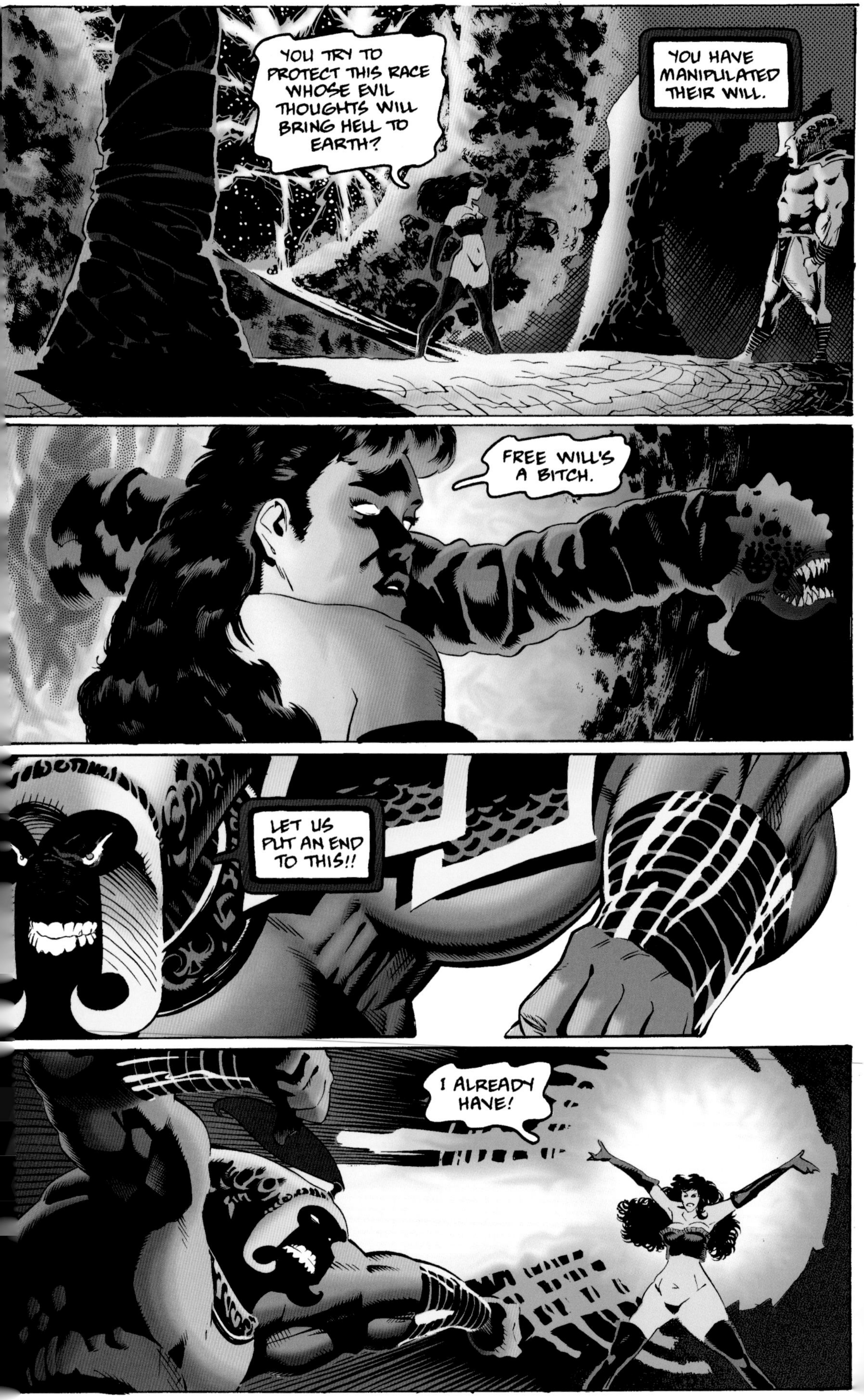
YOU TRY TO PROTECT THIS RACE WHOSE EVIL THOUGHTS WILL BRING HELL TO EARTH?
YOU HAVE MANIPULATED THEIR WILL.
FREE WILL'S A BITCH.
LET US PUT AN END TO THIS!!
I ALREADY HAVE!

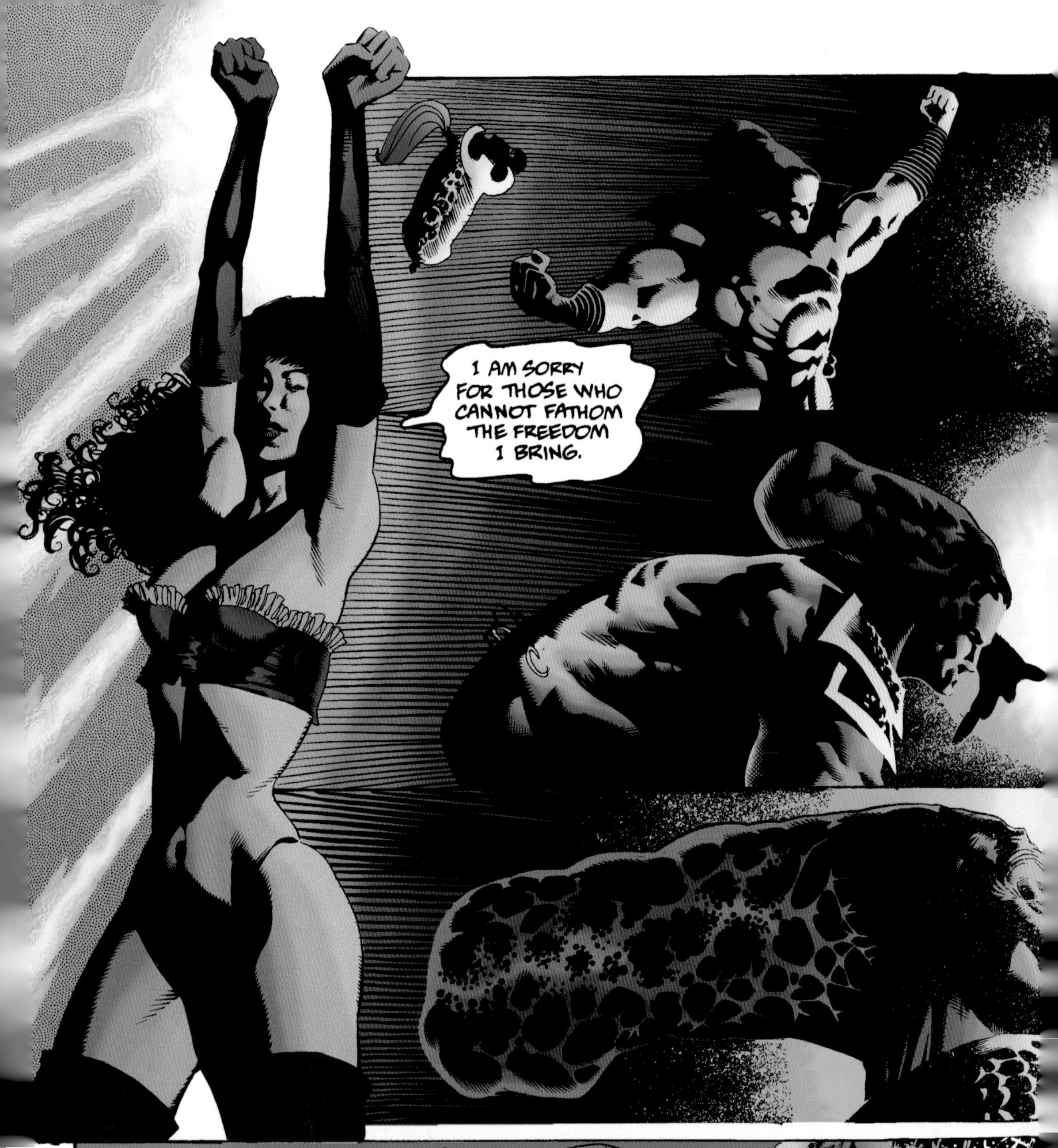
I AM SORRY FOR THOSE WHO CANNOT FATHOM THE FREEDOM I BRING.

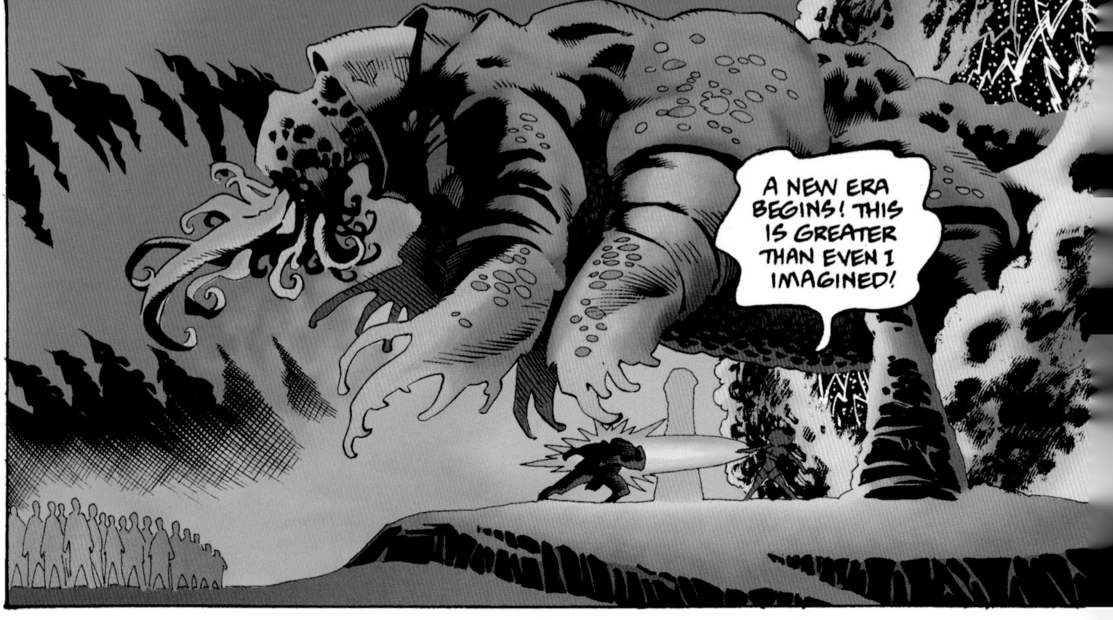
A NEW ERA BEGINS! THIS IS GREATER THAN EVEN I IMAGINED!

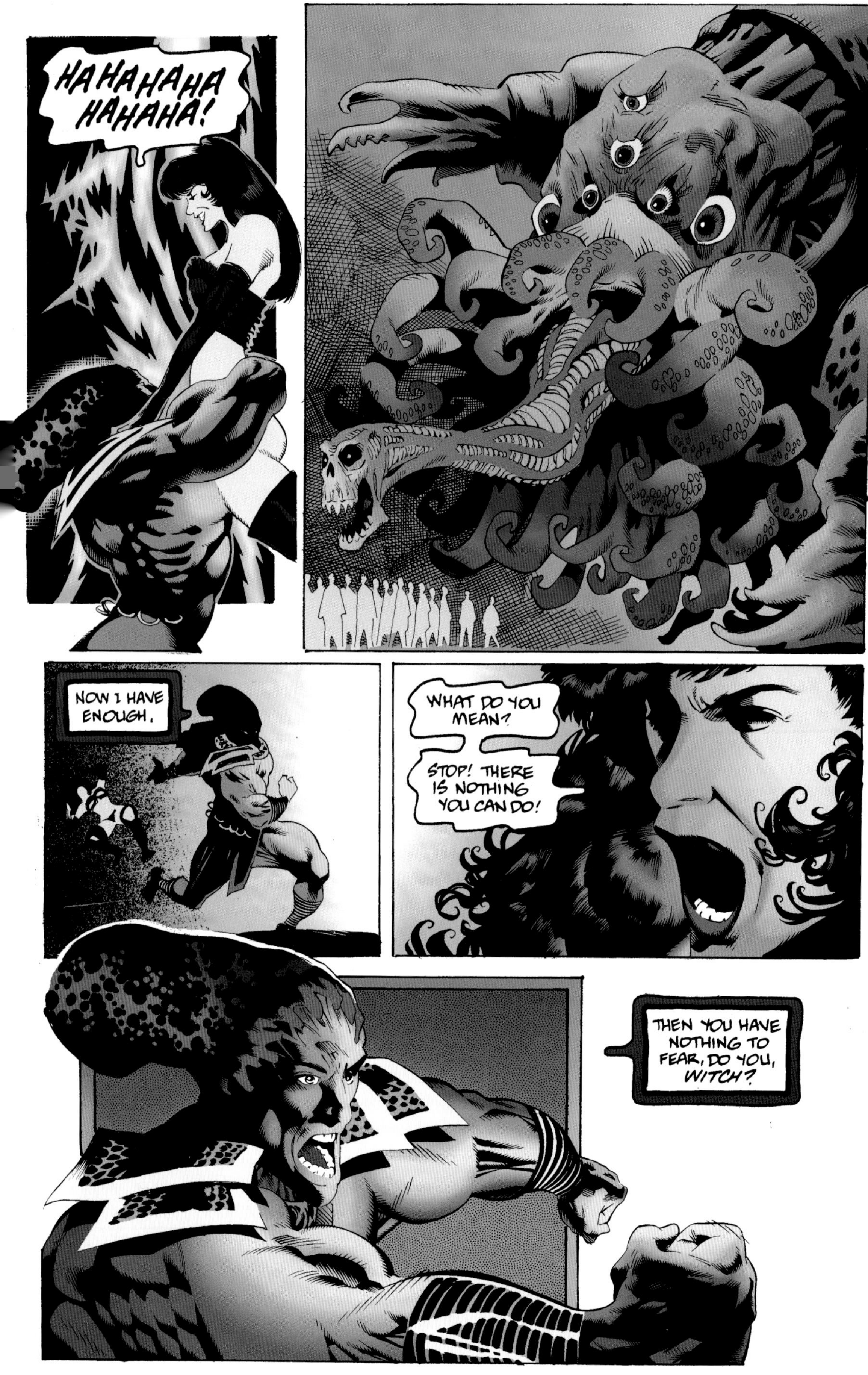
HAHAHAHAHA
HAHAHA!
NOW I HAVE ENOUGH.
WHAT DO YOU MEAN?
STOP! THERE IS NOTHING YOU CAN DO!
THEN YOU HAVE NOTHING TO FEAR, DO YOU, *WITCH?*

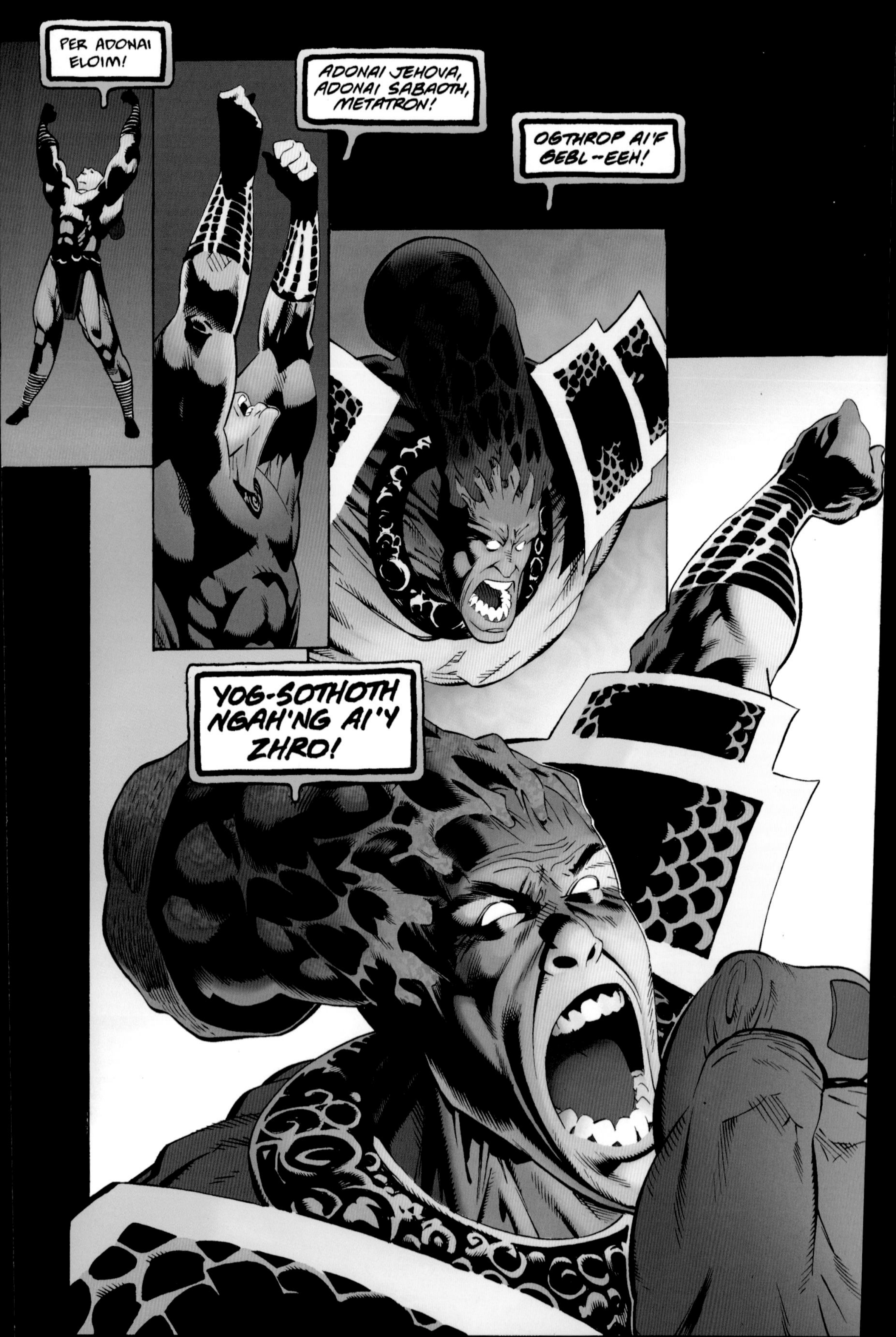
PER ADONAI ELOIM!
ADONAI JEHOVA, ADONAI SABAOTH, METATRON!
OGTHROP AI'F GEBL--EEH!
YOG-SOTHOTH NGAH'NG AI'Y ZHRO!

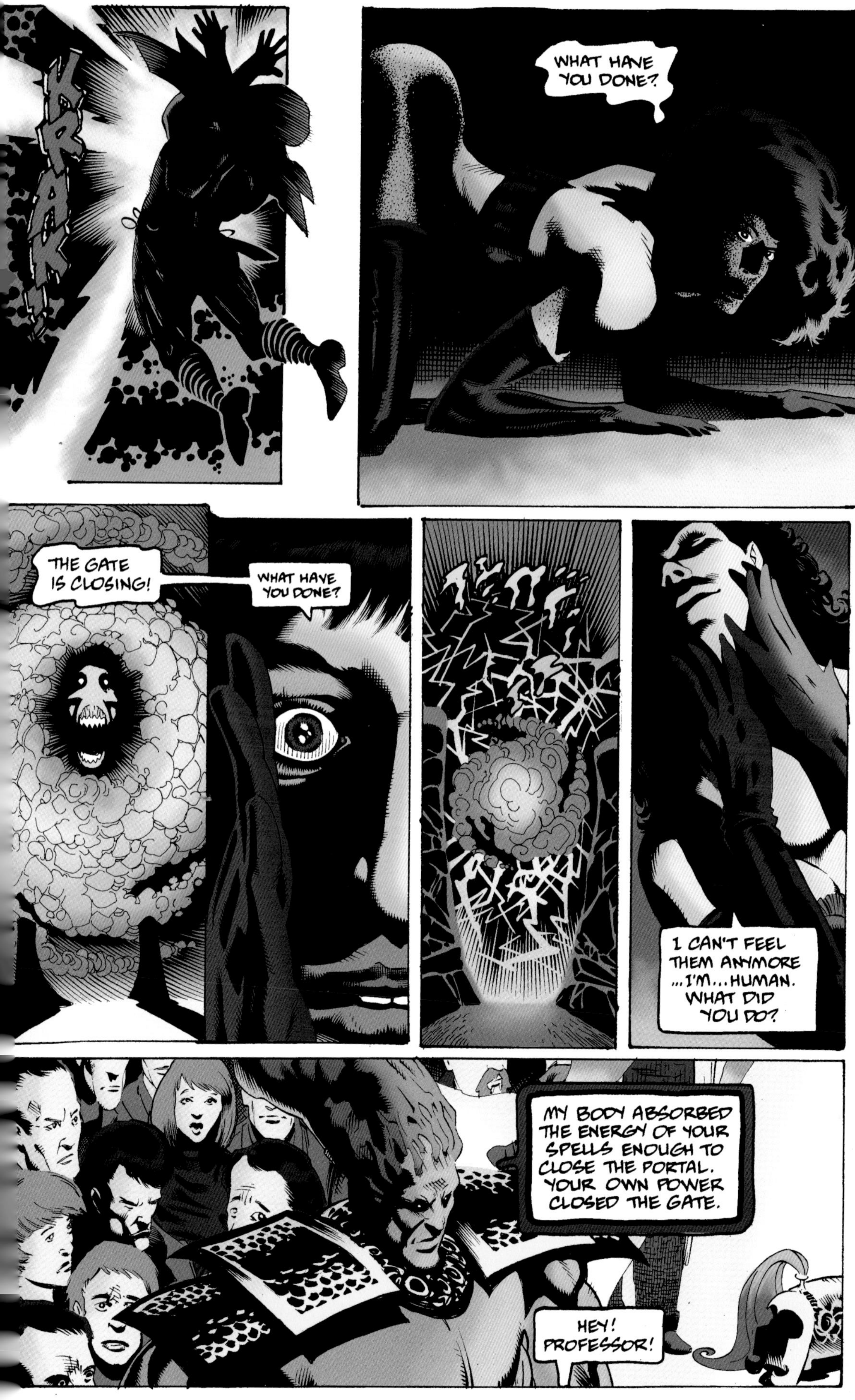
KRAK
WHAT HAVE YOU DONE?
THE GATE IS CLOSING!
WHAT HAVE YOU DONE?
I CAN'T FEEL THEM ANYMORE ...I'M...HUMAN. WHAT DID YOU DO?
MY BODY ABSORBED THE ENERGY OF YOUR SPELLS ENOUGH TO CLOSE THE PORTAL. YOUR OWN POWER CLOSED THE GATE.
HEY! PROFESSOR!

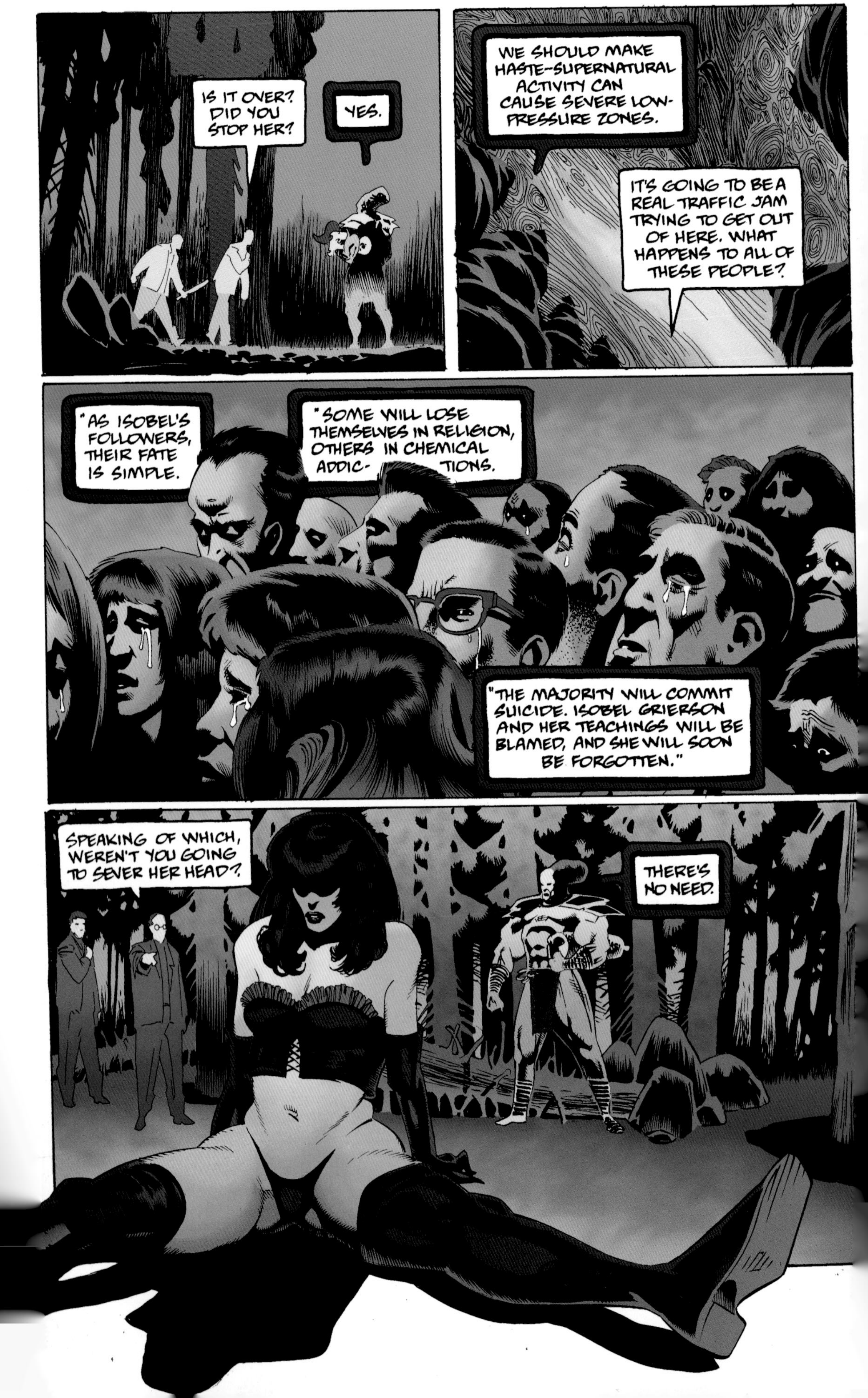
IS IT OVER? DID YOU STOP HER?
YES.
WE SHOULD MAKE HASTE--SUPERNATURAL ACTIVITY CAN CAUSE SEVERE LOW-PRESSURE ZONES.
IT'S GOING TO BE A REAL TRAFFIC JAM TRYING TO GET OUT OF HERE. WHAT HAPPENS TO ALL OF THESE PEOPLE?
"AS ISOBEL'S FOLLOWERS, THEIR FATE IS SIMPLE.
"SOME WILL LOSE THEMSELVES IN RELIGION, OTHERS IN CHEMICAL ADDIC- TIONS.
"THE MAJORITY WILL COMMIT SUICIDE. ISOBEL GRIERSON AND HER TEACHINGS WILL BE BLAMED, AND SHE WILL SOON BE FORGOTTEN."
SPEAKING OF WHICH, WEREN'T YOU GOING TO SEVER HER HEAD?
THERE'S NO NEED.

SHE IS ONLY HUMAN NOW. SHE CAN NEVER AGAIN BE OF ANY TROUBLE. HER MIND WAS CUT OFF FROM THE OLD ONES WHEN THE GATE CLOSED.

I BELIEVE SEVERING HER HEAD AND BURNING HER BODY WOULD BE POINTLESS.

THAT SOUNDS ALMOST HUMAN.

VENGEANCE IS NOT IN MY NATURE.

SO, ALL'S WELL THAT ENDS WELL.

I'VE GOT TO ADMIT I HAVE HAD MY DOUBTS ABOUT YOU.

YOU BEING ALIEN MADE ME NOT TRUST YOU OR YOUR MOTIVES.

I, AH, HOPE YOU CAN FORGIVE MY PREJUDICE.

REALIZE, YOU ARE ALL ALIEN TO ME. I COULD NOT AFFORD DISBELIEF. THE RISKS WERE TOO HIGH. I'VE HAD TO KEEP SECRETS FROM YOU TO MAKE YOU ACCEPT YOUR ROLES IN THIS, JUST AS PROFESSOR WILCOX WAS DENIED SOME ANSWERS...

...AND TOLD ONE GREAT LIE.

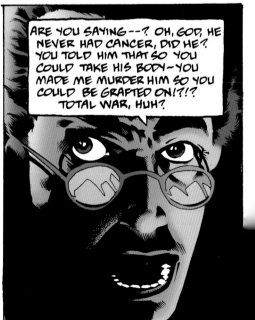

ARE YOU SAYING --? OH, GOD, HE NEVER HAD CANCER, DID HE? YOU TOLD HIM THAT SO YOU COULD TAKE HIS BODY~YOU MADE ME MURDER HIM SO YOU COULD BE GRAFTED ON!?!? TOTAL WAR, HUH?

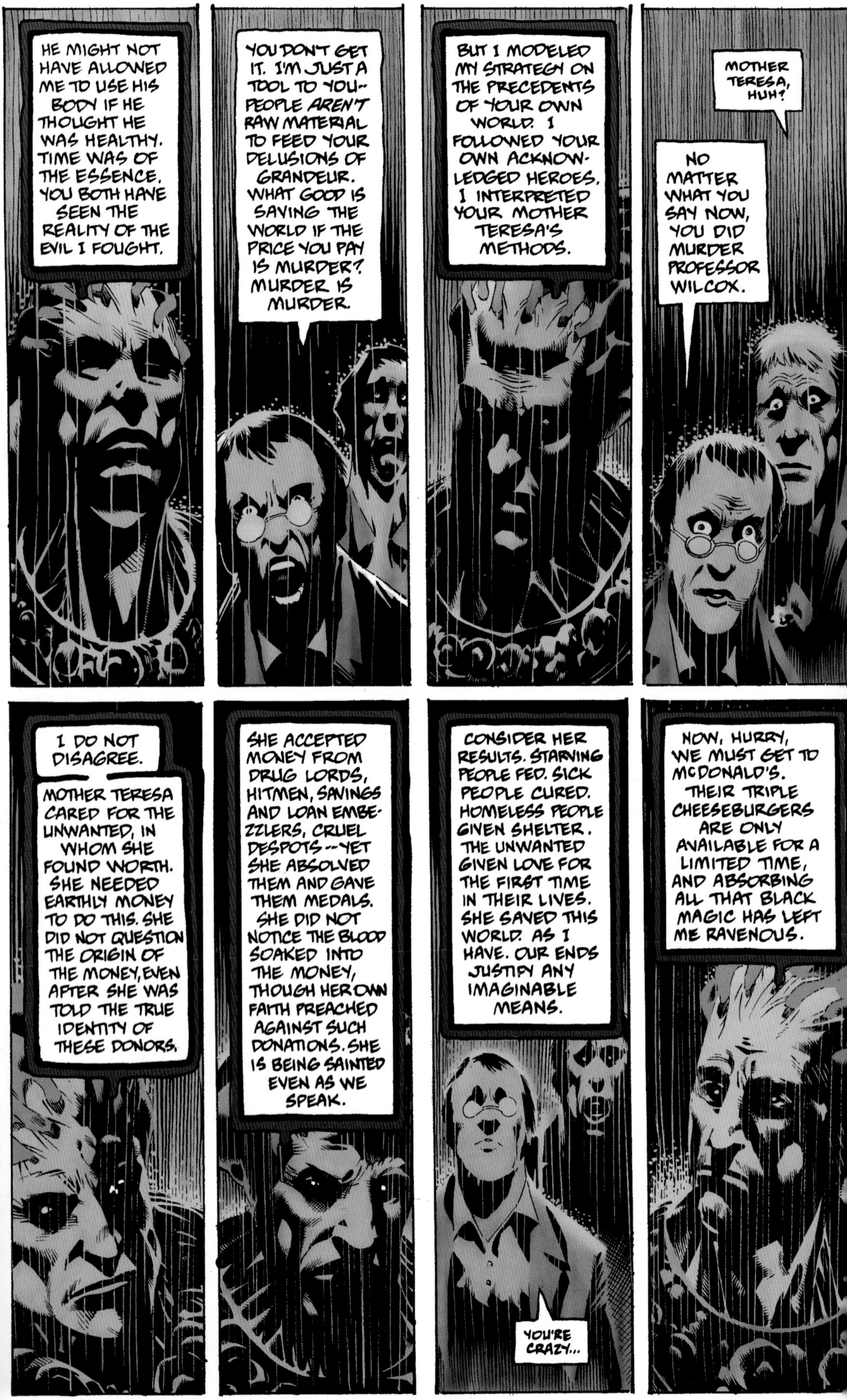
HE MIGHT NOT HAVE ALLOWED ME TO USE HIS BODY IF HE THOUGHT HE WAS HEALTHY. TIME WAS OF THE ESSENCE. YOU BOTH HAVE SEEN THE REALITY OF THE EVIL I FOUGHT.
YOU DON'T GET IT. I'M JUST A TOOL TO YOU-- PEOPLE *AREN'T* RAW MATERIAL TO FEED YOUR DELUSIONS OF GRANDEUR. WHAT GOOD IS SAVING THE WORLD IF THE PRICE YOU PAY IS MURDER? MURDER IS MURDER.
BUT I MODELED MY STRATEGY ON THE PRECEDENTS OF YOUR OWN WORLD. I FOLLOWED YOUR OWN ACKNOWLEDGED HEROES. I INTERPRETED YOUR MOTHER TERESA'S METHODS.
MOTHER TERESA, HUH?
NO MATTER WHAT YOU SAY NOW, YOU DID MURDER PROFESSOR WILCOX.
I DO NOT DISAGREE.
MOTHER TERESA CARED FOR THE UNWANTED, IN WHOM SHE FOUND WORTH. SHE NEEDED EARTHLY MONEY TO DO THIS. SHE DID NOT QUESTION THE ORIGIN OF THE MONEY, EVEN AFTER SHE WAS TOLD THE TRUE IDENTITY OF THESE DONORS.
SHE ACCEPTED MONEY FROM DRUG LORDS, HITMEN, SAVINGS AND LOAN EMBEZZLERS, CRUEL DESPOTS--YET SHE ABSOLVED THEM AND GAVE THEM MEDALS. SHE DID NOT NOTICE THE BLOOD SOAKED INTO THE MONEY, THOUGH HER OWN FAITH PREACHED AGAINST SUCH DONATIONS. SHE IS BEING SAINTED EVEN AS WE SPEAK.
CONSIDER HER RESULTS. STARVING PEOPLE FED. SICK PEOPLE CURED. HOMELESS PEOPLE GIVEN SHELTER. THE UNWANTED GIVEN LOVE FOR THE FIRST TIME IN THEIR LIVES. SHE SAVED THIS WORLD. AS I HAVE. OUR ENDS JUSTIFY ANY IMAGINABLE MEANS.
YOU'RE CRAZY...
NOW, HURRY, WE MUST GET TO McDONALD'S. THEIR TRIPLE CHEESEBURGERS ARE ONLY AVAILABLE FOR A LIMITED TIME, AND ABSORBING ALL THAT BLACK MAGIC HAS LEFT ME RAVENOUS.

Montgomery, Alabama. Seven years later.

SHUT UP, YOU LITTLE CREEPS, OR I'LL TAN YOUR HIDES.

HEY, WHEN'S SUPPER? I'M STARVING! I NEED MY STRENGTH!

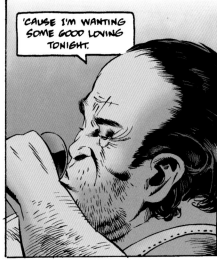

'CAUSE I'M WANTING SOME GOOD LOVING TONIGHT.

SORRY ABOUT THE BLACK EYE, BUT YOU KNOW NOT TO PISS ME OFF WHEN THE RAZORBACKS LOSE. BUT, REMEMBER, I'M YOUR DREAM COME TRUE, HONEY. THAT'S WHAT YOU SAID WHEN WE MET. GUESS YOU DIDN'T KNOW WHAT KIND OF DREAM, HUH?

DAMMIT! SHUT THEM KIDS UP OR I'M GONNA LIGHT THEIR LITTLE BUTTS ON FIRE! I'M GONNA BRING HELL TO EARTH, ISOBEL, YOU HEAR ME?!?

The End

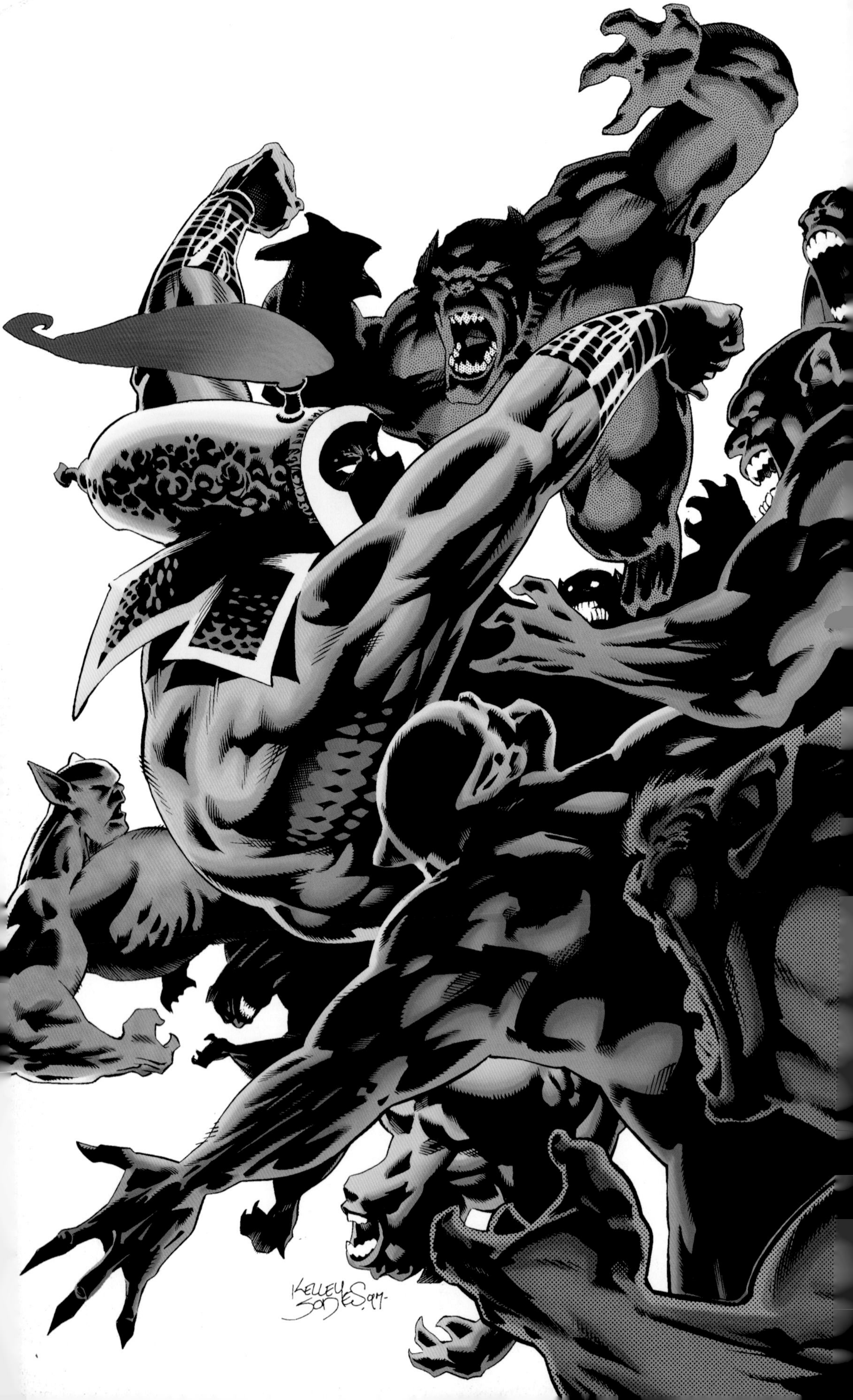

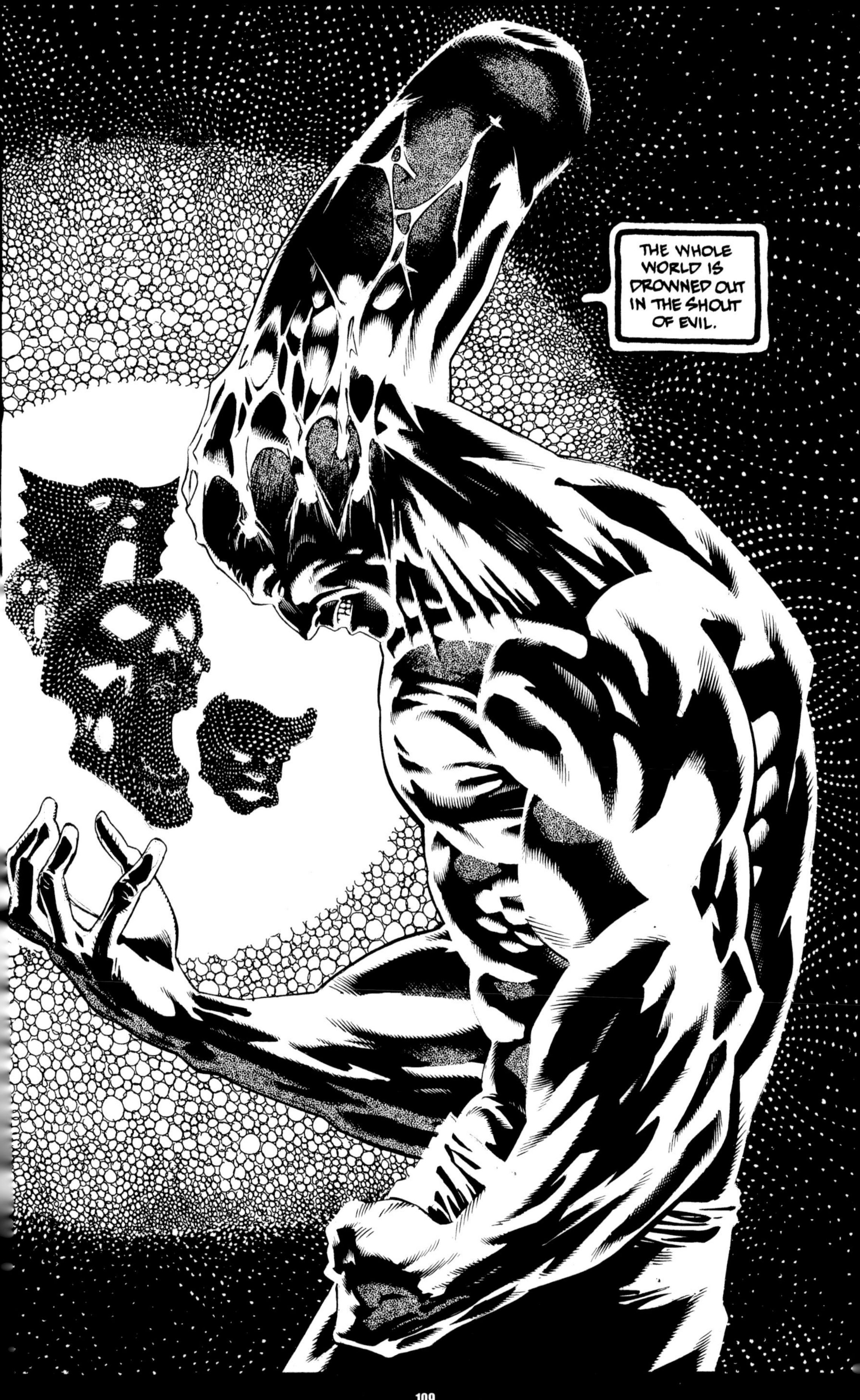
THE WHOLE WORLD IS DROWNED OUT IN THE SHOUT OF EVIL.

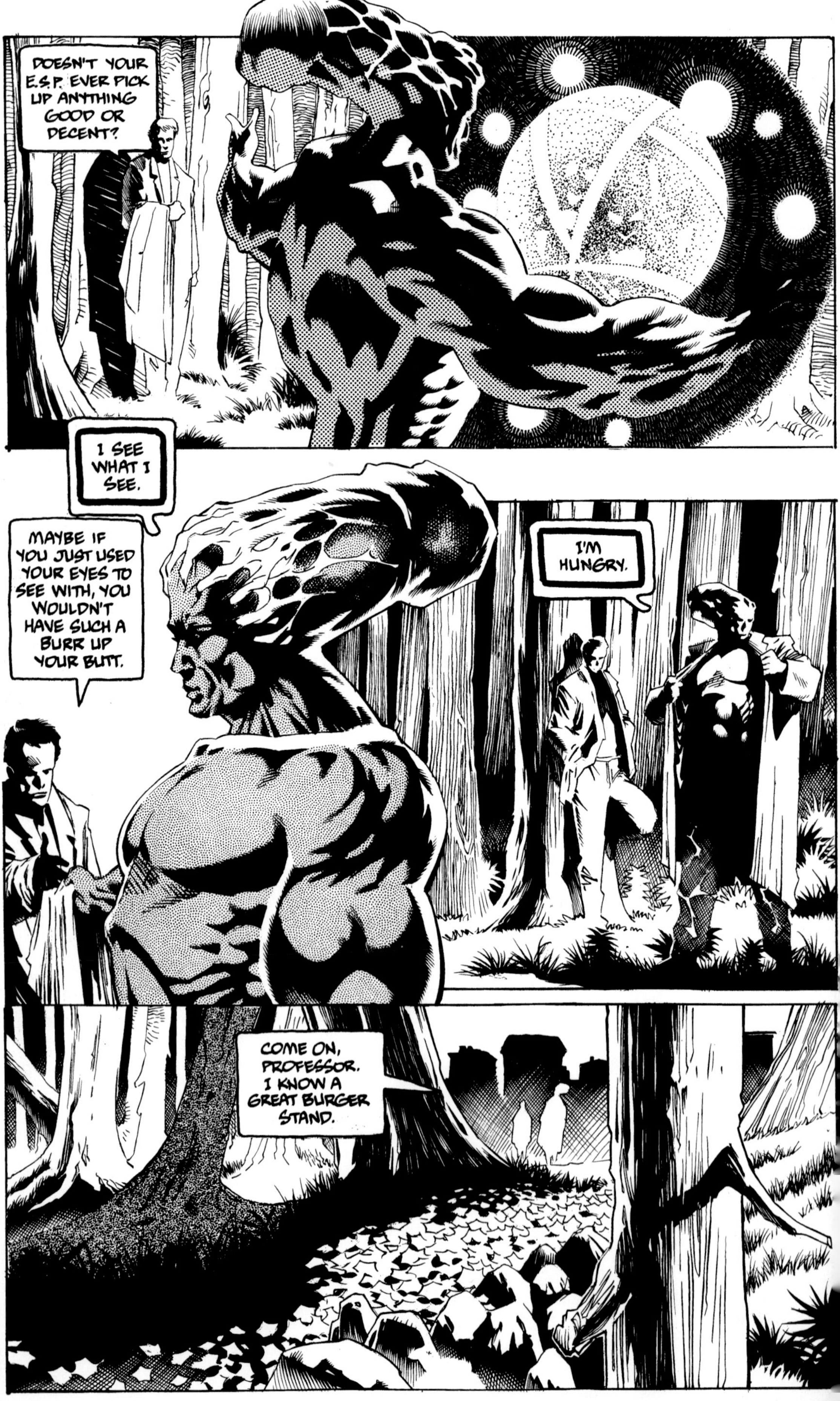
DOESN'T YOUR E.S.P. EVER PICK UP ANYTHING GOOD OR DECENT?
I SEE WHAT I SEE.
MAYBE IF YOU JUST USED YOUR EYES TO SEE WITH, YOU WOULDN'T HAVE SUCH A BURR UP YOUR BUTT.
I'M HUNGRY.
COME ON, PROFESSOR. I KNOW A GREAT BURGER STAND.

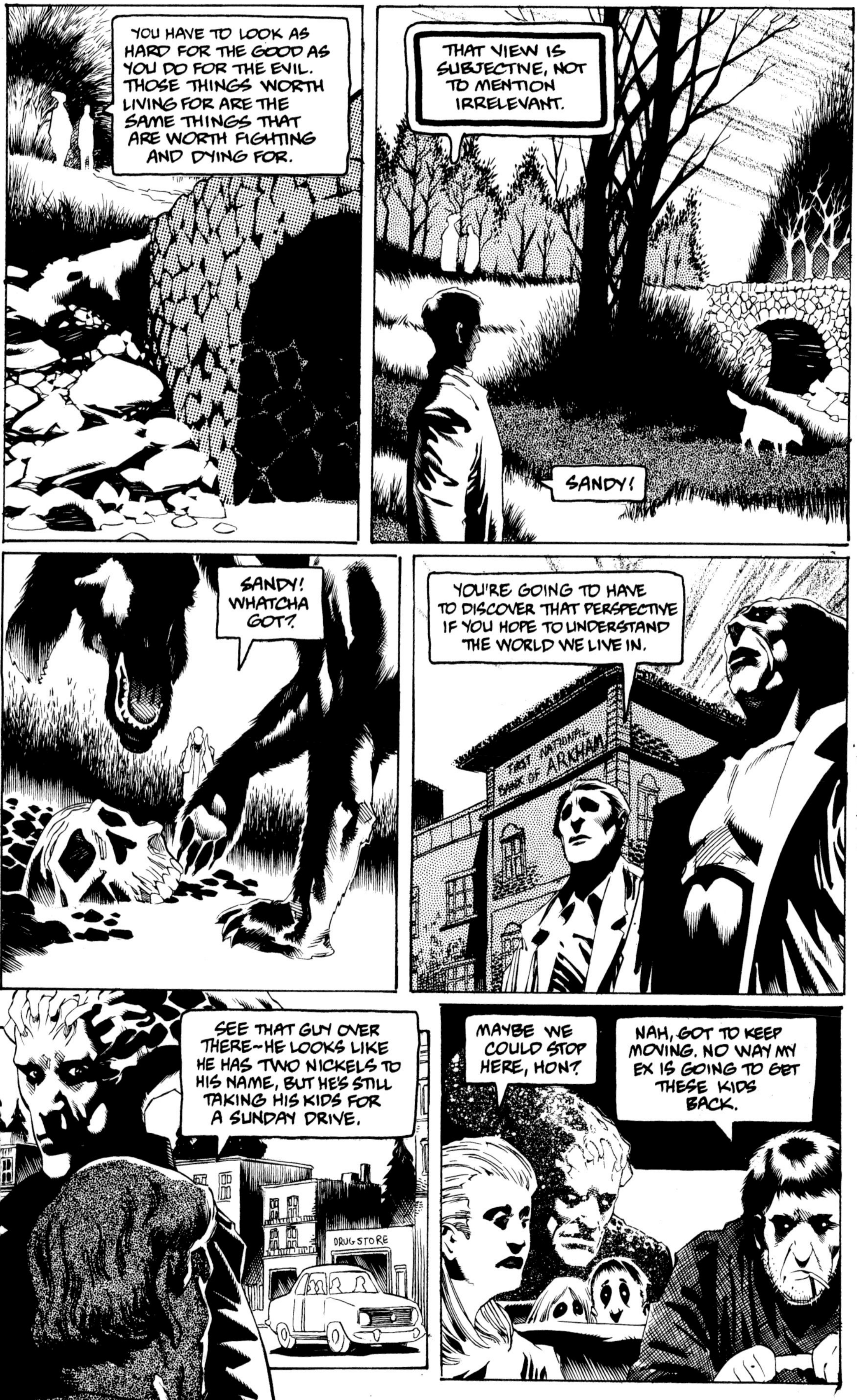
YOU HAVE TO LOOK AS HARD FOR THE GOOD AS YOU DO FOR THE EVIL. THOSE THINGS WORTH LIVING FOR ARE THE SAME THINGS THAT ARE WORTH FIGHTING AND DYING FOR.
THAT VIEW IS SUBJECTIVE, NOT TO MENTION IRRELEVANT.
SANDY!
SANDY! WHATCHA GOT?
YOU'RE GOING TO HAVE TO DISCOVER THAT PERSPECTIVE IF YOU HOPE TO UNDERSTAND THE WORLD WE LIVE IN.
SEE THAT GUY OVER THERE--HE LOOKS LIKE HE HAS TWO NICKELS TO HIS NAME, BUT HE'S STILL TAKING HIS KIDS FOR A SUNDAY DRIVE.
DRUGSTORE
MAYBE WE COULD STOP HERE, HON?
NAH, GOT TO KEEP MOVING. NO WAY MY EX IS GOING TO GET THESE KIDS BACK.

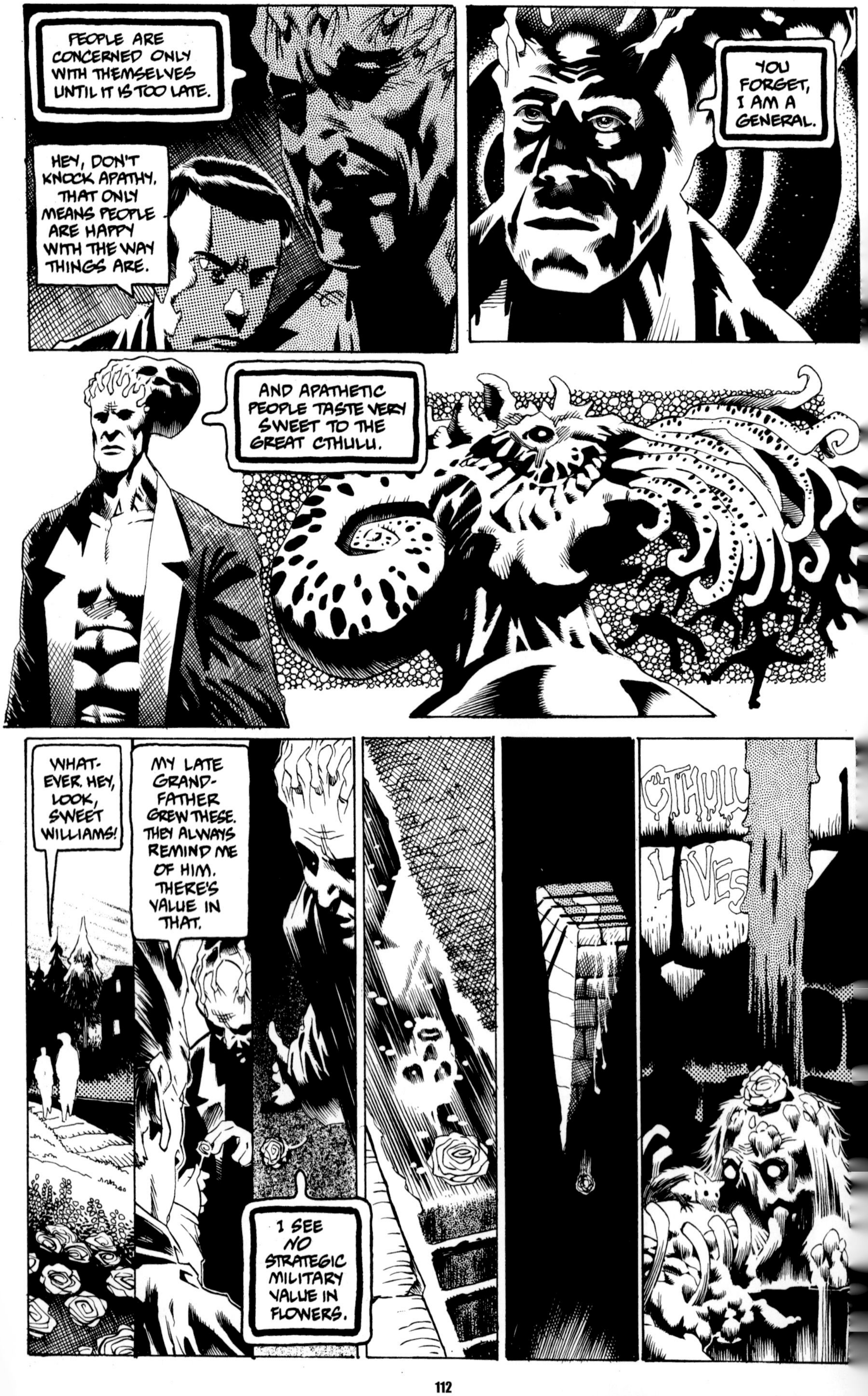
PEOPLE ARE CONCERNED ONLY WITH THEMSELVES UNTIL IT IS TOO LATE.
HEY, DON'T KNOCK APATHY. THAT ONLY MEANS PEOPLE ARE HAPPY WITH THE WAY THINGS ARE.
YOU FORGET, I AM A GENERAL.
AND APATHETIC PEOPLE TASTE VERY SWEET TO THE GREAT CTHULU.
WHAT-EVER. HEY, LOOK, SWEET WILLIAMS!
MY LATE GRAND-FATHER GREW THESE. THEY ALWAYS REMIND ME OF HIM. THERE'S VALUE IN THAT.
I SEE NO STRATEGIC MILITARY VALUE IN FLOWERS.
CTHULU
LIVES

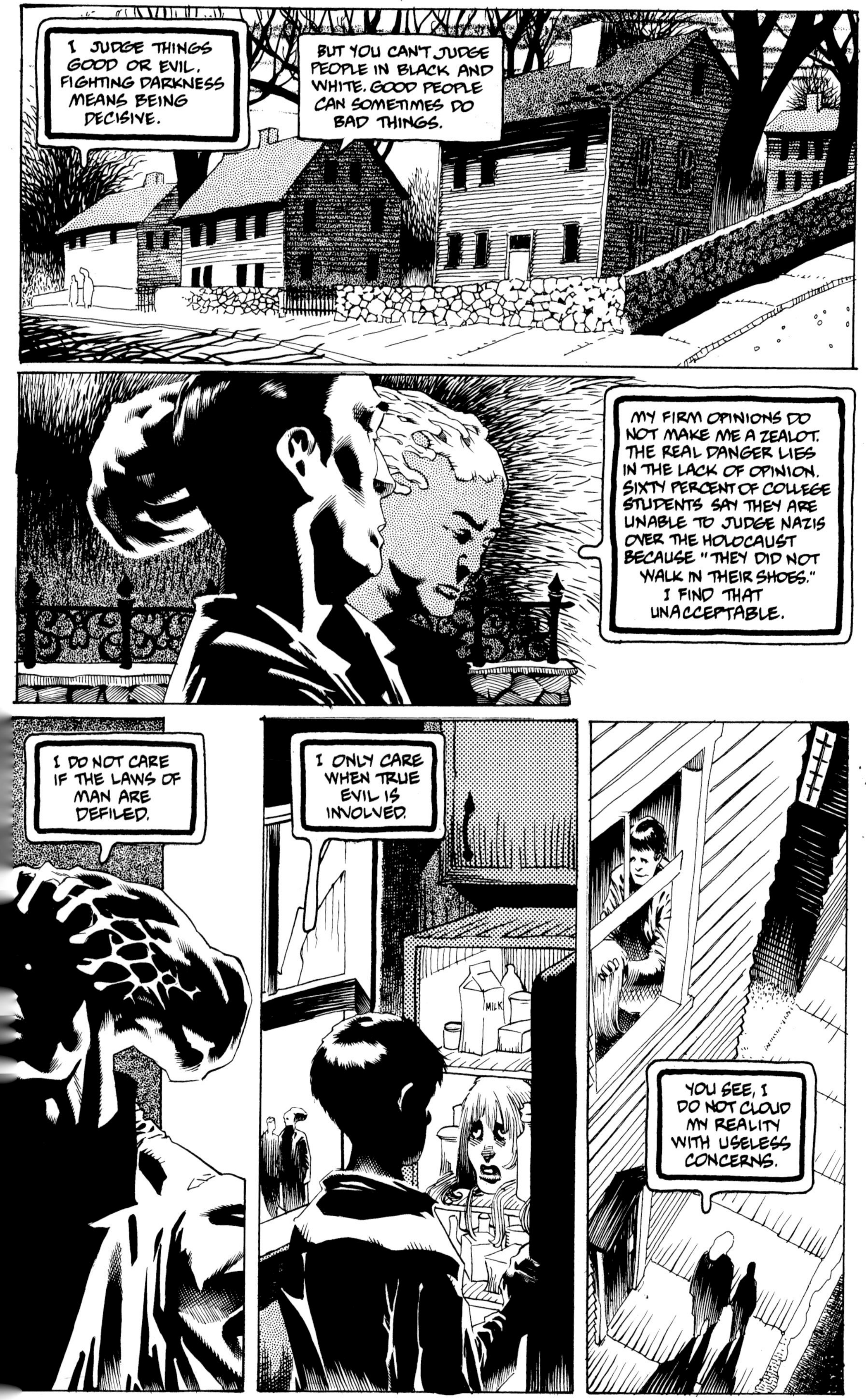
I JUDGE THINGS GOOD OR EVIL. FIGHTING DARKNESS MEANS BEING DECISIVE.
BUT YOU CAN'T JUDGE PEOPLE IN BLACK AND WHITE. GOOD PEOPLE CAN SOMETIMES DO BAD THINGS.
MY FIRM OPINIONS DO NOT MAKE ME A ZEALOT. THE REAL DANGER LIES IN THE LACK OF OPINION. SIXTY PERCENT OF COLLEGE STUDENTS SAY THEY ARE UNABLE TO JUDGE NAZIS OVER THE HOLOCAUST BECAUSE "THEY DID NOT WALK IN THEIR SHOES." I FIND THAT UNACCEPTABLE.
I DO NOT CARE IF THE LAWS OF MAN ARE DEFILED.
I ONLY CARE WHEN TRUE EVIL IS INVOLVED.
MILK
YOU SEE, I DO NOT CLOUD MY REALITY WITH USELESS CONCERNS.

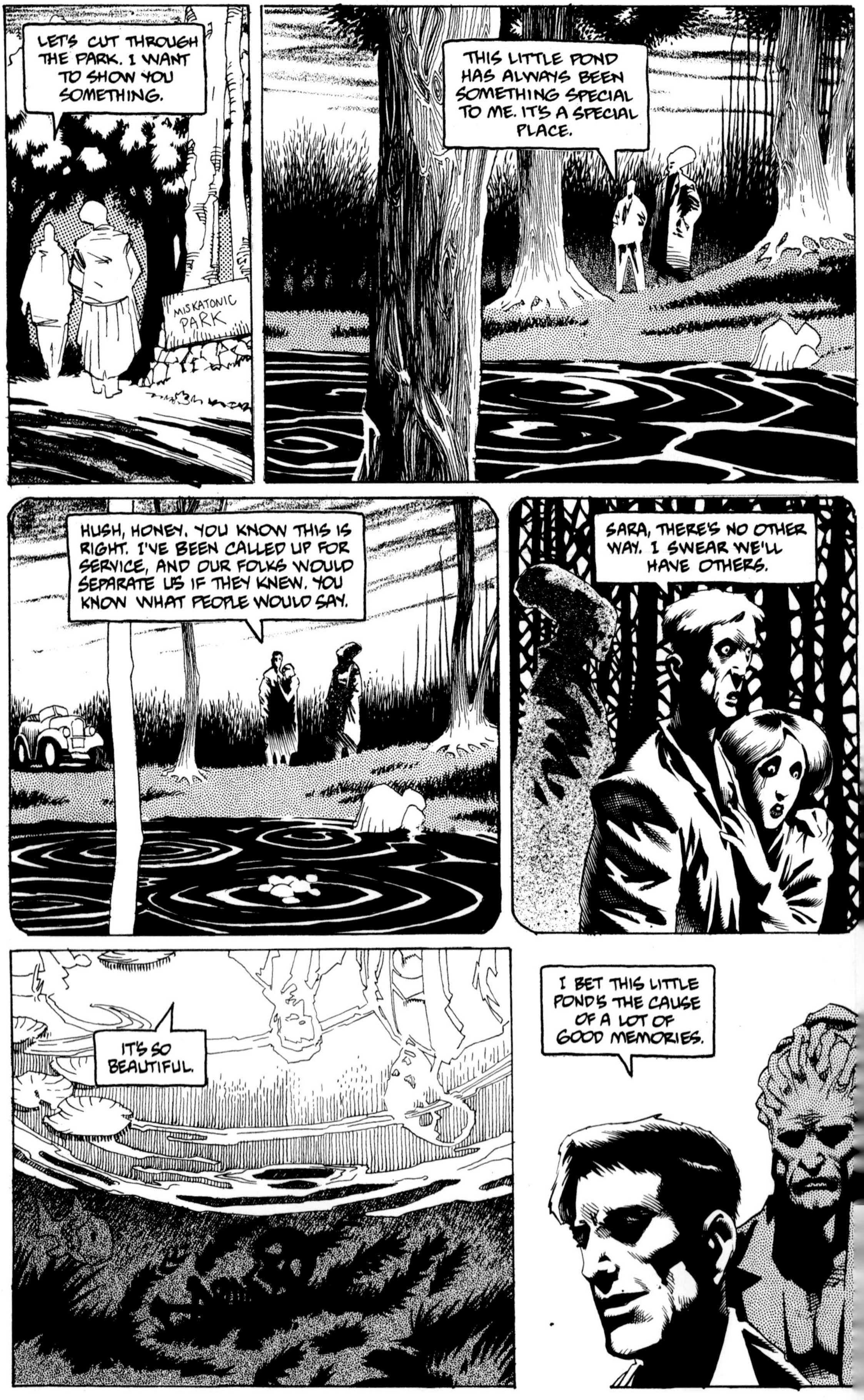
LET'S CUT THROUGH THE PARK. I WANT TO SHOW YOU SOMETHING.
MISKATONIC PARK
THIS LITTLE POND HAS ALWAYS BEEN SOMETHING SPECIAL TO ME. IT'S A SPECIAL PLACE.
HUSH, HONEY. YOU KNOW THIS IS RIGHT. I'VE BEEN CALLED UP FOR SERVICE, AND OUR FOLKS WOULD SEPARATE US IF THEY KNEW. YOU KNOW WHAT PEOPLE WOULD SAY.
SARA, THERE'S NO OTHER WAY. I SWEAR WE'LL HAVE OTHERS.
IT'S SO BEAUTIFUL.
I BET THIS LITTLE POND'S THE CAUSE OF A LOT OF GOOD MEMORIES.

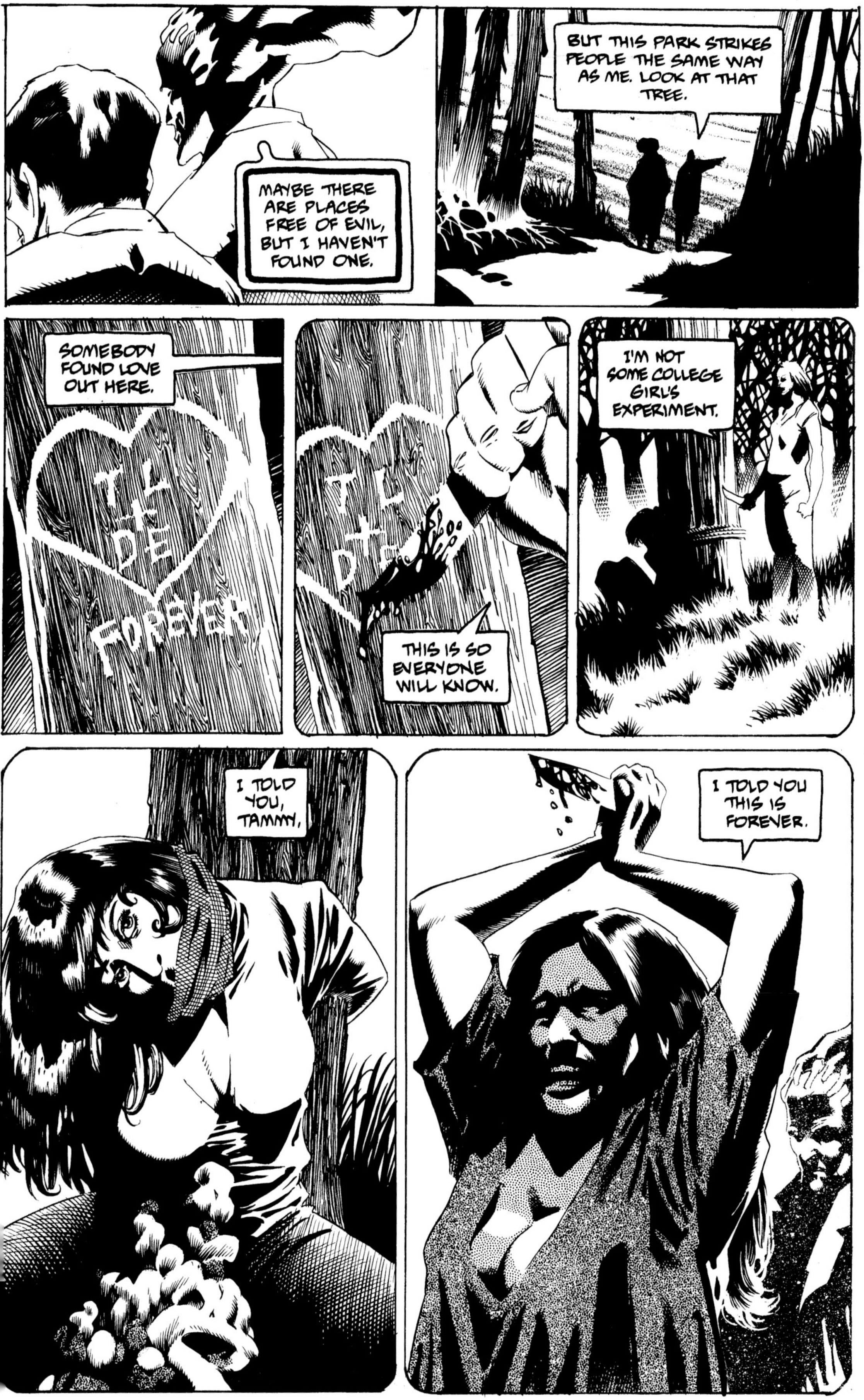
MAYBE THERE ARE PLACES FREE OF EVIL, BUT I HAVEN'T FOUND ONE.
BUT THIS PARK STRIKES PEOPLE THE SAME WAY AS ME. LOOK AT THAT TREE.
SOMEBODY FOUND LOVE OUT HERE.
TL
DE
FOREVER
THIS IS SO EVERYONE WILL KNOW.
I'M NOT SOME COLLEGE GIRL'S EXPERIMENT.
I TOLD YOU, TAMMY,
I TOLD YOU THIS IS FOREVER.

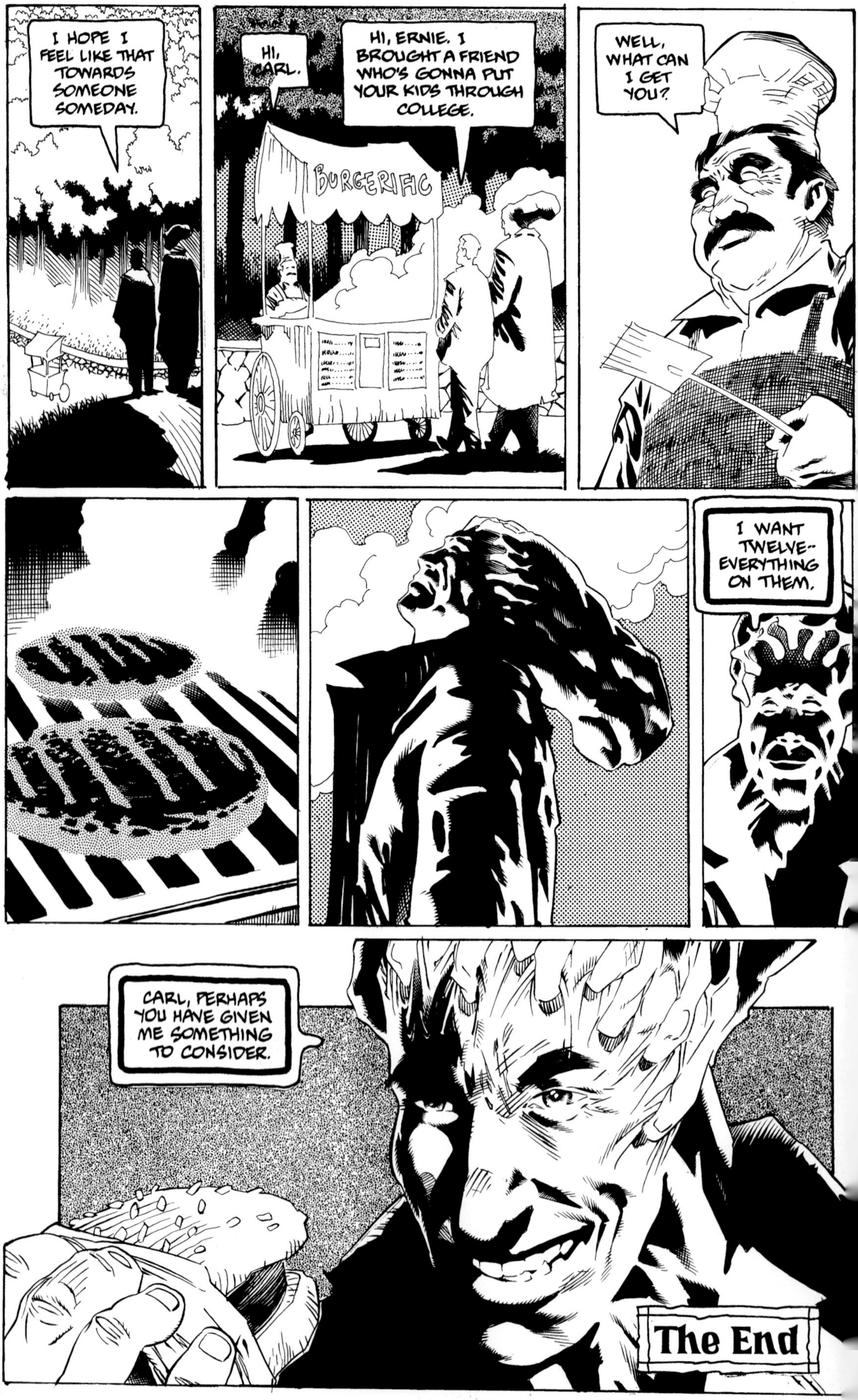
I HOPE I FEEL LIKE THAT TOWARDS SOMEONE SOMEDAY.
HI, CARL.
HI, ERNIE. I BROUGHT A FRIEND WHO'S GONNA PUT YOUR KIDS THROUGH COLLEGE.
BURGERIFIC
WELL, WHAT CAN I GET YOU?
I WANT TWELVE-- EVERYTHING ON THEM.
CARL, PERHAPS YOU HAVE GIVEN ME SOMETHING TO CONSIDER.
The End

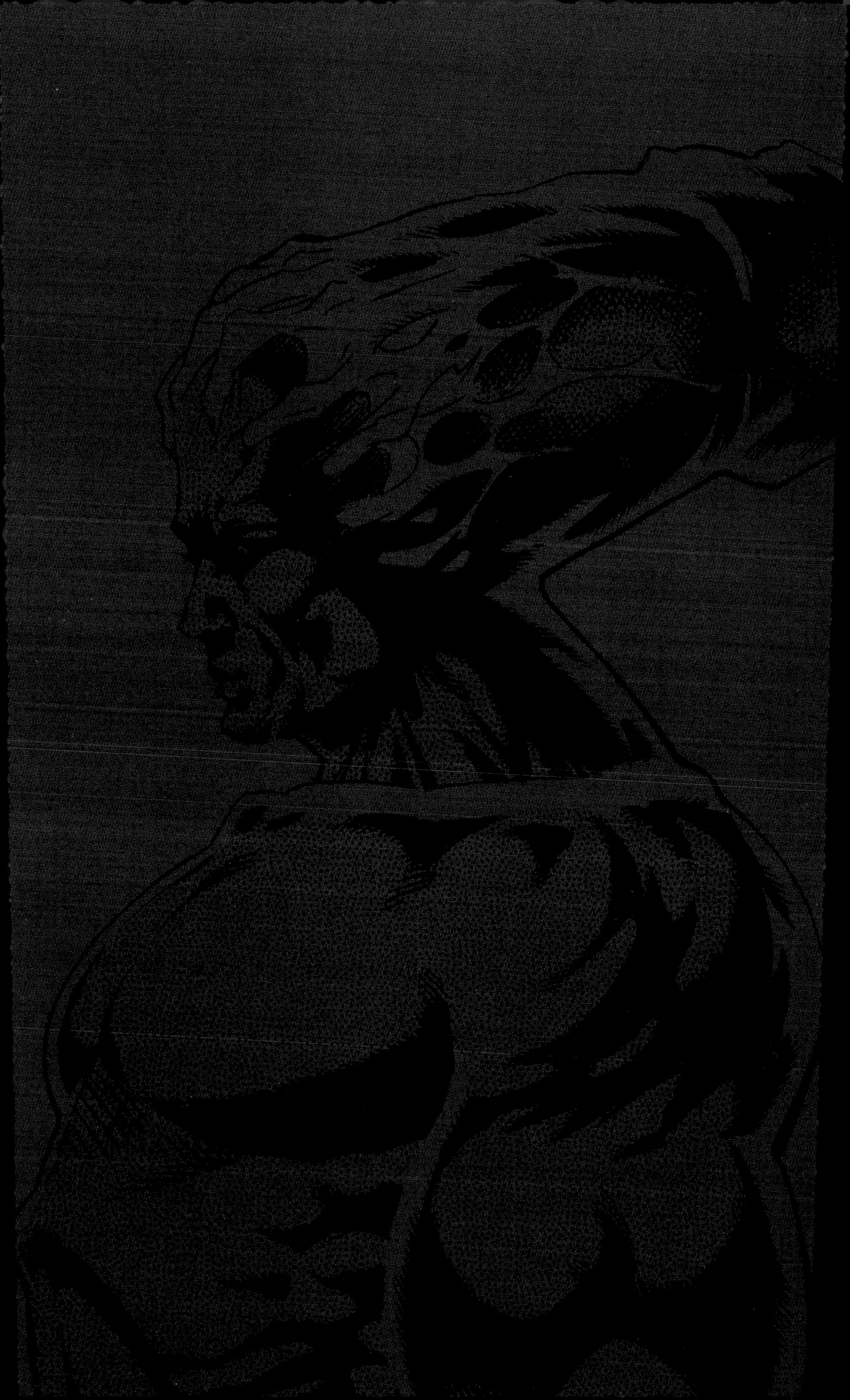

KELLEYJONES 98

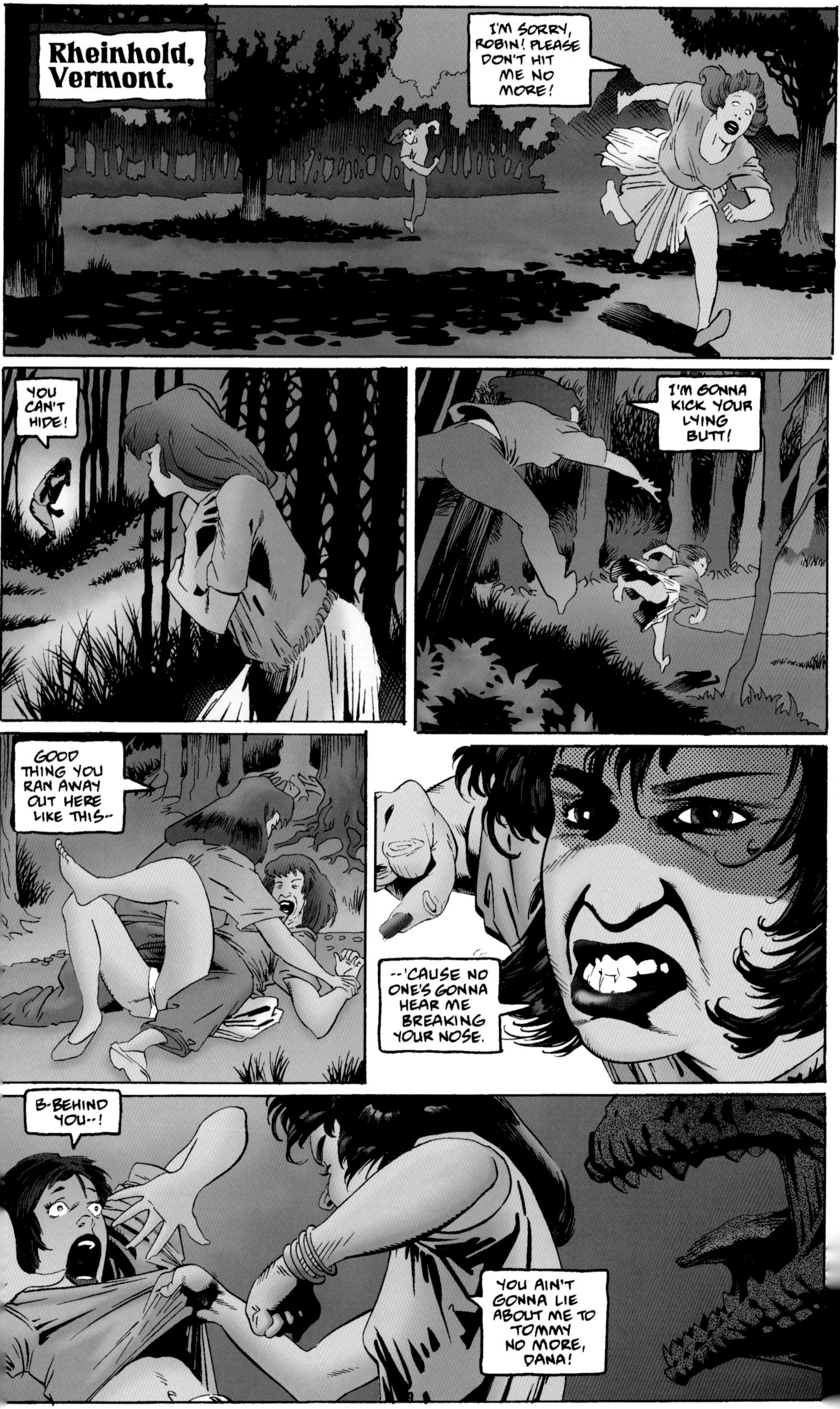
Rheinhold, Vermont.
I'M SORRY, ROBIN! PLEASE DON'T HIT ME NO MORE!
YOU CAN'T HIDE!
I'M GONNA KICK YOUR LYING BUTT!
GOOD THING YOU RAN AWAY OUT HERE LIKE THIS--
--'CAUSE NO ONE'S GONNA HEAR ME BREAKING YOUR NOSE.
B-BEHIND YOU--!
YOU AIN'T GONNA LIE ABOUT ME TO TOMMY NO MORE, DANA!

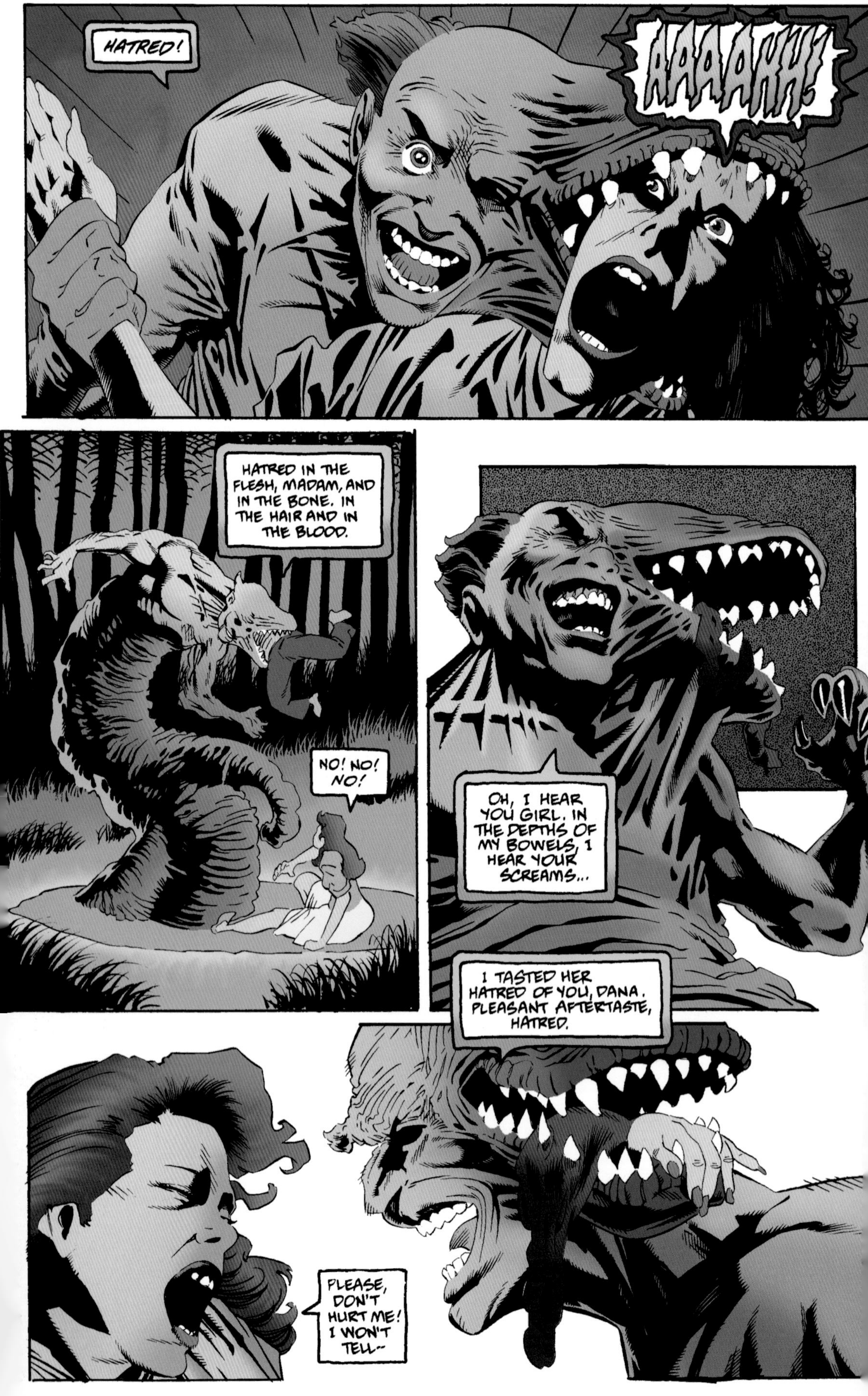
HATRED!
AAAAKH!
HATRED IN THE FLESH, MADAM, AND IN THE BONE. IN THE HAIR AND IN THE BLOOD.
NO! NO! NO!
OH, I HEAR YOU GIRL. IN THE DEPTHS OF MY BOWELS, I HEAR YOUR SCREAMS...
I TASTED HER HATRED OF YOU, DANA. PLEASANT AFTERTASTE, HATRED.
PLEASE, DON'T HURT ME! I WON'T TELL--

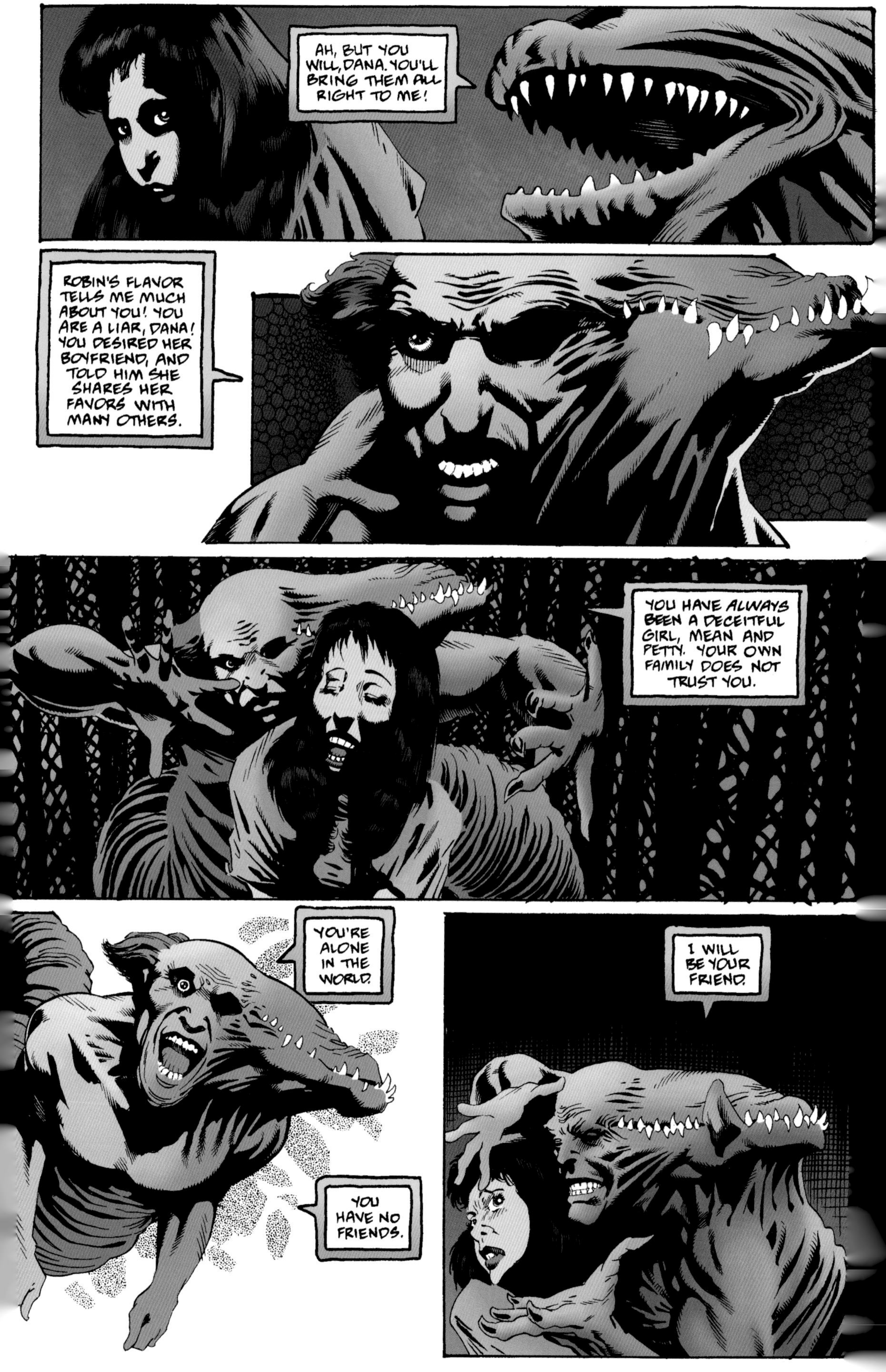
AH, BUT YOU WILL, DANA. YOU'LL BRING THEM ALL RIGHT TO ME!
ROBIN'S FLAVOR TELLS ME MUCH ABOUT YOU! YOU ARE A LIAR, DANA! YOU DESIRED HER BOYFRIEND, AND TOLD HIM SHE SHARES HER FAVORS WITH MANY OTHERS.
YOU HAVE ALWAYS BEEN A DECEITFUL GIRL, MEAN AND PETTY. YOUR OWN FAMILY DOES NOT TRUST YOU.
YOU'RE ALONE IN THE WORLD.
YOU HAVE NO FRIENDS.
I WILL BE YOUR FRIEND.

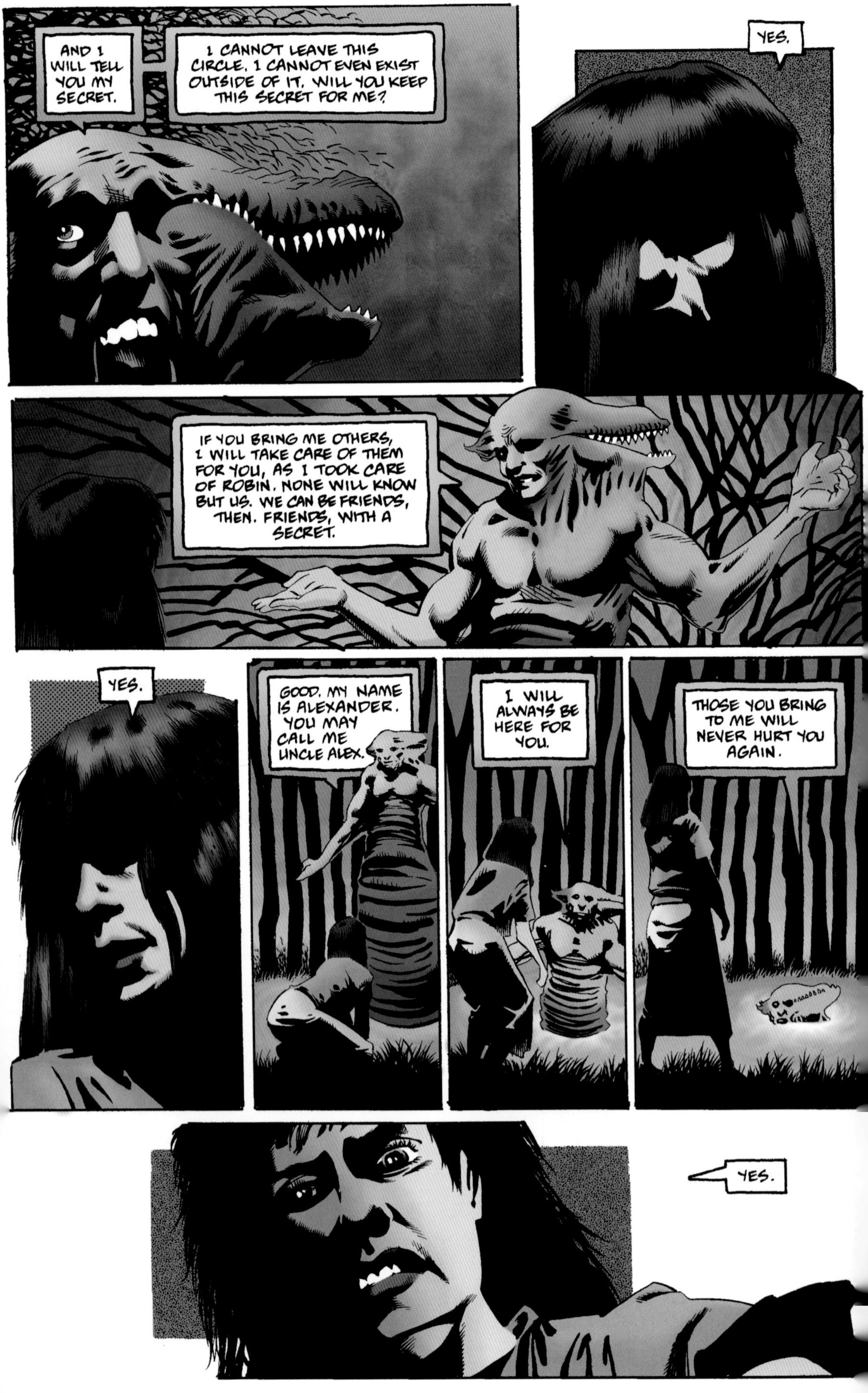
AND I WILL TELL YOU MY SECRET.
I CANNOT LEAVE THIS CIRCLE. I CANNOT EVEN EXIST OUTSIDE OF IT. WILL YOU KEEP THIS SECRET FOR ME?
YES.
IF YOU BRING ME OTHERS, I WILL TAKE CARE OF THEM FOR YOU, AS I TOOK CARE OF ROBIN. NONE WILL KNOW BUT US. WE CAN BE FRIENDS, THEN. FRIENDS, WITH A SECRET.
YES.
GOOD. MY NAME IS ALEXANDER. YOU MAY CALL ME UNCLE ALEX.
I WILL ALWAYS BE HERE FOR YOU.
THOSE YOU BRING TO ME WILL NEVER HURT YOU AGAIN.
YES.

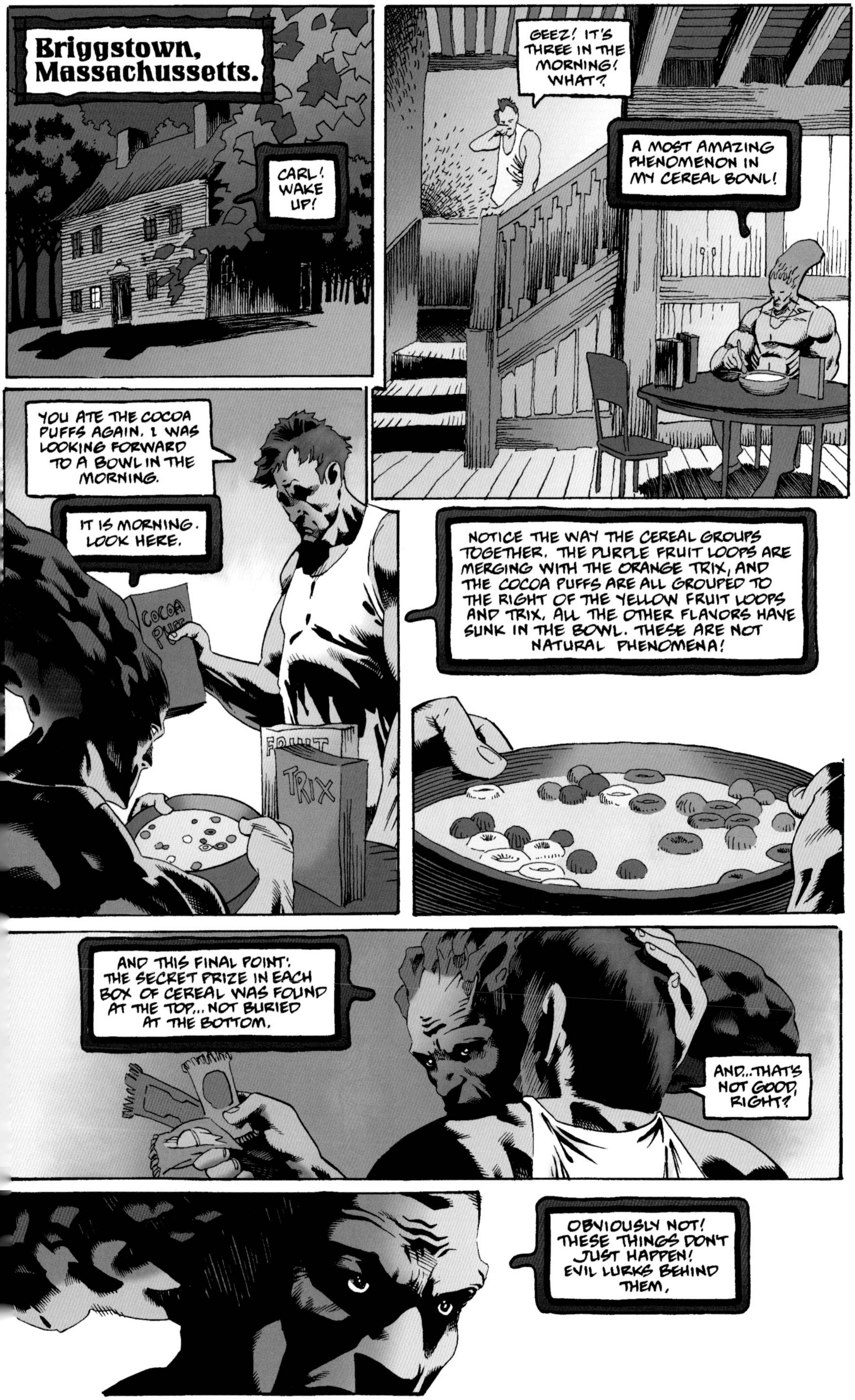
Briggstown, Massachussetts.
CARL! WAKE UP!
GEEZ! IT'S THREE IN THE MORNING! WHAT?
A MOST AMAZING PHENOMENON IN MY CEREAL BOWL!
YOU ATE THE COCOA PUFFS AGAIN. I WAS LOOKING FORWARD TO A BOWL IN THE MORNING.
IT IS MORNING. LOOK HERE.
COCOA PUFF
FRUIT
TRIX
NOTICE THE WAY THE CEREAL GROUPS TOGETHER. THE PURPLE FRUIT LOOPS ARE MERGING WITH THE ORANGE TRIX, AND THE COCOA PUFFS ARE ALL GROUPED TO THE RIGHT OF THE YELLOW FRUIT LOOPS AND TRIX. ALL THE OTHER FLAVORS HAVE SUNK IN THE BOWL. THESE ARE NOT NATURAL PHENOMENA!
AND THIS FINAL POINT: THE SECRET PRIZE IN EACH BOX OF CEREAL WAS FOUND AT THE TOP... NOT BURIED AT THE BOTTOM.
AND...THAT'S NOT GOOD, RIGHT?
OBVIOUSLY NOT! THESE THINGS DON'T JUST HAPPEN! EVIL LURKS BEHIND THEM.

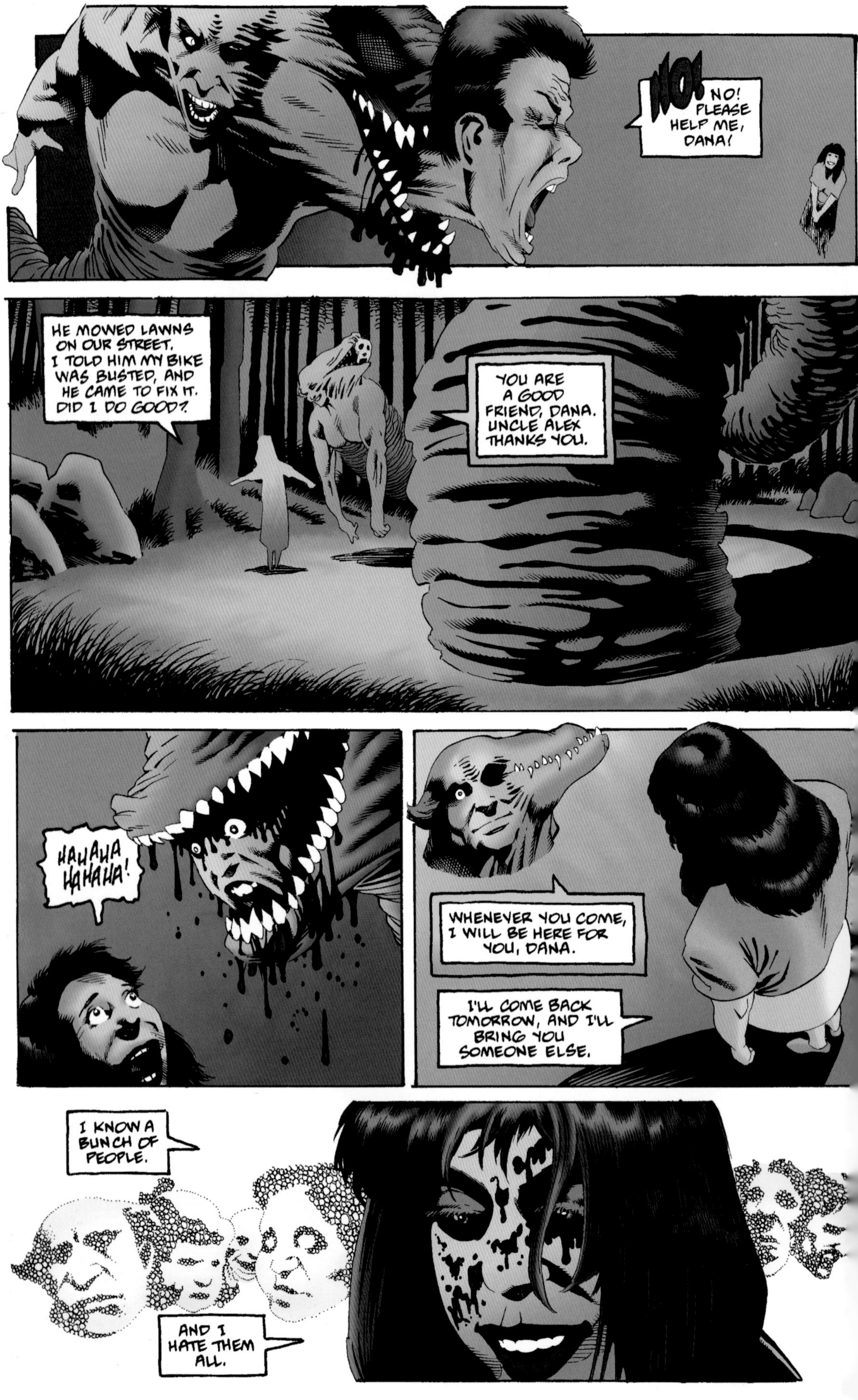
NO!
NO! PLEASE HELP ME, DANA!
HE MOWED LAWNS ON OUR STREET. I TOLD HIM MY BIKE WAS BUSTED, AND HE CAME TO FIX IT. DID I DO GOOD?
YOU ARE A GOOD FRIEND, DANA. UNCLE ALEX THANKS YOU.
HAHAHA HAHAHA!
WHENEVER YOU COME, I WILL BE HERE FOR YOU, DANA.
I'LL COME BACK TOMORROW, AND I'LL BRING YOU SOMEONE ELSE.
I KNOW A BUNCH OF PEOPLE.
AND I HATE THEM ALL.

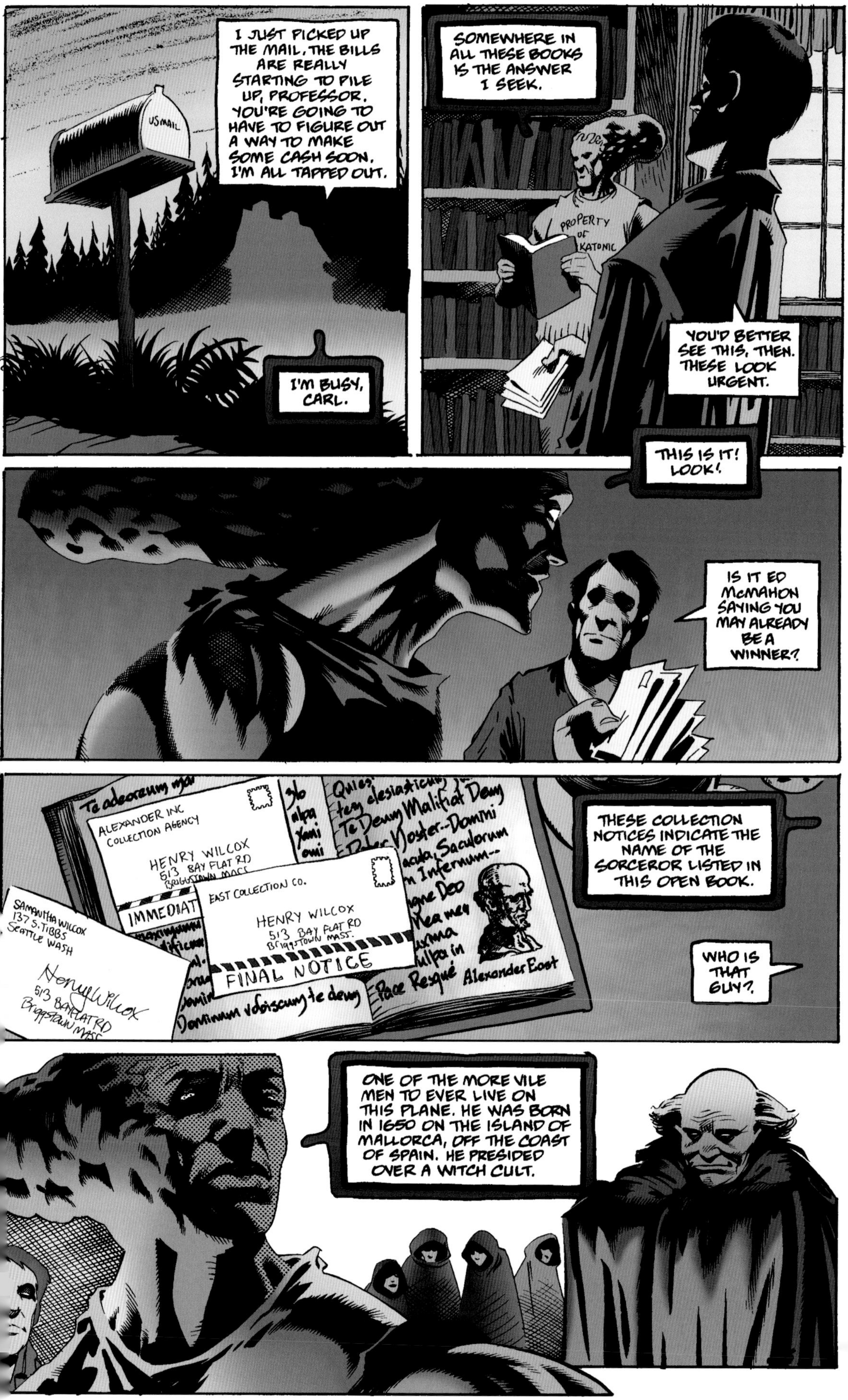
US MAIL
I JUST PICKED UP THE MAIL. THE BILLS ARE REALLY STARTING TO PILE UP, PROFESSOR. YOU'RE GOING TO HAVE TO FIGURE OUT A WAY TO MAKE SOME CASH SOON. I'M ALL TAPPED OUT.
I'M BUSY, CARL.
SOMEWHERE IN ALL THESE BOOKS IS THE ANSWER I SEEK.
PROPERTY OF
KATONIC
YOU'D BETTER SEE THIS, THEN. THESE LOOK URGENT.
THIS IS IT! LOOK!
IS IT ED McMAHON SAYING YOU MAY ALREADY BE A WINNER?
ALEXANDER INC
COLLECTION AGENCY
HENRY WILCOX
513 BAY FLAT RD
IMMEDIAT
EAST COLLECTION CO.
HENRY WILCOX
513 BAY FLAT RD
BRIGGSTOWN MASS.
FINAL NOTICE
SAMANTHA WILCOX
137 S. TIBBS
SEATTLE WASH
Alexander East
THESE COLLECTION NOTICES INDICATE THE NAME OF THE SORCEROR LISTED IN THIS OPEN BOOK.
WHO IS THAT GUY?
ONE OF THE MORE VILE MEN TO EVER LIVE ON THIS PLANE. HE WAS BORN IN 1650 ON THE ISLAND OF MALLORCA, OFF THE COAST OF SPAIN. HE PRESIDED OVER A WITCH CULT.

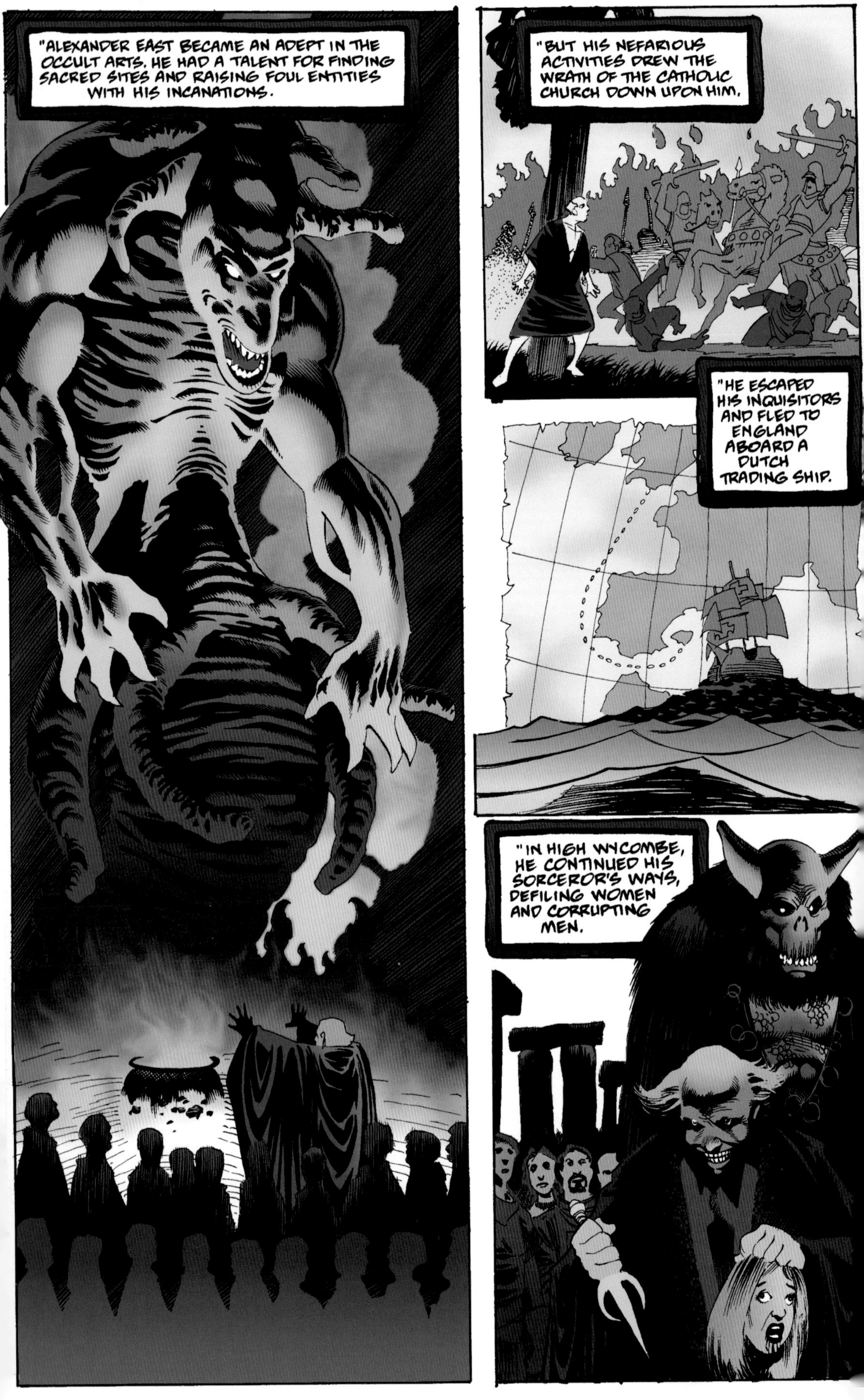
"ALEXANDER EAST BECAME AN ADEPT IN THE OCCULT ARTS. HE HAD A TALENT FOR FINDING SACRED SITES AND RAISING FOUL ENTITIES WITH HIS INCANATIONS.
"BUT HIS NEFARIOUS ACTIVITIES DREW THE WRATH OF THE CATHOLIC CHURCH DOWN UPON HIM.
"HE ESCAPED HIS INQUISITORS AND FLED TO ENGLAND ABOARD A DUTCH TRADING SHIP.
"IN HIGH WYCOMBE, HE CONTINUED HIS SORCEROR'S WAYS, DEFILING WOMEN AND CORRUPTING MEN.

"BUT, ONE BY ONE, HIS COVEN WAS BURNED.

"KING JAMES II ORDERED HIS EXECUTION. HE FLED AGAIN, THIS TIME, TO AMERICA,

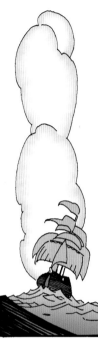

"HE ESTABLISHED HIMSELF AS THE REVEREND ALEXANDER EAST...

"...AND CONTINUED WITH HIS EVIL PRACTICES.

"HIS FOLLOWERS SAY HE RAISED THAT WHICH COULD NOT BE PUT BACK."

"NOTHING WAS HEARD FROM HIM AGAIN.

UNTIL NOW.

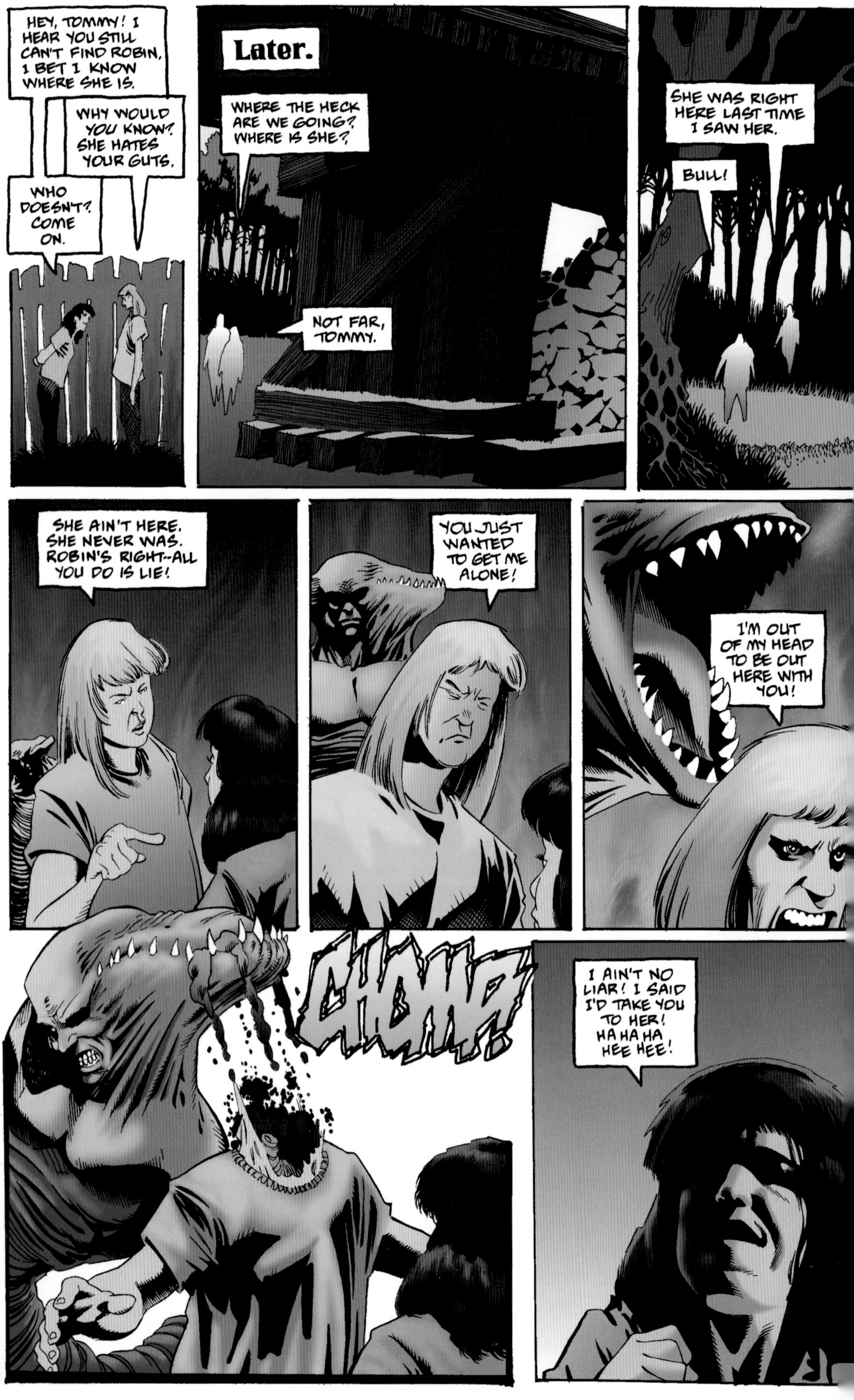
HEY, TOMMY! I HEAR YOU STILL CAN'T FIND ROBIN, I BET I KNOW WHERE SHE IS.
WHY WOULD YOU KNOW? SHE HATES YOUR GUTS.
WHO DOESN'T? COME ON.
Later.
WHERE THE HECK ARE WE GOING? WHERE IS SHE?
NOT FAR, TOMMY.
SHE WAS RIGHT HERE LAST TIME I SAW HER.
BULL!
SHE AIN'T HERE. SHE NEVER WAS. ROBIN'S RIGHT--ALL YOU DO IS LIE!
YOU JUST WANTED TO GET ME ALONE!
I'M OUT OF MY HEAD TO BE OUT HERE WITH YOU!
CHOMP!
I AIN'T NO LIAR! I SAID I'D TAKE YOU TO HER! HA HA HA HEE HEE!

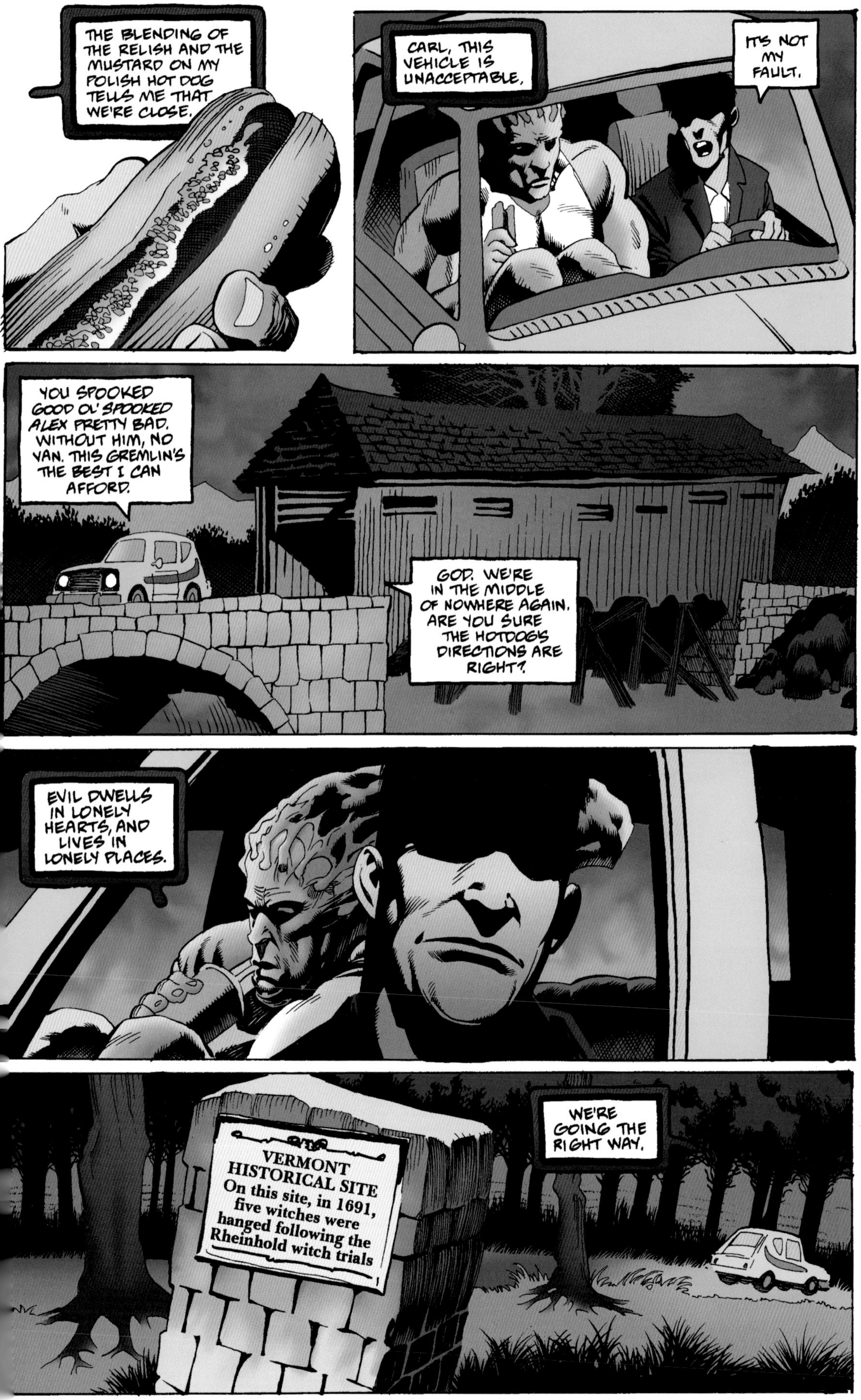
THE BLENDING OF THE RELISH AND THE MUSTARD ON MY POLISH HOT DOG TELLS ME THAT WE'RE CLOSE.
CARL, THIS VEHICLE IS UNACCEPTABLE.
IT'S NOT MY FAULT.
YOU SPOOKED GOOD OL' SPOOKED ALEX PRETTY BAD. WITHOUT HIM, NO VAN. THIS GREMLIN'S THE BEST I CAN AFFORD.
GOD. WE'RE IN THE MIDDLE OF NOWHERE AGAIN. ARE YOU SURE THE HOTDOG'S DIRECTIONS ARE RIGHT?
EVIL DWELLS IN LONELY HEARTS, AND LIVES IN LONELY PLACES.
VERMONT HISTORICAL SITE
On this site, in 1691, five witches were hanged following the Rheinhold witch trials
WE'RE GOING THE RIGHT WAY.

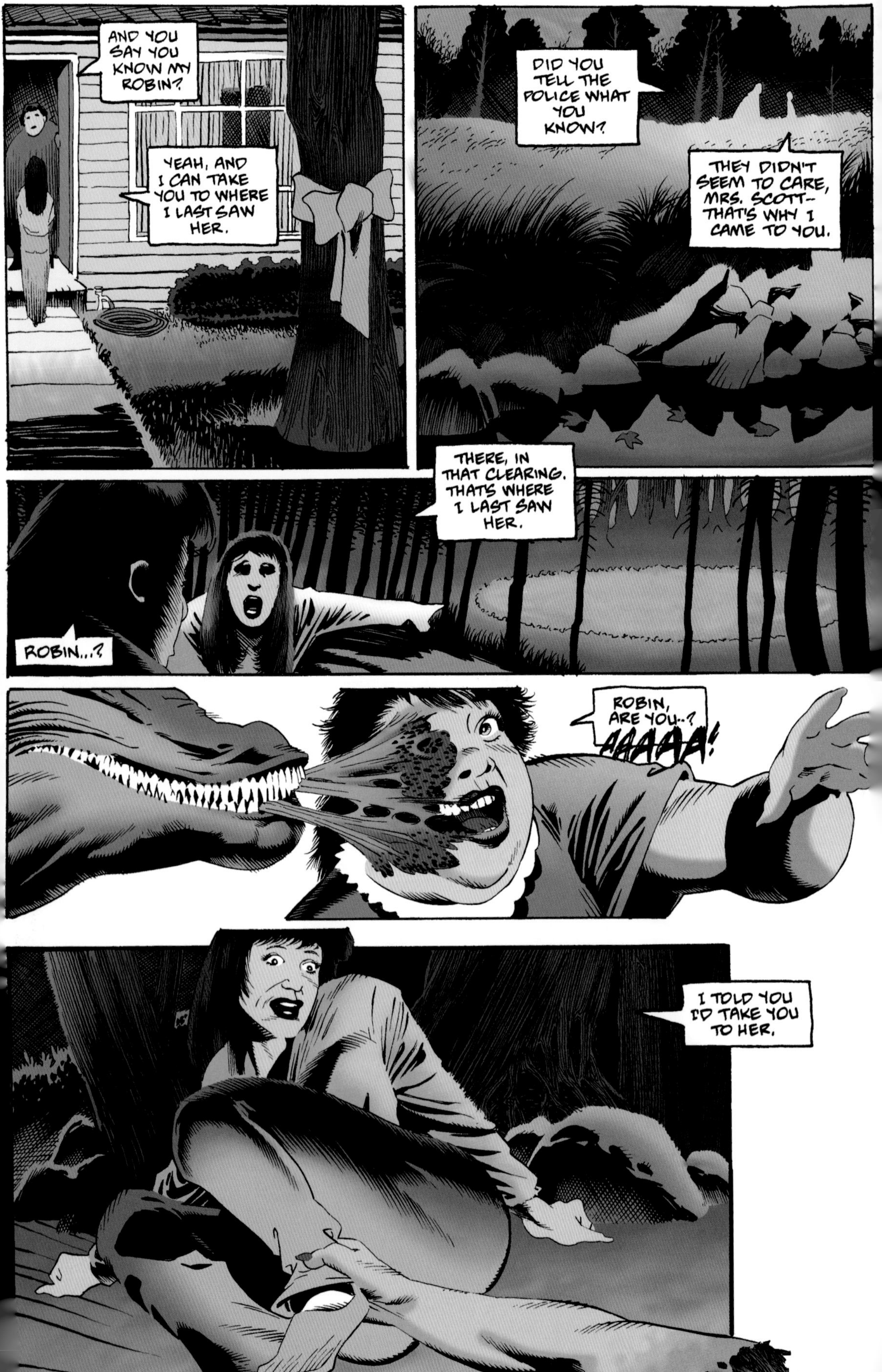
AND YOU SAY YOU KNOW MY ROBIN?
YEAH, AND I CAN TAKE YOU TO WHERE I LAST SAW HER.
DID YOU TELL THE POLICE WHAT YOU KNOW?
THEY DIDN'T SEEM TO CARE, MRS. SCOTT-- THAT'S WHY I CAME TO YOU.
THERE, IN THAT CLEARING. THAT'S WHERE I LAST SAW HER.
ROBIN...?
ROBIN, ARE YOU..?
AAAAA!
I TOLD YOU I'D TAKE YOU TO HER.

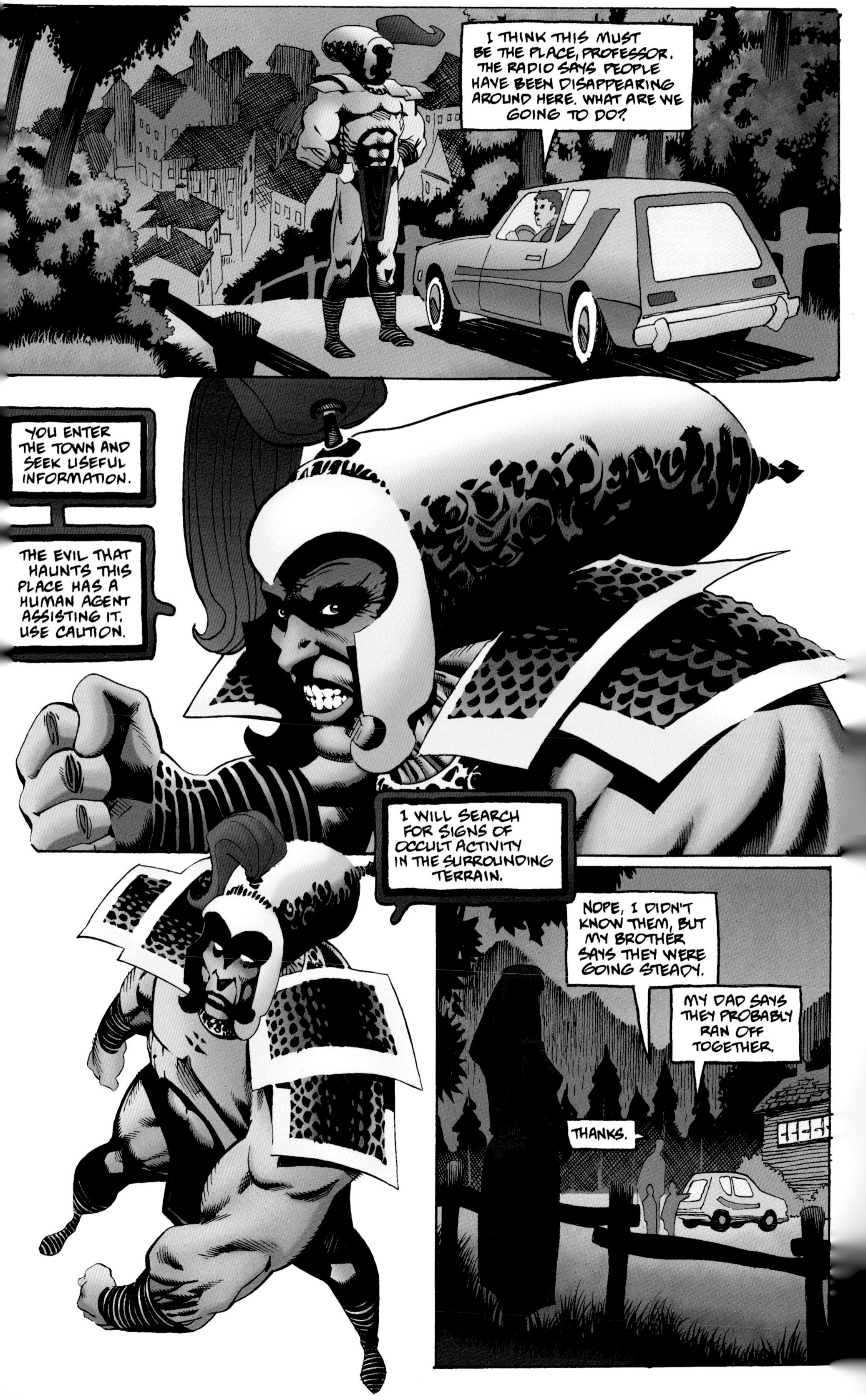
I THINK THIS MUST BE THE PLACE, PROFESSOR. THE RADIO SAYS PEOPLE HAVE BEEN DISAPPEARING AROUND HERE. WHAT ARE WE GOING TO DO?
YOU ENTER THE TOWN AND SEEK USEFUL INFORMATION.
THE EVIL THAT HAUNTS THIS PLACE HAS A HUMAN AGENT ASSISTING IT. USE CAUTION.
I WILL SEARCH FOR SIGNS OF OCCULT ACTIVITY IN THE SURROUNDING TERRAIN.
NOPE, I DIDN'T KNOW THEM, BUT MY BROTHER SAYS THEY WERE GOING STEADY.
MY DAD SAYS THEY PROBABLY RAN OFF TOGETHER.
THANKS.

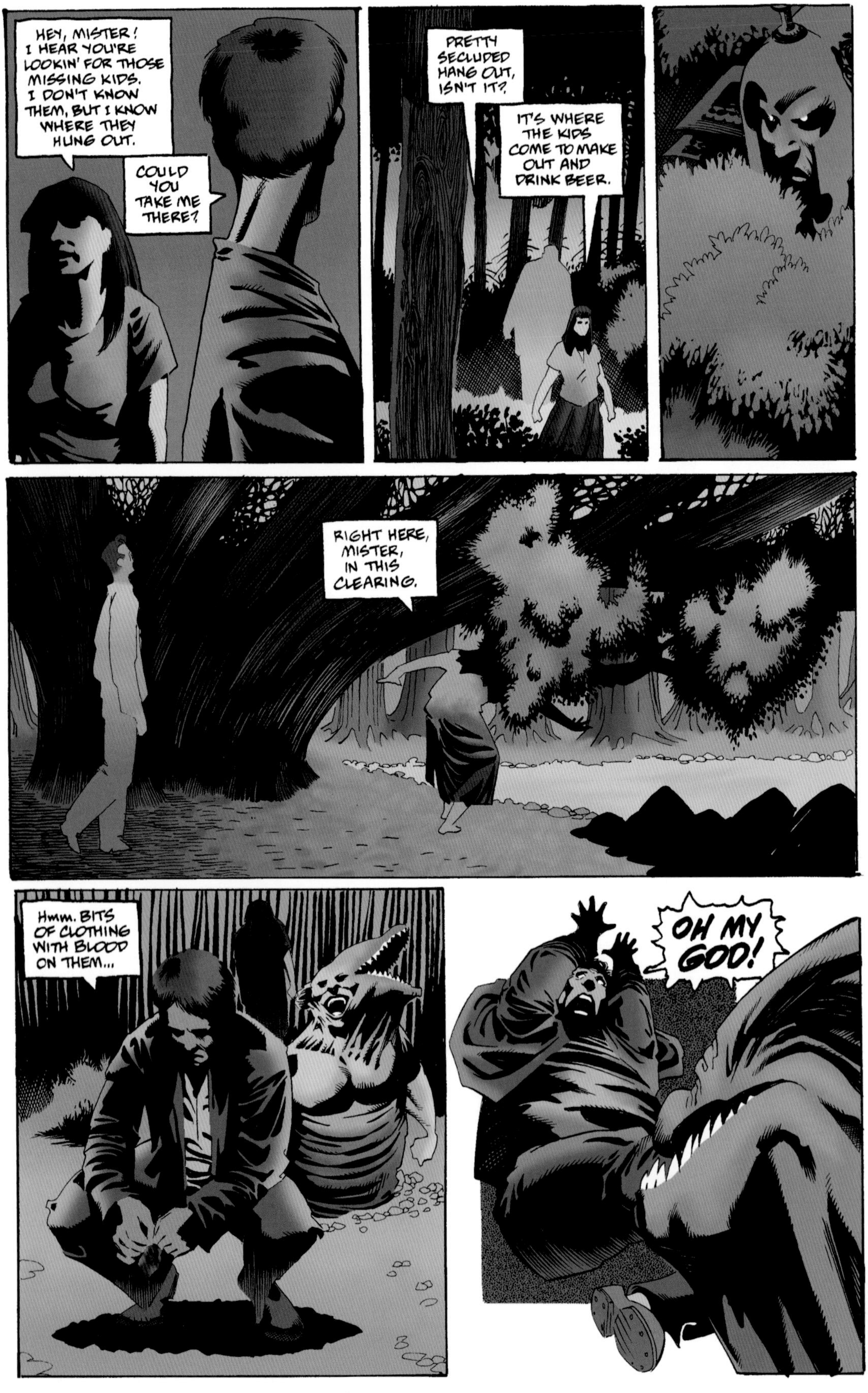
HEY, MISTER! I HEAR YOU'RE LOOKIN' FOR THOSE MISSING KIDS. I DON'T KNOW THEM, BUT I KNOW WHERE THEY HUNG OUT.
COULD YOU TAKE ME THERE?
PRETTY SECLUDED HANG OUT, ISN'T IT?
IT'S WHERE THE KIDS COME TO MAKE OUT AND DRINK BEER.
RIGHT HERE, MISTER, IN THIS CLEARING.
Hmm. BITS OF CLOTHING WITH BLOOD ON THEM...
OH MY GOD!

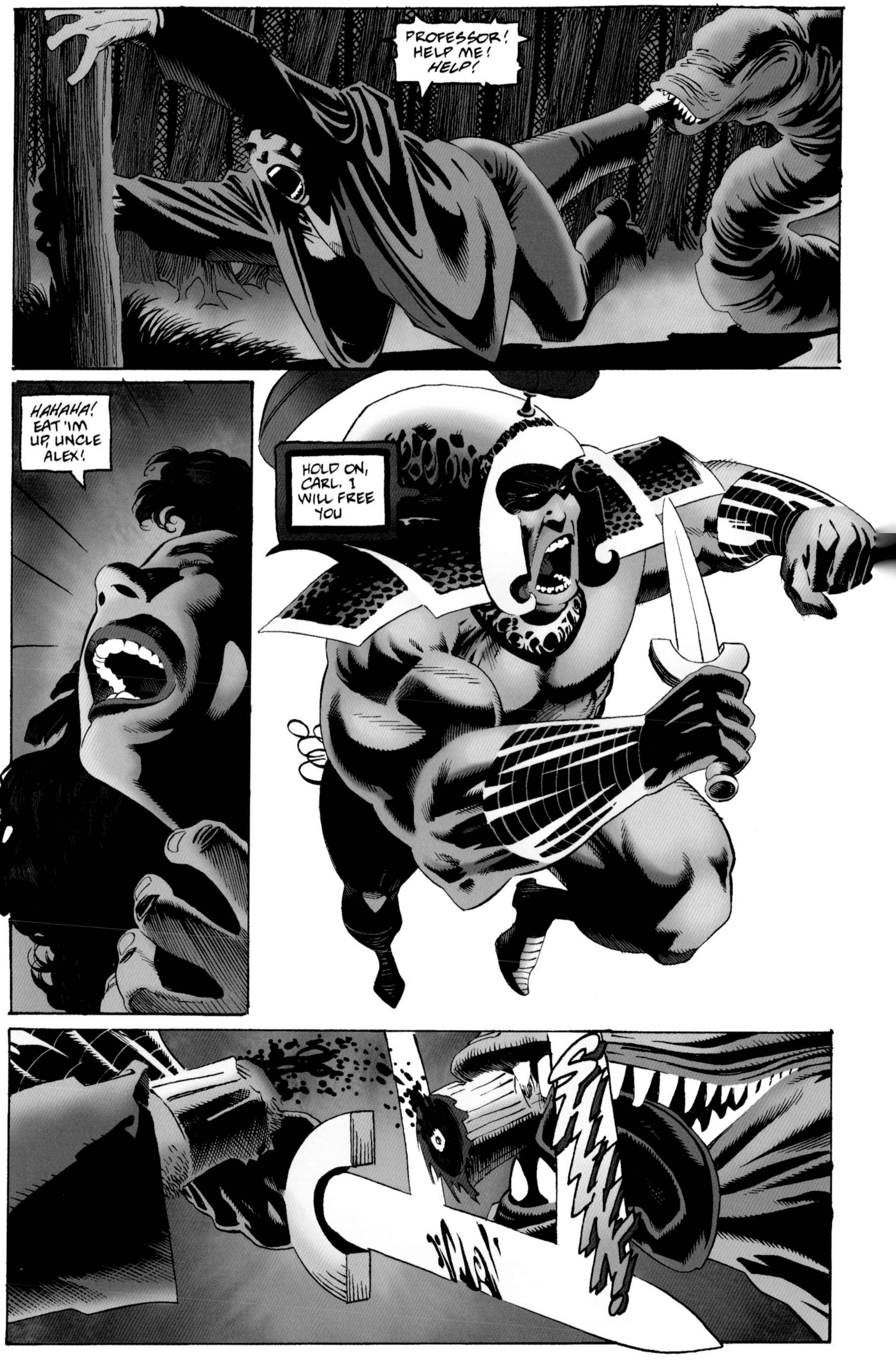
PROFESSOR! HELP ME! HELP!
HAHAHA! EAT 'IM UP, UNCLE ALEX!
HOLD ON, CARL. I WILL FREE YOU

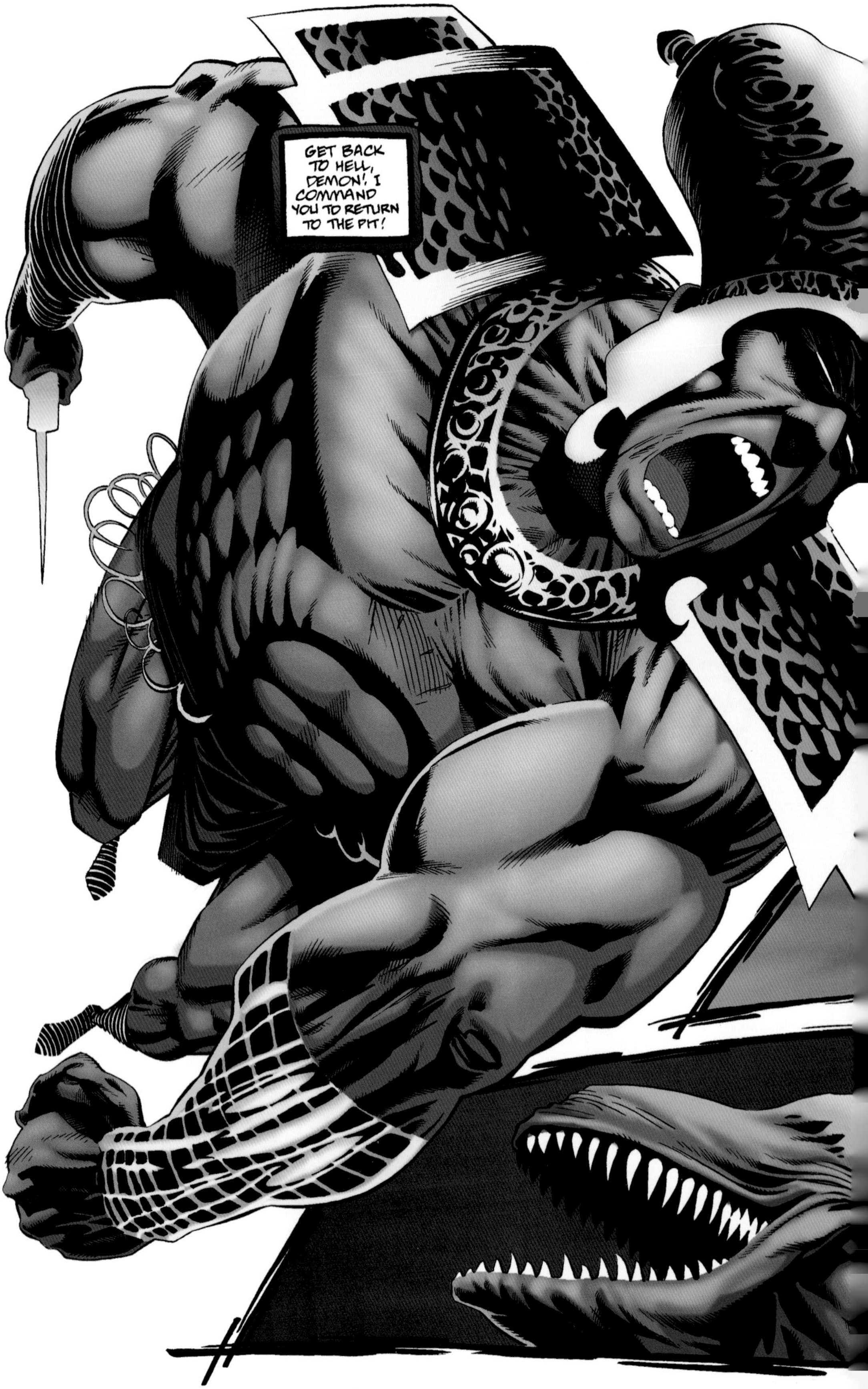
GET BACK TO HELL, DEMON! I COMMAND YOU TO RETURN TO THE PIT!

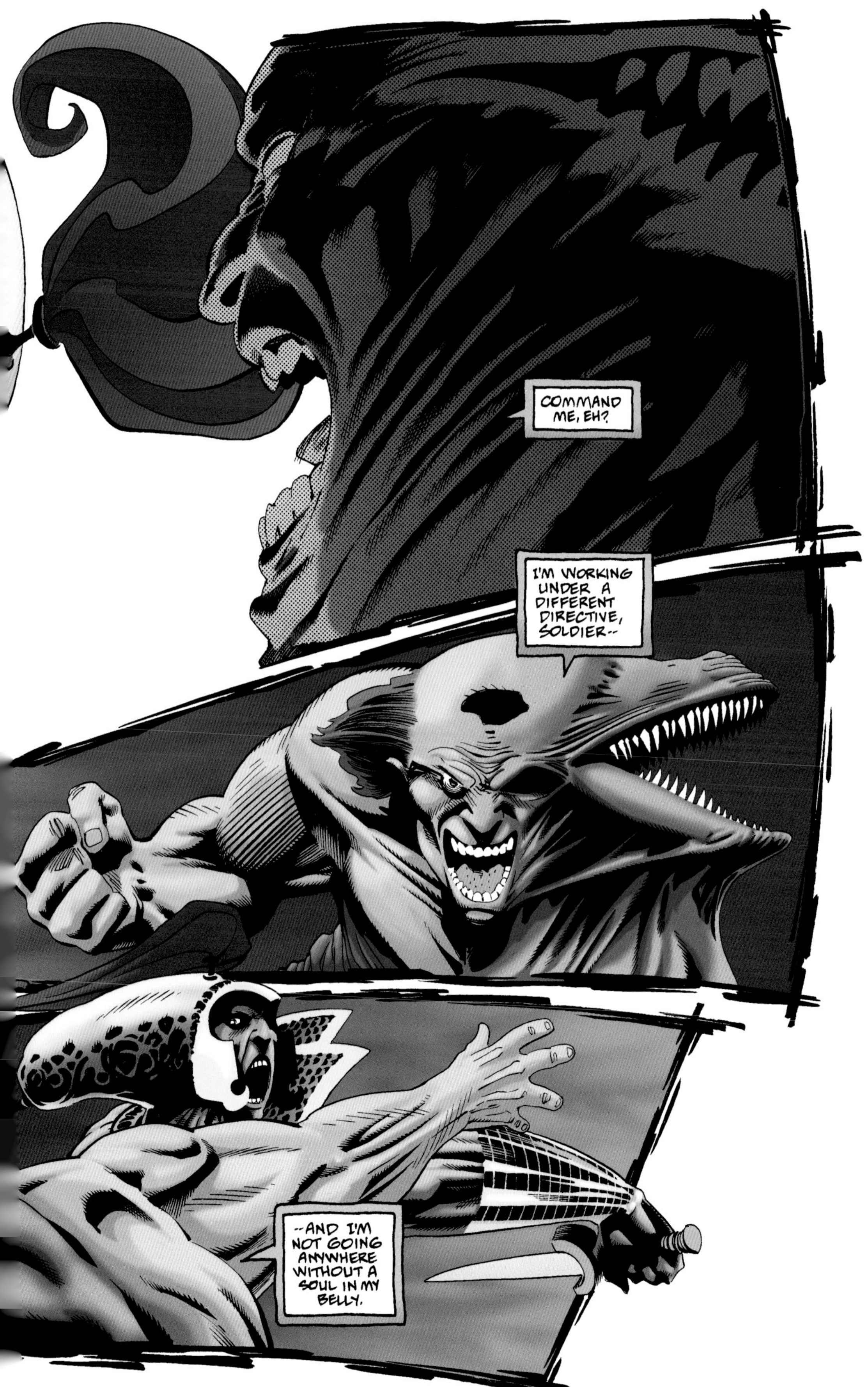
COMMAND ME, EH?
I'M WORKING UNDER A DIFFERENT DIRECTIVE, SOLDIER--
--AND I'M NOT GOING ANYWHERE WITHOUT A SOUL IN MY BELLY.

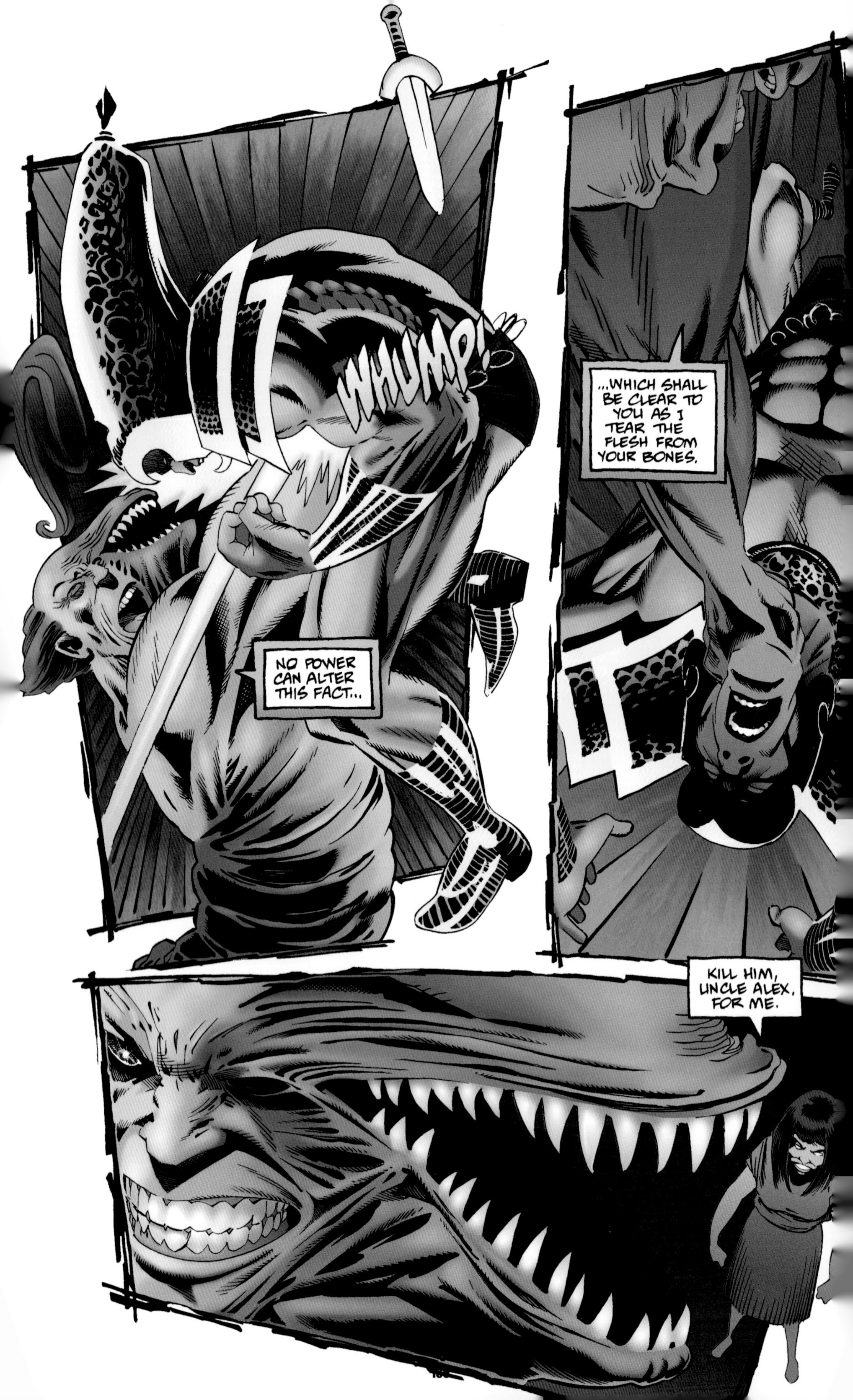
WHUMP!
NO POWER CAN ALTER THIS FACT...
...WHICH SHALL BE CLEAR TO YOU AS I TEAR THE FLESH FROM YOUR BONES.
KILL HIM, UNCLE ALEX, FOR ME.

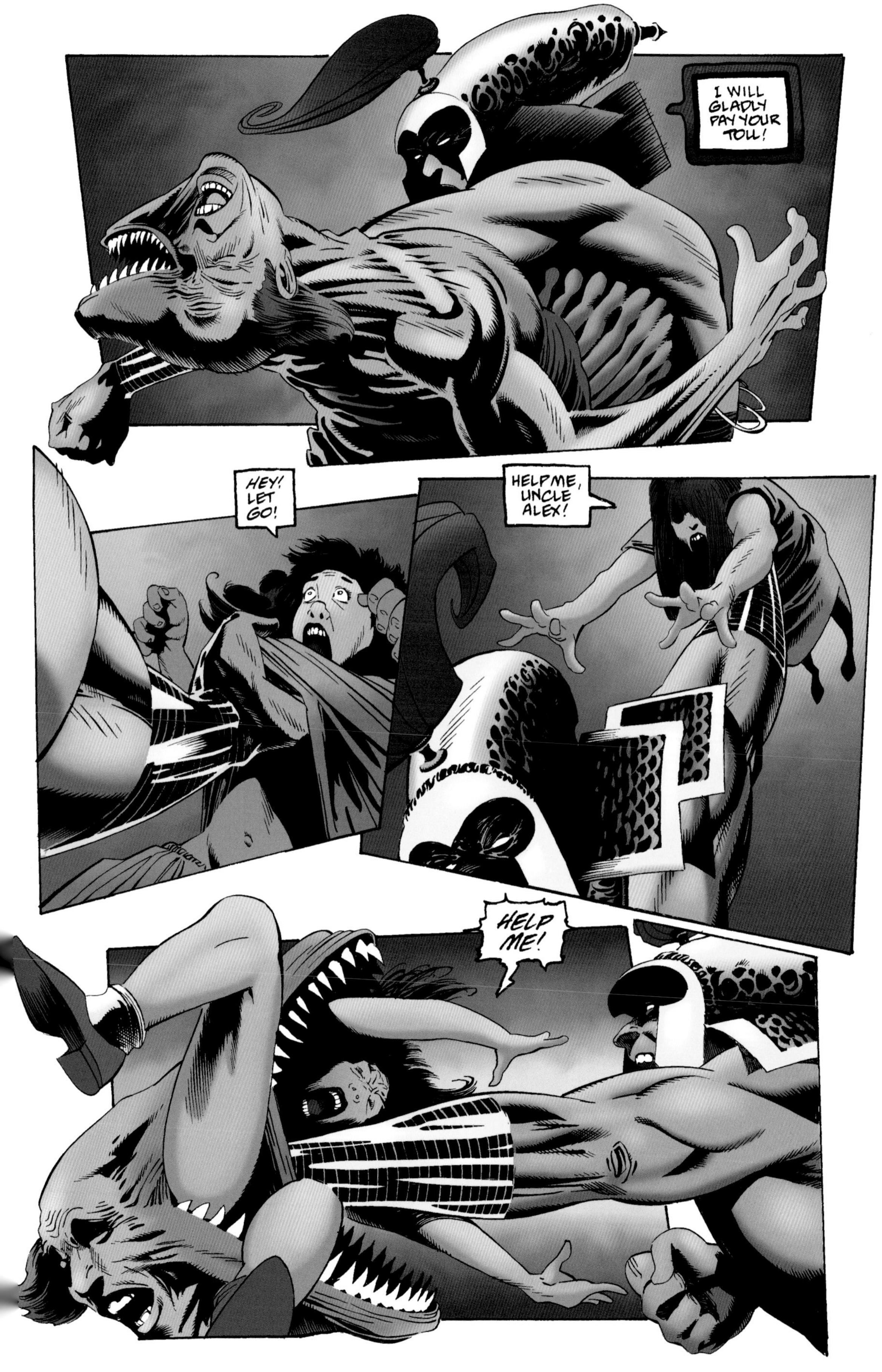
I WILL GLADLY PAY YOUR TOLL!
HEY! LET GO!
HELP ME, UNCLE ALEX!
HELP ME!

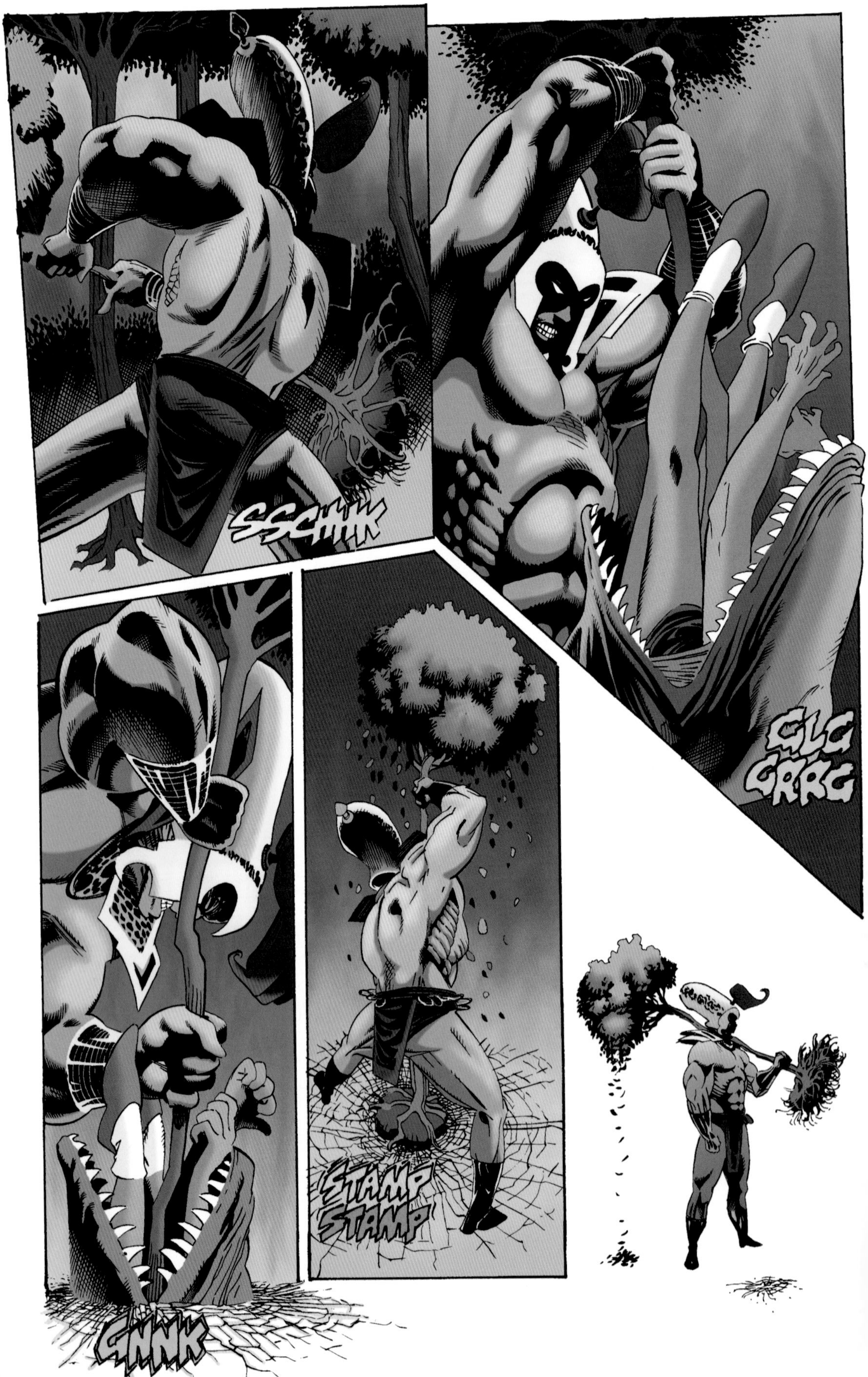
SSCHUK
GLG GRRG
GNNK
STAMP STAMP

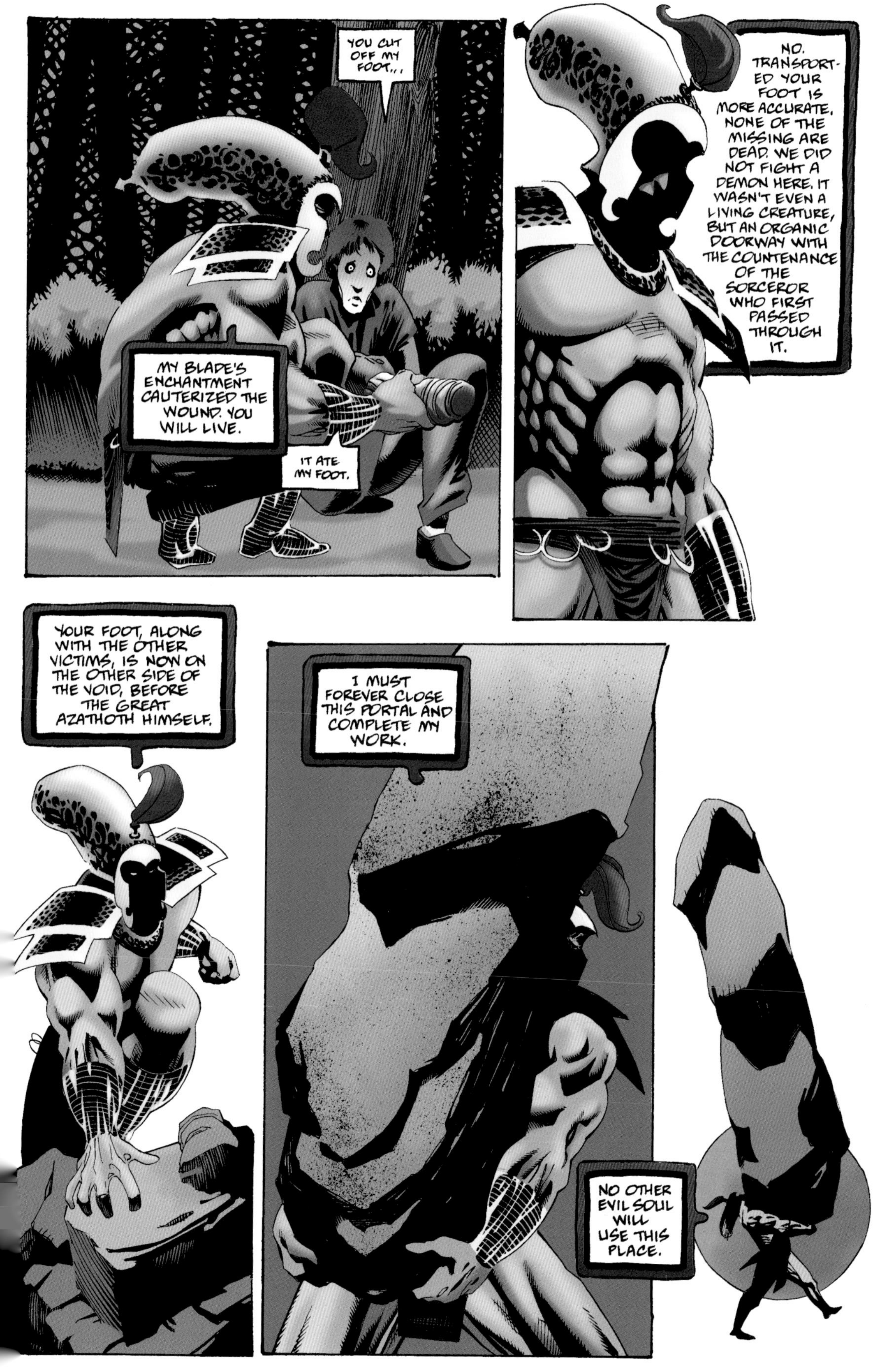
YOU CUT OFF MY FOOT...
MY BLADE'S ENCHANTMENT CAUTERIZED THE WOUND. YOU WILL LIVE.
IT ATE MY FOOT.
NO. TRANSPORTED YOUR FOOT IS MORE ACCURATE. NONE OF THE MISSING ARE DEAD. WE DID NOT FIGHT A DEMON HERE. IT WASN'T EVEN A LIVING CREATURE, BUT AN ORGANIC DOORWAY WITH THE COUNTENANCE OF THE SORCEROR WHO FIRST PASSED THROUGH IT.
YOUR FOOT, ALONG WITH THE OTHER VICTIMS, IS NOW ON THE OTHER SIDE OF THE VOID, BEFORE THE GREAT AZATHOTH HIMSELF.
I MUST FOREVER CLOSE THIS PORTAL AND COMPLETE MY WORK.
NO OTHER EVIL SOUL WILL USE THIS PLACE.

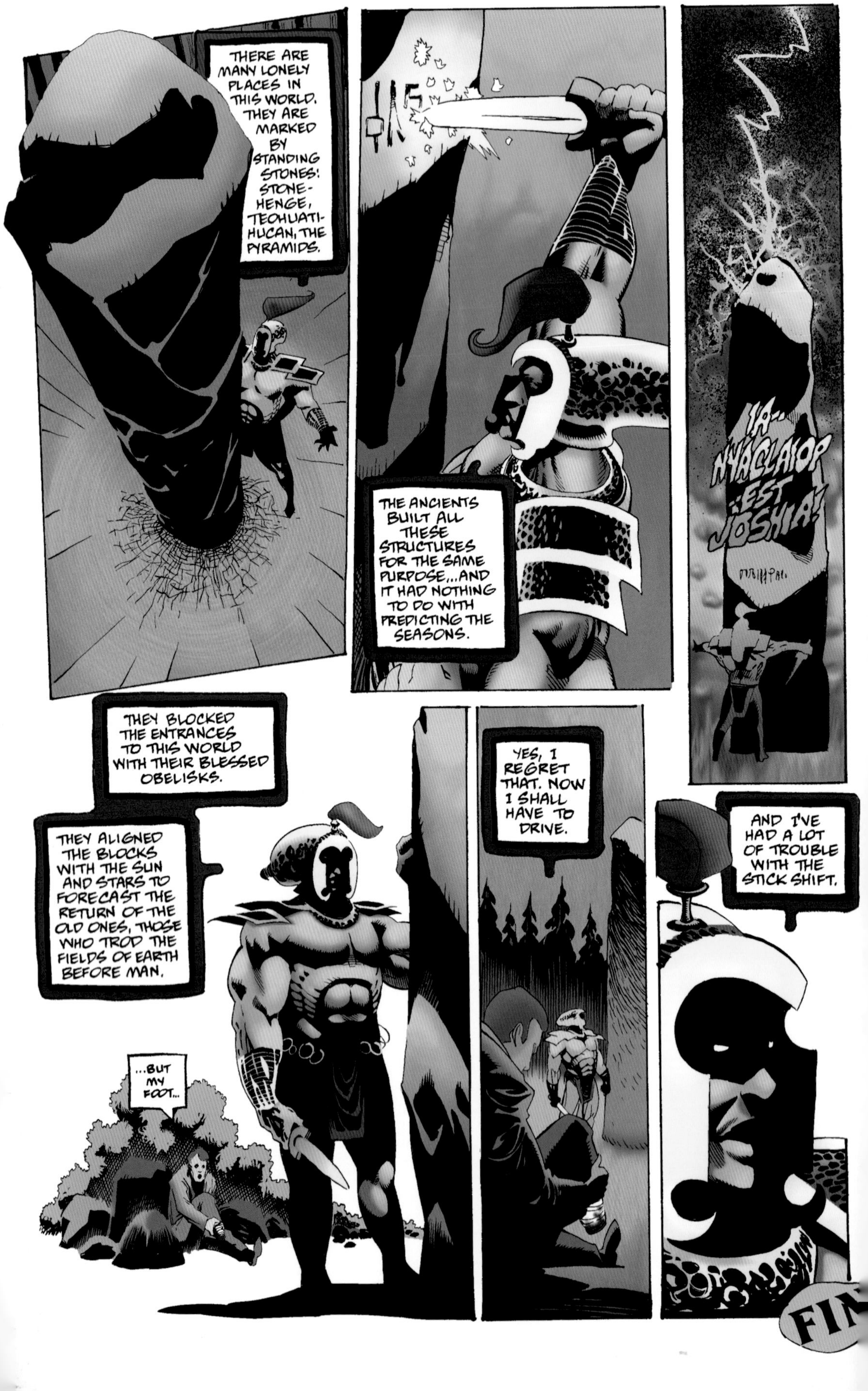
THERE ARE MANY LONELY PLACES IN THIS WORLD. THEY ARE MARKED BY STANDING STONES: STONE-HENGE, TEOHUATI-HUCAN, THE PYRAMIDS.
THE ANCIENTS BUILT ALL THESE STRUCTURES FOR THE SAME PURPOSE,...AND IT HAD NOTHING TO DO WITH PREDICTING THE SEASONS.
IA-NYACLAIOP-EST JOSHIA!
THEY BLOCKED THE ENTRANCES TO THIS WORLD WITH THEIR BLESSED OBELISKS.
THEY ALIGNED THE BLOCKS WITH THE SUN AND STARS TO FORECAST THE RETURN OF THE OLD ONES, THOSE WHO TROD THE FIELDS OF EARTH BEFORE MAN.
...BUT MY FOOT...
YES, I REGRET THAT. NOW I SHALL HAVE TO DRIVE.
AND I'VE HAD A LOT OF TROUBLE WITH THE STICK SHIFT.
FIN

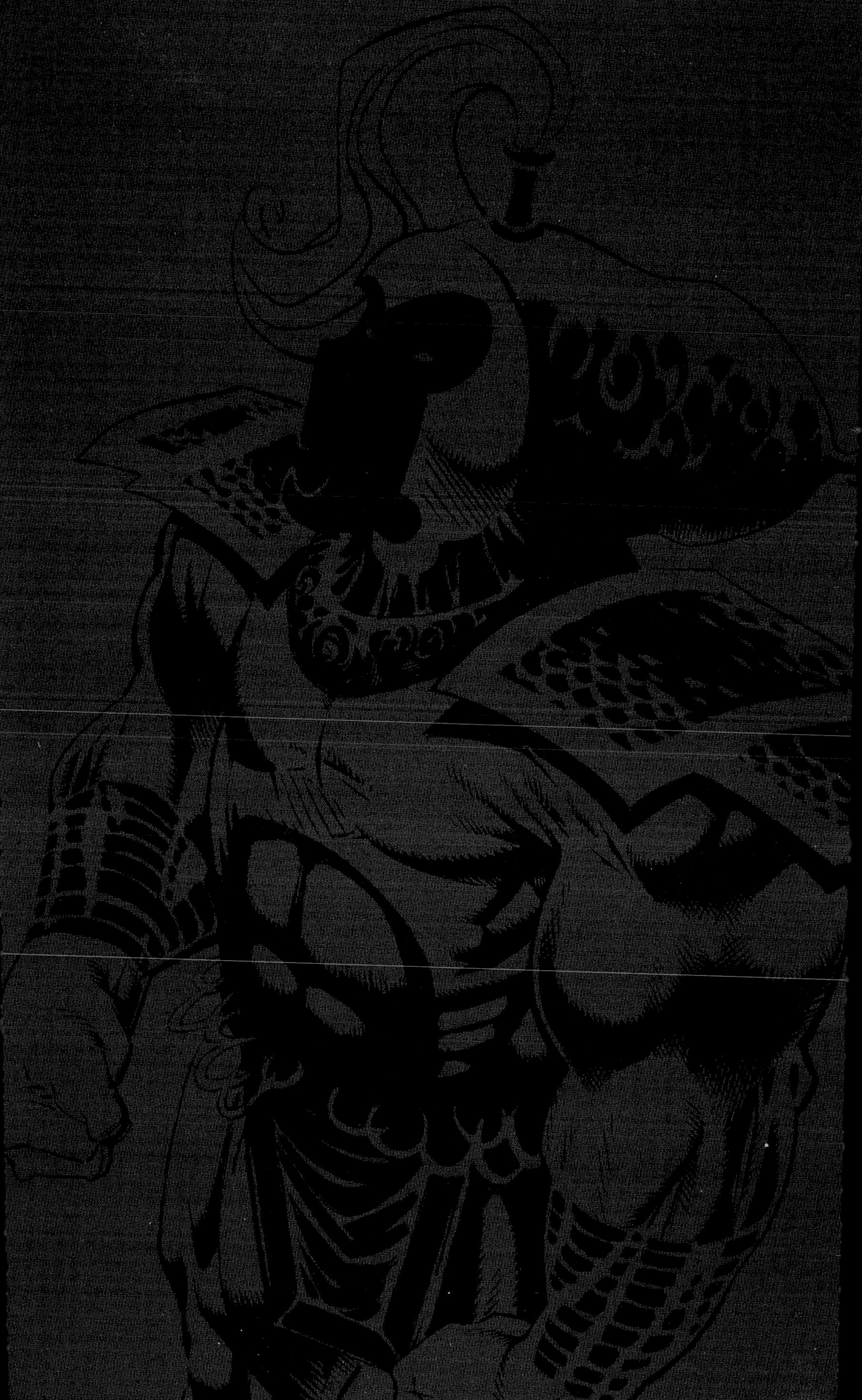

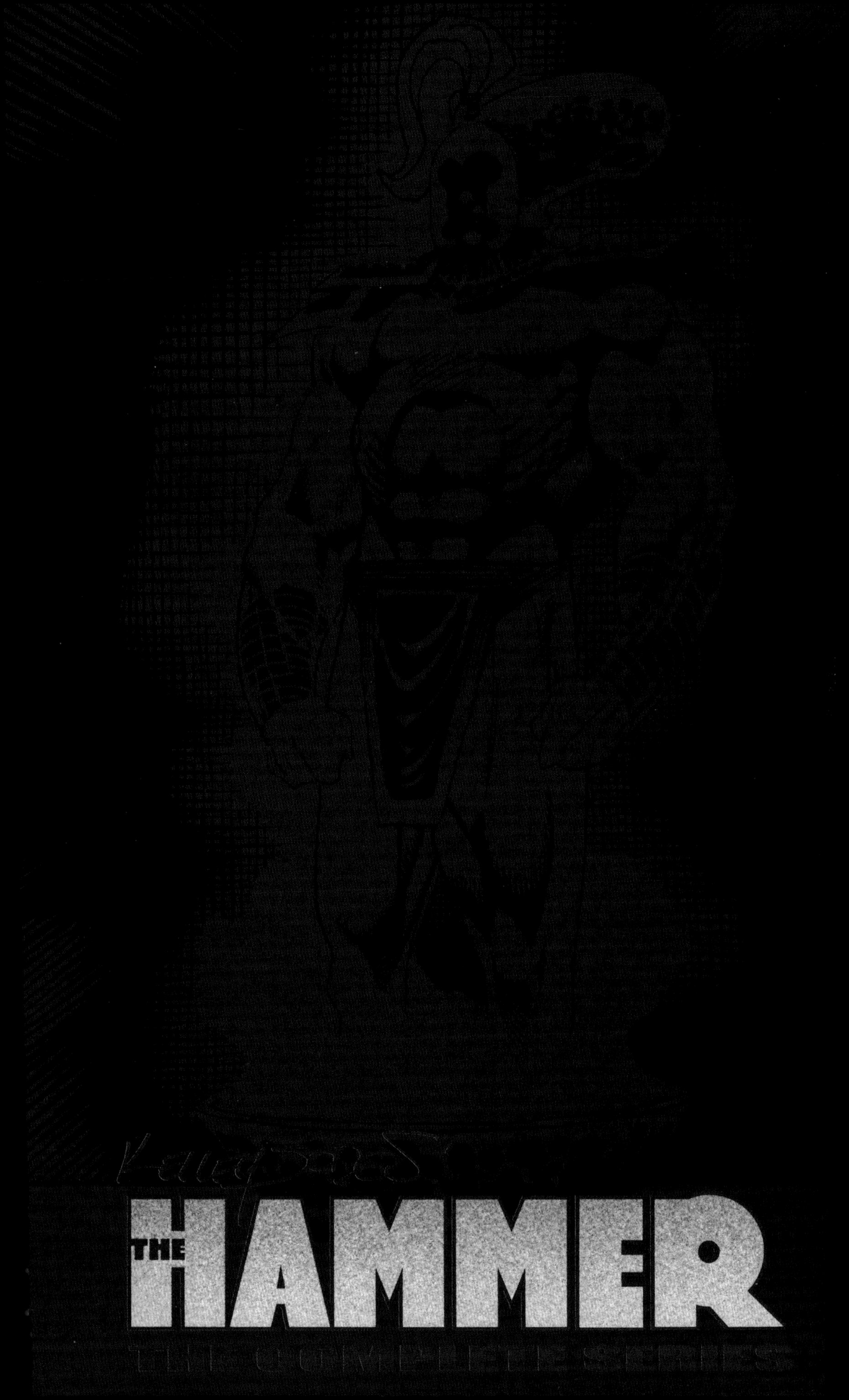
THE HAMMER
THE COMPLETE SERIES

ALL RIGHT, MADEOLINE. WE'VE MADE ALL OUR PREPARATIONS.

I HAVE WHAT WE NEED.

ΛΠΛι ΠΛiΗΠΛΚ μΠiΗνΥ beiΗμii δ°αΗiεινieΠΙe

143

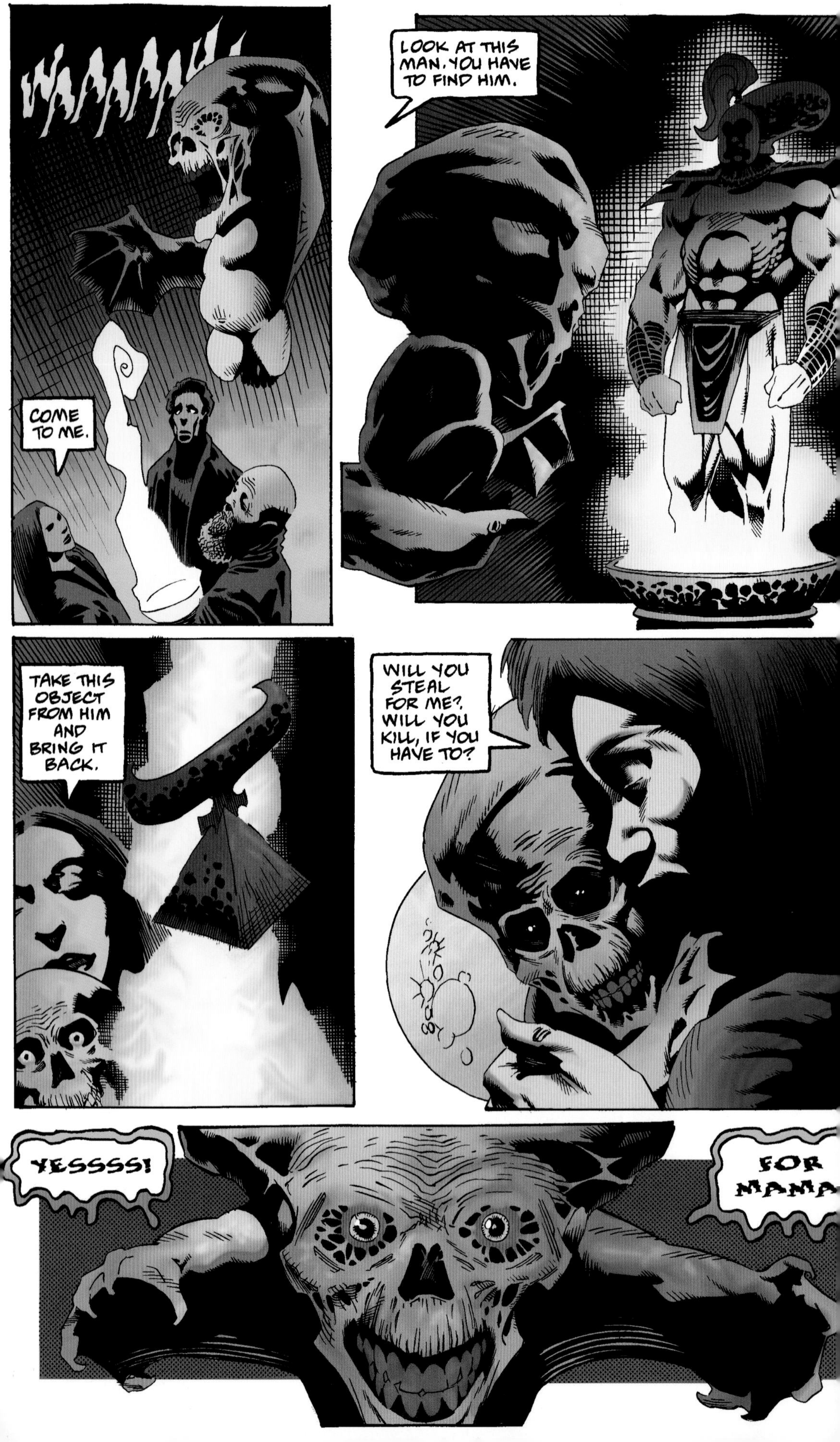

WAAAAAH!
COME TO ME.
LOOK AT THIS MAN. YOU HAVE TO FIND HIM.
TAKE THIS OBJECT FROM HIM AND BRING IT BACK.
WILL YOU STEAL FOR ME? WILL YOU KILL, IF YOU HAVE TO?
YESSSS!
FOR MAMA

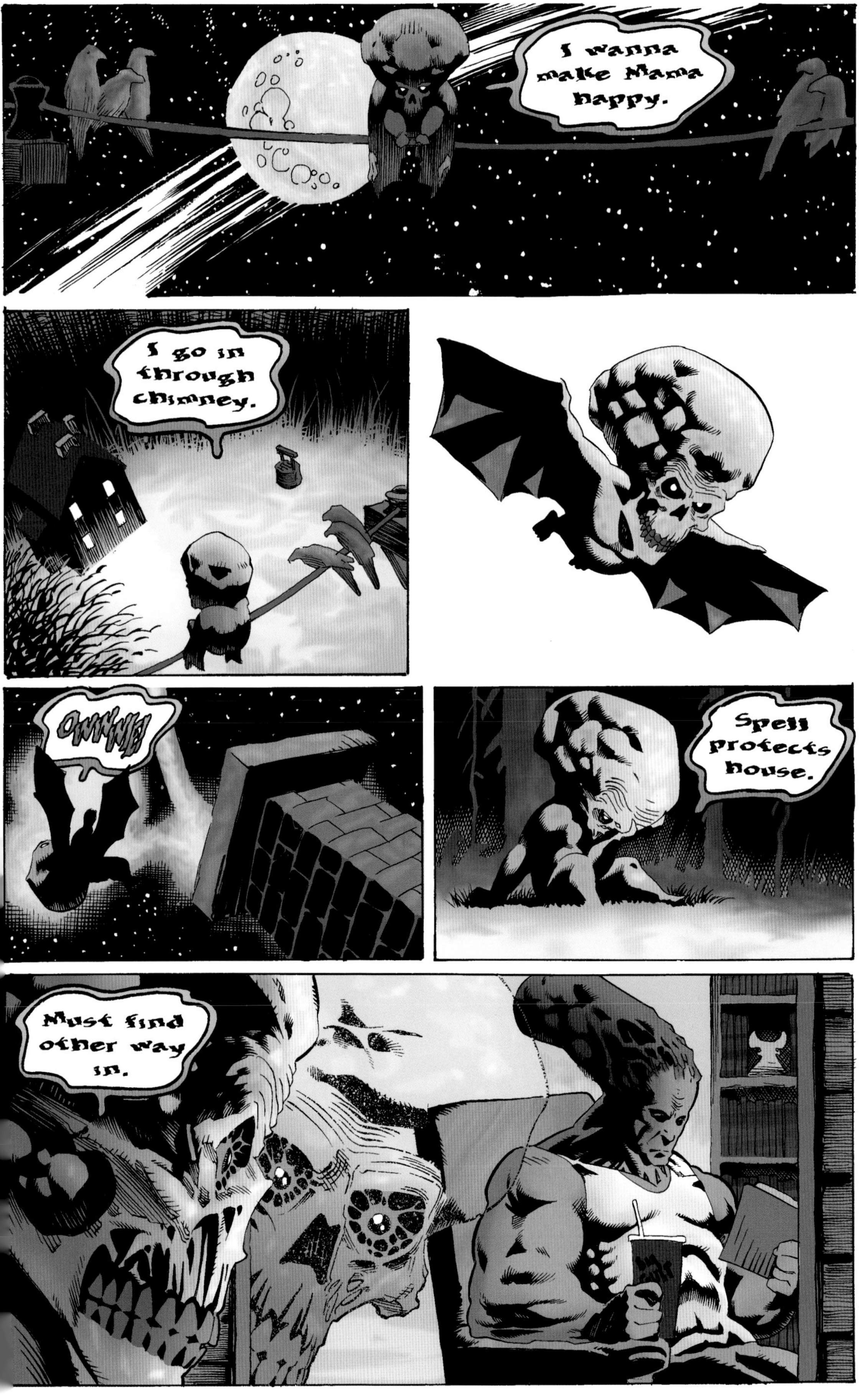
I wanna make Mama happy.
I go in through chimney.
Spell protects house.
Must find other way in.

I'VE ONLY DRUNK FOUR BIG GULPS AND I ALREADY FEEL THE NEED TO URINATE.

HUMAN BLADDERS ARE FAR TOO SMALL.

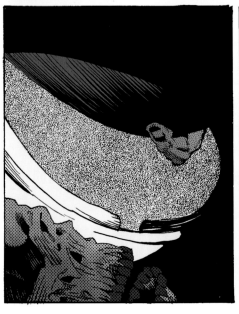

YEAH!

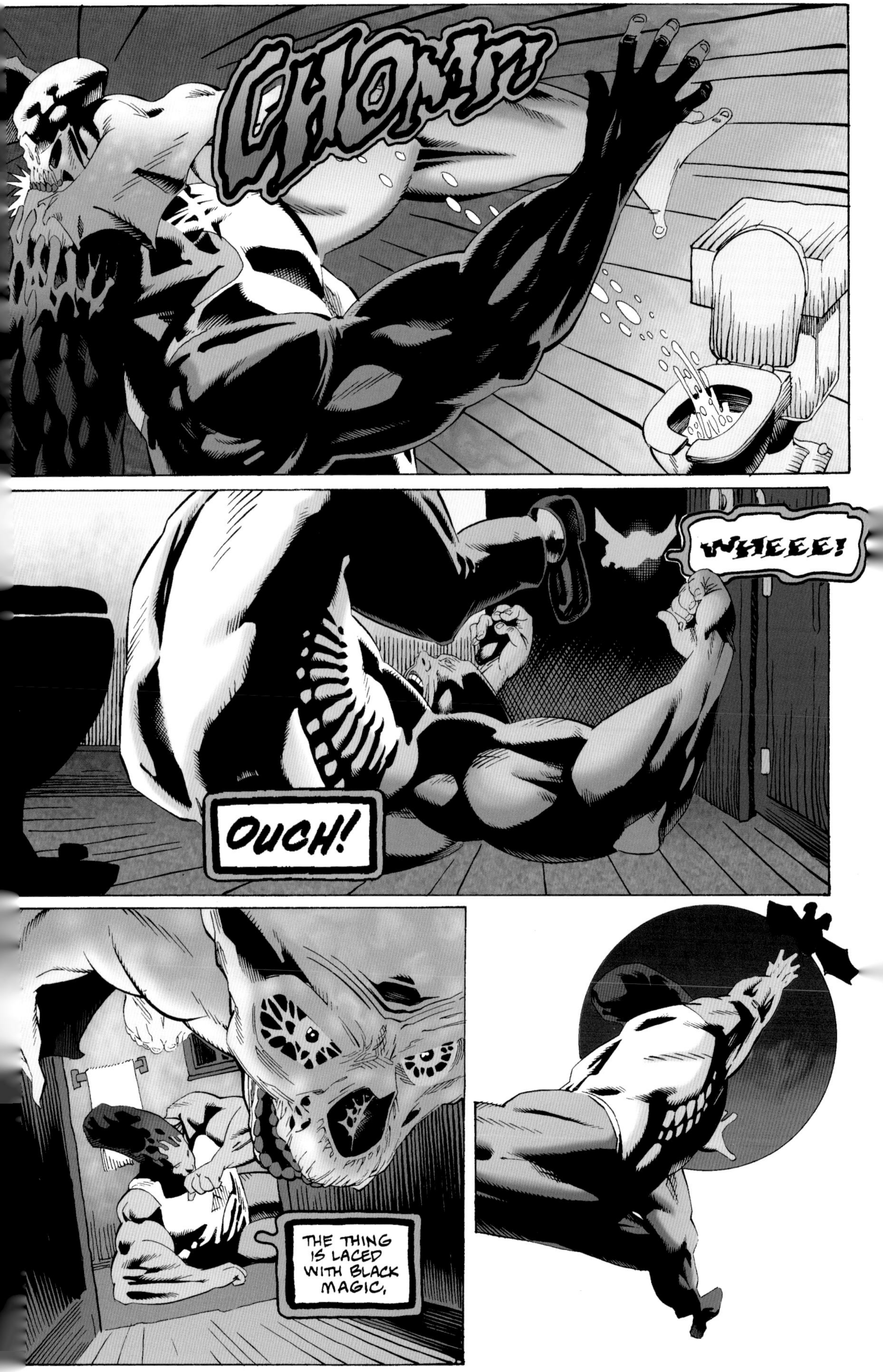
CHOMP
WHEEE!
OUCH!
THE THING IS LACED WITH BLACK MAGIC,

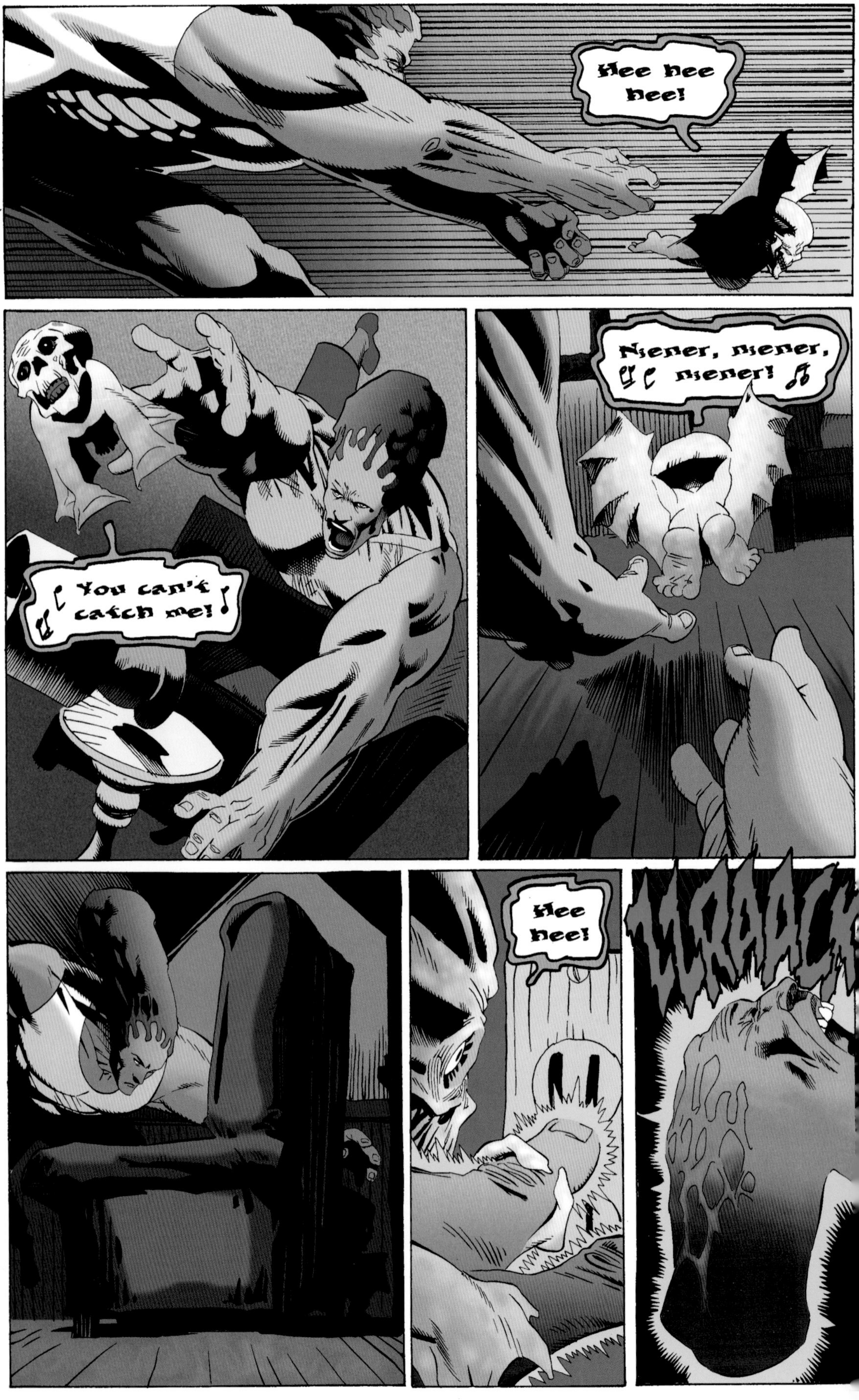
Hee hee hee!
You can't catch me!
Nyener, nyener, nyener!
Hee hee!
KRAACK

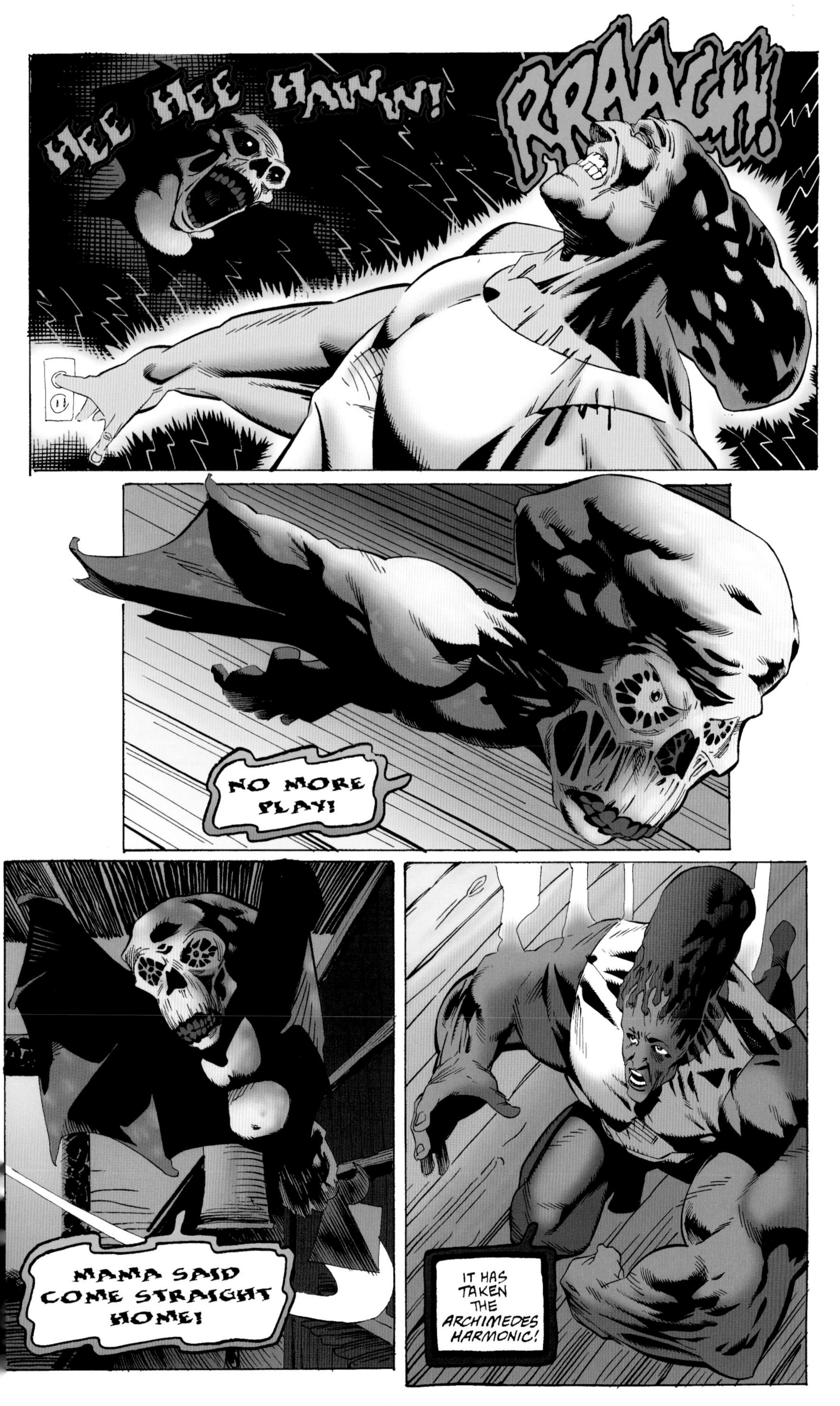
HEE HEE HAWW!
RRAAGH!
NO MORE PLAY!
MAMA SAID COME STRAIGHT HOME!
IT HAS TAKEN THE ARCHIMEDES HARMONIC!

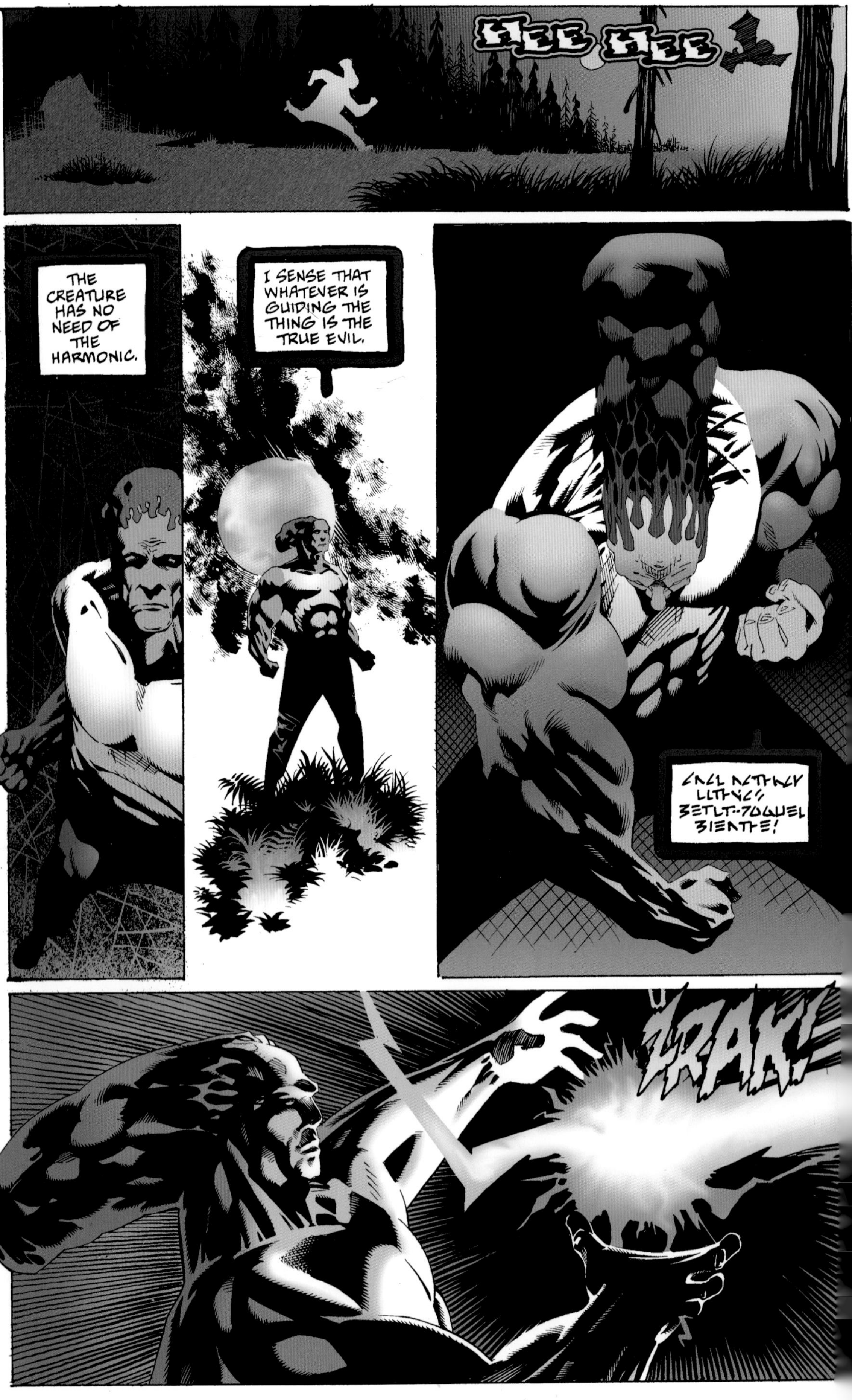
HEE HEE
THE CREATURE HAS NO NEED OF THE HARMONIC.
I SENSE THAT WHATEVER IS GUIDING THE THING IS THE TRUE EVIL.
ZRAK!

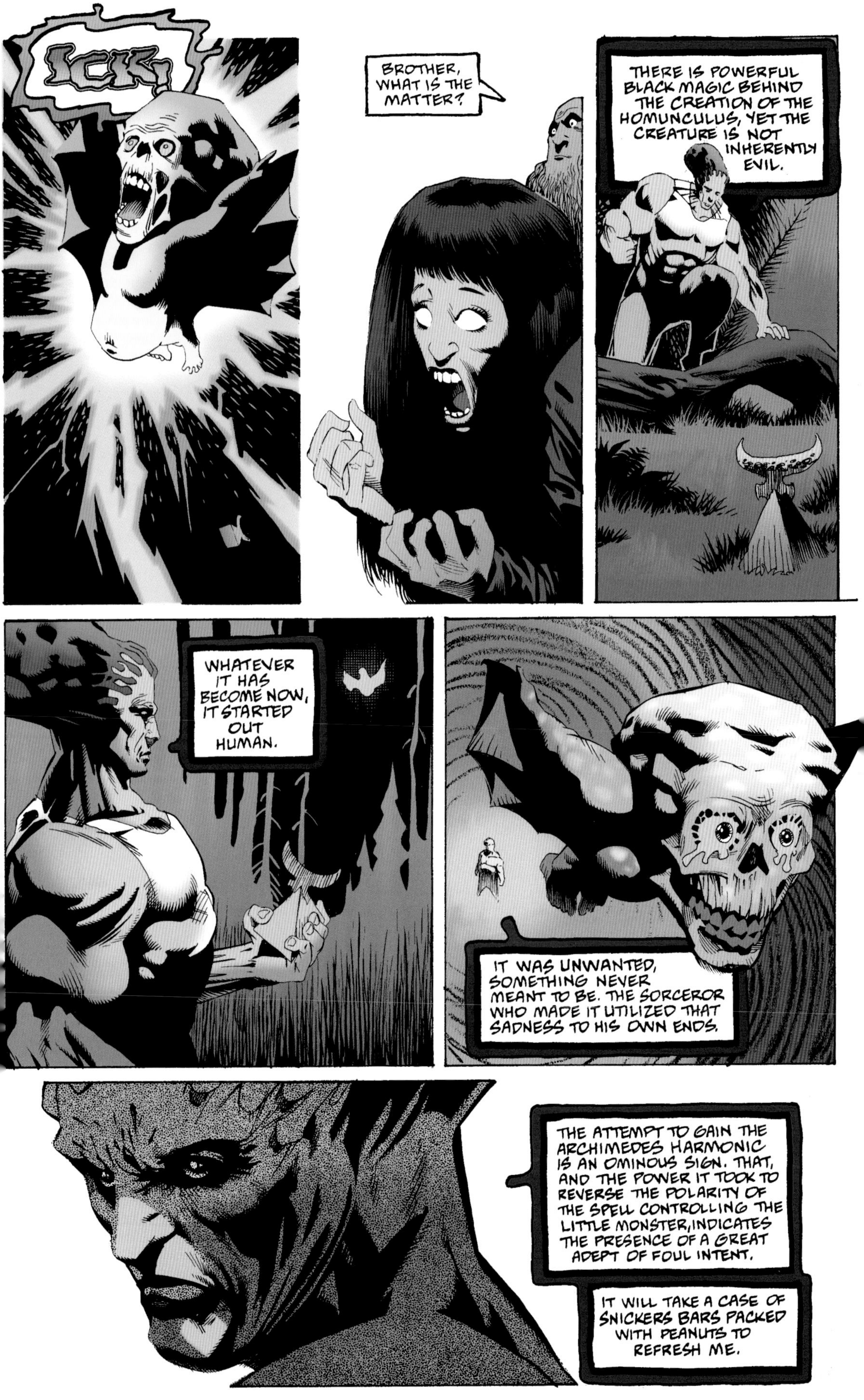
ICK!
BROTHER, WHAT IS THE MATTER?
THERE IS POWERFUL BLACK MAGIC BEHIND THE CREATION OF THE HOMUNCULUS, YET THE CREATURE IS NOT INHERENTLY EVIL.
WHATEVER IT HAS BECOME NOW, IT STARTED OUT HUMAN.
IT WAS UNWANTED, SOMETHING NEVER MEANT TO BE. THE SORCEROR WHO MADE IT UTILIZED THAT SADNESS TO HIS OWN ENDS.
THE ATTEMPT TO GAIN THE ARCHIMEDES HARMONIC IS AN OMINOUS SIGN. THAT, AND THE POWER IT TOOK TO REVERSE THE POLARITY OF THE SPELL CONTROLLING THE LITTLE MONSTER, INDICATES THE PRESENCE OF A GREAT ADEPT OF FOUL INTENT.
IT WILL TAKE A CASE OF SNICKERS BARS PACKED WITH PEANUTS TO REFRESH ME.

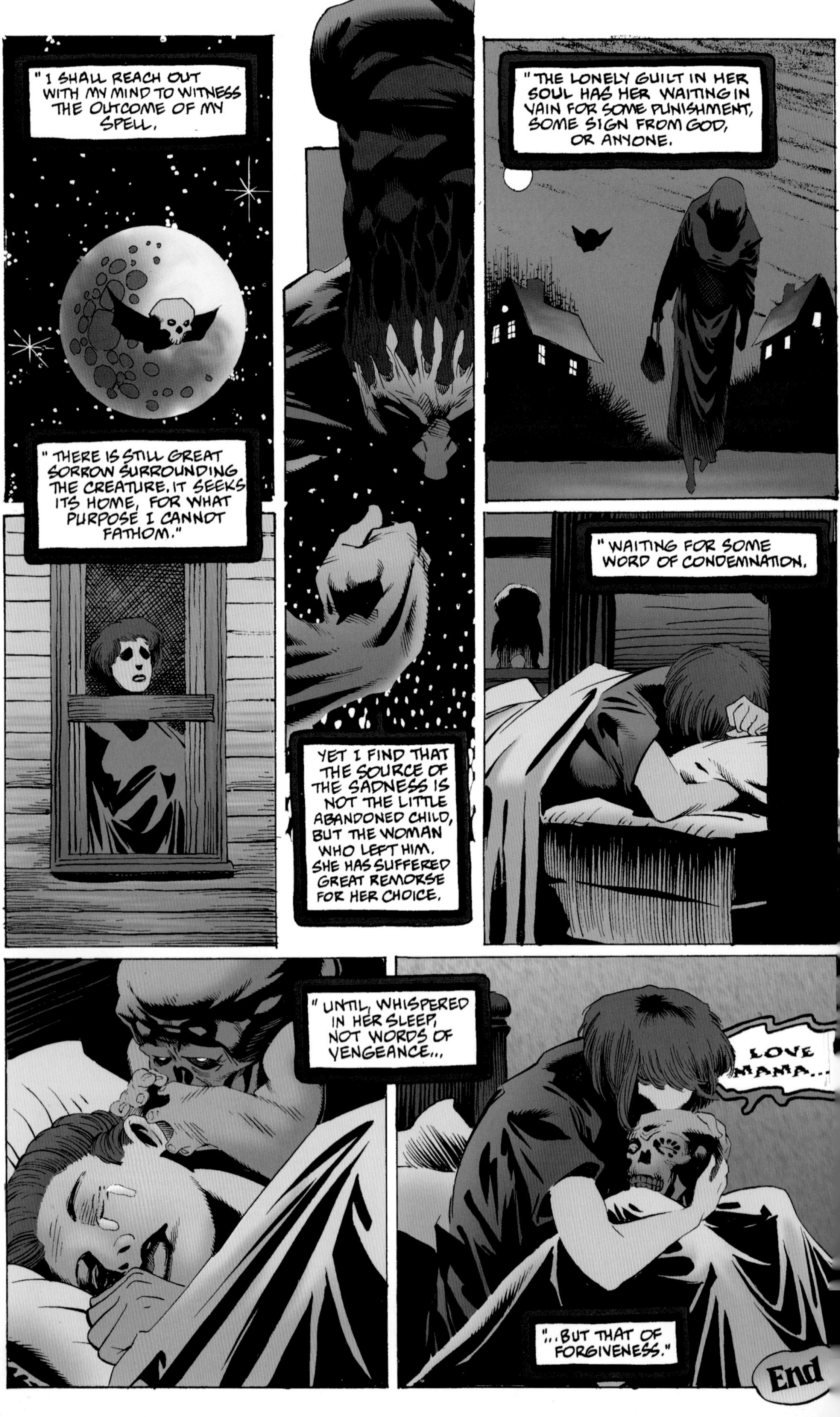
"I SHALL REACH OUT WITH MY MIND TO WITNESS THE OUTCOME OF MY SPELL.
"THERE IS STILL GREAT SORROW SURROUNDING THE CREATURE. IT SEEKS ITS HOME, FOR WHAT PURPOSE I CANNOT FATHOM."
YET I FIND THAT THE SOURCE OF THE SADNESS IS NOT THE LITTLE ABANDONED CHILD, BUT THE WOMAN WHO LEFT HIM. SHE HAS SUFFERED GREAT REMORSE FOR HER CHOICE.
"THE LONELY GUILT IN HER SOUL HAS HER WAITING IN VAIN FOR SOME PUNISHMENT, SOME SIGN FROM GOD, OR ANYONE.
"WAITING FOR SOME WORD OF CONDEMNATION.
"UNTIL, WHISPERED IN HER SLEEP, NOT WORDS OF VENGEANCE...
LOVE MAMA...
"...BUT THAT OF FORGIVENESS."
End

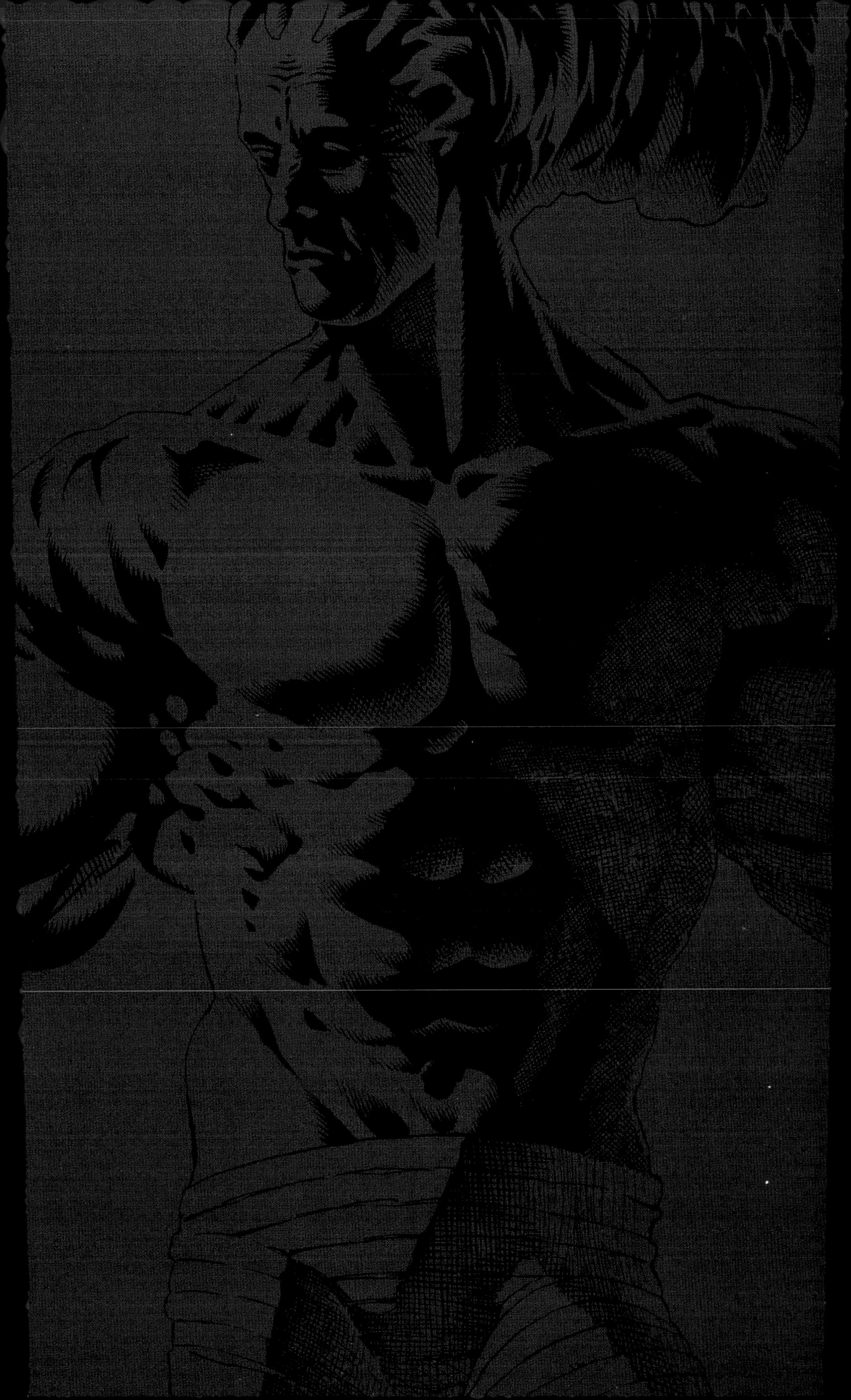

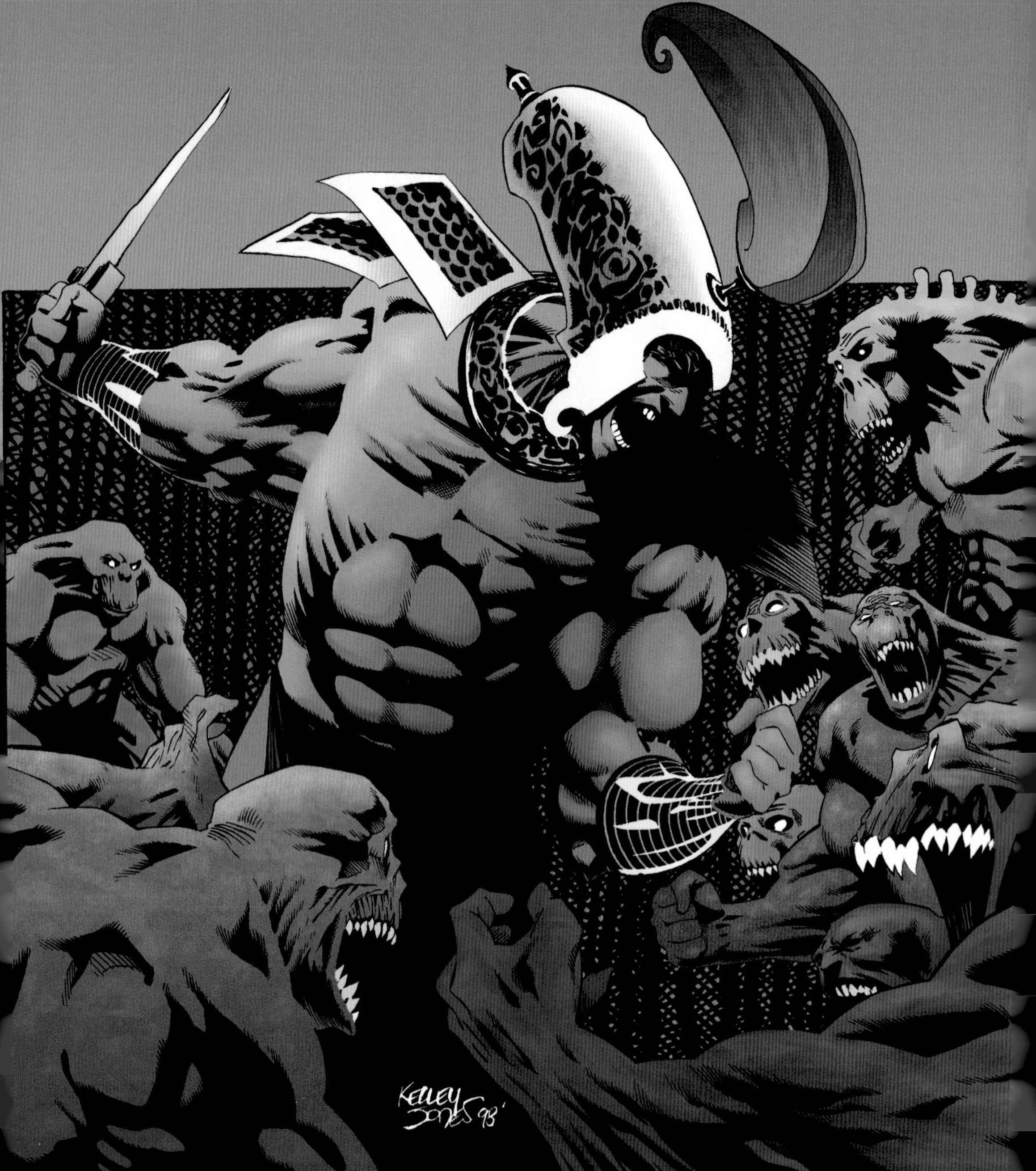
KELLEY JONES '93

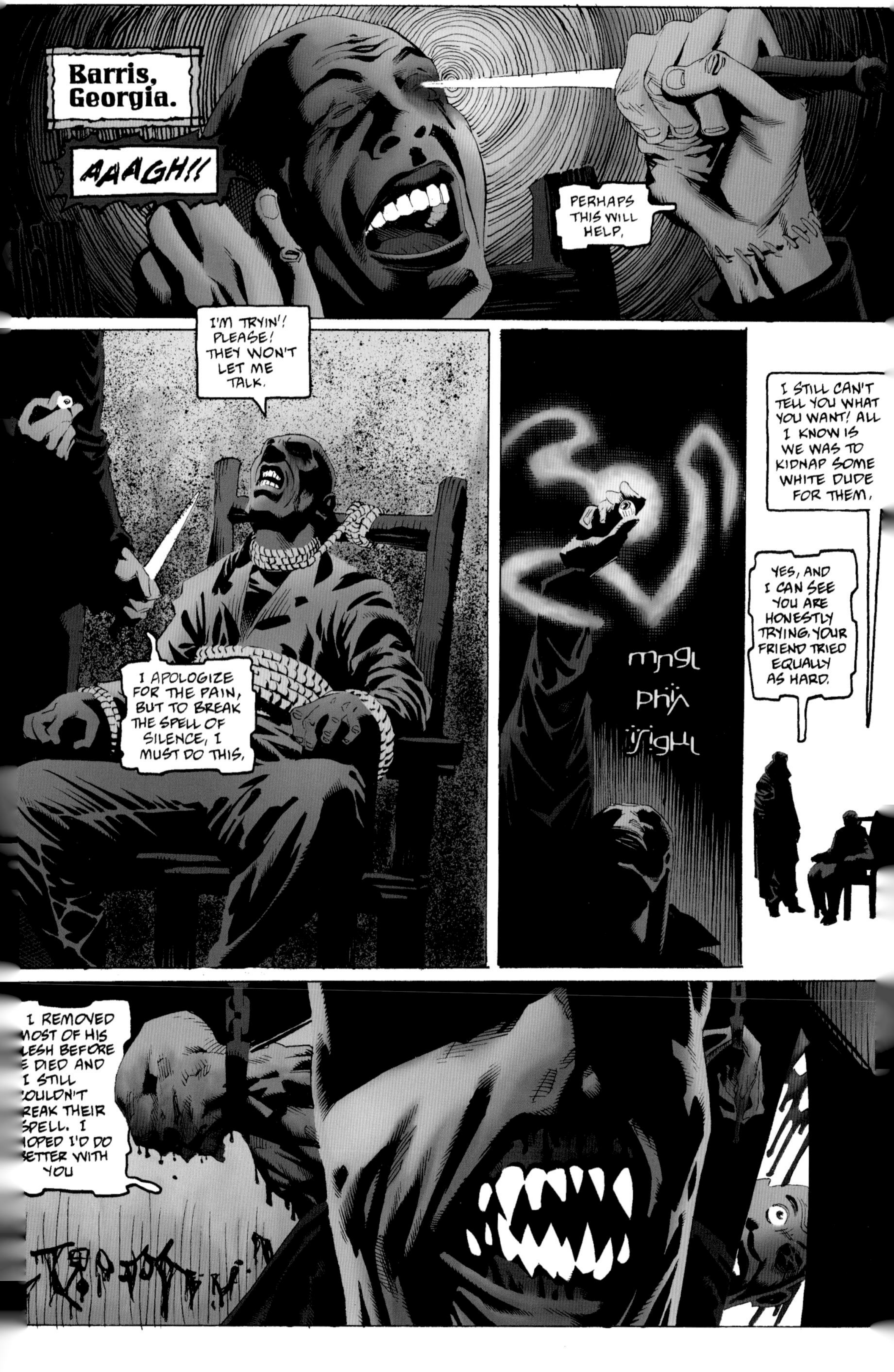
Barris, Georgia.
AAAGH!!
PERHAPS THIS WILL HELP.
I'M TRYIN'! PLEASE! THEY WON'T LET ME TALK.
I APOLOGIZE FOR THE PAIN, BUT TO BREAK THE SPELL OF SILENCE, I MUST DO THIS.
I STILL CAN'T TELL YOU WHAT YOU WANT! ALL I KNOW IS WE WAS TO KIDNAP SOME WHITE DUDE FOR THEM.
YES, AND I CAN SEE YOU ARE HONESTLY TRYING. YOUR FRIEND TRIED EQUALLY AS HARD.
I REMOVED MOST OF HIS FLESH BEFORE HE DIED AND I STILL COULDN'T BREAK THEIR SPELL. I HOPED I'D DO BETTER WITH YOU

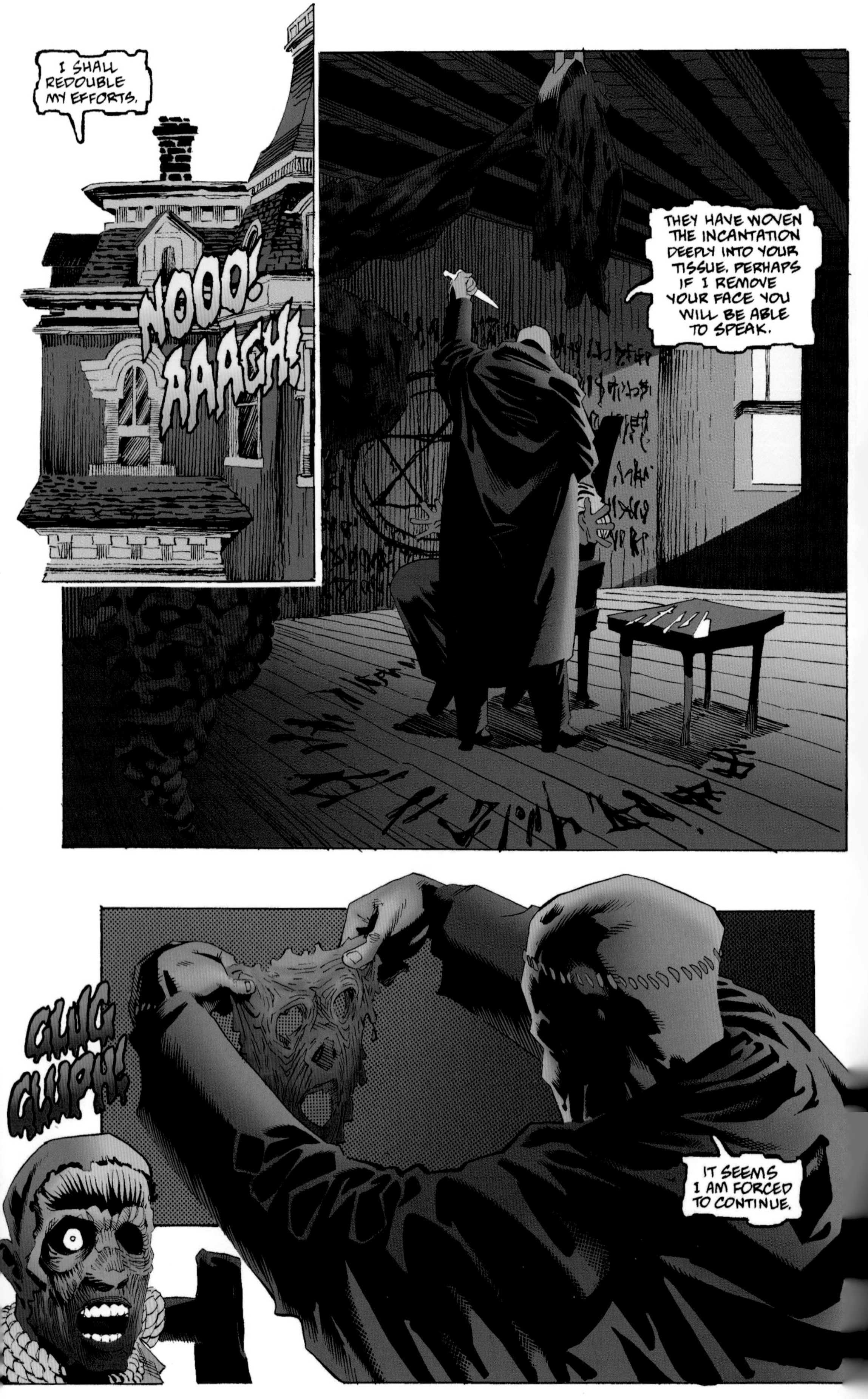
I SHALL REDOUBLE MY EFFORTS.
NOOO! AAAGH!
THEY HAVE WOVEN THE INCANTATION DEEPLY INTO YOUR TISSUE. PERHAPS IF I REMOVE YOUR FACE YOU WILL BE ABLE TO SPEAK.
GLUG GLUPH!
IT SEEMS I AM FORCED TO CONTINUE.

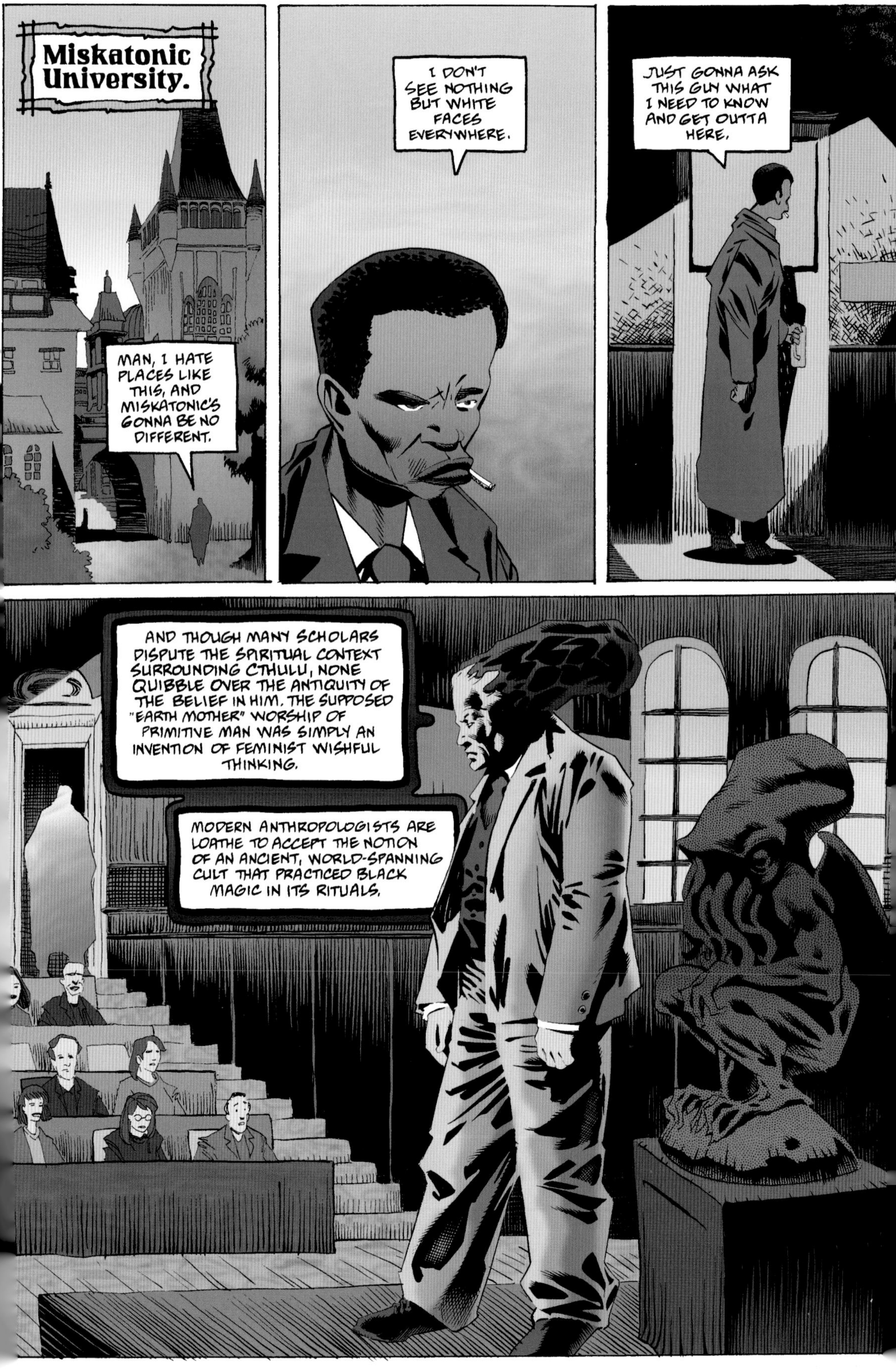
Miskatonic University.
MAN, I HATE PLACES LIKE THIS, AND MISKATONIC'S GONNA BE NO DIFFERENT.
I DON'T SEE NOTHING BUT WHITE FACES EVERYWHERE.
JUST GONNA ASK THIS GUY WHAT I NEED TO KNOW AND GET OUTTA HERE.
AND THOUGH MANY SCHOLARS DISPUTE THE SPIRITUAL CONTEXT SURROUNDING CTHULU, NONE QUIBBLE OVER THE ANTIQUITY OF THE BELIEF IN HIM. THE SUPPOSED "EARTH MOTHER" WORSHIP OF PRIMITIVE MAN WAS SIMPLY AN INVENTION OF FEMINIST WISHFUL THINKING.
MODERN ANTHROPOLOGISTS ARE LOATHE TO ACCEPT THE NOTION OF AN ANCIENT, WORLD-SPANNING CULT THAT PRACTICED BLACK MAGIC IN ITS RITUALS.

St. Augustine, Florida.

THOSE WHO BROUGHT THIS MAN DID WELL.

HEY, MAN, I'LL DO WHATEVER YOU WANT. JUST DON'T HURT ME.

WE HAVE NO INTENTION OF HARMING YOU.

IN FACT, YOU ARE TO BE HONORED.

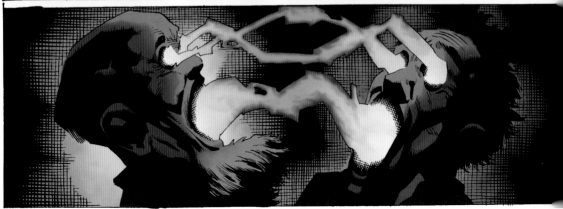

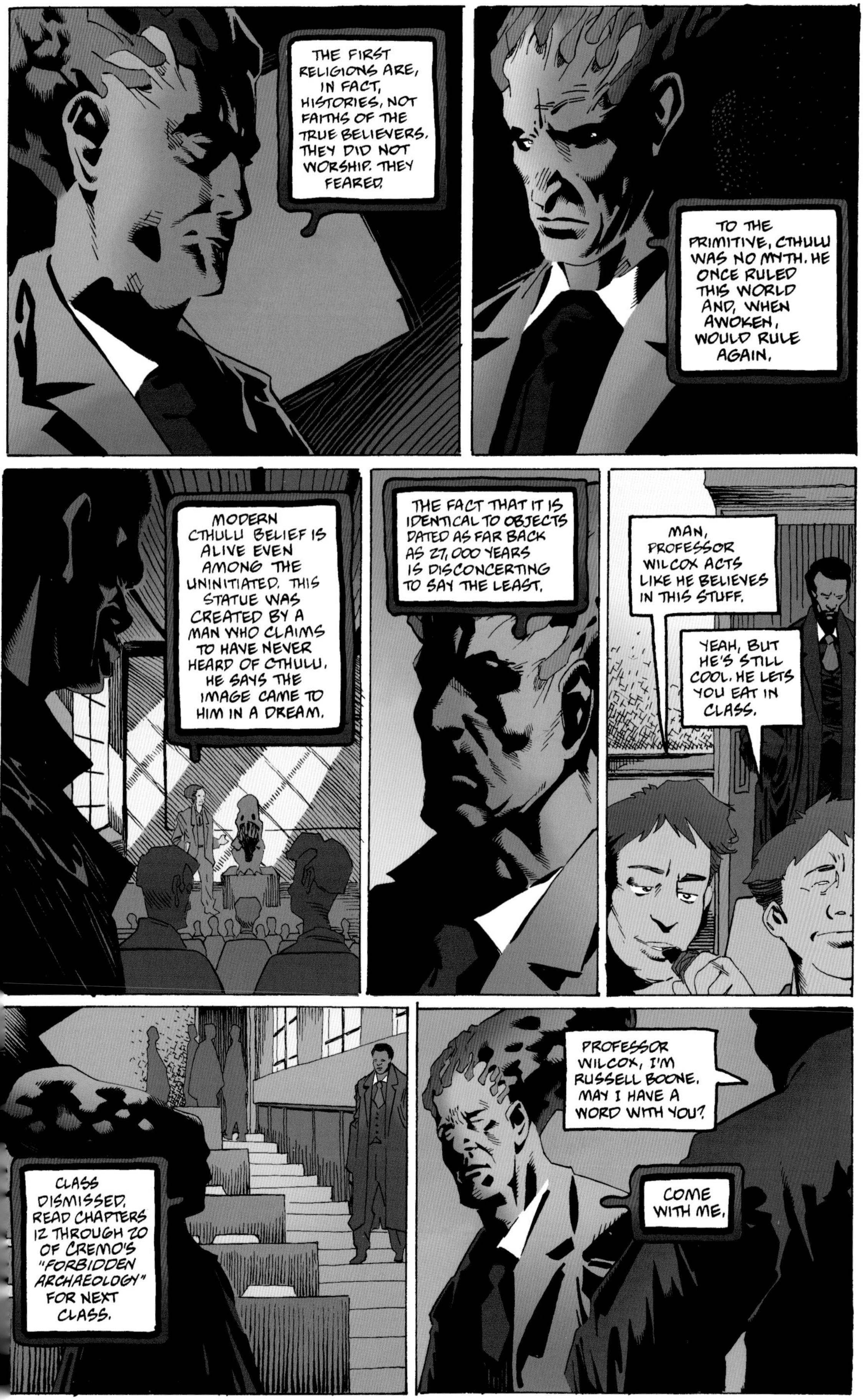
THE FIRST RELIGIONS ARE, IN FACT, HISTORIES, NOT FAITHS OF THE TRUE BELIEVERS. THEY DID NOT WORSHIP. THEY FEARED.
TO THE PRIMITIVE, CTHULU WAS NO MYTH. HE ONCE RULED THIS WORLD AND, WHEN AWOKEN, WOULD RULE AGAIN.
MODERN CTHULU BELIEF IS ALIVE EVEN AMONG THE UNINITIATED. THIS STATUE WAS CREATED BY A MAN WHO CLAIMS TO HAVE NEVER HEARD OF CTHULU. HE SAYS THE IMAGE CAME TO HIM IN A DREAM.
THE FACT THAT IT IS IDENTICAL TO OBJECTS DATED AS FAR BACK AS 27,000 YEARS IS DISCONCERTING TO SAY THE LEAST.
MAN, PROFESSOR WILCOX ACTS LIKE HE BELIEVES IN THIS STUFF.
YEAH, BUT HE'S STILL COOL. HE LETS YOU EAT IN CLASS.
CLASS DISMISSED. READ CHAPTERS 12 THROUGH 20 OF CREMO'S "FORBIDDEN ARCHAEOLOGY" FOR NEXT CLASS.
PROFESSOR WILCOX, I'M RUSSELL BOONE. MAY I HAVE A WORD WITH YOU?
COME WITH ME.

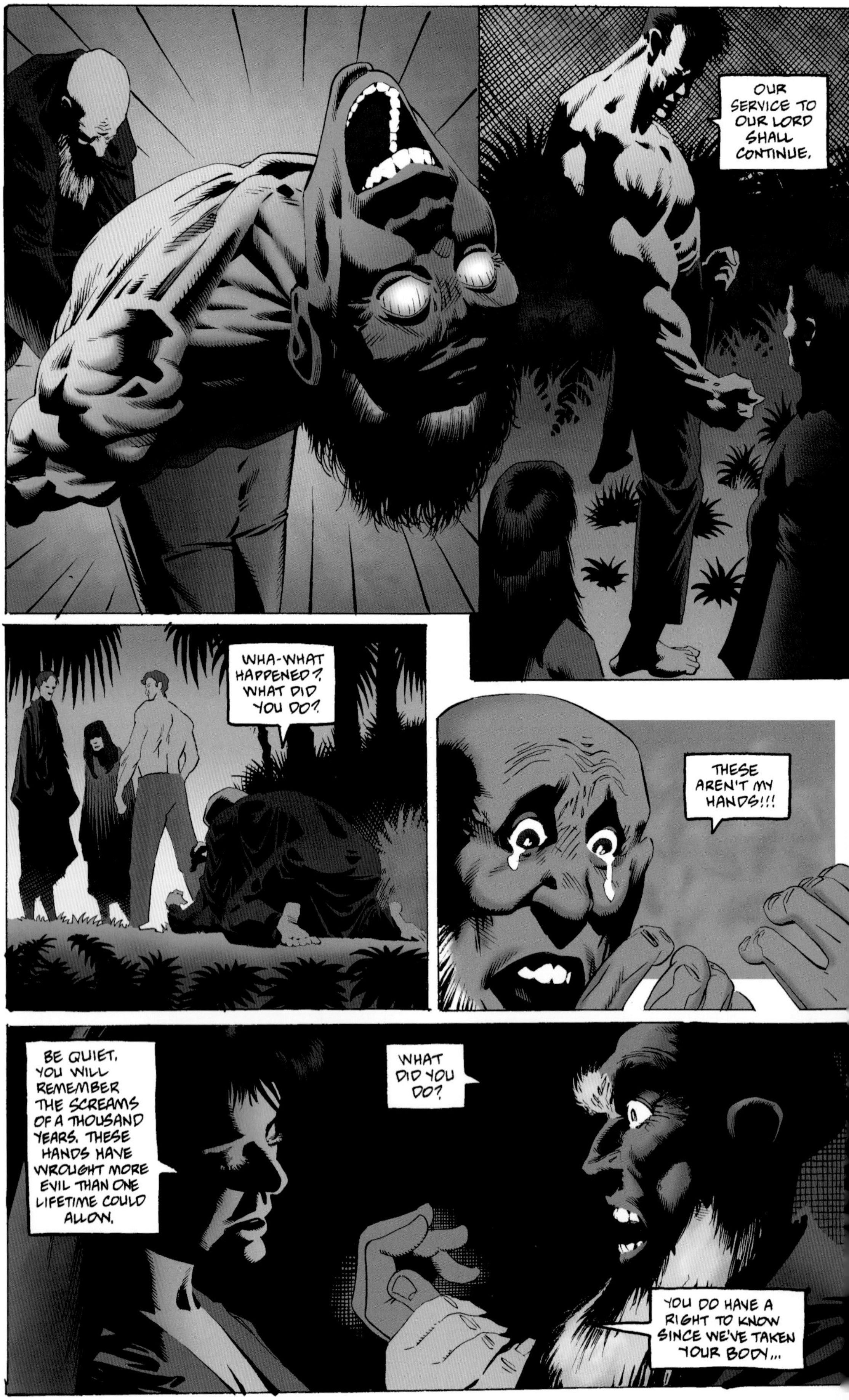
OUR SERVICE TO OUR LORD SHALL CONTINUE.
WHA-WHAT HAPPENED? WHAT DID YOU DO?
THESE AREN'T MY HANDS!!!
BE QUIET. YOU WILL REMEMBER THE SCREAMS OF A THOUSAND YEARS. THESE HANDS HAVE WROUGHT MORE EVIL THAN ONE LIFETIME COULD ALLOW.
WHAT DID YOU DO?
YOU DO HAVE A RIGHT TO KNOW SINCE WE'VE TAKEN YOUR BODY...

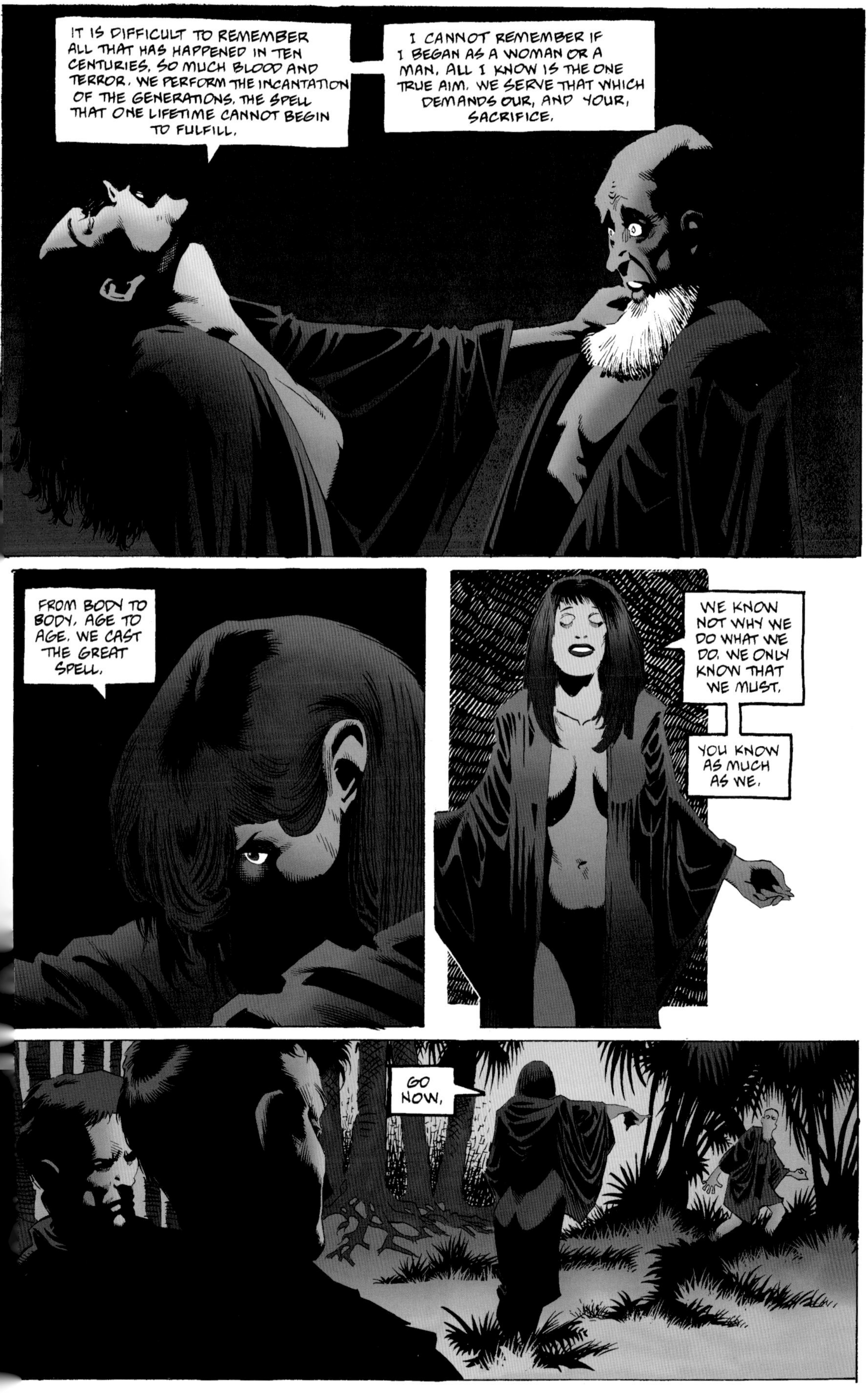
IT IS DIFFICULT TO REMEMBER ALL THAT HAS HAPPENED IN TEN CENTURIES. SO MUCH BLOOD AND TERROR. WE PERFORM THE INCANTATION OF THE GENERATIONS. THE SPELL THAT ONE LIFETIME CANNOT BEGIN TO FULFILL.
I CANNOT REMEMBER IF I BEGAN AS A WOMAN OR A MAN. ALL I KNOW IS THE ONE TRUE AIM. WE SERVE THAT WHICH DEMANDS OUR, AND YOUR, SACRIFICE.
FROM BODY TO BODY, AGE TO AGE. WE CAST THE GREAT SPELL.
WE KNOW NOT WHY WE DO WHAT WE DO. WE ONLY KNOW THAT WE MUST.
YOU KNOW AS MUCH AS WE.
GO NOW.

I WORK FOR THE SOUTHERN LEGAL CENTER, WE FOCUS ON CASES DEALING WITH HATE CRIMES.

WHAT ARE HATE CRIMES?

THEY ARE OFFENSES COMMITTED SOLELY ON THE BASIS OF RACE, SEXUAL PREFERENCE, OR RELIGIOUS BIAS. THEY ARE CRIMES OF BIGOTRY.

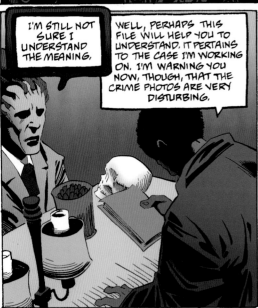

I'M STILL NOT SURE I UNDERSTAND THE MEANING.

WELL, PERHAPS THIS FILE WILL HELP YOU TO UNDERSTAND. IT PERTAINS TO THE CASE I'M WORKING ON. I'M WARNING YOU NOW, THOUGH, THAT THE CRIME PHOTOS ARE VERY DISTURBING.

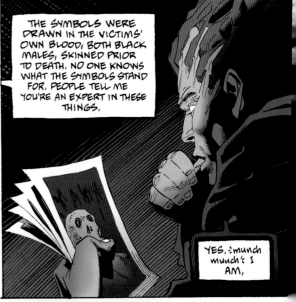

THE SYMBOLS WERE DRAWN IN THE VICTIMS' OWN BLOOD, BOTH BLACK MALES, SKINNED PRIOR TO DEATH. NO ONE KNOWS WHAT THE SYMBOLS STAND FOR. PEOPLE TELL ME YOU'RE AN EXPERT IN THESE THINGS.

YES, ⸨munch munch⸩ I AM.

YOU'VE SEEN THIS KIND OF BRUTALITY BEFORE?

THIS KIND OF EVIL EXISTS EVERYWHERE, MOST JUST FAIL TO SEE IT.

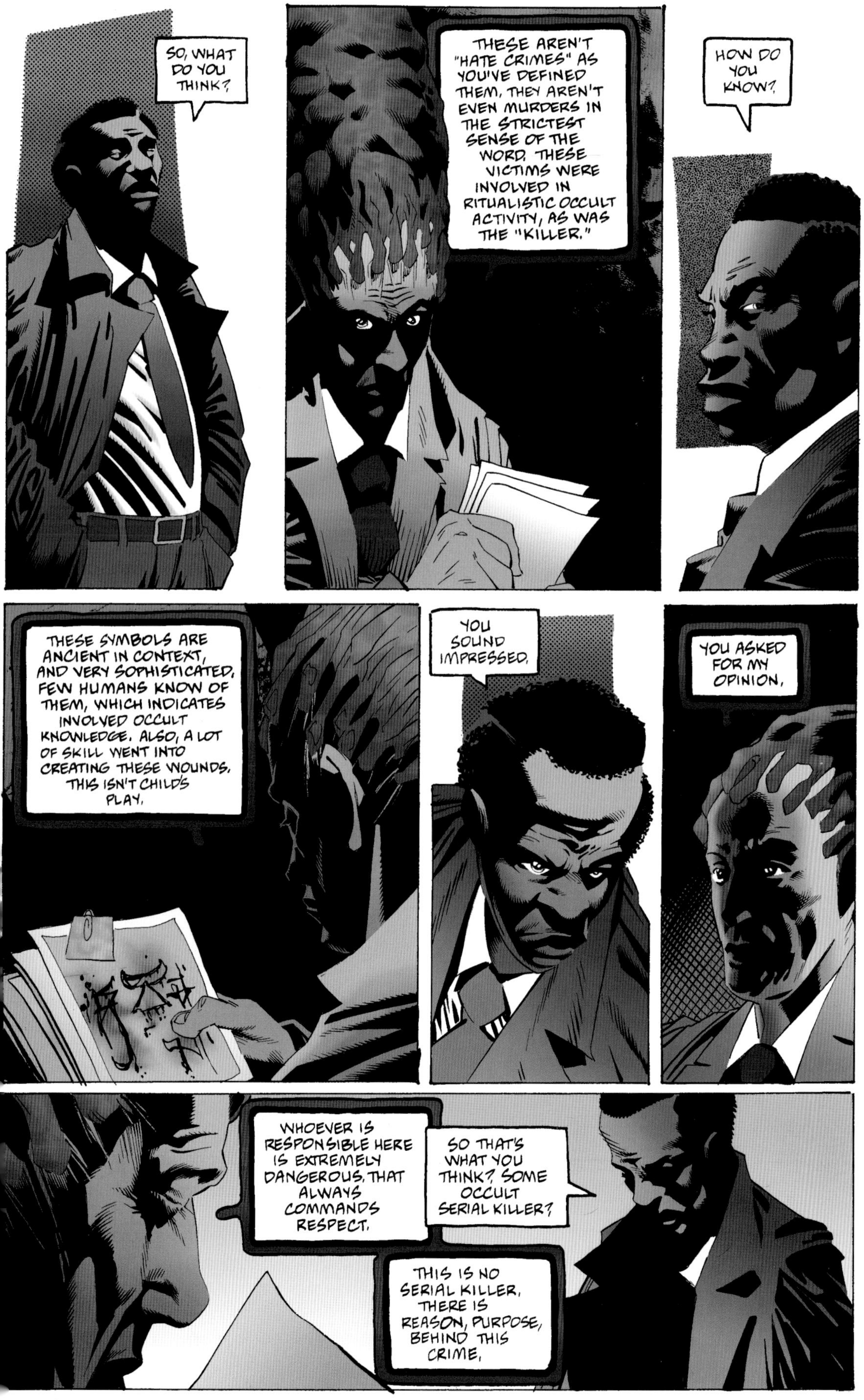
SO, WHAT DO YOU THINK?
THESE AREN'T "HATE CRIMES" AS YOU'VE DEFINED THEM, THEY AREN'T EVEN MURDERS IN THE STRICTEST SENSE OF THE WORD. THESE VICTIMS WERE INVOLVED IN RITUALISTIC OCCULT ACTIVITY, AS WAS THE "KILLER."
HOW DO YOU KNOW?
THESE SYMBOLS ARE ANCIENT IN CONTEXT, AND VERY SOPHISTICATED, FEW HUMANS KNOW OF THEM, WHICH INDICATES INVOLVED OCCULT KNOWLEDGE. ALSO, A LOT OF SKILL WENT INTO CREATING THESE WOUNDS, THIS ISN'T CHILD'S PLAY.
YOU SOUND IMPRESSED.
YOU ASKED FOR MY OPINION.
WHOEVER IS RESPONSIBLE HERE IS EXTREMELY DANGEROUS, THAT ALWAYS COMMANDS RESPECT.
SO THAT'S WHAT YOU THINK? SOME OCCULT SERIAL KILLER?
THIS IS NO SERIAL KILLER, THERE IS REASON, PURPOSE, BEHIND THIS CRIME.

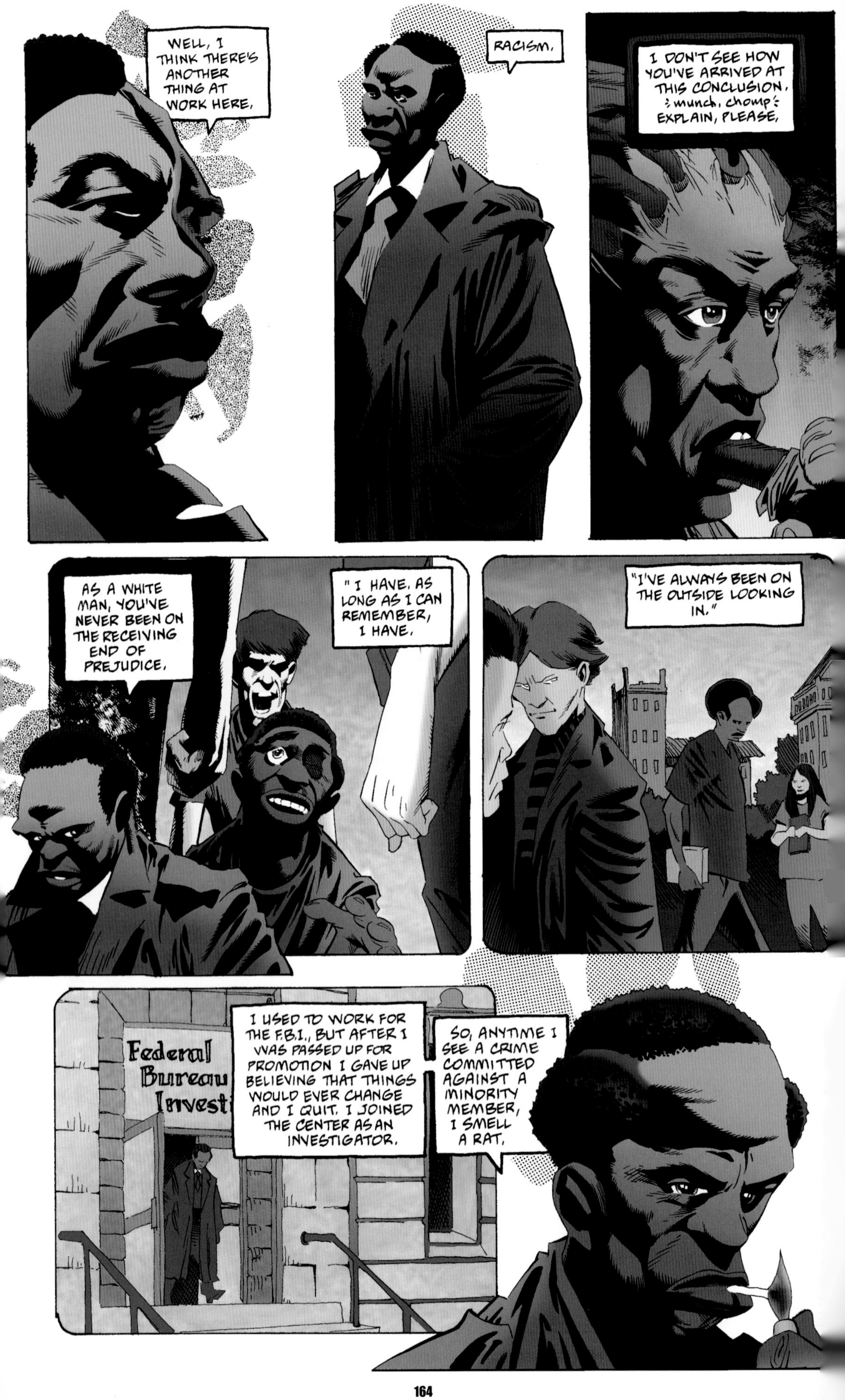

WELL, I THINK THERE'S ANOTHER THING AT WORK HERE.
RACISM.
I DON'T SEE HOW YOU'VE ARRIVED AT THIS CONCLUSION. ⁑munch, chomp⁑ EXPLAIN, PLEASE.
AS A WHITE MAN, YOU'VE NEVER BEEN ON THE RECEIVING END OF PREJUDICE.
"I HAVE. AS LONG AS I CAN REMEMBER, I HAVE.
"I'VE ALWAYS BEEN ON THE OUTSIDE LOOKING IN."
Federal Bureau Invest
I USED TO WORK FOR THE F.B.I., BUT AFTER I WAS PASSED UP FOR PROMOTION I GAVE UP BELIEVING THAT THINGS WOULD EVER CHANGE AND I QUIT. I JOINED THE CENTER AS AN INVESTIGATOR.
SO, ANYTIME I SEE A CRIME COMMITTED AGAINST A MINORITY MEMBER, I SMELL A RAT.

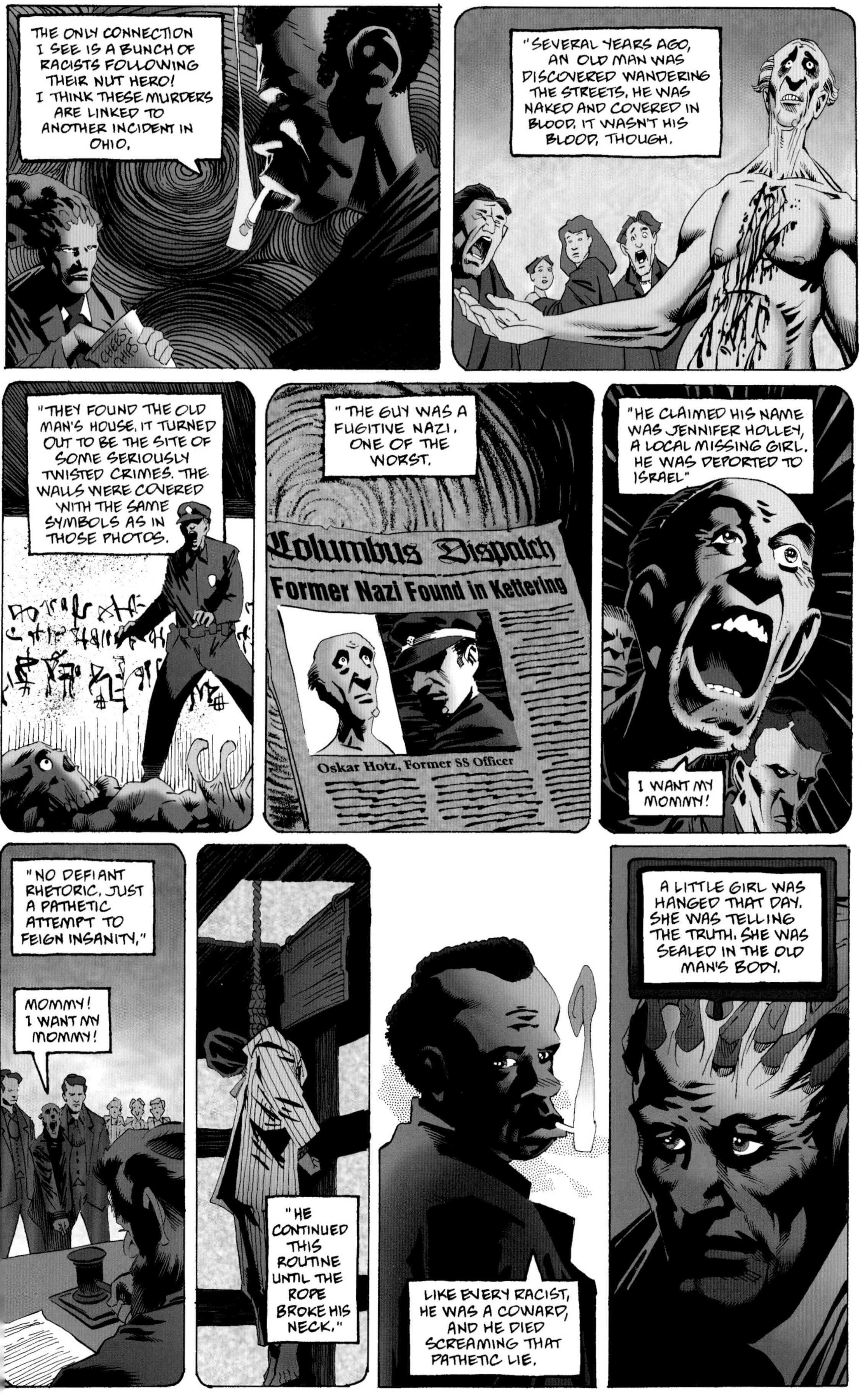
THE ONLY CONNECTION I SEE IS A BUNCH OF RACISTS FOLLOWING THEIR NUT HERO! I THINK THESE MURDERS ARE LINKED TO ANOTHER INCIDENT IN OHIO.
CHEESY CHIPS
"SEVERAL YEARS AGO, AN OLD MAN WAS DISCOVERED WANDERING THE STREETS. HE WAS NAKED AND COVERED IN BLOOD. IT WASN'T HIS BLOOD, THOUGH.
"THEY FOUND THE OLD MAN'S HOUSE. IT TURNED OUT TO BE THE SITE OF SOME SERIOUSLY TWISTED CRIMES. THE WALLS WERE COVERED WITH THE SAME SYMBOLS AS IN THOSE PHOTOS.
"THE GUY WAS A FUGITIVE NAZI, ONE OF THE WORST.
Columbus Dispatch
Former Nazi Found in Kettering
Oskar Hotz, Former SS Officer
"HE CLAIMED HIS NAME WAS JENNIFER HOLLEY, A LOCAL MISSING GIRL. HE WAS DEPORTED TO ISRAEL"
I WANT MY MOMMY!
"NO DEFIANT RHETORIC, JUST A PATHETIC ATTEMPT TO FEIGN INSANITY."
MOMMY! I WANT MY MOMMY!
"HE CONTINUED THIS ROUTINE UNTIL THE ROPE BROKE HIS NECK."
LIKE EVERY RACIST, HE WAS A COWARD, AND HE DIED SCREAMING THAT PATHETIC LIE.
A LITTLE GIRL WAS HANGED THAT DAY. SHE WAS TELLING THE TRUTH. SHE WAS SEALED IN THE OLD MAN'S BODY.

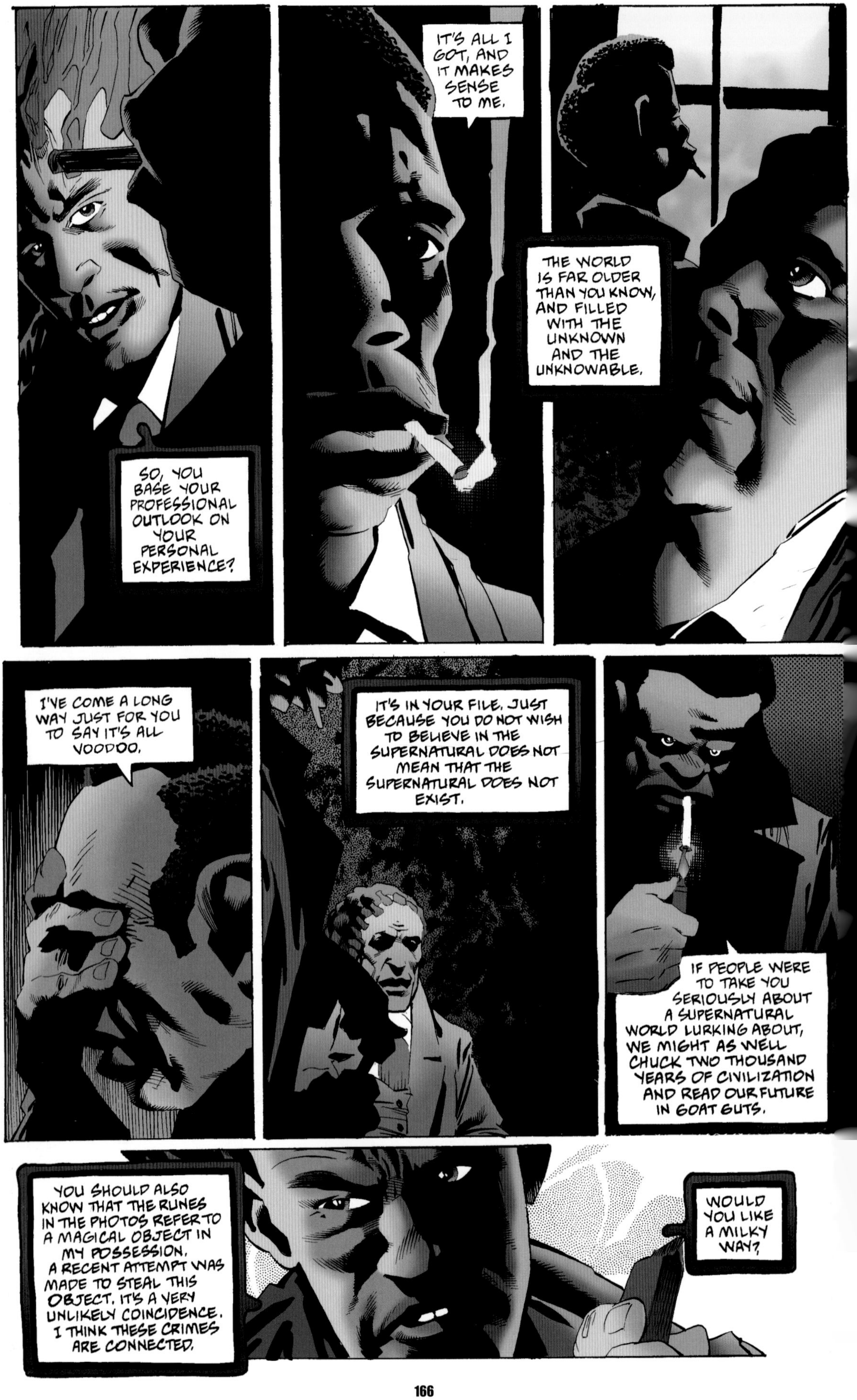

SO, YOU BASE YOUR PROFESSIONAL OUTLOOK ON YOUR PERSONAL EXPERIENCE?
IT'S ALL I GOT, AND IT MAKES SENSE TO ME.
THE WORLD IS FAR OLDER THAN YOU KNOW, AND FILLED WITH THE UNKNOWN AND THE UNKNOWABLE.
I'VE COME A LONG WAY JUST FOR YOU TO SAY IT'S ALL VOODOO.
IT'S IN YOUR FILE. JUST BECAUSE YOU DO NOT WISH TO BELIEVE IN THE SUPERNATURAL DOES NOT MEAN THAT THE SUPERNATURAL DOES NOT EXIST.
IF PEOPLE WERE TO TAKE YOU SERIOUSLY ABOUT A SUPERNATURAL WORLD LURKING ABOUT, WE MIGHT AS WELL CHUCK TWO THOUSAND YEARS OF CIVILIZATION AND READ OUR FUTURE IN GOAT GUTS.
YOU SHOULD ALSO KNOW THAT THE RUNES IN THE PHOTOS REFER TO A MAGICAL OBJECT IN MY POSSESSION.
A RECENT ATTEMPT WAS MADE TO STEAL THIS OBJECT. IT'S A VERY UNLIKELY COINCIDENCE. I THINK THESE CRIMES ARE CONNECTED.
WOULD YOU LIKE A MILKY WAY?

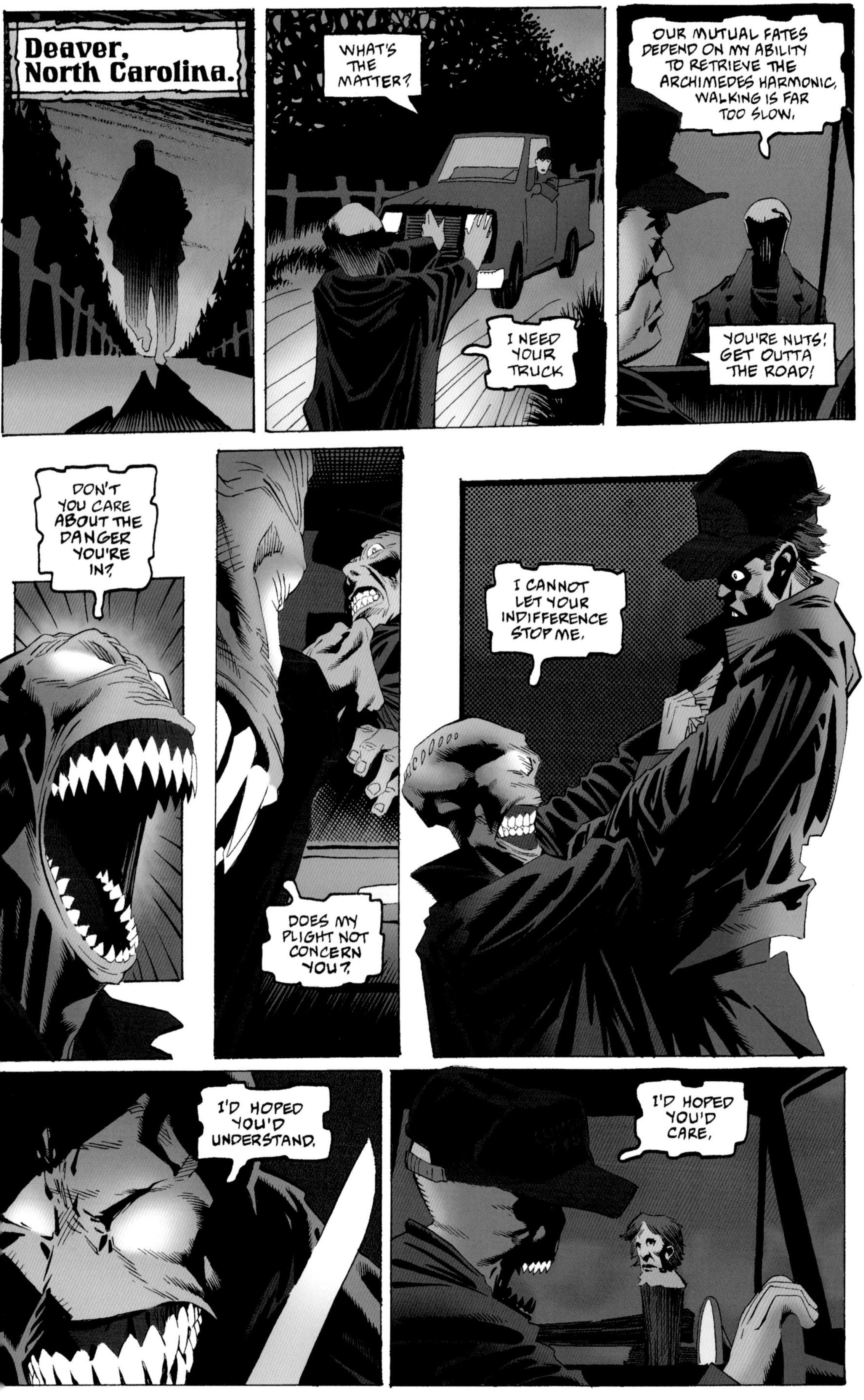

Deaver, North Carolina.
WHAT'S THE MATTER?
I NEED YOUR TRUCK
OUR MUTUAL FATES DEPEND ON MY ABILITY TO RETRIEVE THE ARCHIMEDES HARMONIC, WALKING IS FAR TOO SLOW.
YOU'RE NUTS! GET OUTTA THE ROAD!
DON'T YOU CARE ABOUT THE DANGER YOU'RE IN?
DOES MY PLIGHT NOT CONCERN YOU?
I CANNOT LET YOUR INDIFFERENCE STOP ME.
I'D HOPED YOU'D UNDERSTAND.
I'D HOPED YOU'D CARE.

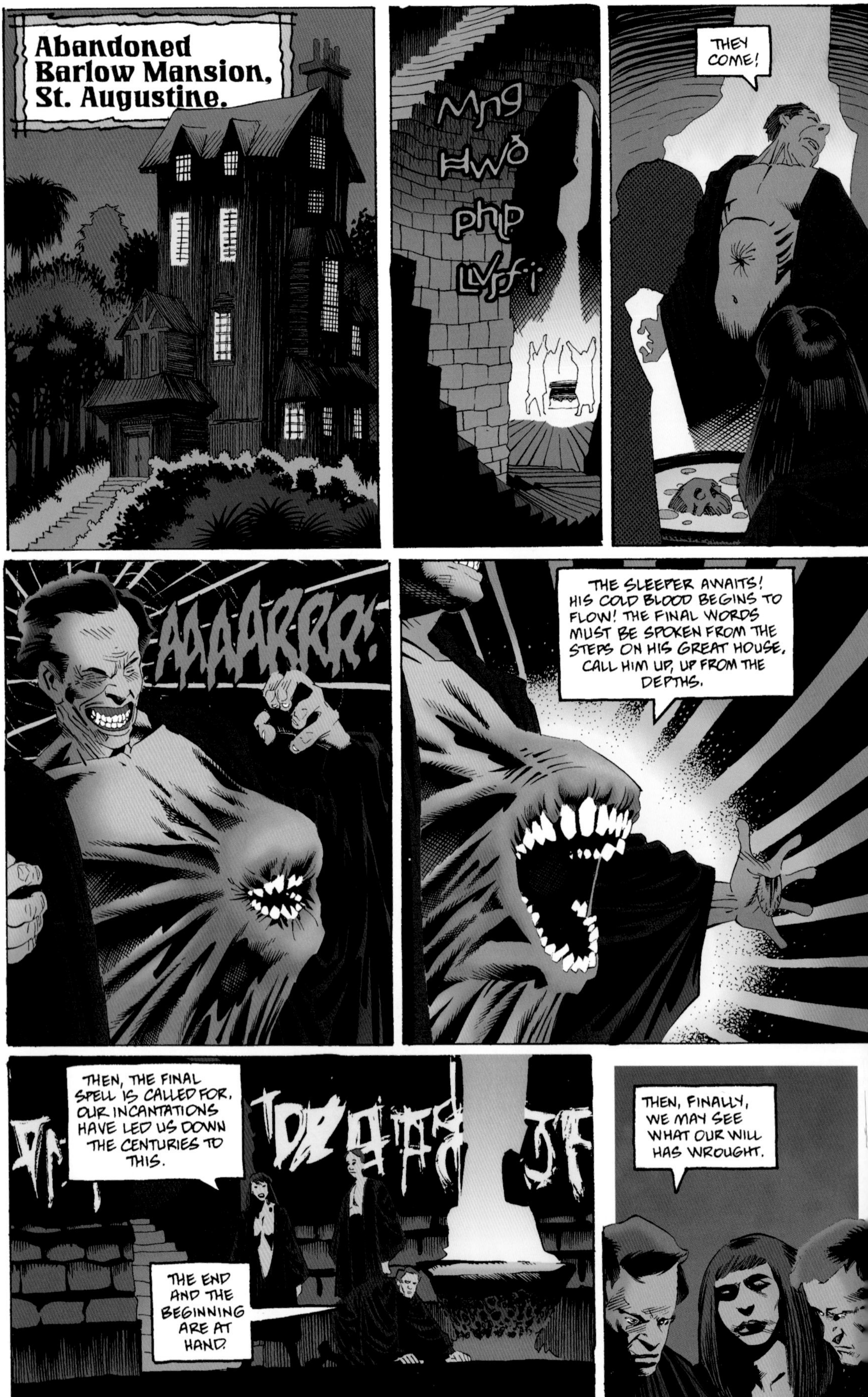
Abandoned Barlow Mansion, St. Augustine.
THEY COME!
AAAARRR!
THE SLEEPER AWAITS! HIS COLD BLOOD BEGINS TO FLOW! THE FINAL WORDS MUST BE SPOKEN FROM THE STEPS ON HIS GREAT HOUSE, CALL HIM UP, UP FROM THE DEPTHS.
THEN, THE FINAL SPELL IS CALLED FOR, OUR INCANTATIONS HAVE LED US DOWN THE CENTURIES TO THIS.
THE END AND THE BEGINNING ARE AT HAND.
THEN, FINALLY, WE MAY SEE WHAT OUR WILL HAS WROUGHT.

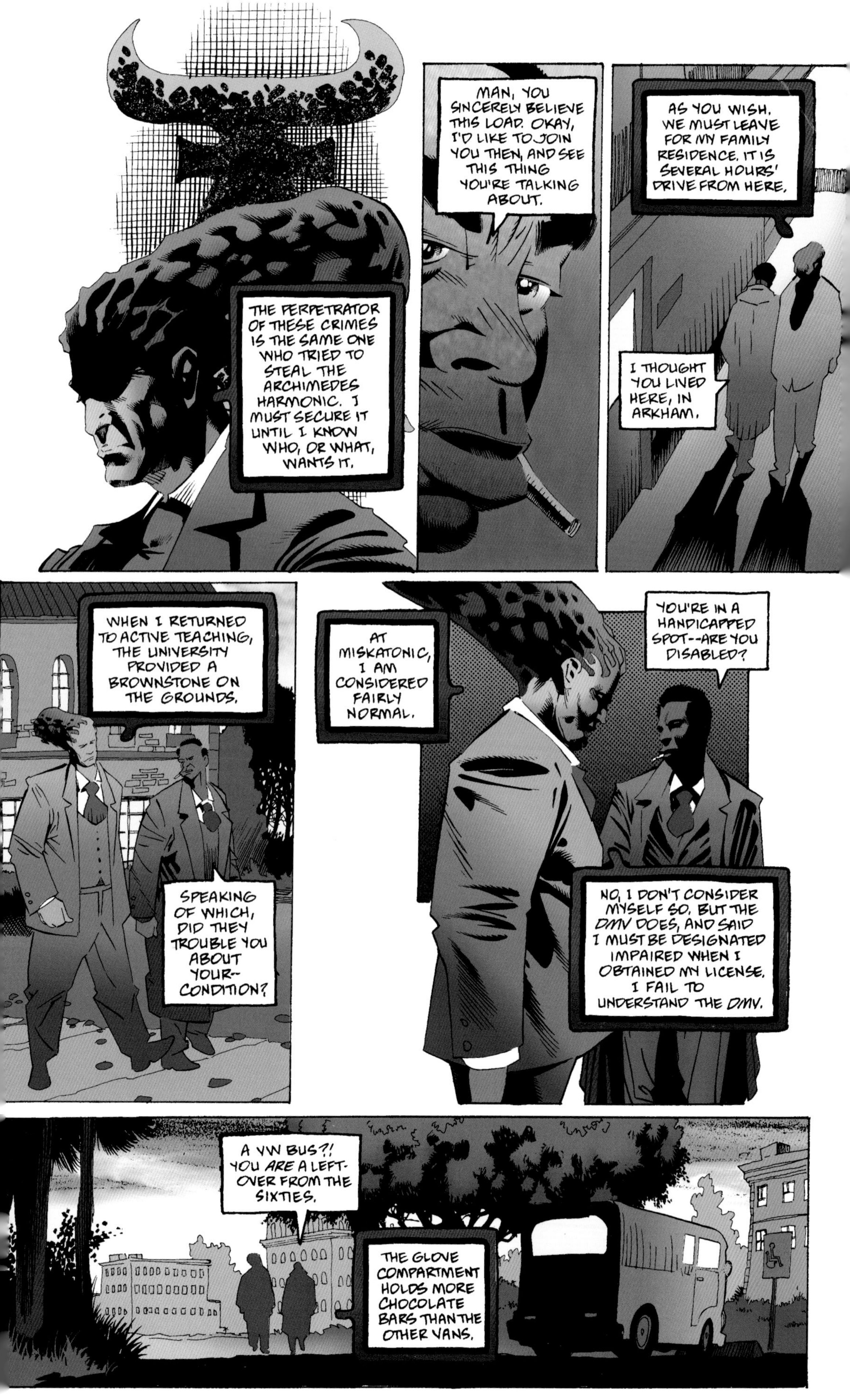
THE PERPETRATOR OF THESE CRIMES IS THE SAME ONE WHO TRIED TO STEAL THE ARCHIMEDES HARMONIC. I MUST SECURE IT UNTIL I KNOW WHO, OR WHAT, WANTS IT.
MAN, YOU SINCERELY BELIEVE THIS LOAD. OKAY, I'D LIKE TO JOIN YOU THEN, AND SEE THIS THING YOU'RE TALKING ABOUT.
AS YOU WISH. WE MUST LEAVE FOR MY FAMILY RESIDENCE. IT IS SEVERAL HOURS' DRIVE FROM HERE.
I THOUGHT YOU LIVED HERE, IN ARKHAM.
WHEN I RETURNED TO ACTIVE TEACHING, THE UNIVERSITY PROVIDED A BROWNSTONE ON THE GROUNDS.
SPEAKING OF WHICH, DID THEY TROUBLE YOU ABOUT YOUR--CONDITION?
AT MISKATONIC, I AM CONSIDERED FAIRLY NORMAL.
YOU'RE IN A HANDICAPPED SPOT--ARE YOU DISABLED?
NO, I DON'T CONSIDER MYSELF SO. BUT THE *DMV* DOES, AND SAID I MUST BE DESIGNATED IMPAIRED WHEN I OBTAINED MY LICENSE. I FAIL TO UNDERSTAND THE *DMV*.
A VW BUS?! YOU *ARE* A LEFT-OVER FROM THE SIXTIES.
THE GLOVE COMPARTMENT HOLDS MORE CHOCOLATE BARS THAN THE OTHER VANS.

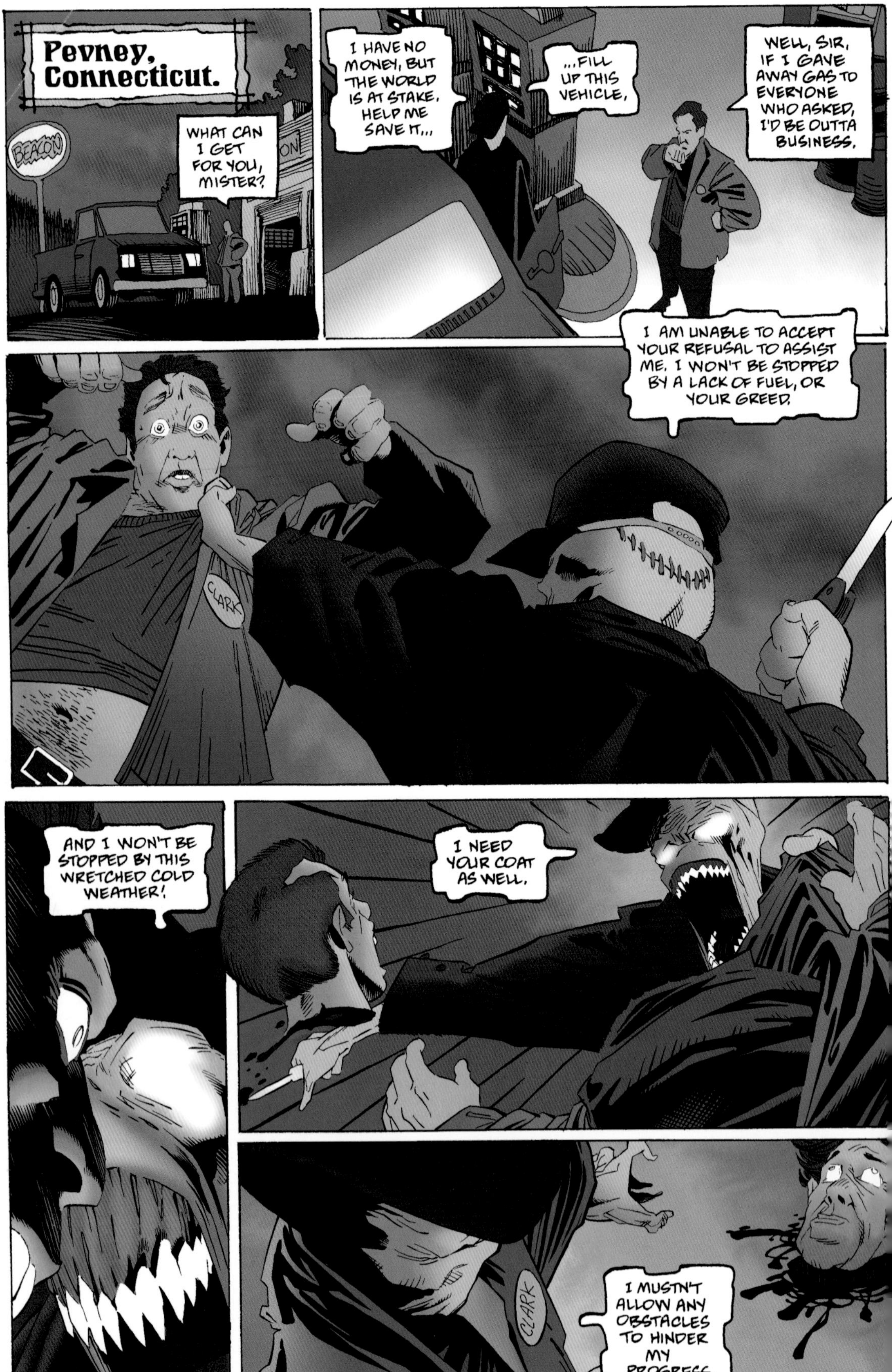
Pevney, Connecticut.
BEACON
WHAT CAN I GET FOR YOU, MISTER?
I HAVE NO MONEY, BUT THE WORLD IS AT STAKE. HELP ME SAVE IT...
...FILL UP THIS VEHICLE.
WELL, SIR, IF I GAVE AWAY GAS TO EVERYONE WHO ASKED, I'D BE OUTTA BUSINESS.
I AM UNABLE TO ACCEPT YOUR REFUSAL TO ASSIST ME. I WON'T BE STOPPED BY A LACK OF FUEL, OR YOUR GREED.
CLARK
AND I WON'T BE STOPPED BY THIS WRETCHED COLD WEATHER!
I NEED YOUR COAT AS WELL.
CLARK
I MUSTN'T ALLOW ANY OBSTACLES TO HINDER MY PROGRESS.

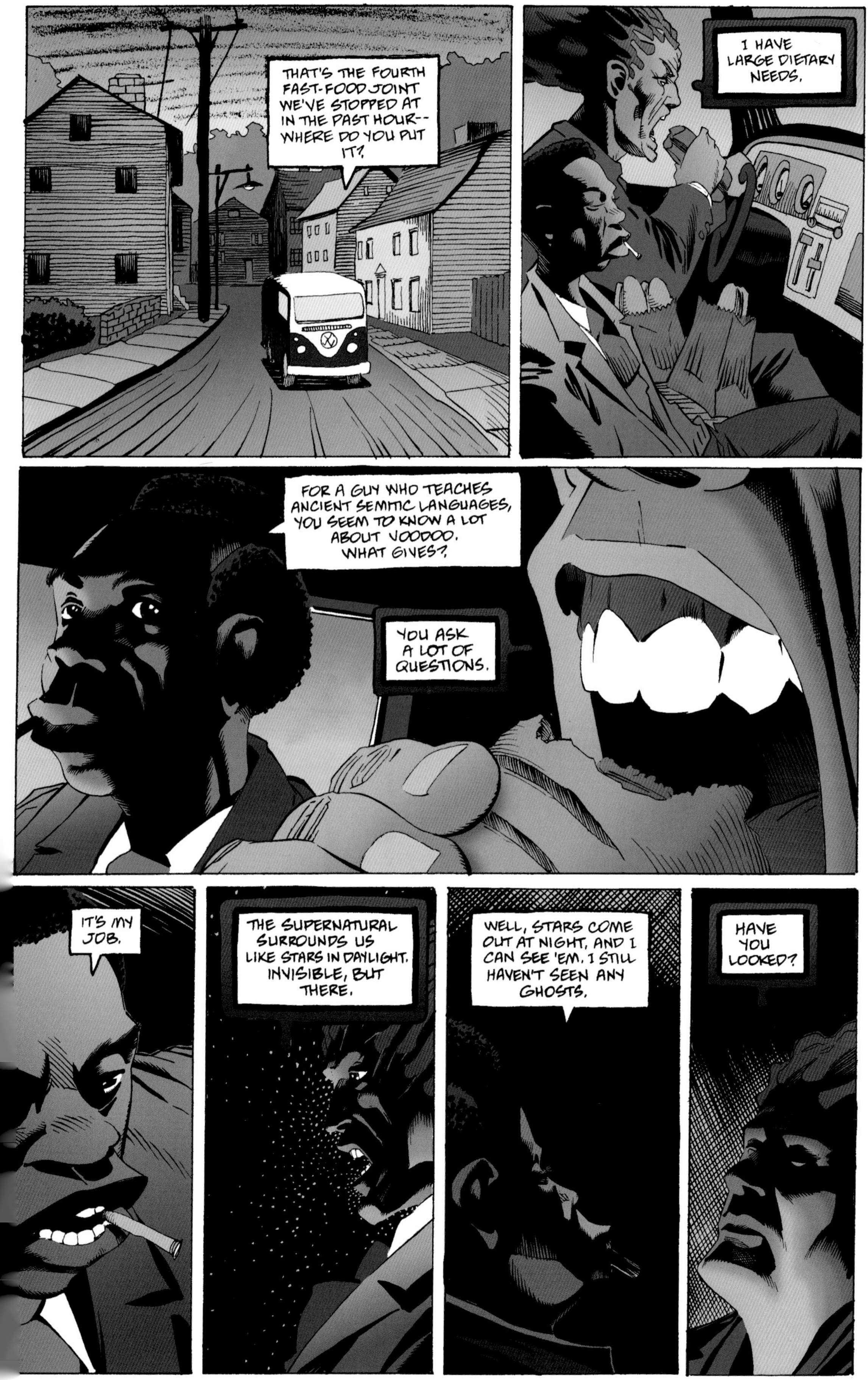
THAT'S THE FOURTH FAST-FOOD JOINT WE'VE STOPPED AT IN THE PAST HOUR-- WHERE DO YOU PUT IT?
I HAVE LARGE DIETARY NEEDS.
FOR A GUY WHO TEACHES ANCIENT SEMITIC LANGUAGES, YOU SEEM TO KNOW A LOT ABOUT VOODOO. WHAT GIVES?
YOU ASK A LOT OF QUESTIONS.
IT'S MY JOB.
THE SUPERNATURAL SURROUNDS US LIKE STARS IN DAYLIGHT. INVISIBLE, BUT THERE.
WELL, STARS COME OUT AT NIGHT, AND I CAN SEE 'EM. I STILL HAVEN'T SEEN ANY GHOSTS.
HAVE YOU LOOKED?

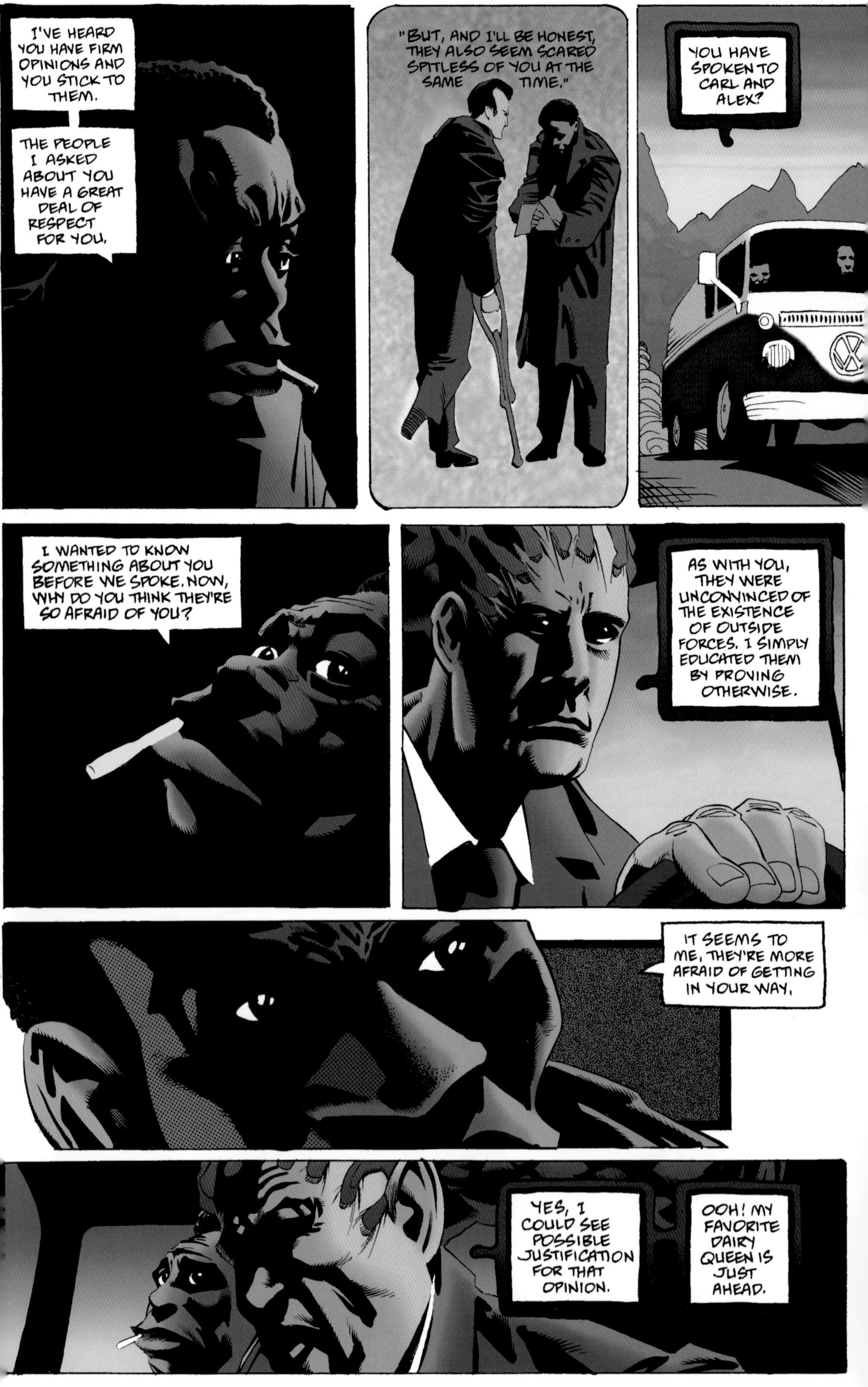

I'VE HEARD YOU HAVE FIRM OPINIONS AND YOU STICK TO THEM.
THE PEOPLE I ASKED ABOUT YOU HAVE A GREAT DEAL OF RESPECT FOR YOU.
"BUT, AND I'LL BE HONEST, THEY ALSO SEEM SCARED SPITLESS OF YOU AT THE SAME TIME."
YOU HAVE SPOKEN TO CARL AND ALEX?
I WANTED TO KNOW SOMETHING ABOUT YOU BEFORE WE SPOKE. NOW, WHY DO YOU THINK THEY'RE SO AFRAID OF YOU?
AS WITH YOU, THEY WERE UNCONVINCED OF THE EXISTENCE OF OUTSIDE FORCES. I SIMPLY EDUCATED THEM BY PROVING OTHERWISE.
IT SEEMS TO ME, THEY'RE MORE AFRAID OF GETTING IN YOUR WAY.
YES, I COULD SEE POSSIBLE JUSTIFICATION FOR THAT OPINION.
OOH! MY FAVORITE DAIRY QUEEN IS JUST AHEAD.

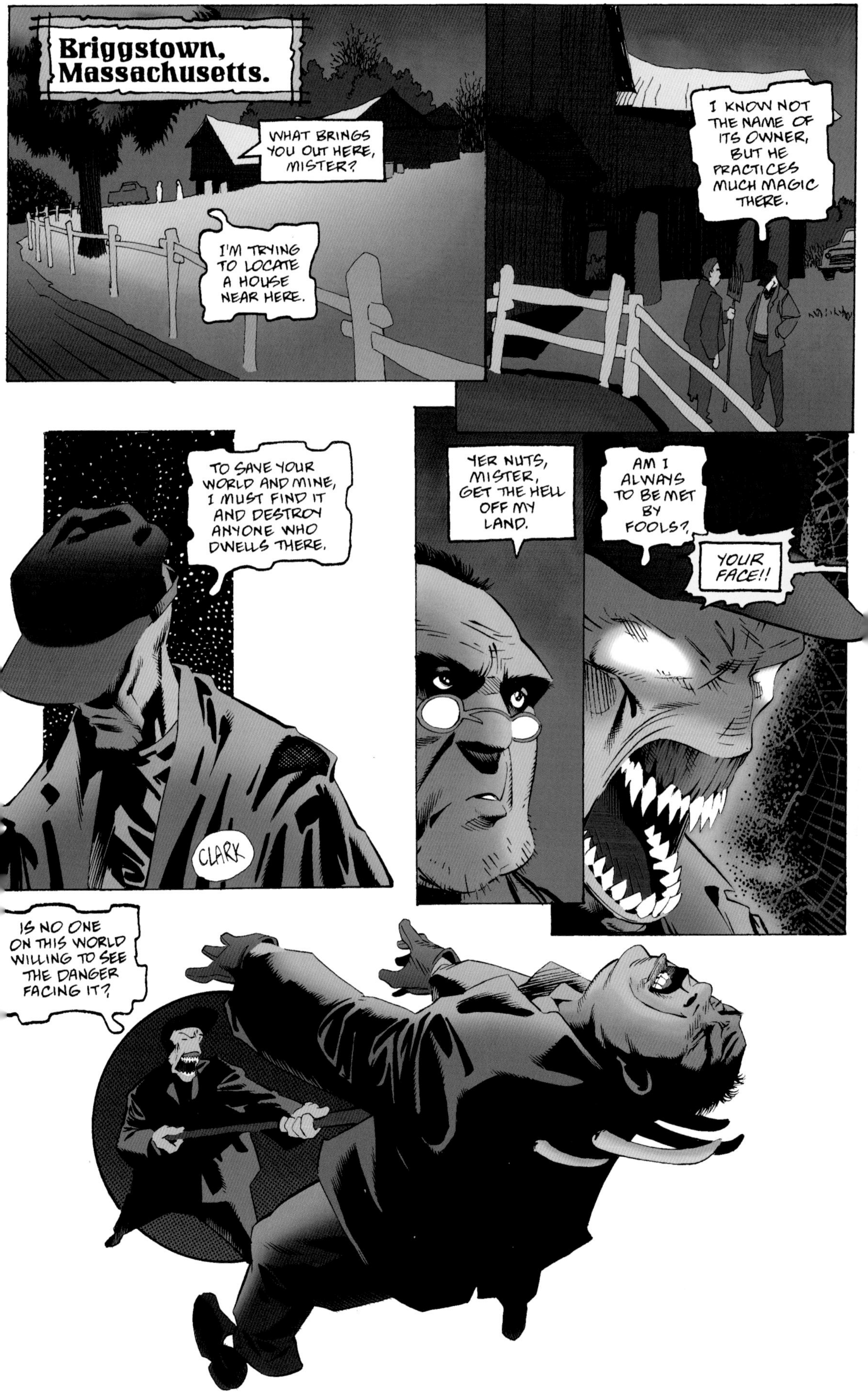
Briggstown, Massachusetts.
WHAT BRINGS YOU OUT HERE, MISTER?
I'M TRYING TO LOCATE A HOUSE NEAR HERE.
I KNOW NOT THE NAME OF ITS OWNER, BUT HE PRACTICES MUCH MAGIC THERE.
TO SAVE YOUR WORLD AND MINE, I MUST FIND IT AND DESTROY ANYONE WHO DWELLS THERE.
CLARK
YER NUTS, MISTER, GET THE HELL OFF MY LAND.
AM I ALWAYS TO BE MET BY FOOLS?
YOUR FACE!!
IS NO ONE ON THIS WORLD WILLING TO SEE THE DANGER FACING IT?

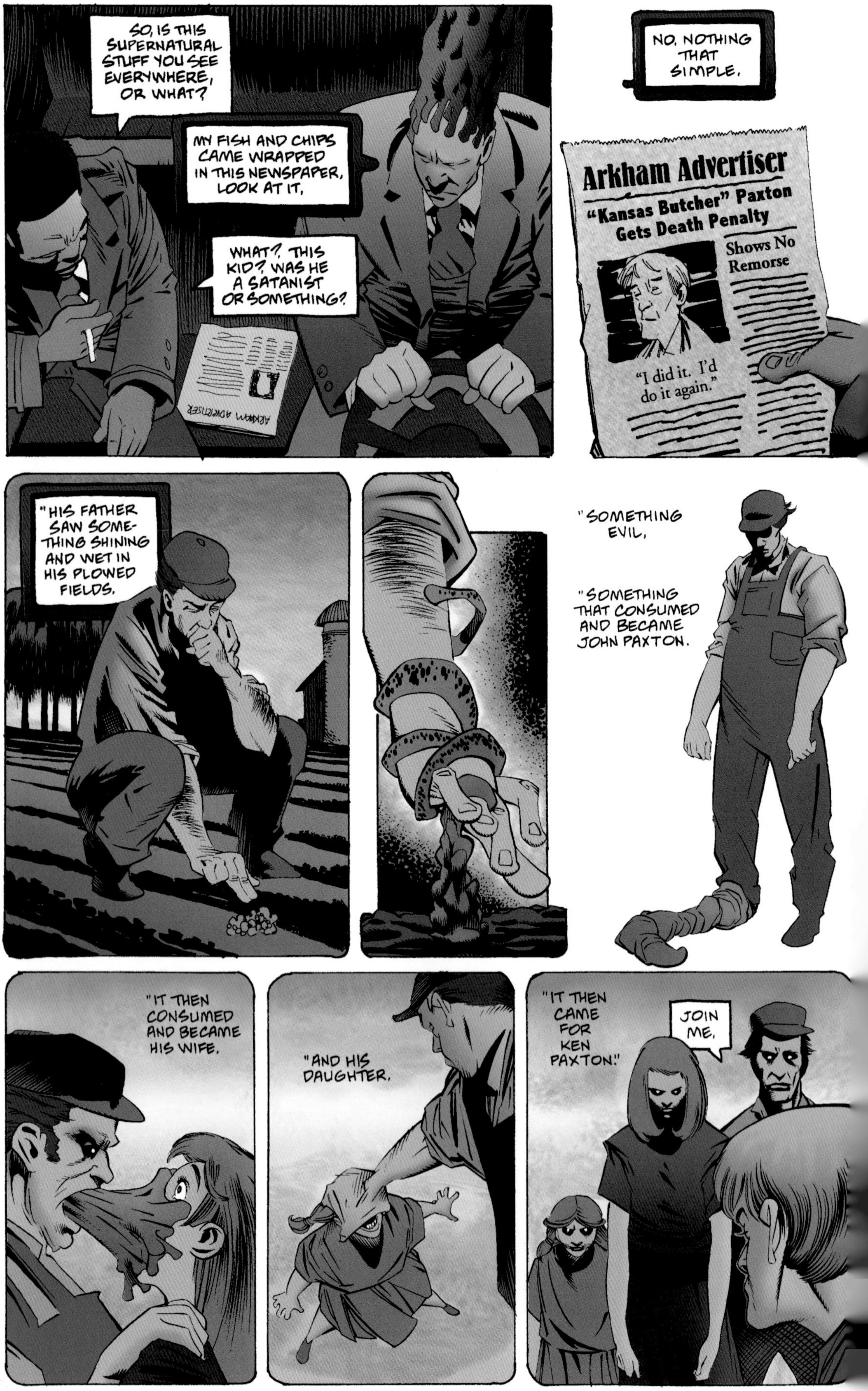
SO, IS THIS SUPERNATURAL STUFF YOU SEE EVERYWHERE, OR WHAT?
MY FISH AND CHIPS CAME WRAPPED IN THIS NEWSPAPER, LOOK AT IT.
WHAT? THIS KID? WAS HE A SATANIST OR SOMETHING?
ARKHAM ADVERTISER
NO, NOTHING THAT SIMPLE.
Arkham Advertiser
"Kansas Butcher" Paxton Gets Death Penalty
Shows No Remorse
"I did it. I'd do it again."
"HIS FATHER SAW SOMETHING SHINING AND WET IN HIS PLOWED FIELDS.
"SOMETHING EVIL.
"SOMETHING THAT CONSUMED AND BECAME JOHN PAXTON.
"IT THEN CONSUMED AND BECAME HIS WIFE.
"AND HIS DAUGHTER.
"IT THEN CAME FOR KEN PAXTON."
JOIN ME.

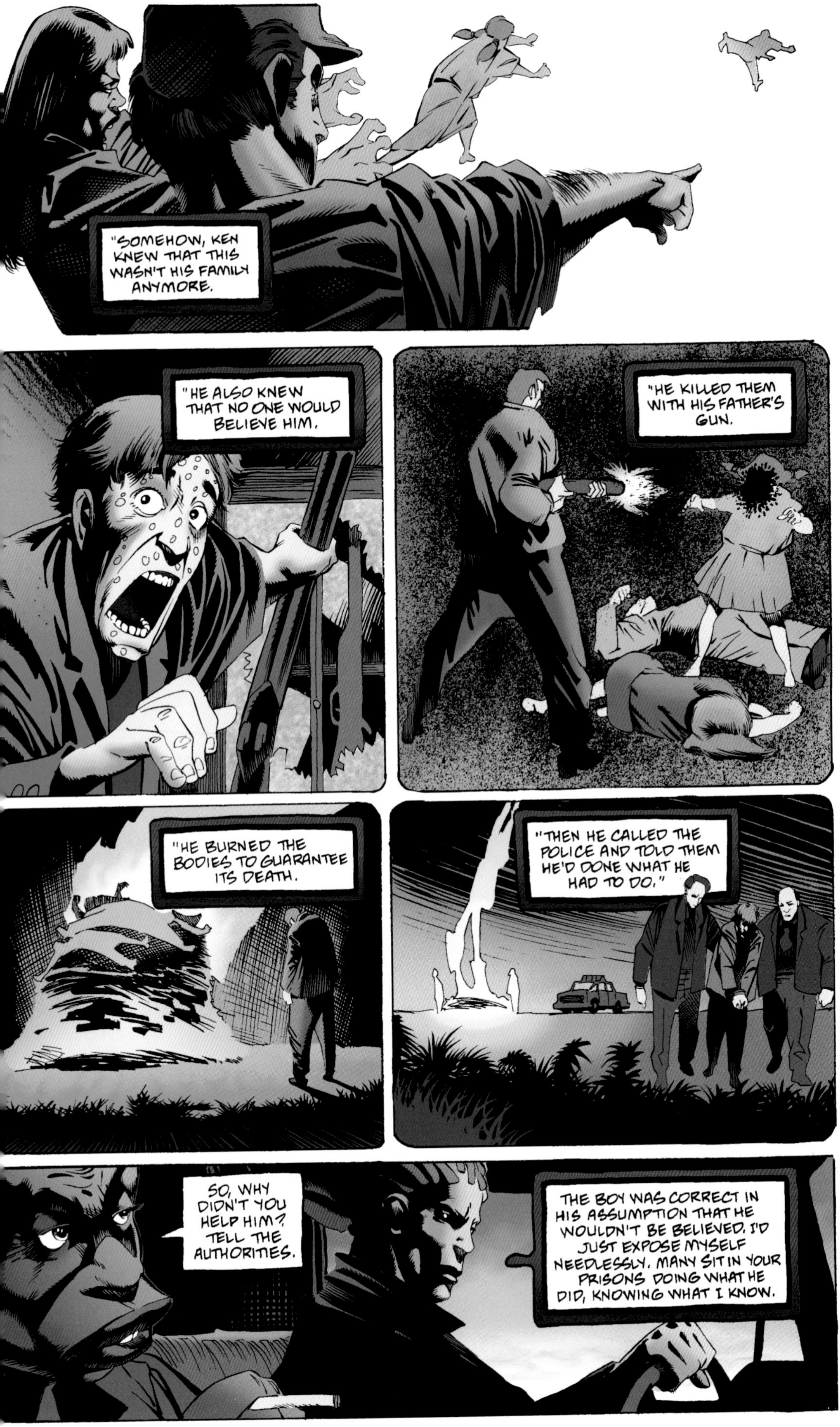
"SOMEHOW, KEN KNEW THAT THIS WASN'T HIS FAMILY ANYMORE.
"HE ALSO KNEW THAT NO ONE WOULD BELIEVE HIM.
"HE KILLED THEM WITH HIS FATHER'S GUN.
"HE BURNED THE BODIES TO GUARANTEE ITS DEATH.
"THEN HE CALLED THE POLICE AND TOLD THEM HE'D DONE WHAT HE HAD TO DO."
SO, WHY DIDN'T YOU HELP HIM? TELL THE AUTHORITIES.
THE BOY WAS CORRECT IN HIS ASSUMPTION THAT HE WOULDN'T BE BELIEVED. I'D JUST EXPOSE MYSELF NEEDLESSLY. MANY SIT IN YOUR PRISONS DOING WHAT HE DID, KNOWING WHAT I KNOW.

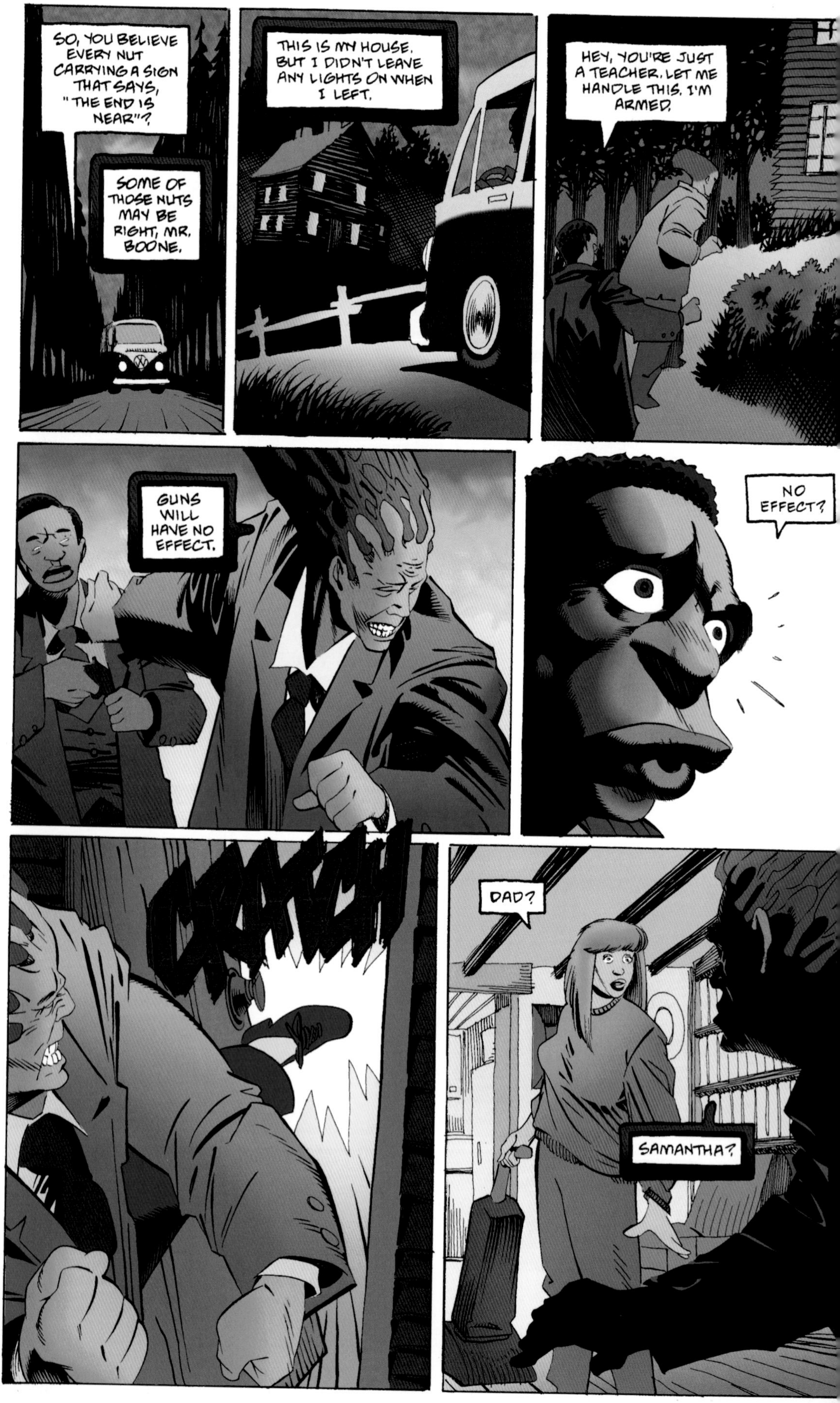
SO, YOU BELIEVE EVERY NUT CARRYING A SIGN THAT SAYS, "THE END IS NEAR"?
SOME OF THOSE NUTS MAY BE RIGHT, MR. BOONE.
THIS IS MY HOUSE, BUT I DIDN'T LEAVE ANY LIGHTS ON WHEN I LEFT.
HEY, YOU'RE JUST A TEACHER. LET ME HANDLE THIS. I'M ARMED.
GUNS WILL HAVE NO EFFECT.
NO EFFECT?
CRAAACH!
DAD?
SAMANTHA?

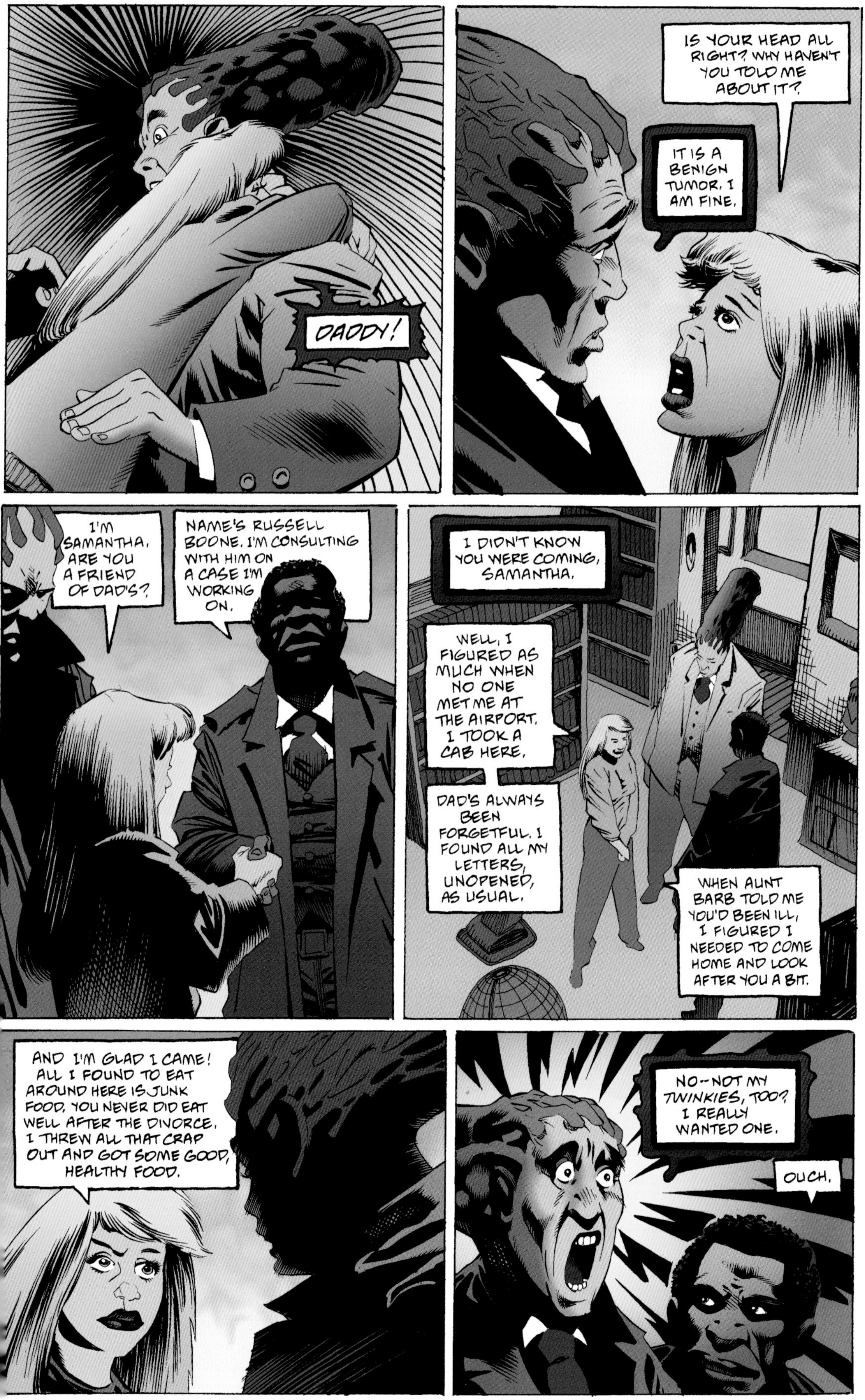
DADDY!
IS YOUR HEAD ALL RIGHT? WHY HAVEN'T YOU TOLD ME ABOUT IT?
IT IS A BENIGN TUMOR. I AM FINE.
I'M SAMANTHA. ARE YOU A FRIEND OF DAD'S?
NAME'S RUSSELL BOONE. I'M CONSULTING WITH HIM ON A CASE I'M WORKING ON.
I DIDN'T KNOW YOU WERE COMING, SAMANTHA.
WELL, I FIGURED AS MUCH WHEN NO ONE MET ME AT THE AIRPORT. I TOOK A CAB HERE.
DAD'S ALWAYS BEEN FORGETFUL. I FOUND ALL MY LETTERS, UNOPENED, AS USUAL.
WHEN AUNT BARB TOLD ME YOU'D BEEN ILL, I FIGURED I NEEDED TO COME HOME AND LOOK AFTER YOU A BIT.
AND I'M GLAD I CAME! ALL I FOUND TO EAT AROUND HERE IS JUNK FOOD. YOU NEVER DID EAT WELL AFTER THE DIVORCE. I THREW ALL THAT CRAP OUT AND GOT SOME GOOD, HEALTHY FOOD.
NO--NOT MY TWINKIES, TOO? I REALLY WANTED ONE.
OUCH.

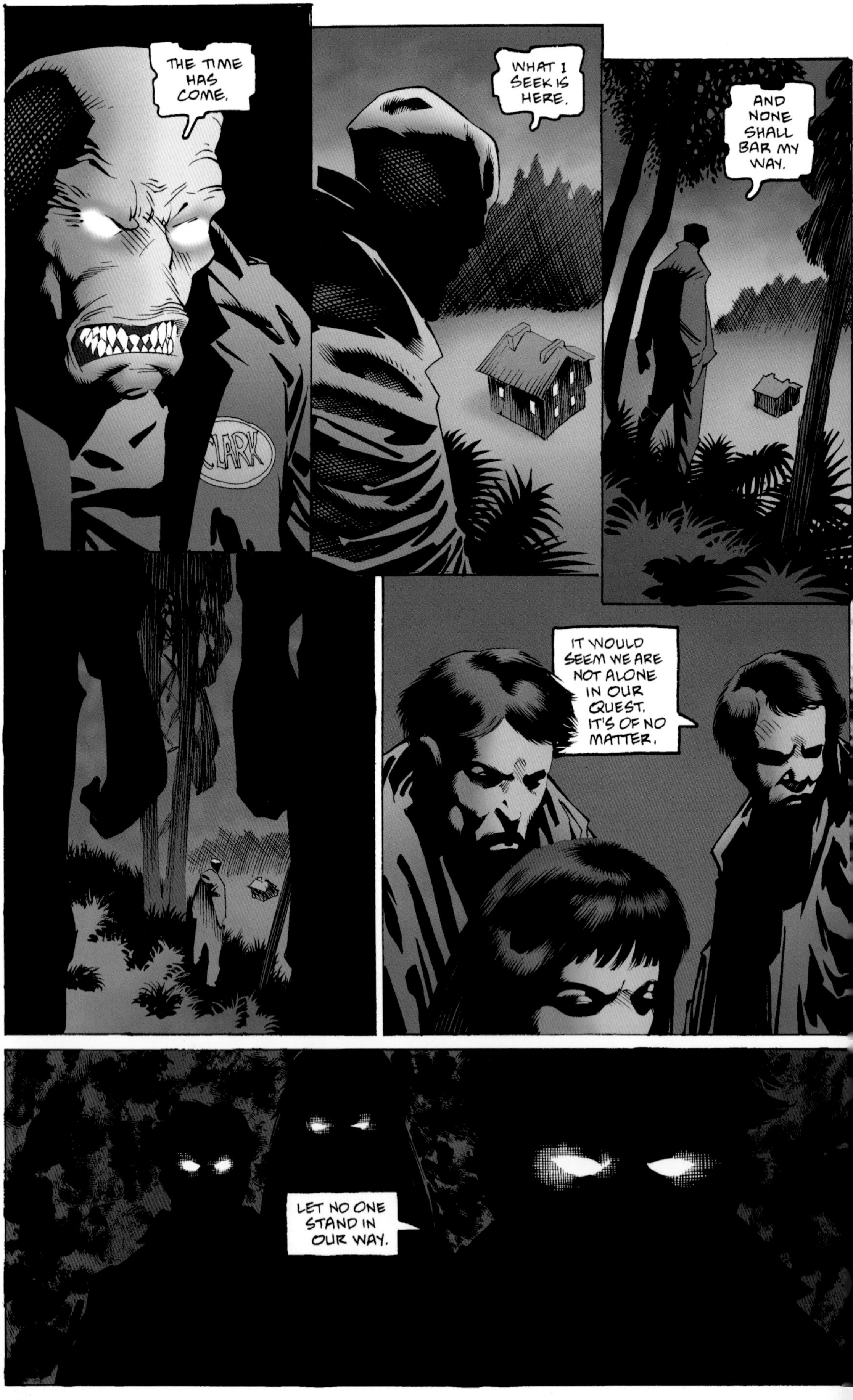

THE TIME HAS COME.
CLARK
WHAT I SEEK IS HERE.
AND NONE SHALL BAR MY WAY.
IT WOULD SEEM WE ARE NOT ALONE IN OUR QUEST. IT'S OF NO MATTER.
LET NO ONE STAND IN OUR WAY.

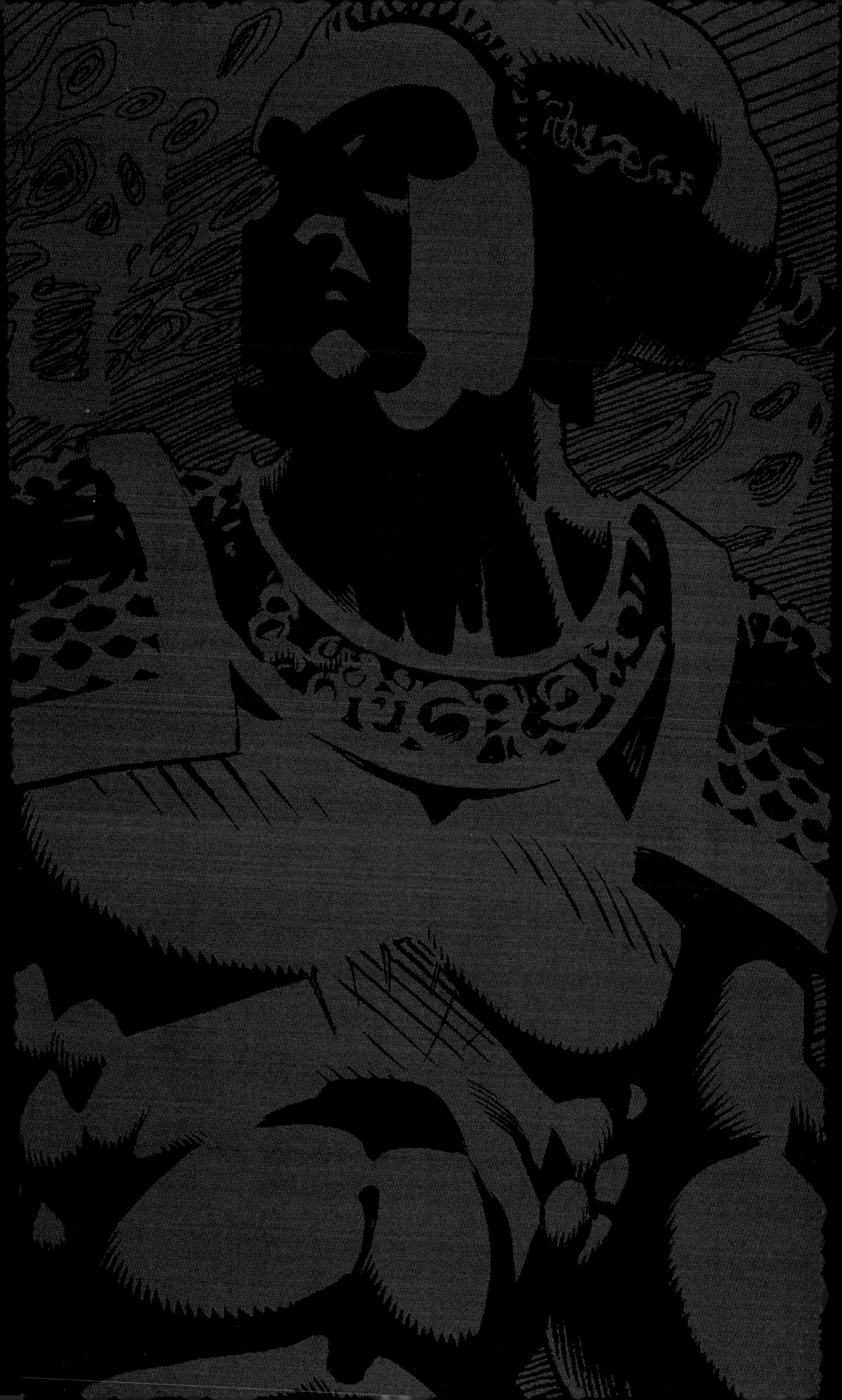

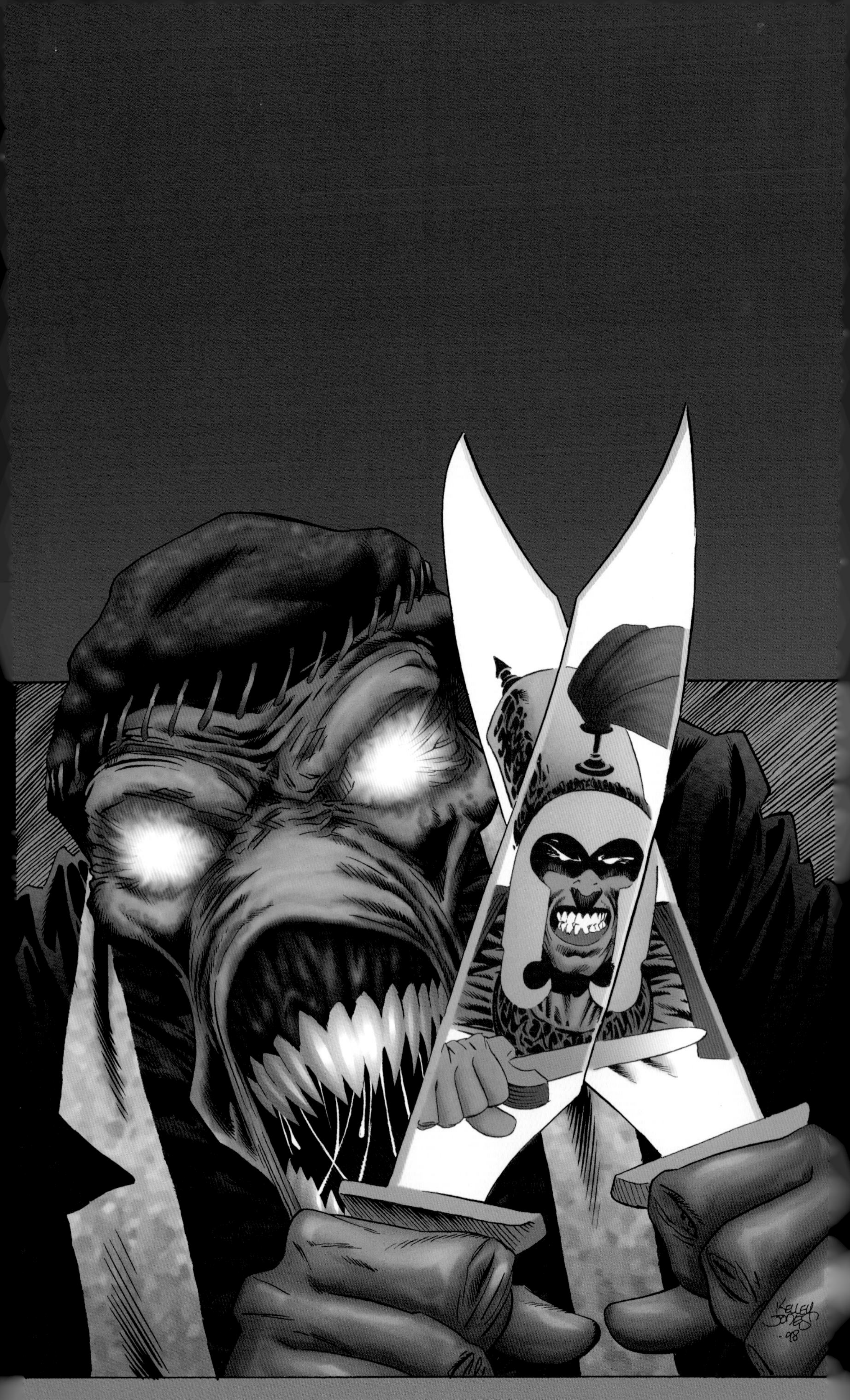
KELLEY JONES -98

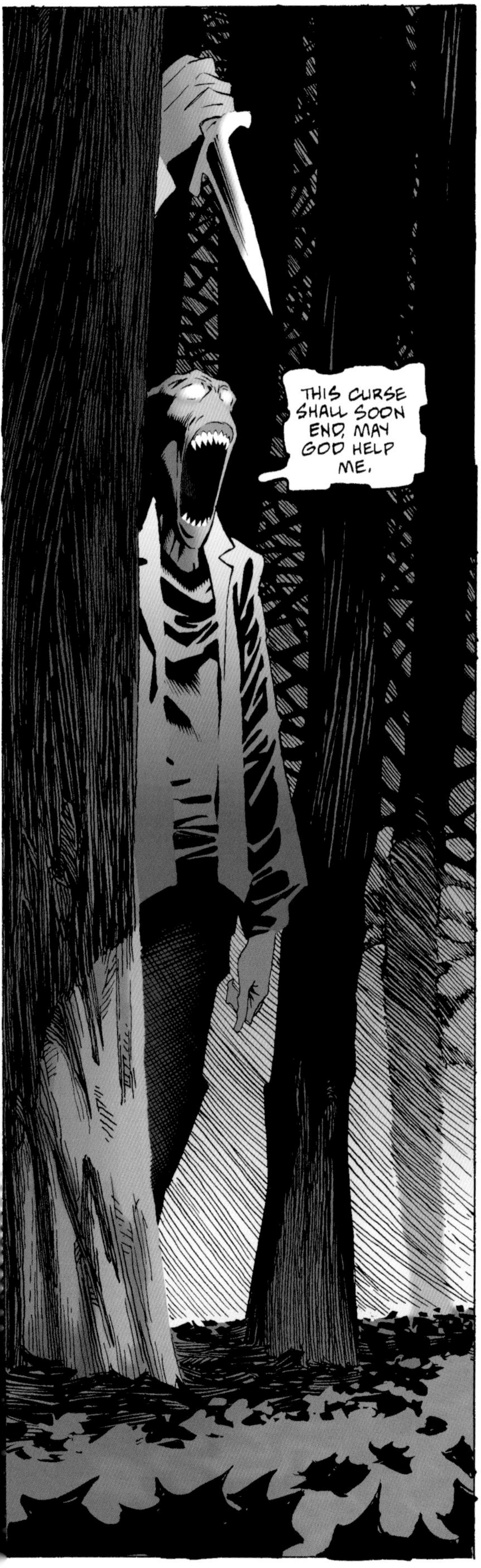
THIS CURSE SHALL SOON END, MAY GOD HELP ME.

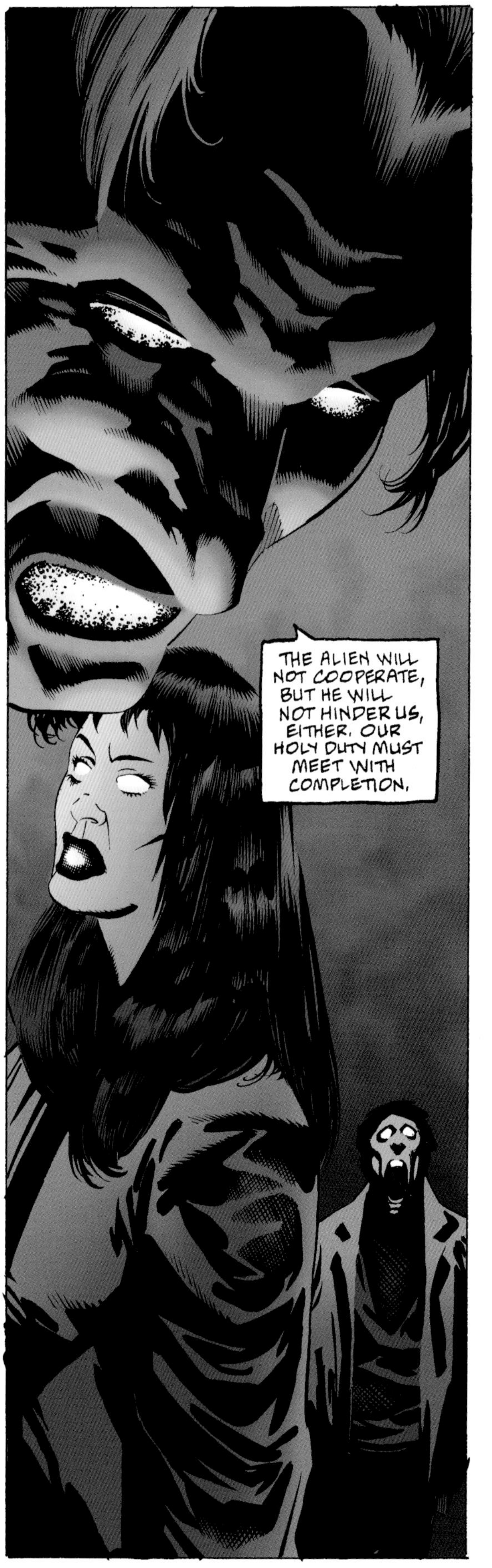
THE ALIEN WILL NOT COOPERATE, BUT HE WILL NOT HINDER US, EITHER. OUR HOLY DUTY MUST MEET WITH COMPLETION.

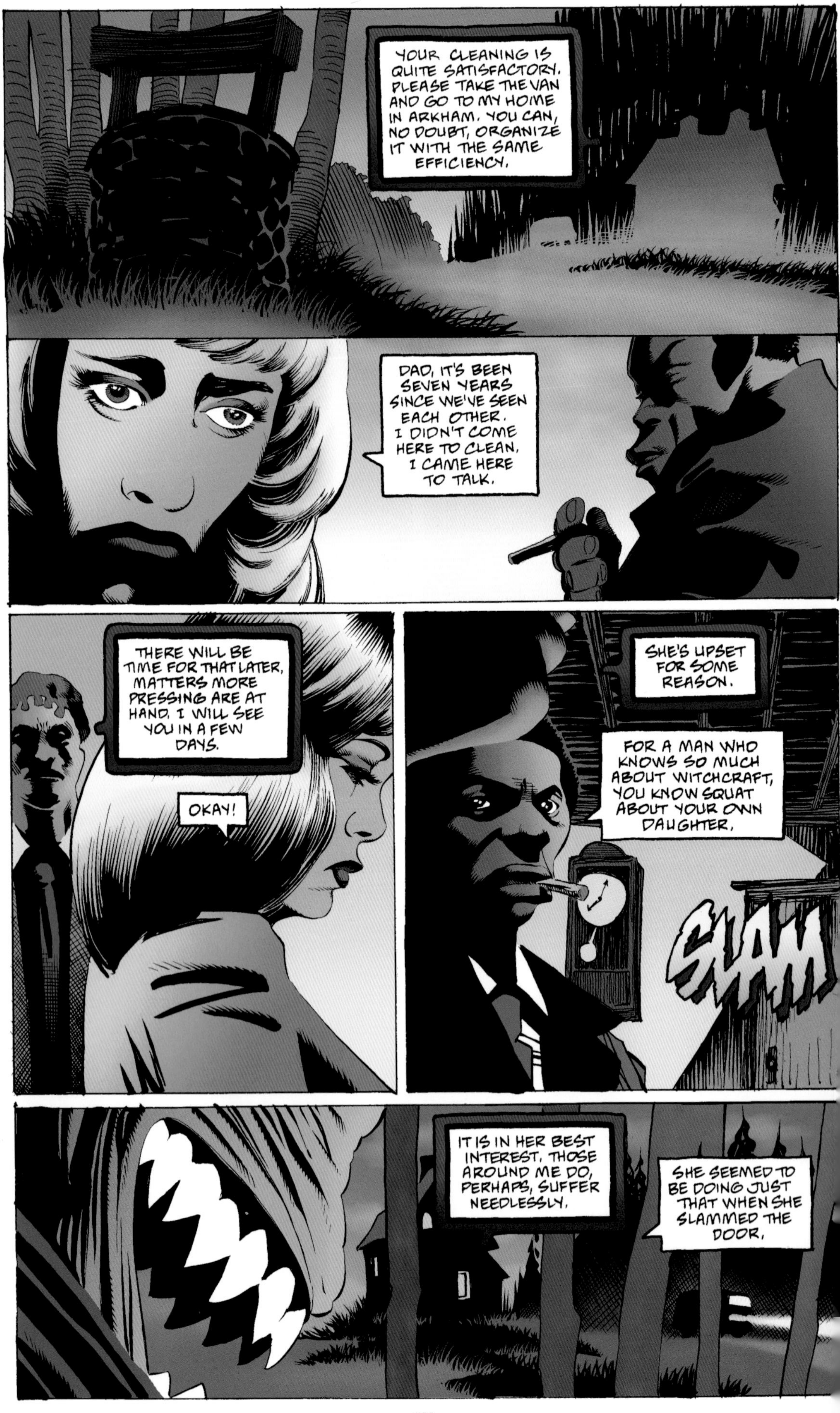
YOUR CLEANING IS QUITE SATISFACTORY. PLEASE TAKE THE VAN AND GO TO MY HOME IN ARKHAM. YOU CAN, NO DOUBT, ORGANIZE IT WITH THE SAME EFFICIENCY.
DAD, IT'S BEEN SEVEN YEARS SINCE WE'VE SEEN EACH OTHER. I DIDN'T COME HERE TO CLEAN, I CAME HERE TO TALK.
THERE WILL BE TIME FOR THAT LATER, MATTERS MORE PRESSING ARE AT HAND. I WILL SEE YOU IN A FEW DAYS.
OKAY!
SHE'S UPSET FOR SOME REASON.
FOR A MAN WHO KNOWS SO MUCH ABOUT WITCHCRAFT, YOU KNOW SQUAT ABOUT YOUR OWN DAUGHTER.
SLAM
IT IS IN HER BEST INTEREST. THOSE AROUND ME DO, PERHAPS, SUFFER NEEDLESSLY.
SHE SEEMED TO BE DOING JUST THAT WHEN SHE SLAMMED THE DOOR.

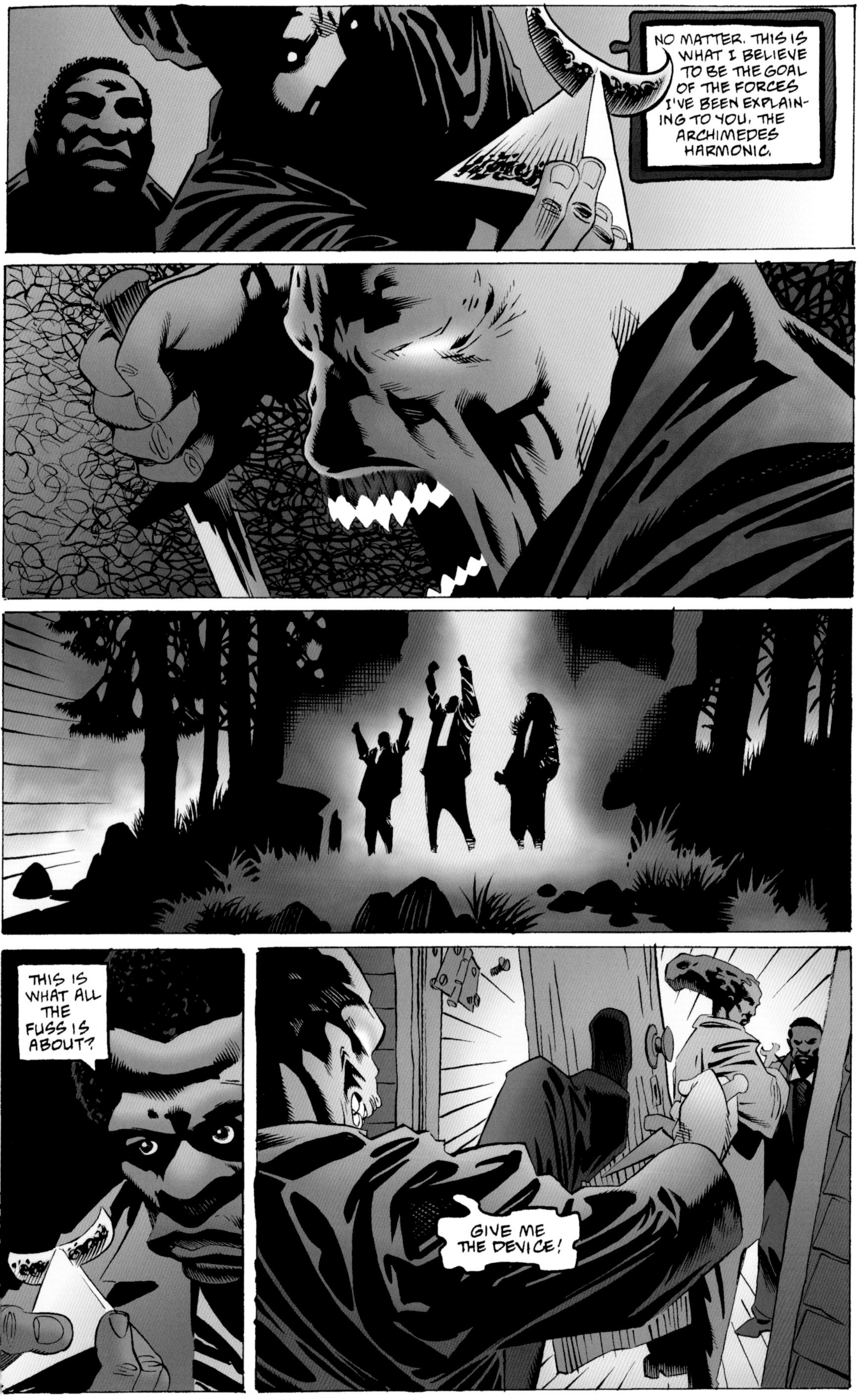
NO MATTER. THIS IS WHAT I BELIEVE TO BE THE GOAL OF THE FORCES I'VE BEEN EXPLAINING TO YOU. THE ARCHIMEDES HARMONIC.
THIS IS WHAT ALL THE FUSS IS ABOUT?
GIVE ME THE DEVICE!

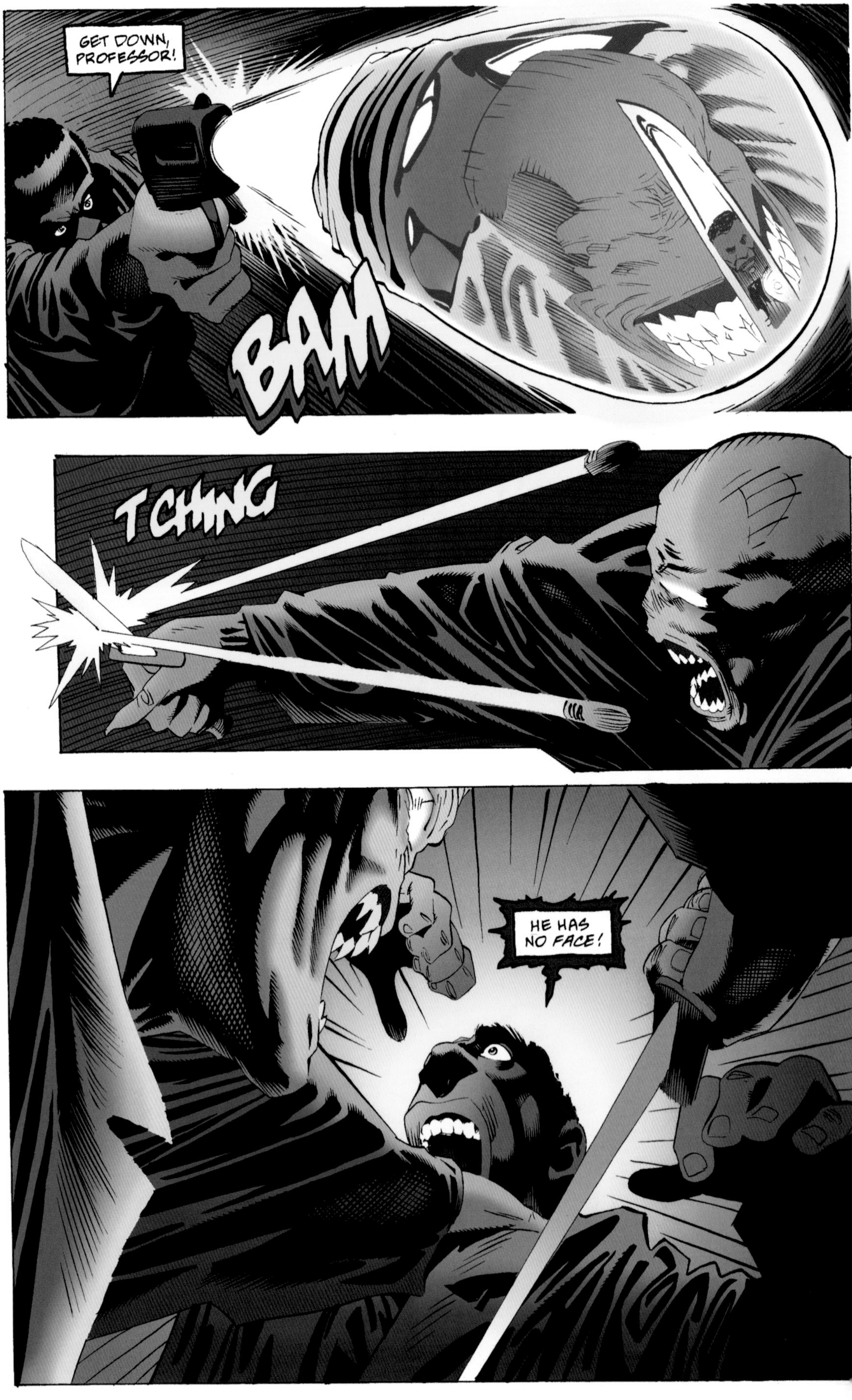
GET DOWN, PROFESSOR!
BAM
T CHING
HE HAS NO FACE!

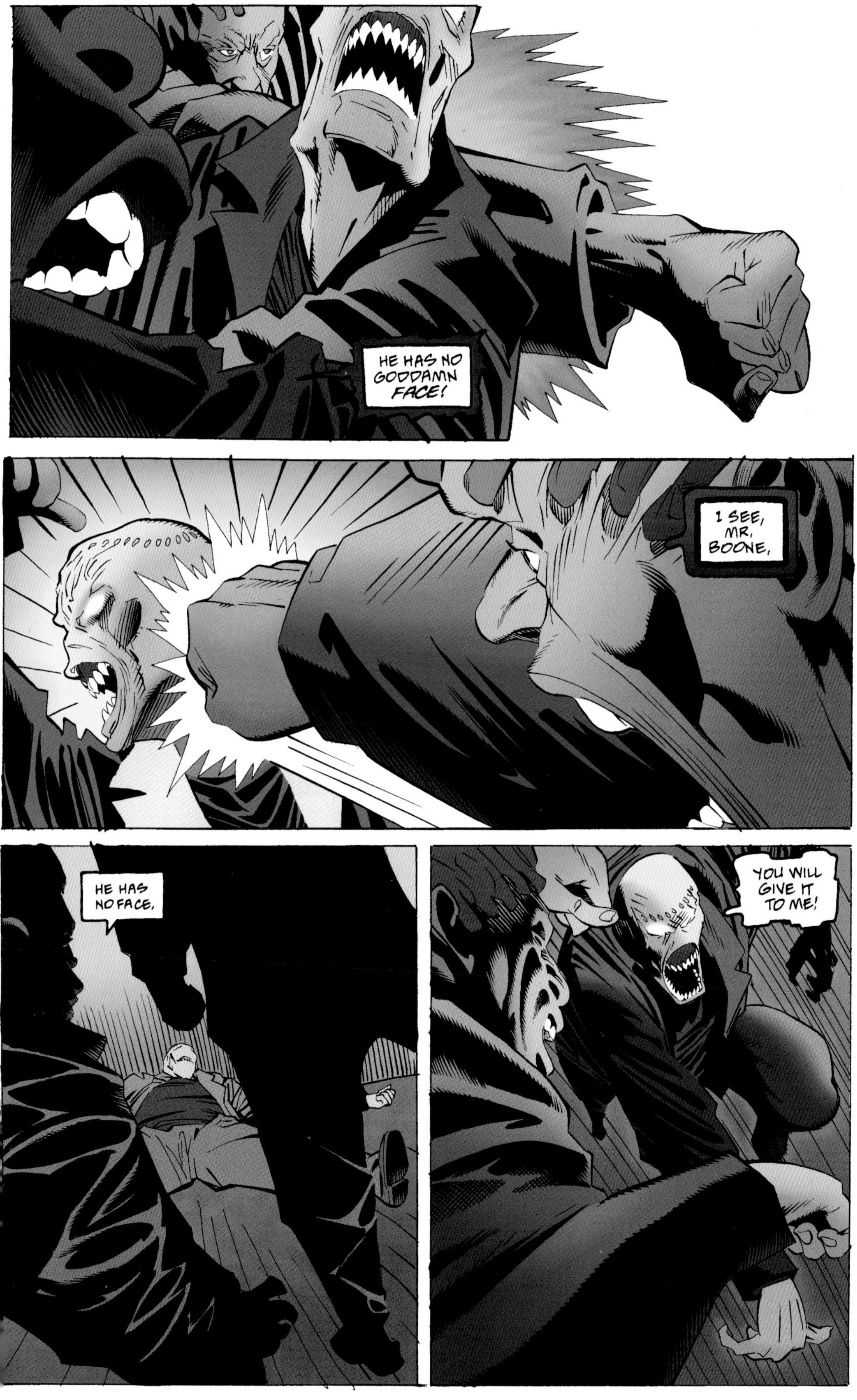
HE HAS NO GODDAMN *FACE!*
I SEE, MR. BOONE.
HE HAS NO FACE.
YOU WILL GIVE IT TO ME!

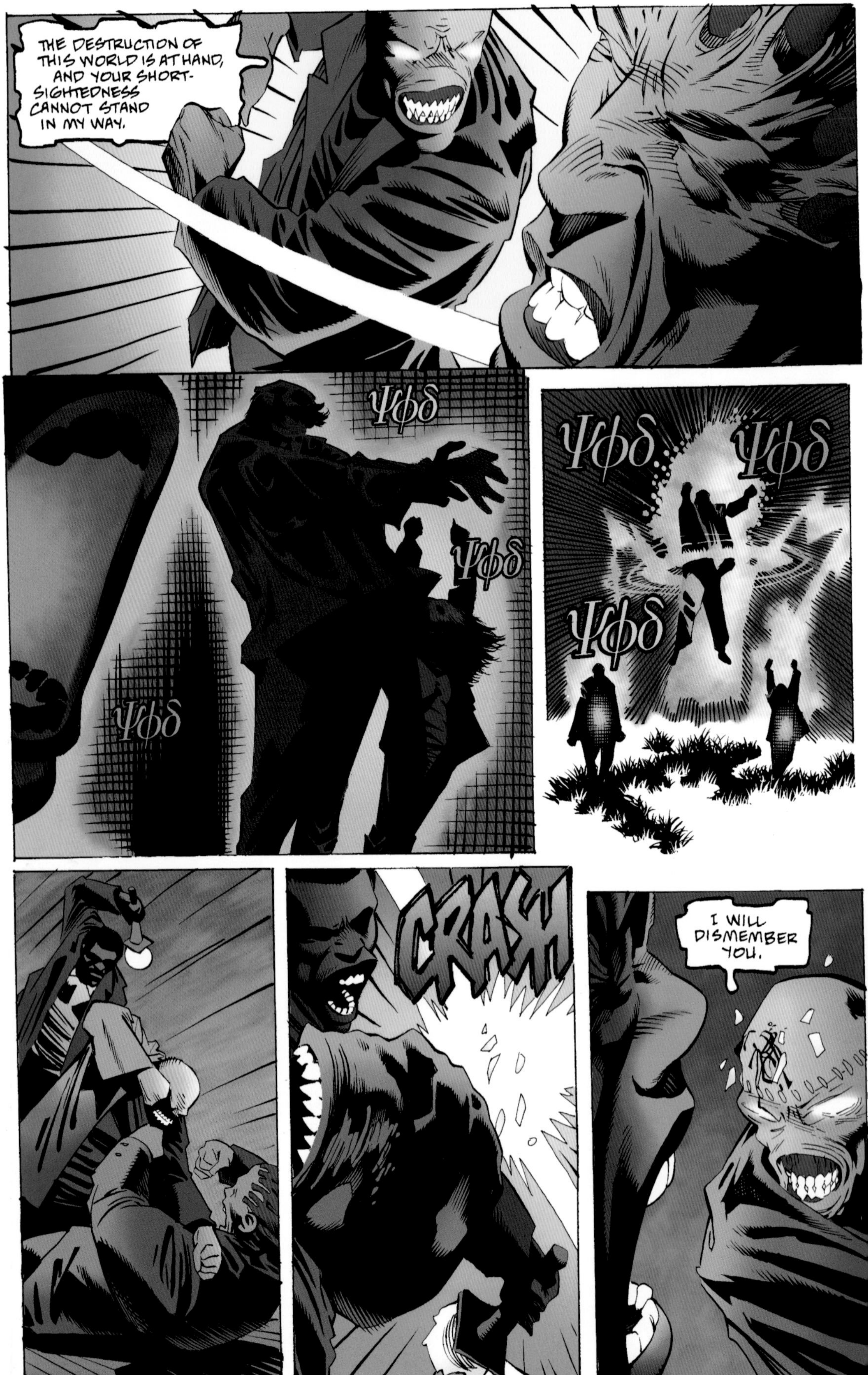
THE DESTRUCTION OF THIS WORLD IS AT HAND, AND YOUR SHORT-SIGHTEDNESS CANNOT STAND IN MY WAY.
Ψφδ
Ψφδ
Ψφδ
Ψφδ
Ψφδ
Ψφδ
CRASH
I WILL DISMEMBER YOU.

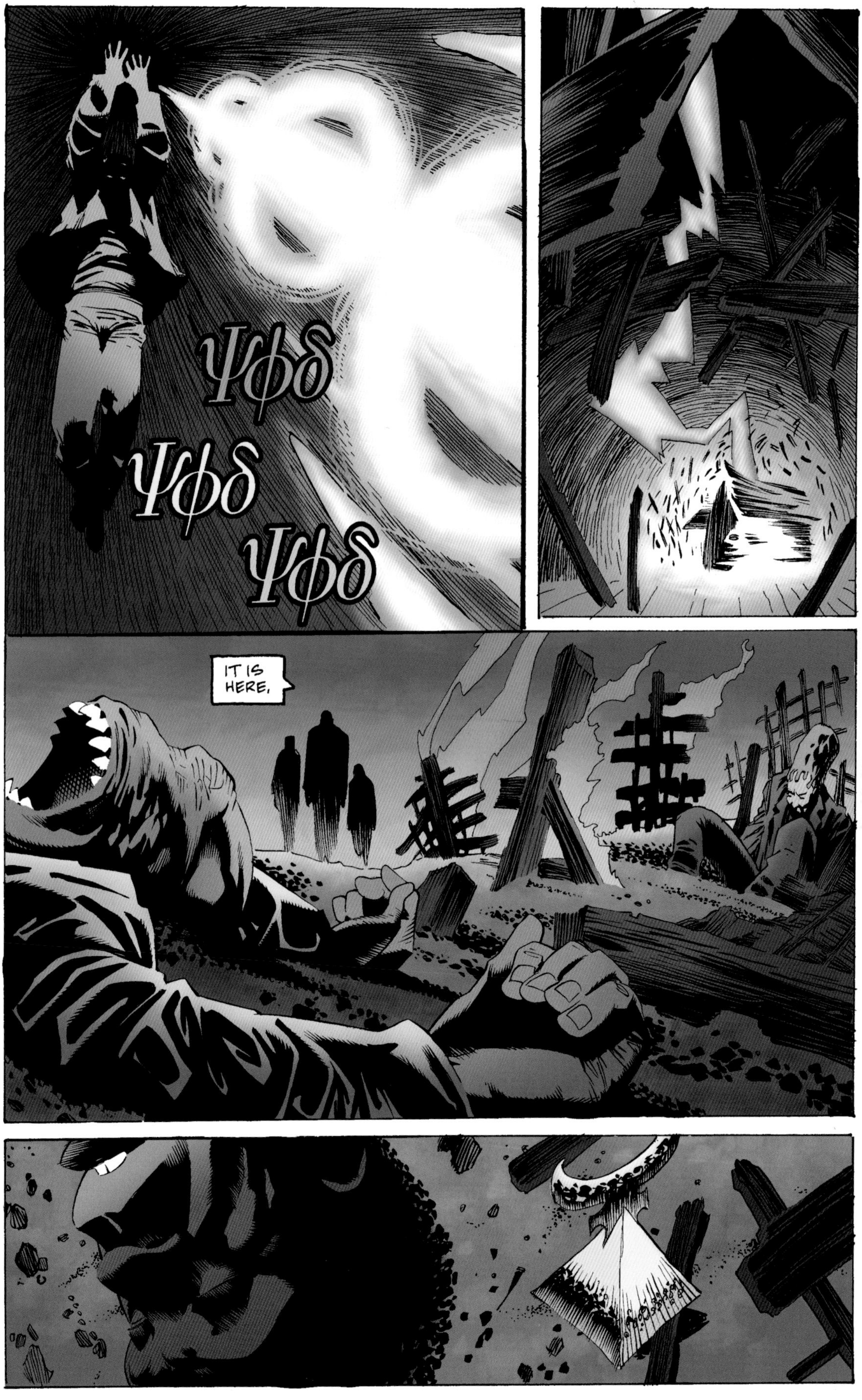
Ψφδ
Ψφδ
Ψφδ
IT IS HERE.

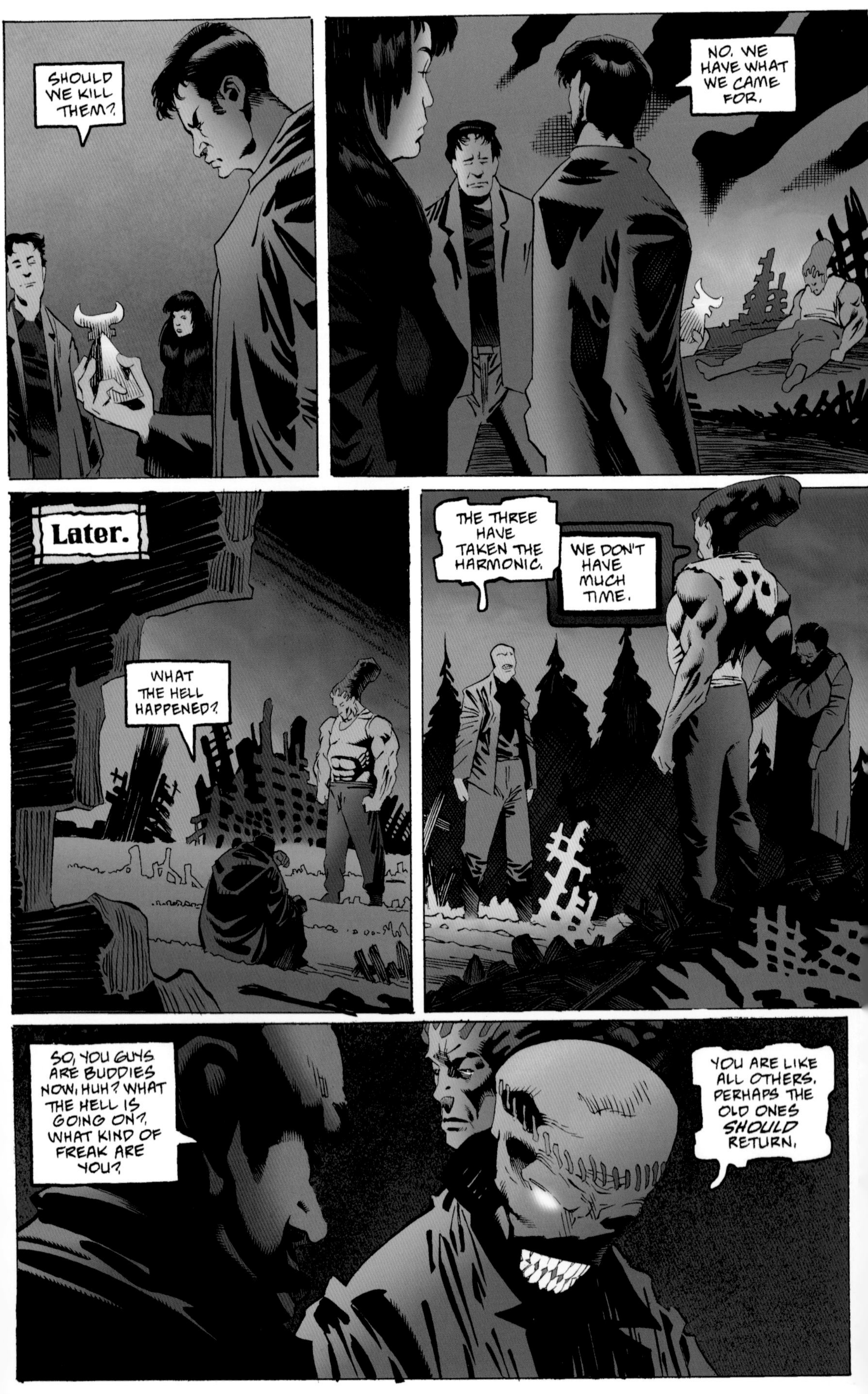

SHOULD WE KILL THEM?
NO. WE HAVE WHAT WE CAME FOR.
Later.
WHAT THE HELL HAPPENED?
THE THREE HAVE TAKEN THE HARMONIC.
WE DON'T HAVE MUCH TIME.
SO, YOU GUYS ARE BUDDIES NOW, HUH? WHAT THE HELL IS GOING ON? WHAT KIND OF FREAK ARE YOU?
YOU ARE LIKE ALL OTHERS. PERHAPS THE OLD ONES *SHOULD* RETURN.

THIS SEEMS TO BE A PLACE WITHOUT VIRTUE. NO WONDER EVIL FLOURISHES HERE.

CLARK

THE PEOPLE ARE SELF-ABSORBED. IT IS AN IMPEDIMENT WHEN BATTLING DARK FORCES.

WE MUST FIND A VEHICLE.

I'M COMIN', TOO. I GOT TO SEE IF THIS BULL IS FOR REAL.

THEN LET US MAKE HASTE.

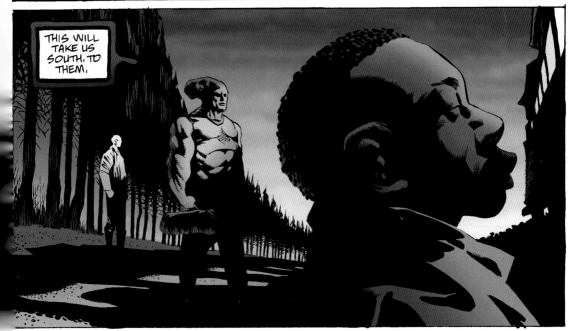

THIS WILL TAKE US SOUTH, TO THEM.

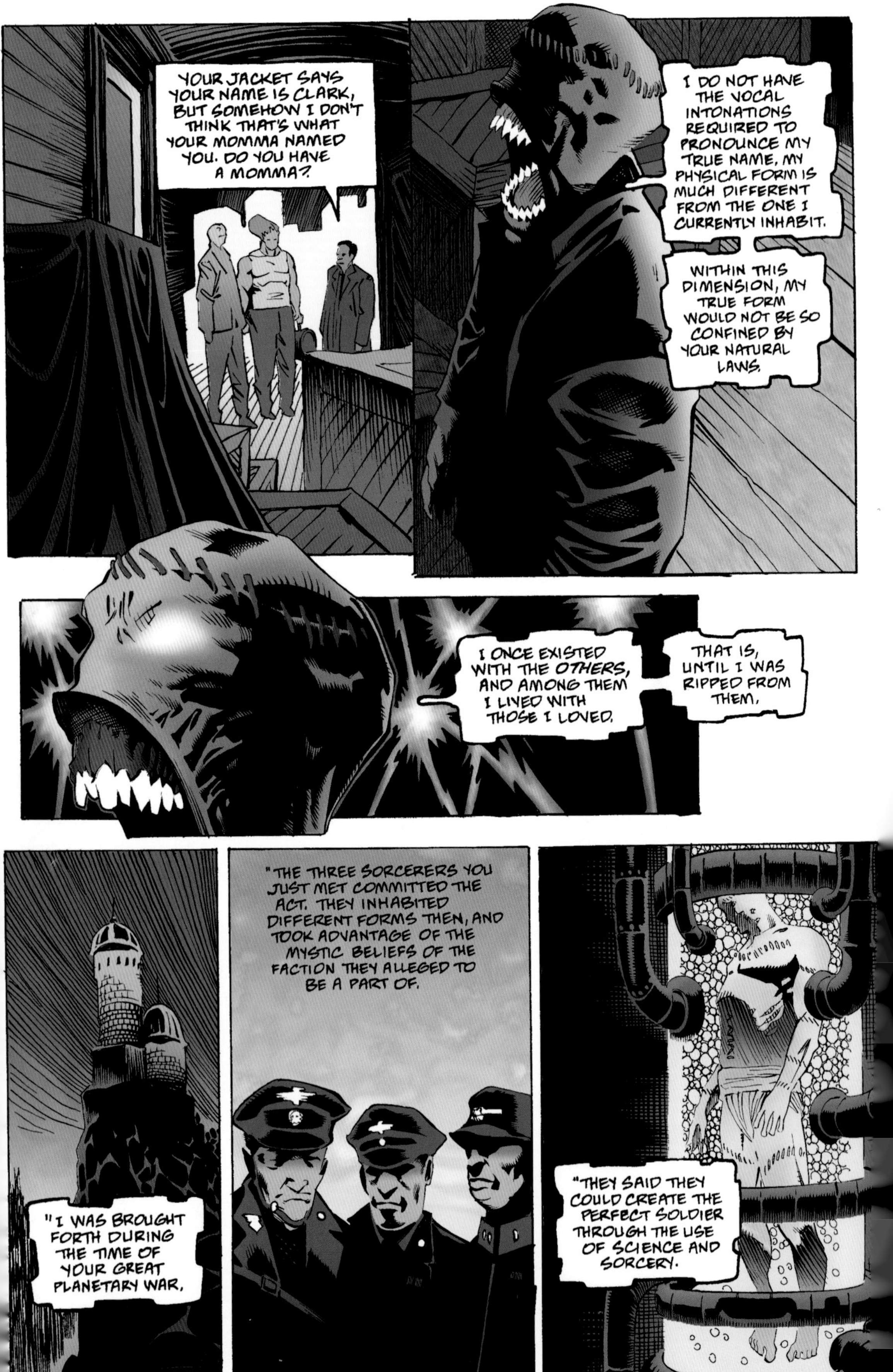
YOUR JACKET SAYS YOUR NAME IS CLARK, BUT SOMEHOW I DON'T THINK THAT'S WHAT YOUR MOMMA NAMED YOU. DO YOU HAVE A MOMMA?
I DO NOT HAVE THE VOCAL INTONATIONS REQUIRED TO PRONOUNCE MY TRUE NAME. MY PHYSICAL FORM IS MUCH DIFFERENT FROM THE ONE I CURRENTLY INHABIT.
WITHIN THIS DIMENSION, MY TRUE FORM WOULD NOT BE SO CONFINED BY YOUR NATURAL LAWS.
I ONCE EXISTED WITH THE *OTHERS*, AND AMONG THEM I LIVED WITH THOSE I LOVED.
THAT IS, UNTIL I WAS RIPPED FROM THEM.
"I WAS BROUGHT FORTH DURING THE TIME OF YOUR GREAT PLANETARY WAR.
"THE THREE SORCERERS YOU JUST MET COMMITTED THE ACT. THEY INHABITED DIFFERENT FORMS THEN, AND TOOK ADVANTAGE OF THE MYSTIC BELIEFS OF THE FACTION THEY ALLEGED TO BE A PART OF.
"THEY SAID THEY COULD CREATE THE PERFECT SOLDIER THROUGH THE USE OF SCIENCE AND SORCERY.

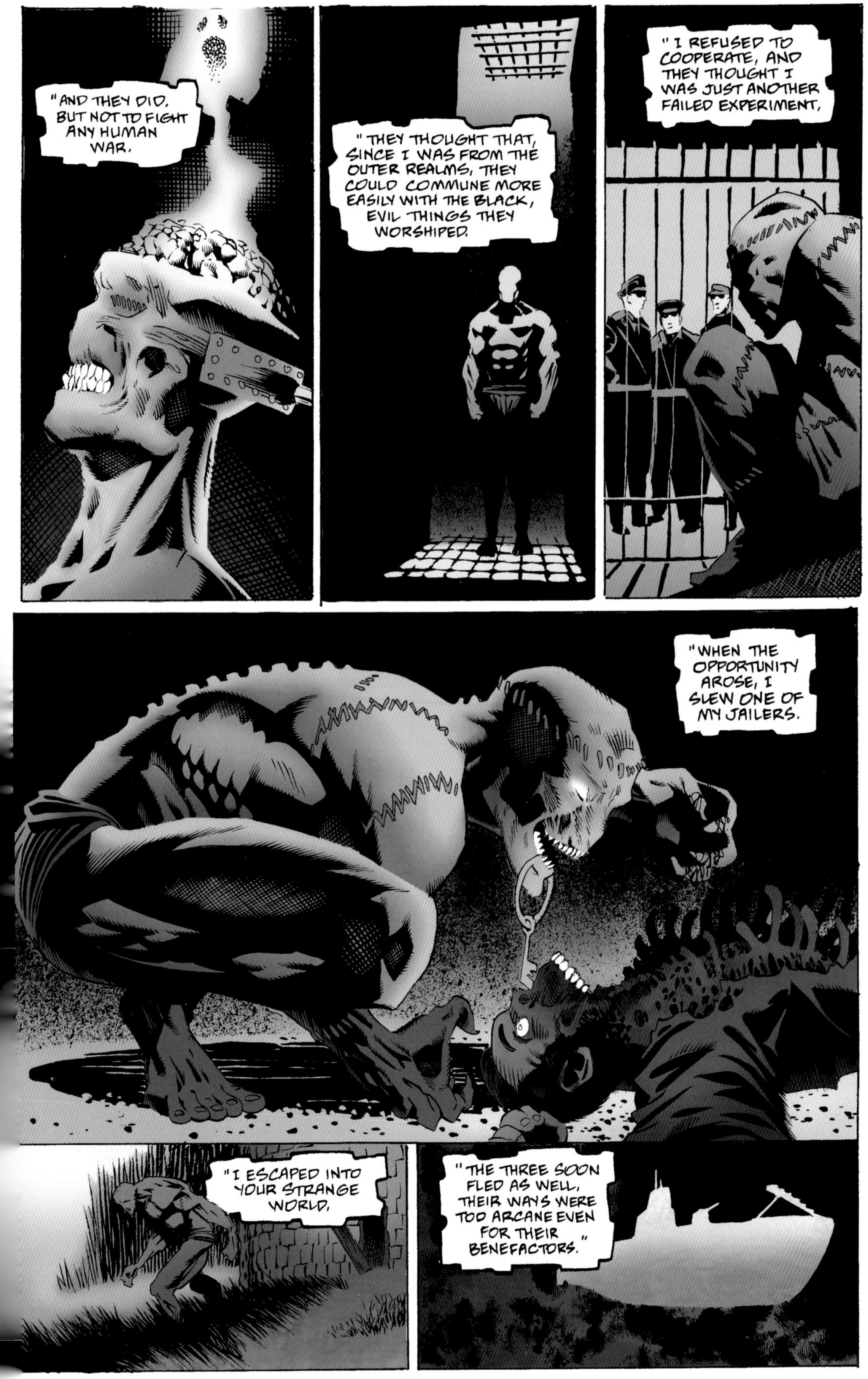
"AND THEY DID, BUT NOT TO FIGHT ANY HUMAN WAR.
"THEY THOUGHT THAT, SINCE I WAS FROM THE OUTER REALMS, THEY COULD COMMUNE MORE EASILY WITH THE BLACK, EVIL THINGS THEY WORSHIPED.
"I REFUSED TO COOPERATE, AND THEY THOUGHT I WAS JUST ANOTHER FAILED EXPERIMENT.
"WHEN THE OPPORTUNITY AROSE, I SLEW ONE OF MY JAILERS.
"I ESCAPED INTO YOUR STRANGE WORLD.
"THE THREE SOON FLED AS WELL. THEIR WAYS WERE TOO ARCANE EVEN FOR THEIR BENEFACTORS."

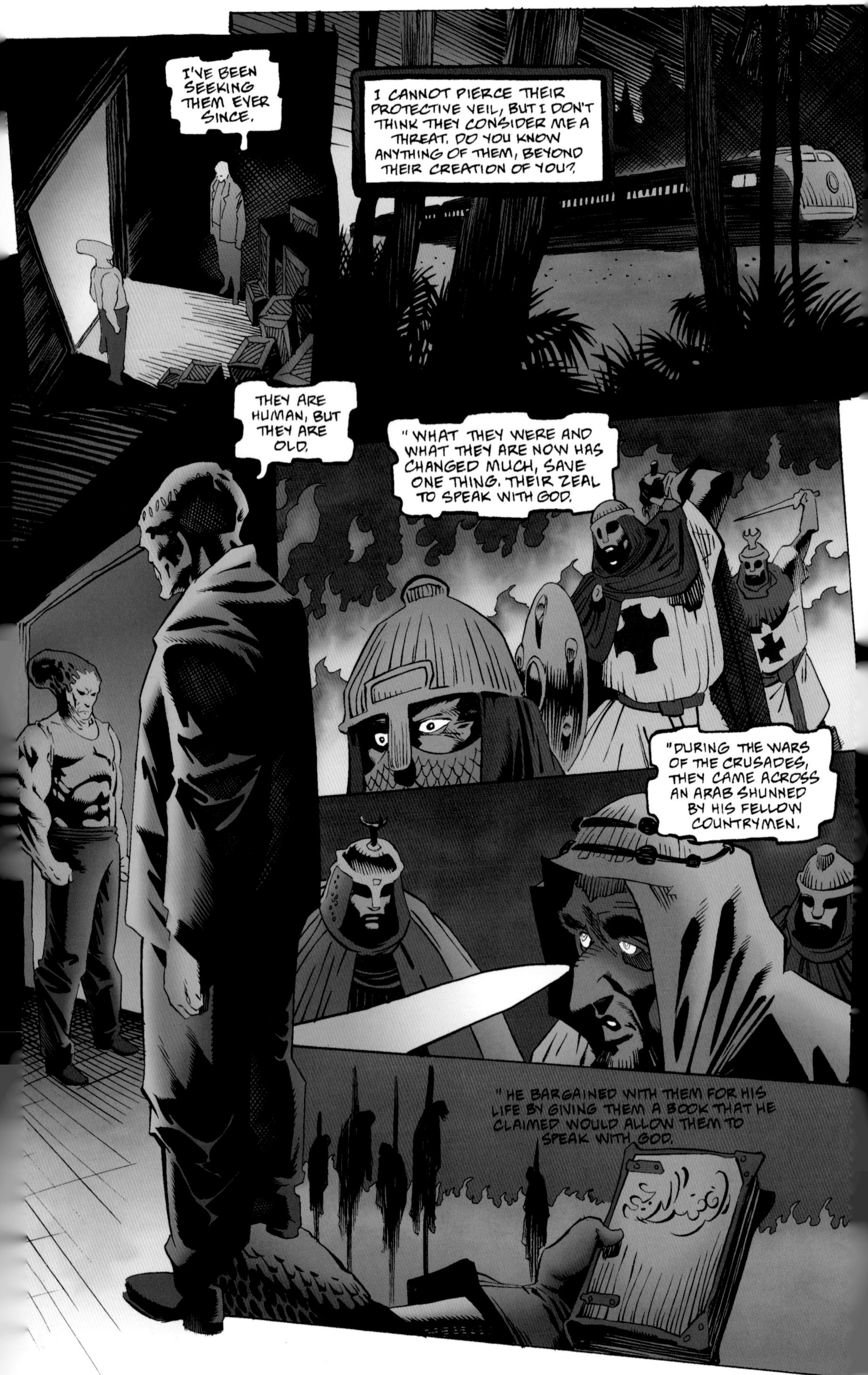
I'VE BEEN SEEKING THEM EVER SINCE.
I CANNOT PIERCE THEIR PROTECTIVE VEIL, BUT I DON'T THINK THEY CONSIDER ME A THREAT. DO YOU KNOW ANYTHING OF THEM, BEYOND THEIR CREATION OF YOU?
THEY ARE HUMAN, BUT THEY ARE OLD.
"WHAT THEY WERE AND WHAT THEY ARE NOW HAS CHANGED MUCH, SAVE ONE THING. THEIR ZEAL TO SPEAK WITH GOD.
"DURING THE WARS OF THE CRUSADES, THEY CAME ACROSS AN ARAB SHUNNED BY HIS FELLOW COUNTRYMEN.
"HE BARGAINED WITH THEM FOR HIS LIFE BY GIVING THEM A BOOK THAT HE CLAIMED WOULD ALLOW THEM TO SPEAK WITH GOD.

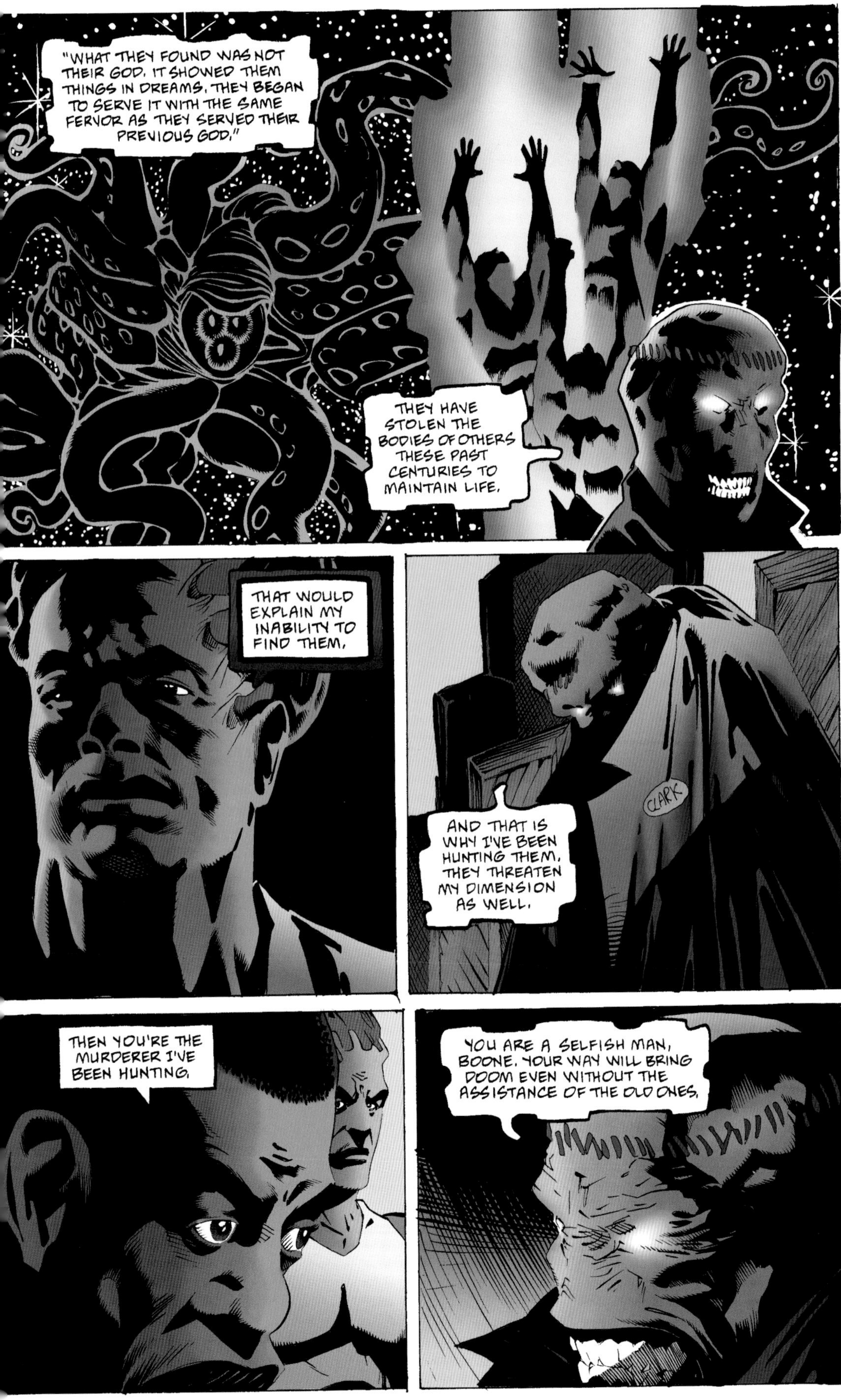
"WHAT THEY FOUND WAS NOT THEIR GOD. IT SHOWED THEM THINGS IN DREAMS. THEY BEGAN TO SERVE IT WITH THE SAME FERVOR AS THEY SERVED THEIR PREVIOUS GOD."
THEY HAVE STOLEN THE BODIES OF OTHERS THESE PAST CENTURIES TO MAINTAIN LIFE.
THAT WOULD EXPLAIN MY INABILITY TO FIND THEM.
CLARK
AND THAT IS WHY I'VE BEEN HUNTING THEM. THEY THREATEN MY DIMENSION AS WELL.
THEN YOU'RE THE MURDERER I'VE BEEN HUNTING.
YOU ARE A SELFISH MAN, BOONE. YOUR WAY WILL BRING DOOM EVEN WITHOUT THE ASSISTANCE OF THE OLD ONES.

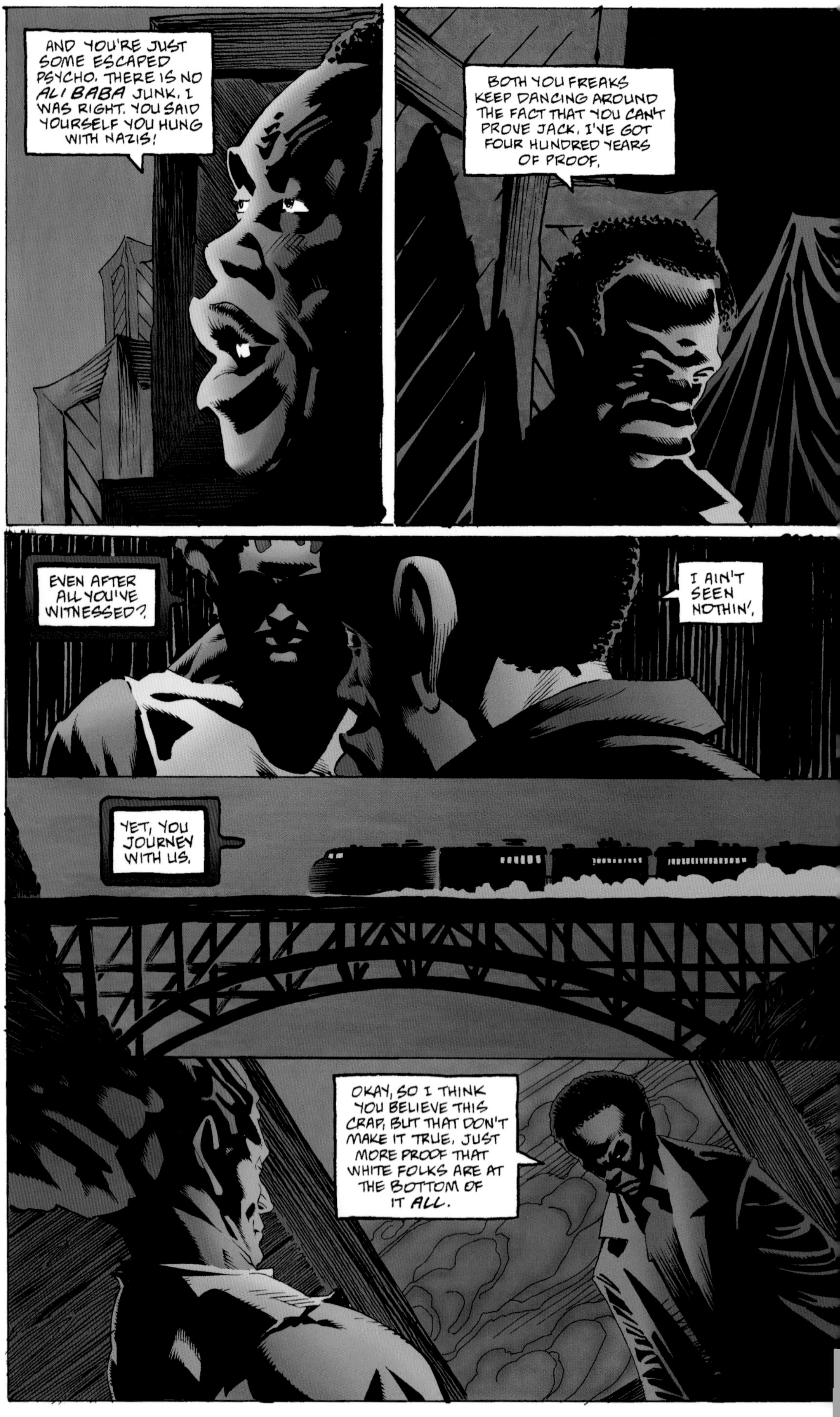
AND YOU'RE JUST SOME ESCAPED PSYCHO. THERE IS NO ALI BABA JUNK. I WAS RIGHT. YOU SAID YOURSELF YOU HUNG WITH NAZIS!
BOTH YOU FREAKS KEEP DANCING AROUND THE FACT THAT YOU CAN'T PROVE JACK. I'VE GOT FOUR HUNDRED YEARS OF PROOF.
EVEN AFTER ALL YOU'VE WITNESSED?
I AIN'T SEEN NOTHIN'.
YET, YOU JOURNEY WITH US.
OKAY, SO I THINK YOU BELIEVE THIS CRAP, BUT THAT DON'T MAKE IT TRUE. JUST MORE PROOF THAT WHITE FOLKS ARE AT THE BOTTOM OF IT ALL.

THEN PERHAPS MORE SHOULD BE REVEALED TO YOU.

YOU PRACTICE THE SAME ARROGANCE YOU CLAIM TO FIGHT. ONCE YOU REALIZE THAT YOUR BIGOTRY IS A CONDITION OF HUMAN NATURE AND NOT RACE, YOU WILL BECOME MORE CIVILIZED.

YOUR LIMITED PERCEPTION DOES NOT ALLOW YOU TO GRASP YOUR OWN KIND, MUCH LESS THE POSSIBILITY OF OTHER INTELLIGENCES.

YOU SEE, I AM ALSO FROM THE STARS.

THE PREVIOUS WORLD THAT I INHABITED WAS VERY DIFFERENT FROM THIS EARTH, COVERED COMPLETELY BY OCEAN, IT SPAWNED LIFE WHICH, TOO, BECAME INTELLIGENT, THEY DID NOT BELIEVE IN THE OLD ONES, EITHER, SO I CAME HERE.

BUT EVEN THE SHAPE I INHABITED THERE WAS NOT MY TRUE FORM. IT WAS A BODY I NEEDED TO CONTINUE MY WORK, A VESSEL TO TAKE ME WHERE I NEEDED TO BE.

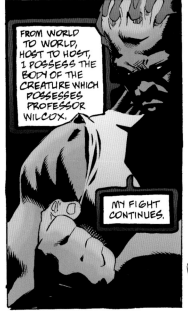

FROM WORLD TO WORLD, HOST TO HOST, I POSSESS THE BODY OF THE CREATURE WHICH POSSESSES PROFESSOR WILCOX.

MY FIGHT CONTINUES.

YOU DON'T SAY—

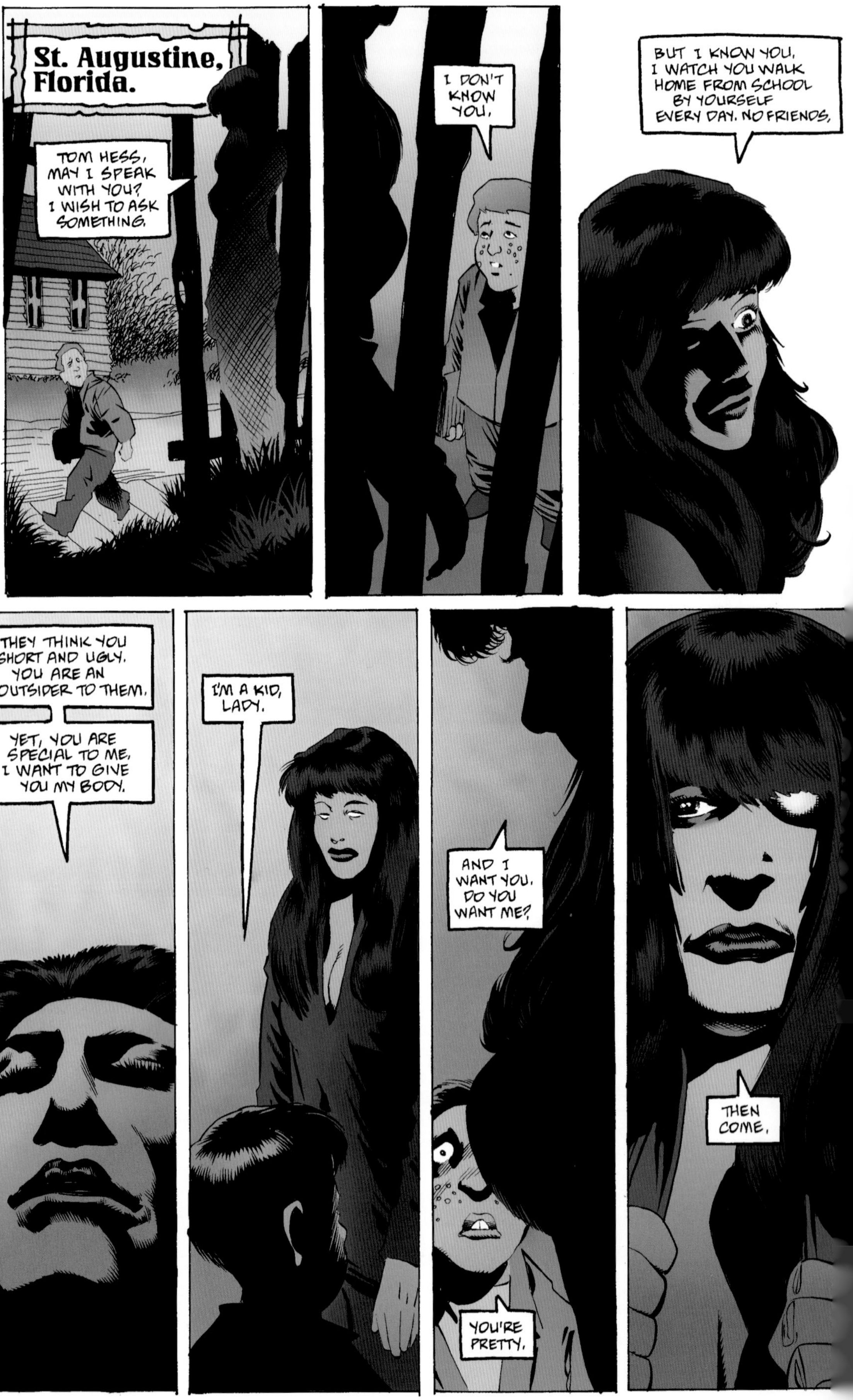
St. Augustine, Florida.
TOM HESS, MAY I SPEAK WITH YOU? I WISH TO ASK SOMETHING.
I DON'T KNOW YOU.
BUT I KNOW YOU. I WATCH YOU WALK HOME FROM SCHOOL BY YOURSELF EVERY DAY. NO FRIENDS.
THEY THINK YOU SHORT AND UGLY. YOU ARE AN OUTSIDER TO THEM.
YET, YOU ARE SPECIAL TO ME. I WANT TO GIVE YOU MY BODY.
I'M A KID, LADY.
AND I WANT YOU. DO YOU WANT ME?
YOU'RE PRETTY.
THEN COME.

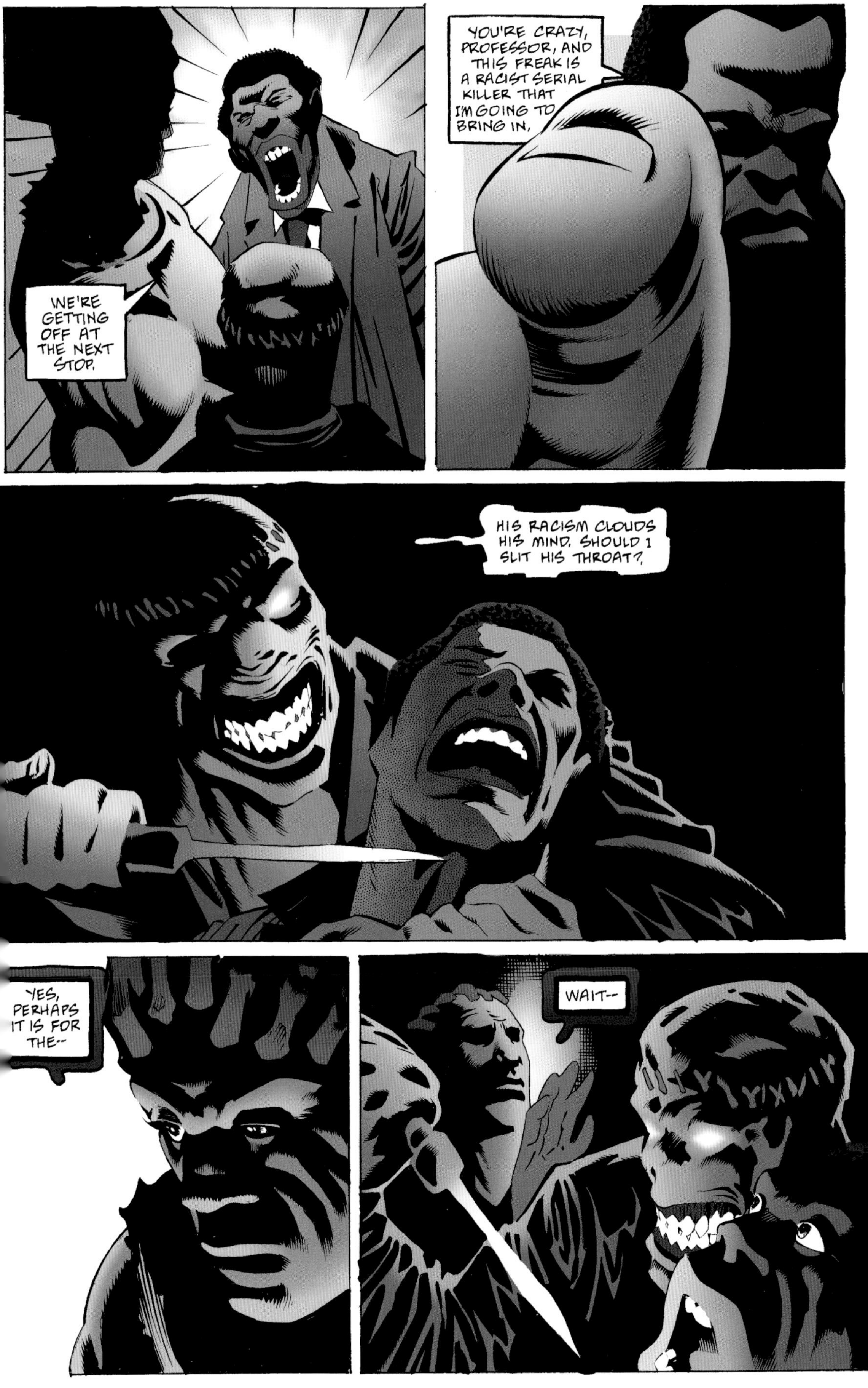
WE'RE GETTING OFF AT THE NEXT STOP.
YOU'RE CRAZY, PROFESSOR, AND THIS FREAK IS A RACIST SERIAL KILLER THAT I'M GOING TO BRING IN.
HIS RACISM CLOUDS HIS MIND. SHOULD I SLIT HIS THROAT?
YES, PERHAPS IT IS FOR THE--
WAIT--

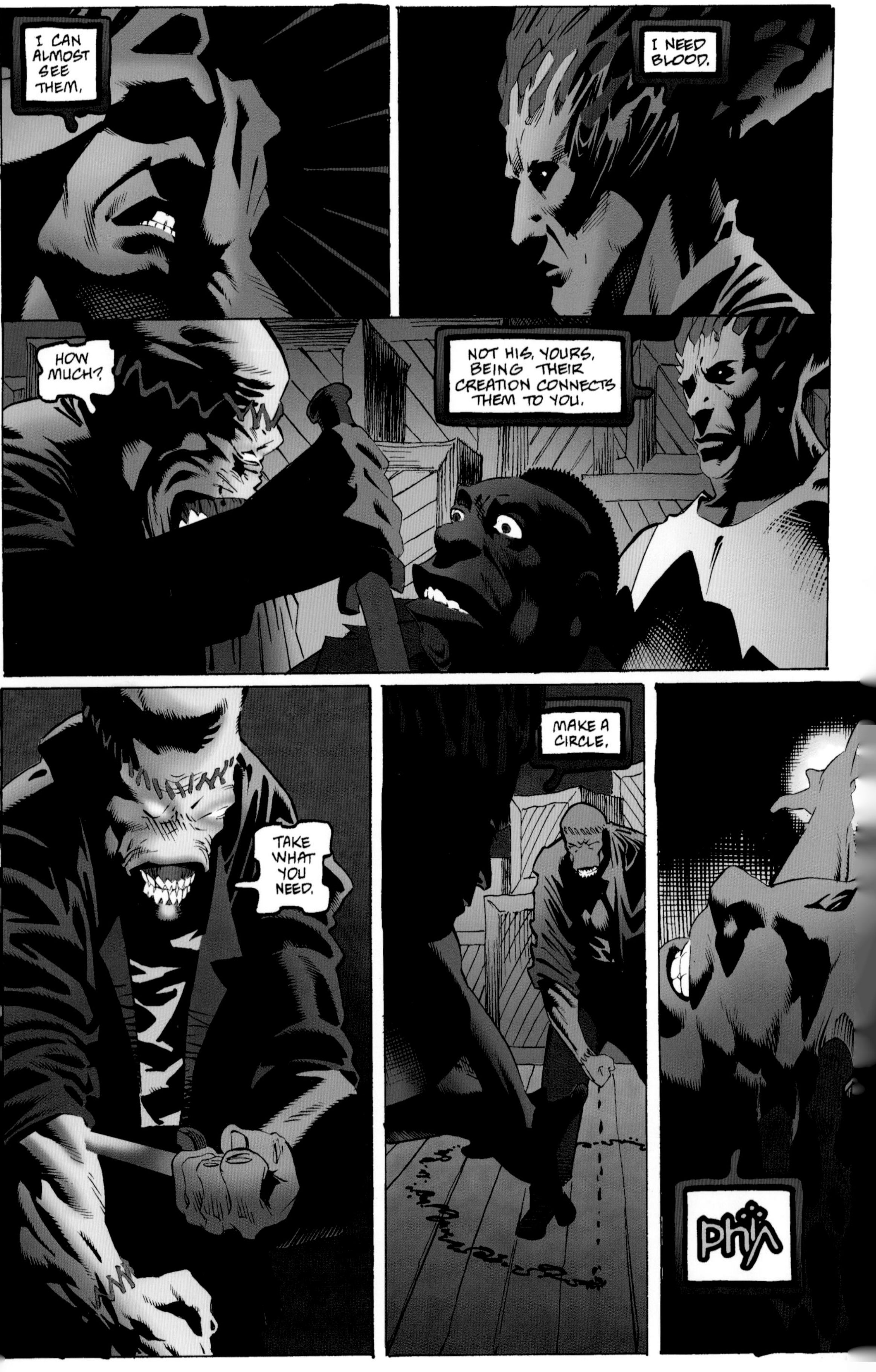
I CAN ALMOST SEE THEM.
I NEED BLOOD.
HOW MUCH?
NOT HIS, YOURS. BEING THEIR CREATION CONNECTS THEM TO YOU.
TAKE WHAT YOU NEED.
MAKE A CIRCLE.

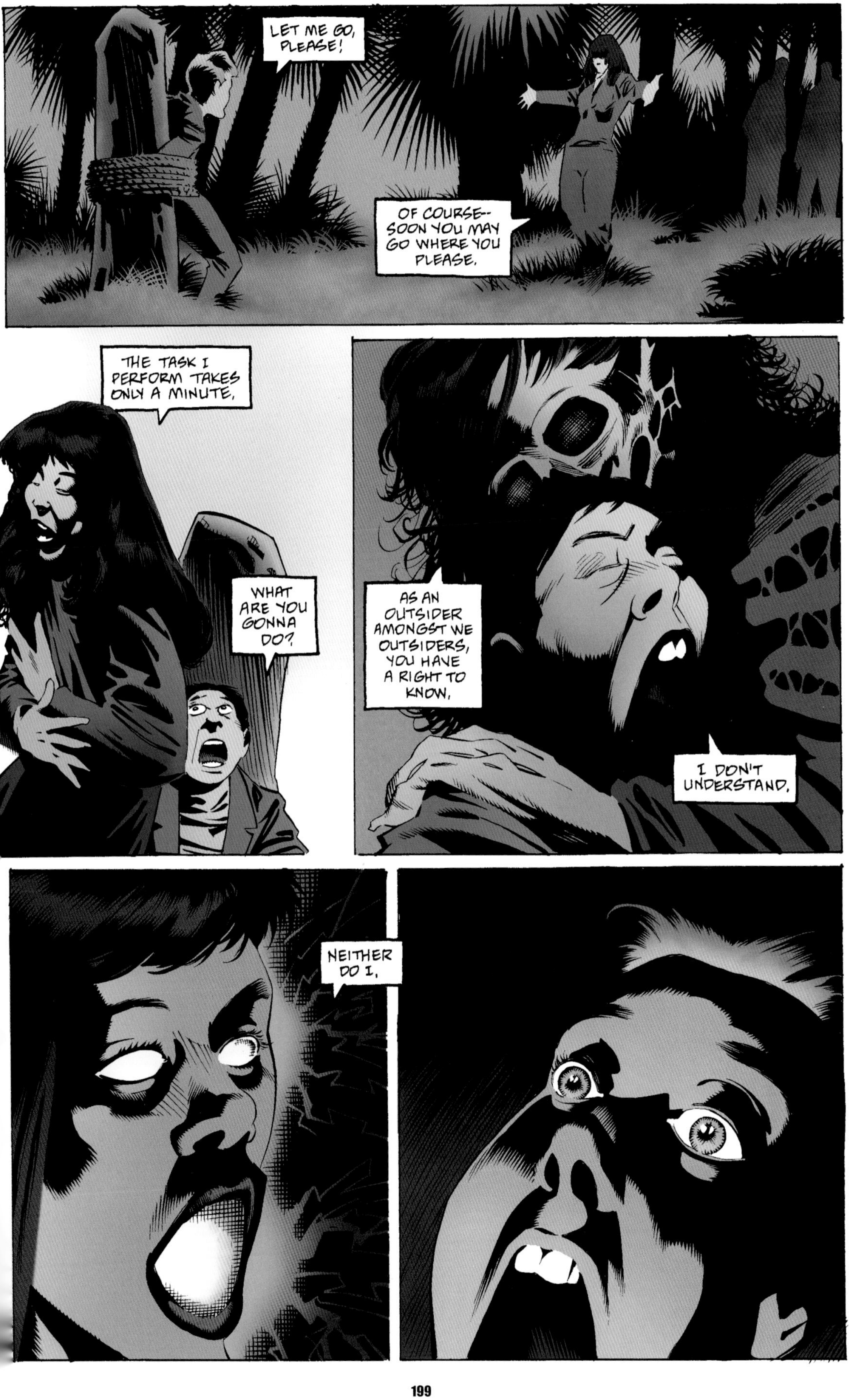
LET ME GO, PLEASE!
OF COURSE-- SOON YOU MAY GO WHERE YOU PLEASE.
THE TASK I PERFORM TAKES ONLY A MINUTE.
WHAT ARE YOU GONNA DO?
AS AN OUTSIDER AMONGST WE OUTSIDERS, YOU HAVE A RIGHT TO KNOW.
I DON'T UNDERSTAND.
NEITHER DO I.

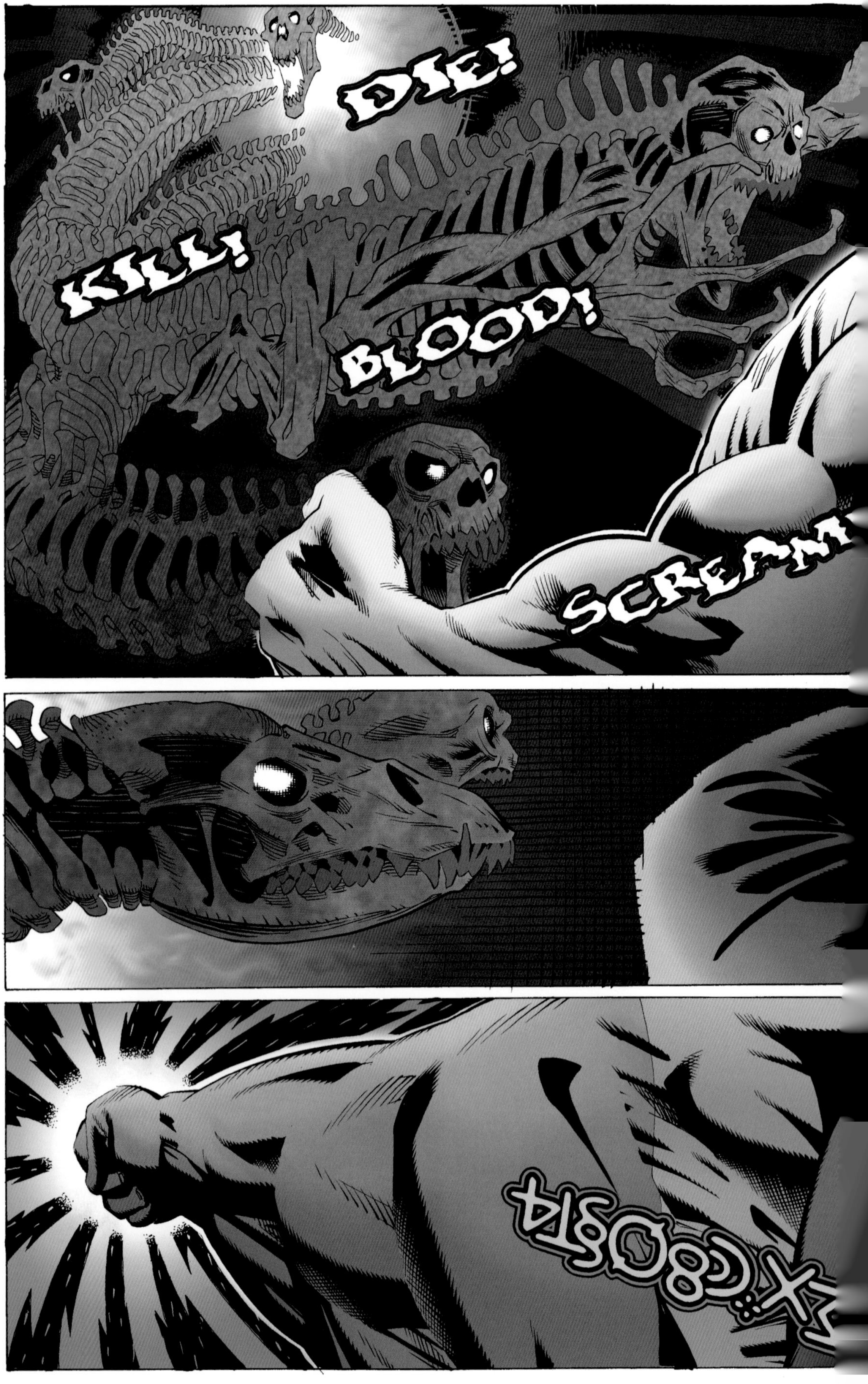
DIE!
KILL!
BLOOD!
SCREAM

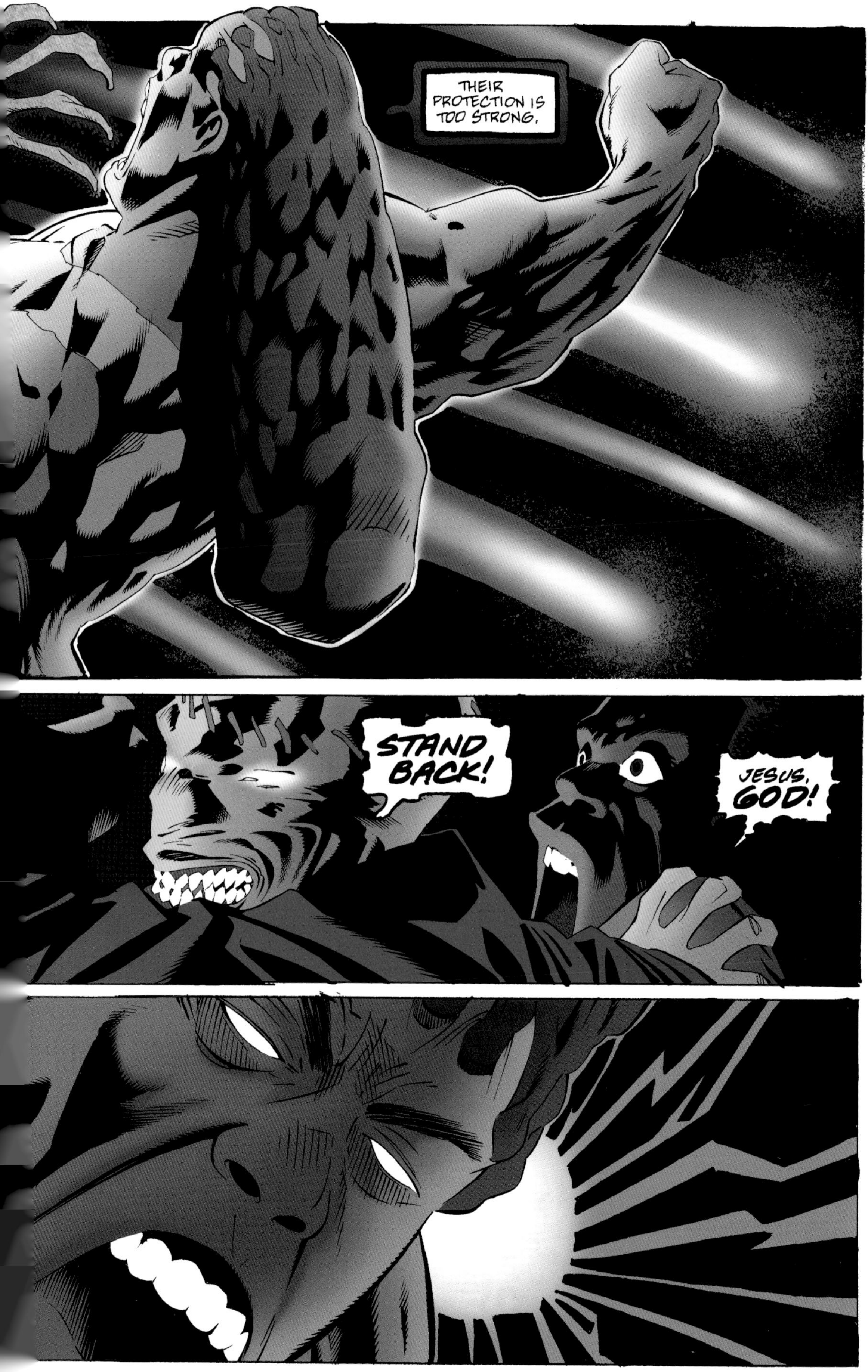
THEIR PROTECTION IS TOO STRONG.
STAND BACK!
JESUS, GOD!

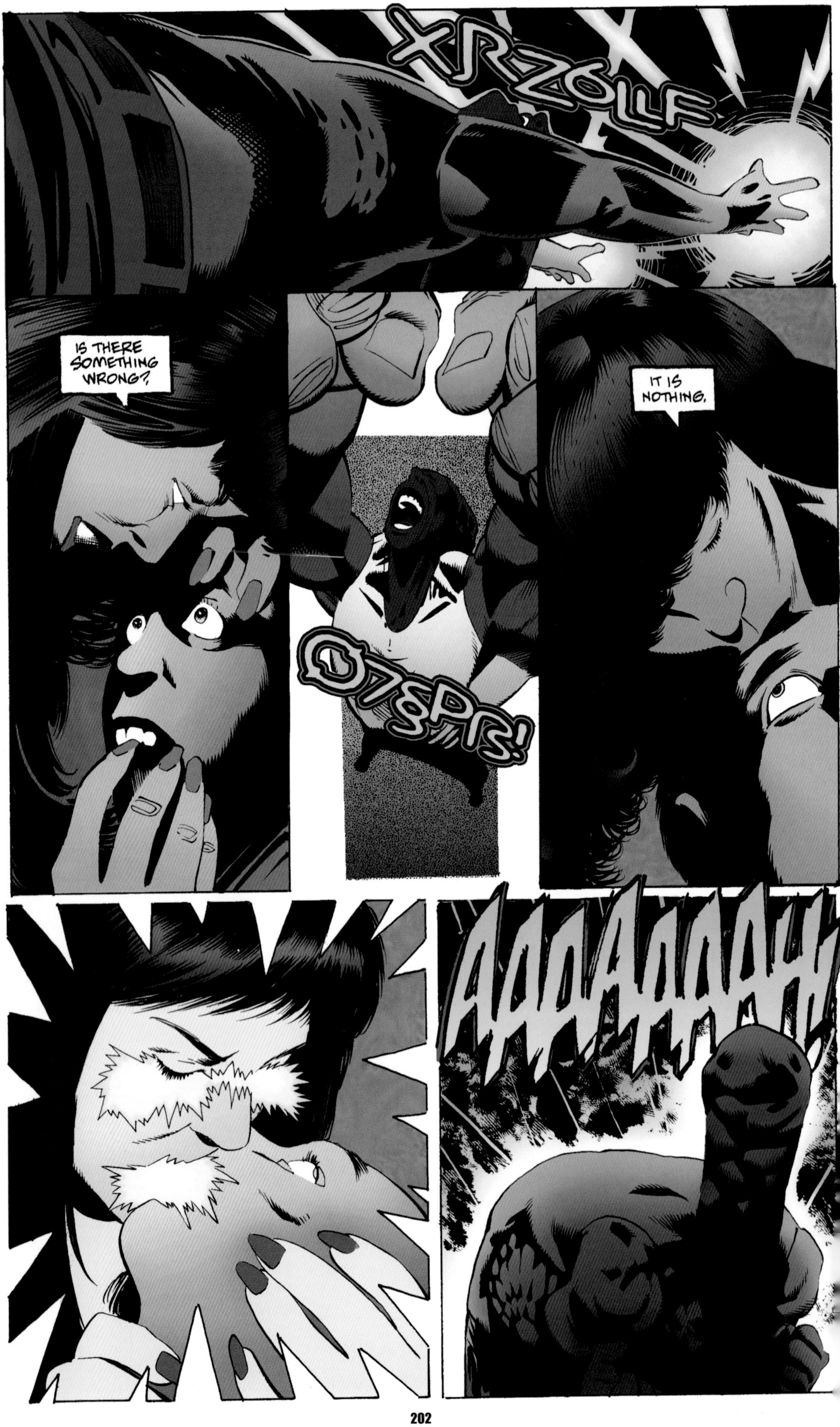
XRZZOLF
IS THERE SOMETHING WRONG?
IT IS NOTHING.
AAAAAAAH

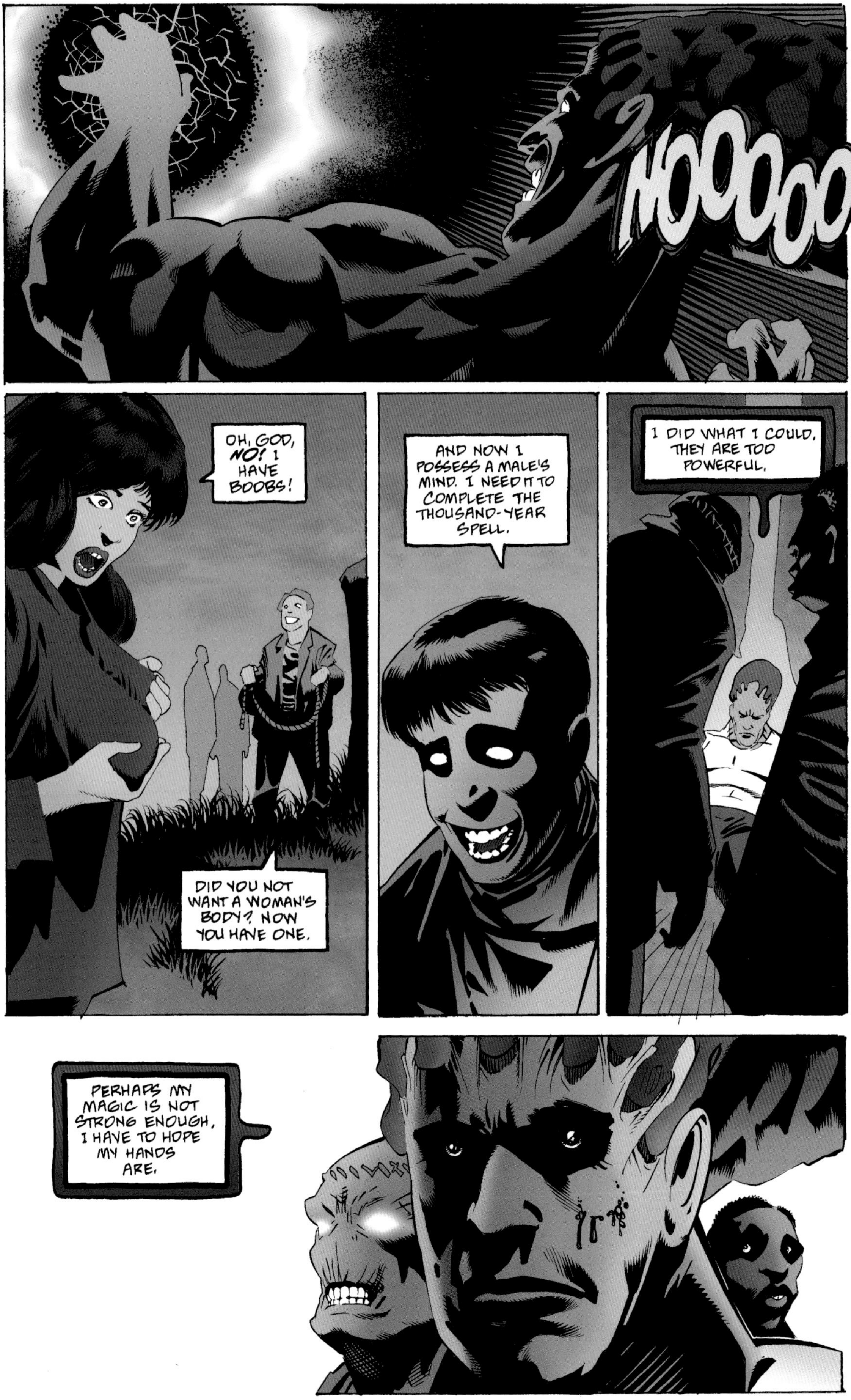
NOOOOO
OH, GOD, NO! I HAVE BOOBS!
DID YOU NOT WANT A WOMAN'S BODY? NOW YOU HAVE ONE.
AND NOW I POSSESS A MALE'S MIND. I NEED IT TO COMPLETE THE THOUSAND-YEAR SPELL.
I DID WHAT I COULD, THEY ARE TOO POWERFUL.
PERHAPS MY MAGIC IS NOT STRONG ENOUGH, I HAVE TO HOPE MY HANDS ARE.

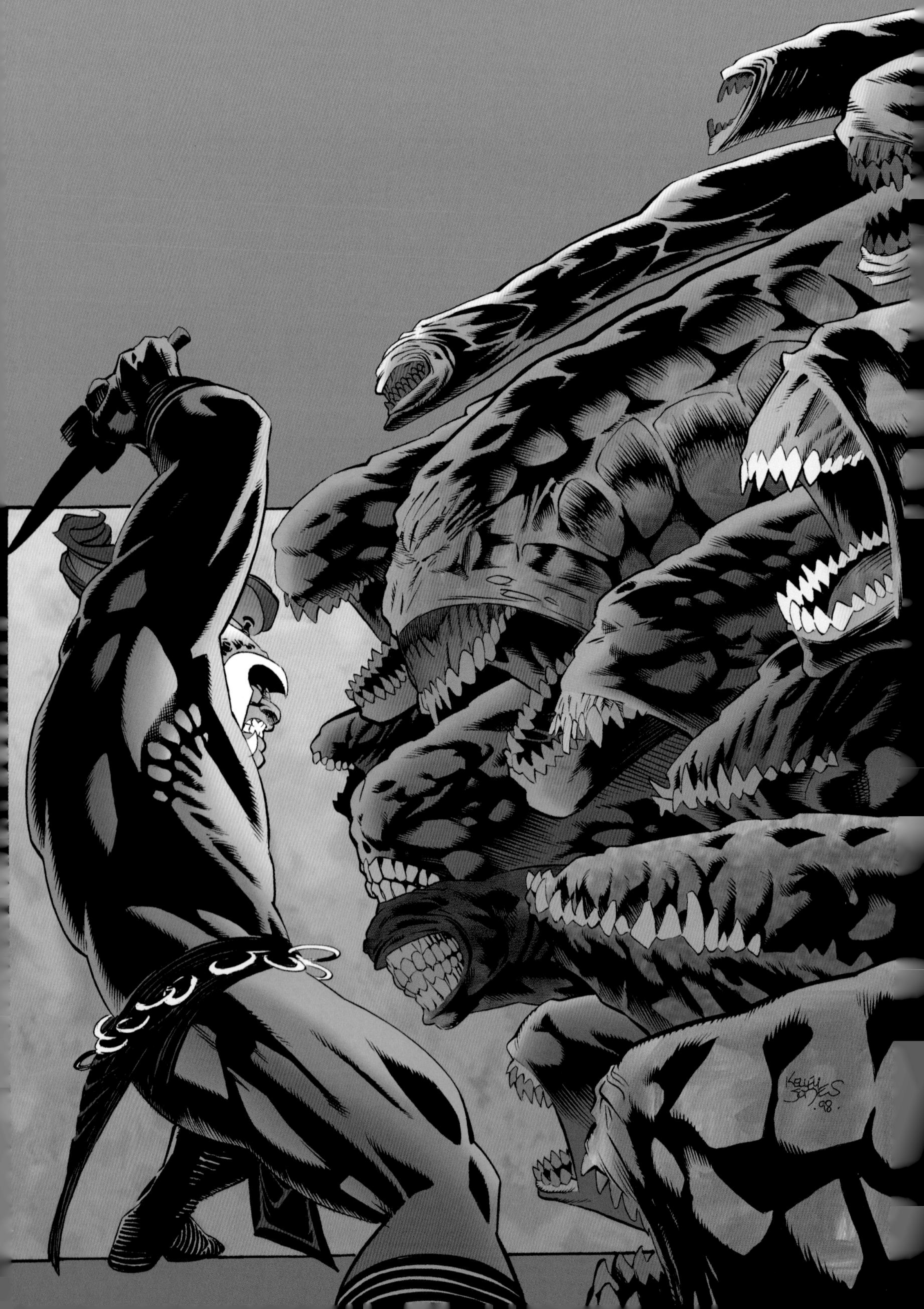

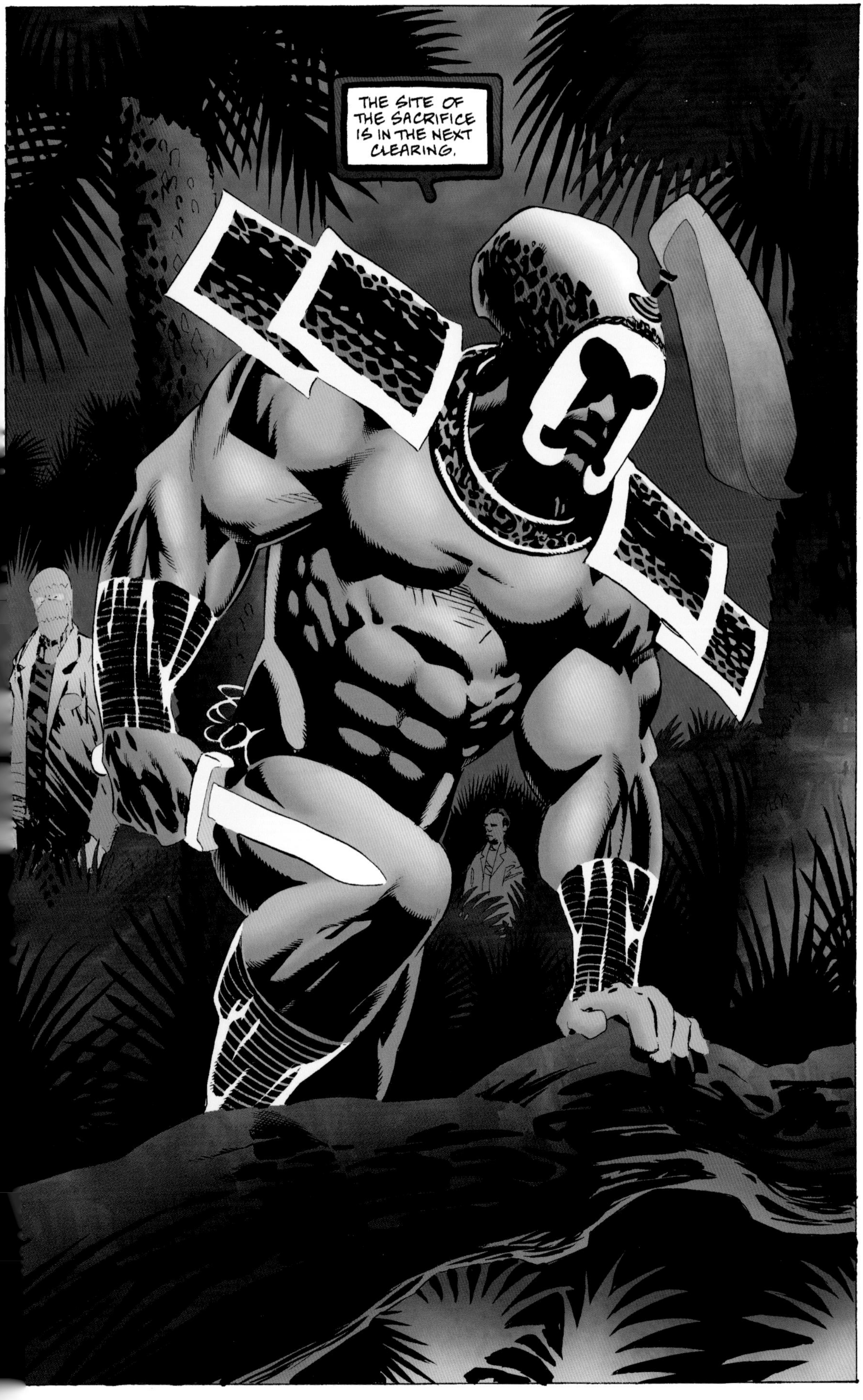
THE SITE OF THE SACRIFICE IS IN THE NEXT CLEARING.

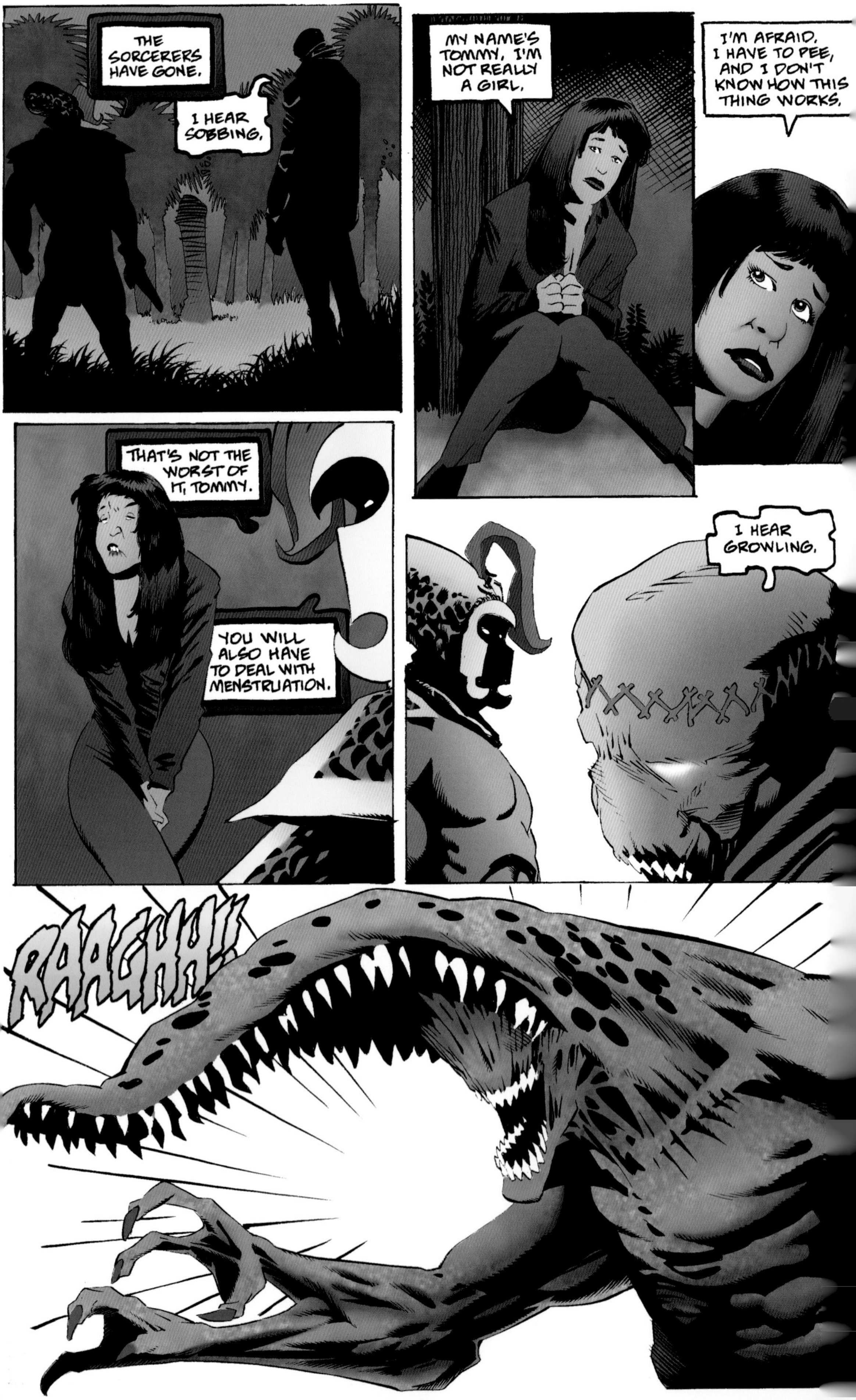
THE SORCERERS HAVE GONE.
I HEAR SOBBING.
MY NAME'S TOMMY, I'M NOT REALLY A GIRL.
I'M AFRAID. I HAVE TO PEE, AND I DON'T KNOW HOW THIS THING WORKS.
THAT'S NOT THE WORST OF IT, TOMMY.
YOU WILL ALSO HAVE TO DEAL WITH MENSTRUATION.
I HEAR GROWLING.
RAAGHH!!

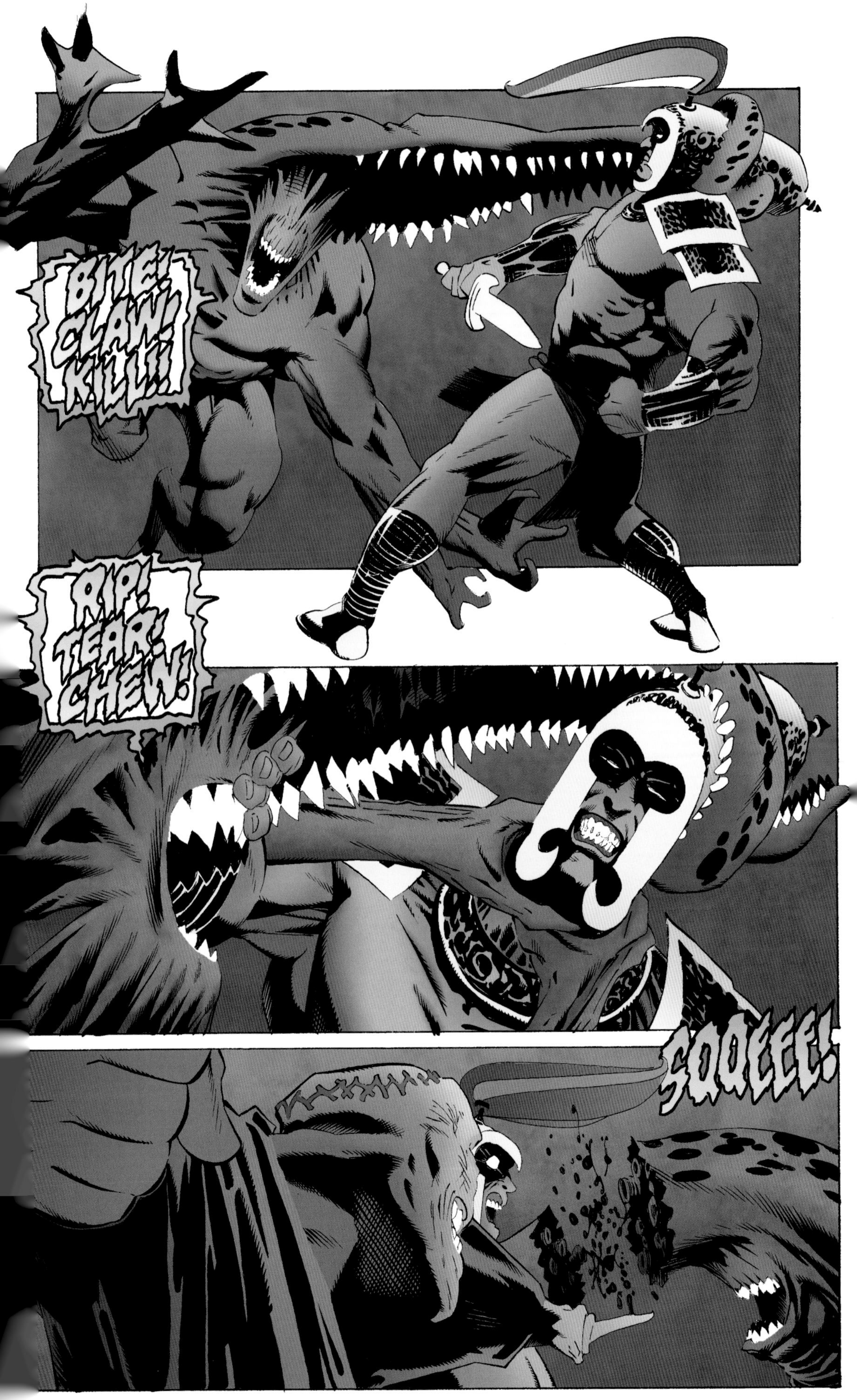

BITE! CLAW! KILL!!
RIP! TEAR! CHEW!
SQEEE!

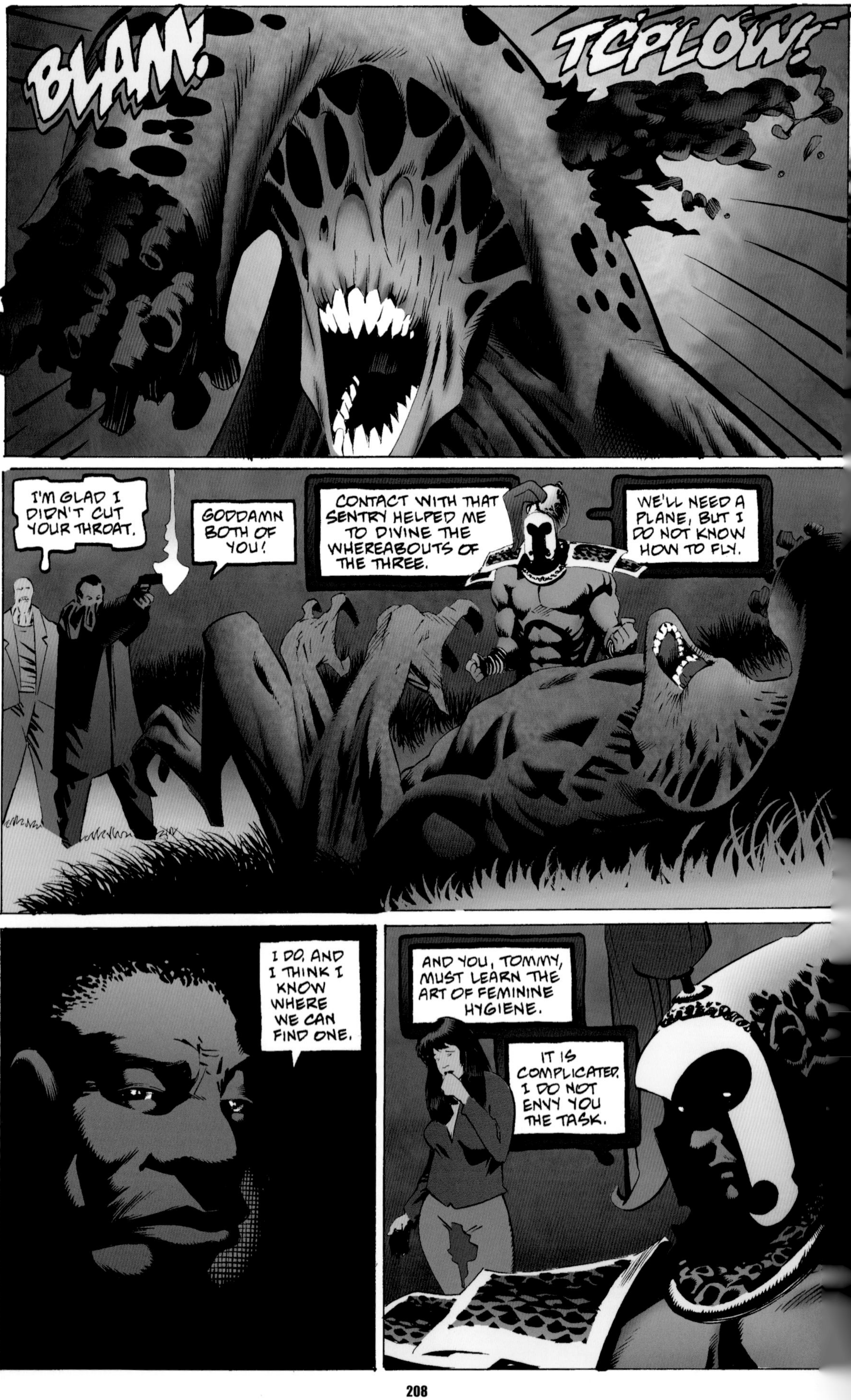
BLAM!
TCPLOW!
I'M GLAD I DIDN'T CUT YOUR THROAT.
GODDAMN BOTH OF YOU!
CONTACT WITH THAT SENTRY HELPED ME TO DIVINE THE WHEREABOUTS OF THE THREE.
WE'LL NEED A PLANE, BUT I DO NOT KNOW HOW TO FLY.
I DO. AND I THINK I KNOW WHERE WE CAN FIND ONE.
AND YOU, TOMMY, MUST LEARN THE ART OF FEMININE HYGIENE.
IT IS COMPLICATED. I DO NOT ENVY YOU THE TASK.

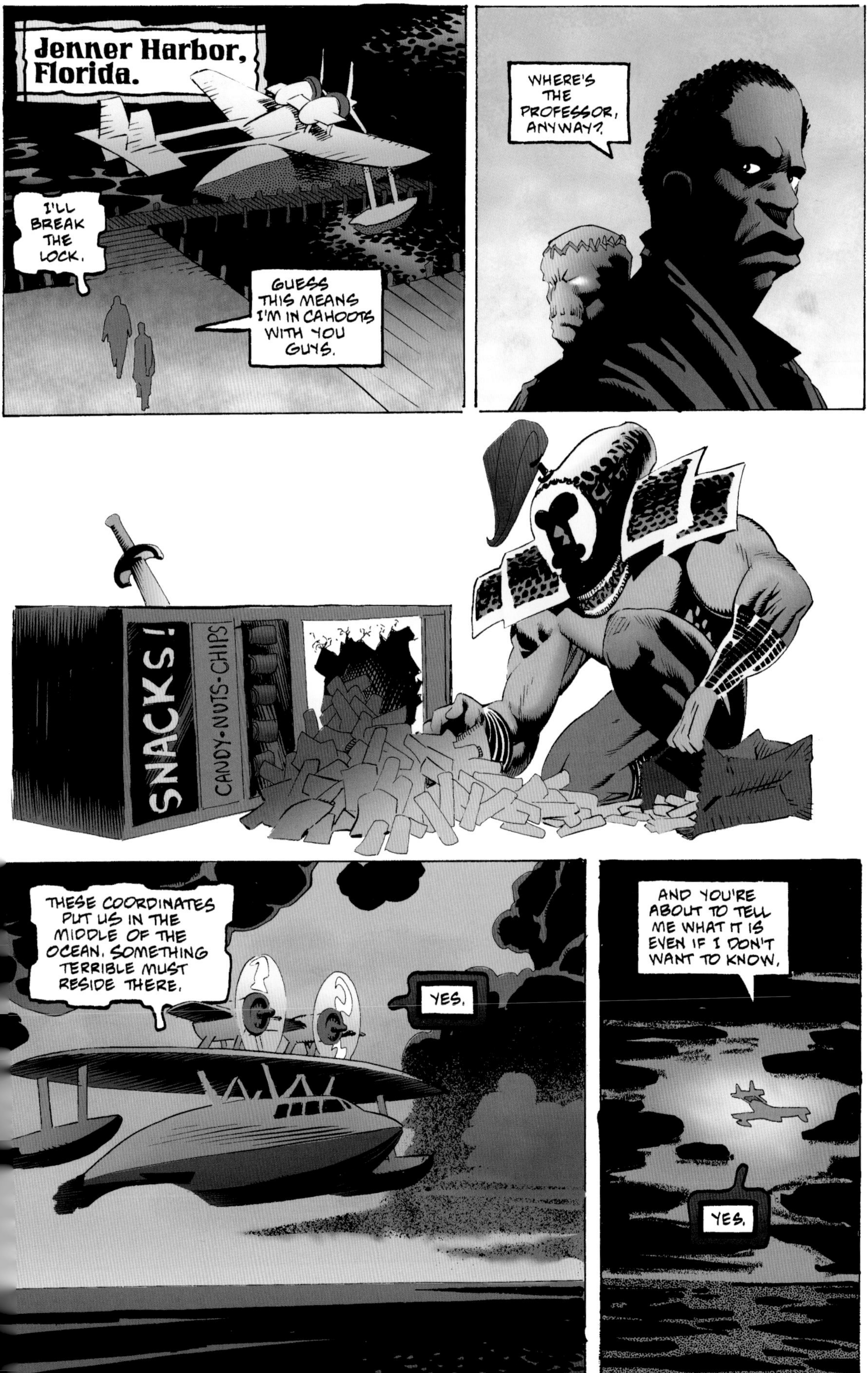
Jenner Harbor, Florida.
I'LL BREAK THE LOCK.
GUESS THIS MEANS I'M IN CAHOOTS WITH YOU GUYS.
WHERE'S THE PROFESSOR, ANYWAY?
SNACKS!
CANDY•NUTS•CHIPS
THESE COORDINATES PUT US IN THE MIDDLE OF THE OCEAN. SOMETHING TERRIBLE MUST RESIDE THERE.
YES.
AND YOU'RE ABOUT TO TELL ME WHAT IT IS EVEN IF I DON'T WANT TO KNOW.
YES.

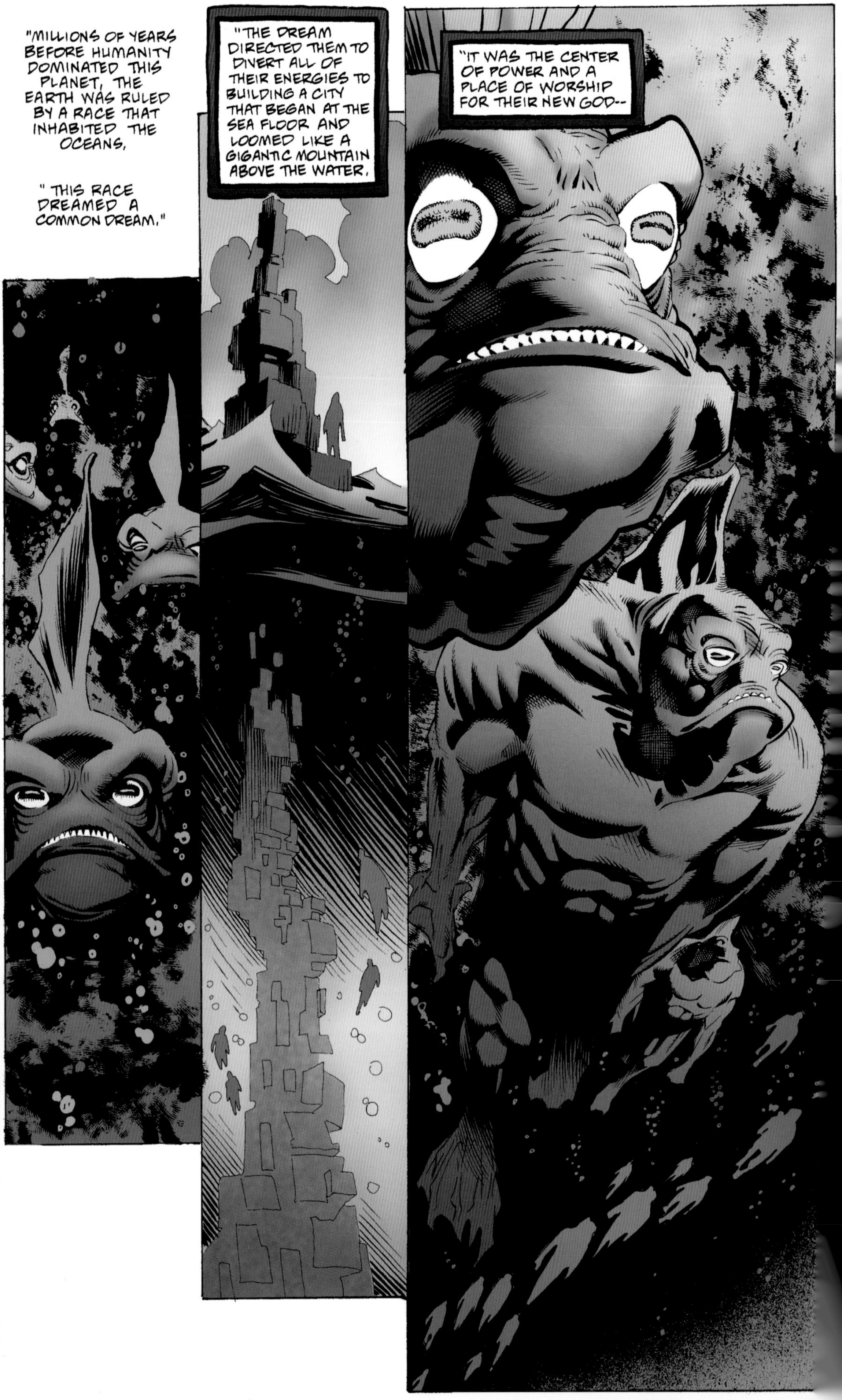
"MILLIONS OF YEARS BEFORE HUMANITY DOMINATED THIS PLANET, THE EARTH WAS RULED BY A RACE THAT INHABITED THE OCEANS.
"THIS RACE DREAMED A COMMON DREAM."
"THE DREAM DIRECTED THEM TO DIVERT ALL OF THEIR ENERGIES TO BUILDING A CITY THAT BEGAN AT THE SEA FLOOR AND LOOMED LIKE A GIGANTIC MOUNTAIN ABOVE THE WATER.
"IT WAS THE CENTER OF POWER AND A PLACE OF WORSHIP FOR THEIR NEW GOD--

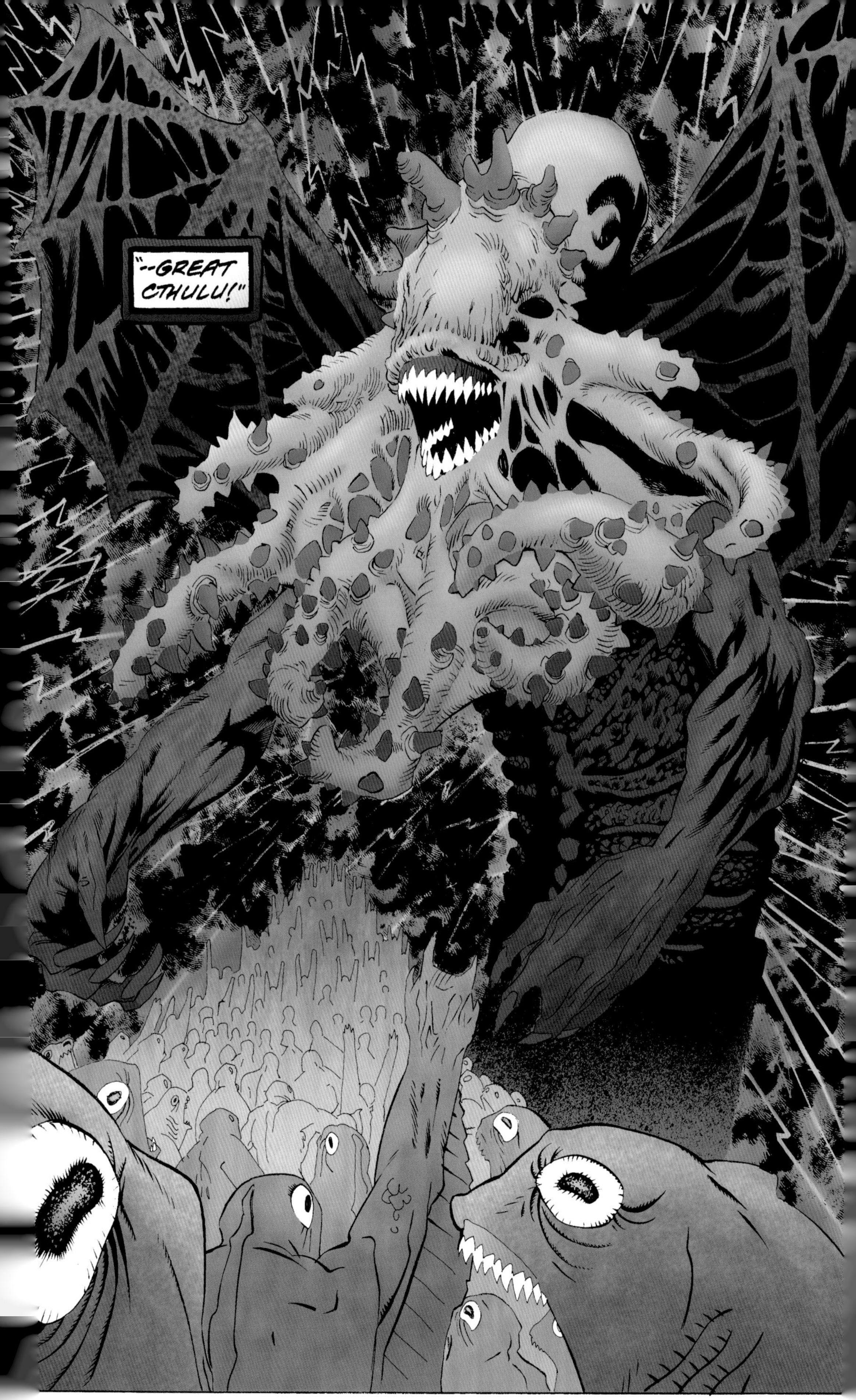
"--GREAT CTHULU!"

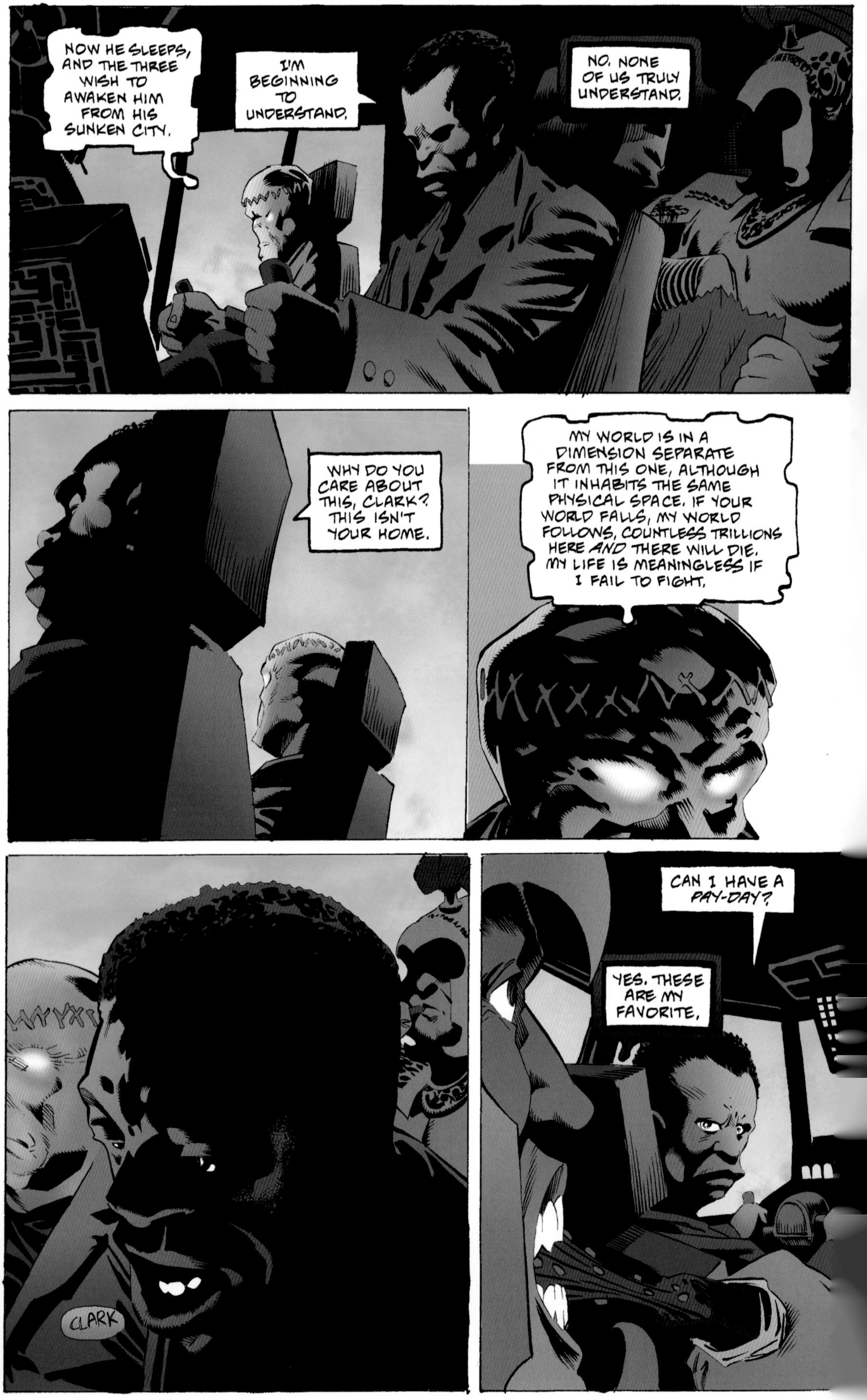
NOW HE SLEEPS, AND THE THREE WISH TO AWAKEN HIM FROM HIS SUNKEN CITY.
I'M BEGINNING TO UNDERSTAND.
NO. NONE OF US TRULY UNDERSTAND.
WHY DO YOU CARE ABOUT THIS, CLARK? THIS ISN'T YOUR HOME.
MY WORLD IS IN A DIMENSION SEPARATE FROM THIS ONE, ALTHOUGH IT INHABITS THE SAME PHYSICAL SPACE. IF YOUR WORLD FALLS, MY WORLD FOLLOWS. COUNTLESS TRILLIONS HERE AND THERE WILL DIE. MY LIFE IS MEANINGLESS IF I FAIL TO FIGHT.
CLARK
CAN I HAVE A PAY-DAY?
YES. THESE ARE MY FAVORITE.

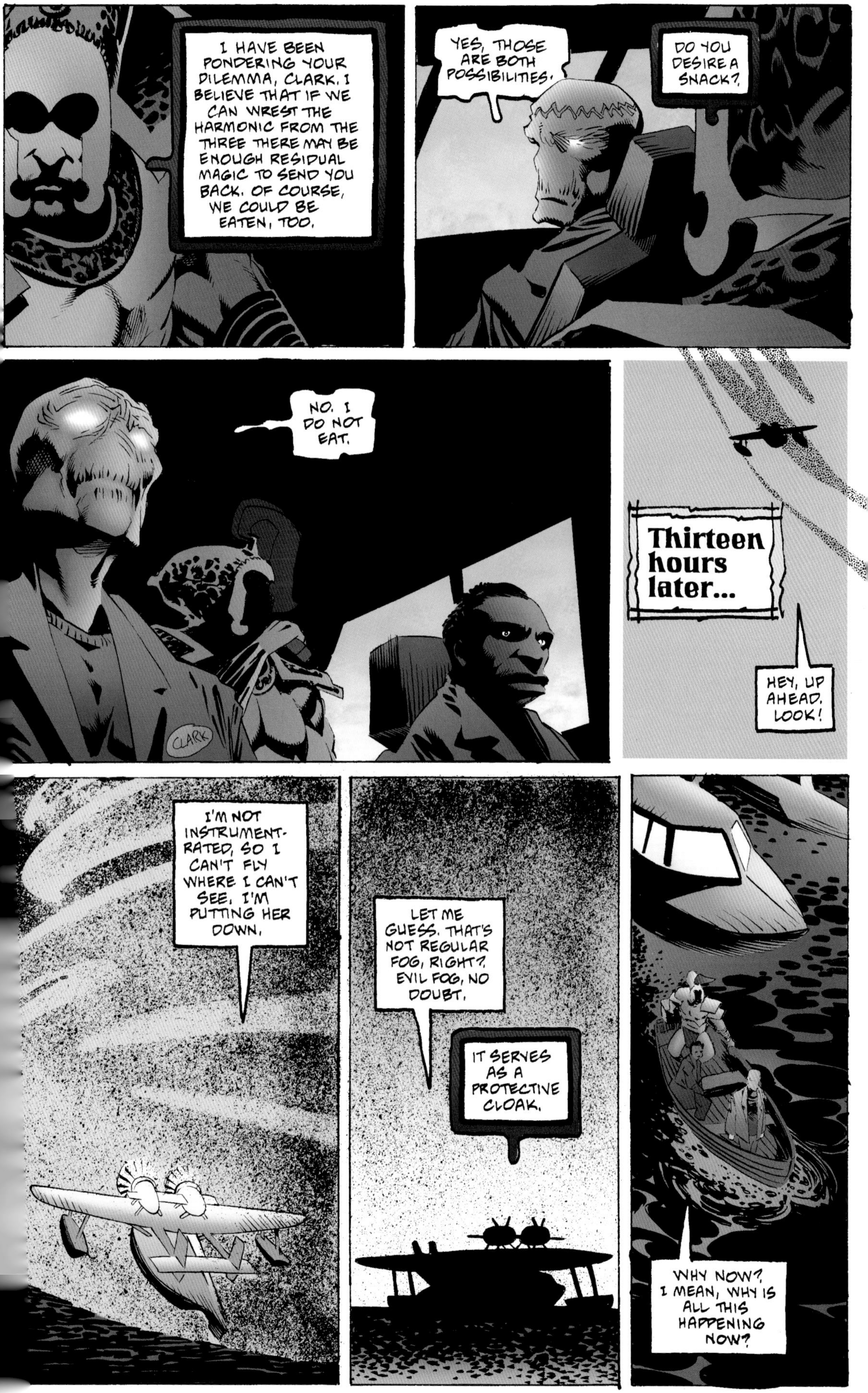
I HAVE BEEN PONDERING YOUR DILEMMA, CLARK. I BELIEVE THAT IF WE CAN WREST THE HARMONIC FROM THE THREE THERE MAY BE ENOUGH RESIDUAL MAGIC TO SEND YOU BACK. OF COURSE, WE COULD BE EATEN, TOO.
YES, THOSE ARE BOTH POSSIBILITIES.
DO YOU DESIRE A SNACK?
NO. I DO NOT EAT.
CLARK
Thirteen hours later...
HEY, UP AHEAD. LOOK!
I'M NOT INSTRUMENT-RATED, SO I CAN'T FLY WHERE I CAN'T SEE. I'M PUTTING HER DOWN.
LET ME GUESS. THAT'S NOT REGULAR FOG, RIGHT? EVIL FOG, NO DOUBT.
IT SERVES AS A PROTECTIVE CLOAK.
WHY NOW? I MEAN, WHY IS ALL THIS HAPPENING NOW?

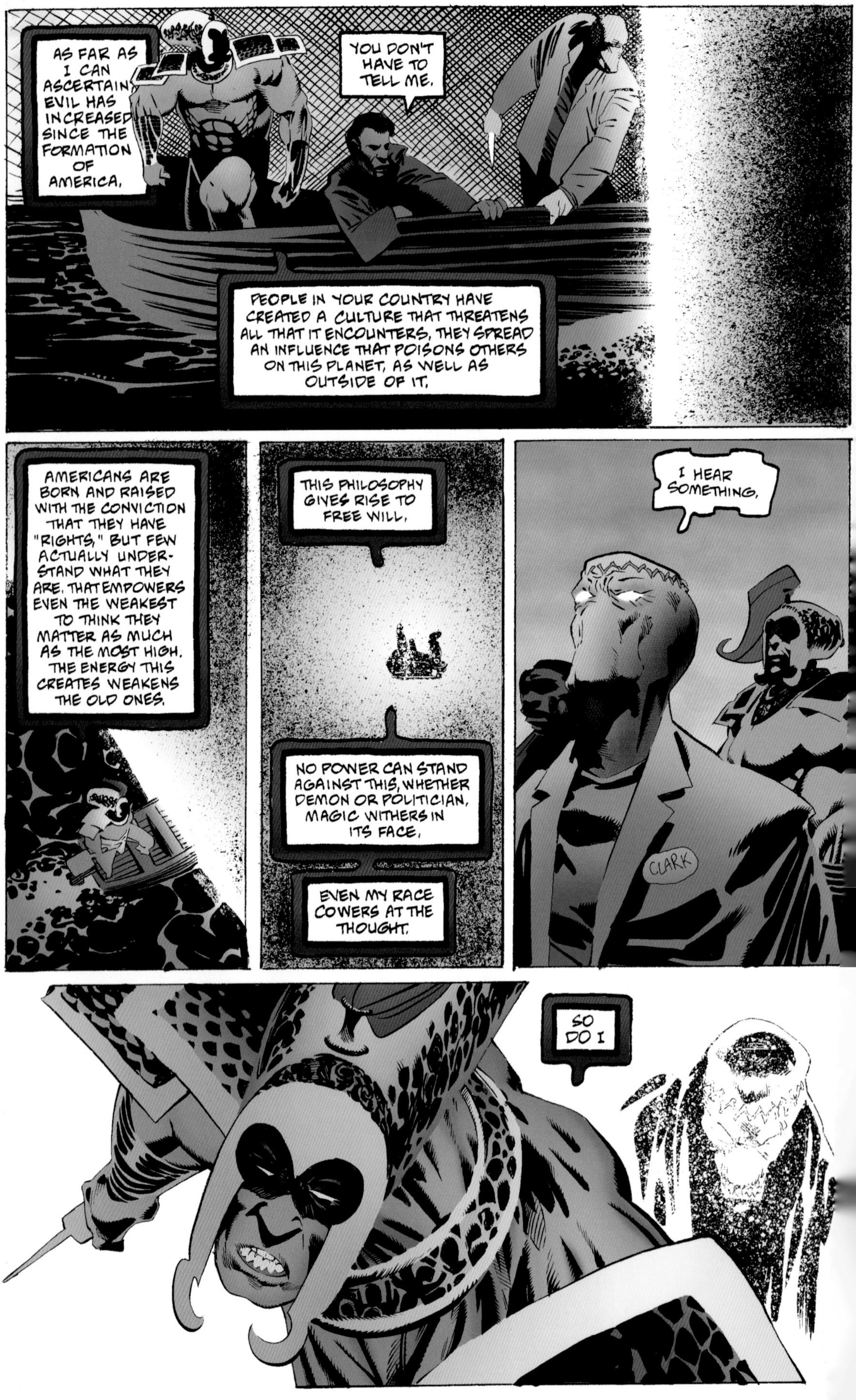
AS FAR AS I CAN ASCERTAIN, EVIL HAS INCREASED SINCE THE FORMATION OF AMERICA,
YOU DON'T HAVE TO TELL ME.
PEOPLE IN YOUR COUNTRY HAVE CREATED A CULTURE THAT THREATENS ALL THAT IT ENCOUNTERS, THEY SPREAD AN INFLUENCE THAT POISONS OTHERS ON THIS PLANET, AS WELL AS OUTSIDE OF IT.
AMERICANS ARE BORN AND RAISED WITH THE CONVICTION THAT THEY HAVE "RIGHTS," BUT FEW ACTUALLY UNDER-STAND WHAT THEY ARE. THAT EMPOWERS EVEN THE WEAKEST TO THINK THEY MATTER AS MUCH AS THE MOST HIGH. THE ENERGY THIS CREATES WEAKENS THE OLD ONES.
THIS PHILOSOPHY GIVES RISE TO FREE WILL,
NO POWER CAN STAND AGAINST THIS, WHETHER DEMON OR POLITICIAN, MAGIC WITHERS IN ITS FACE,
EVEN MY RACE COWERS AT THE THOUGHT.
I HEAR SOMETHING,
CLARK
SO DO I

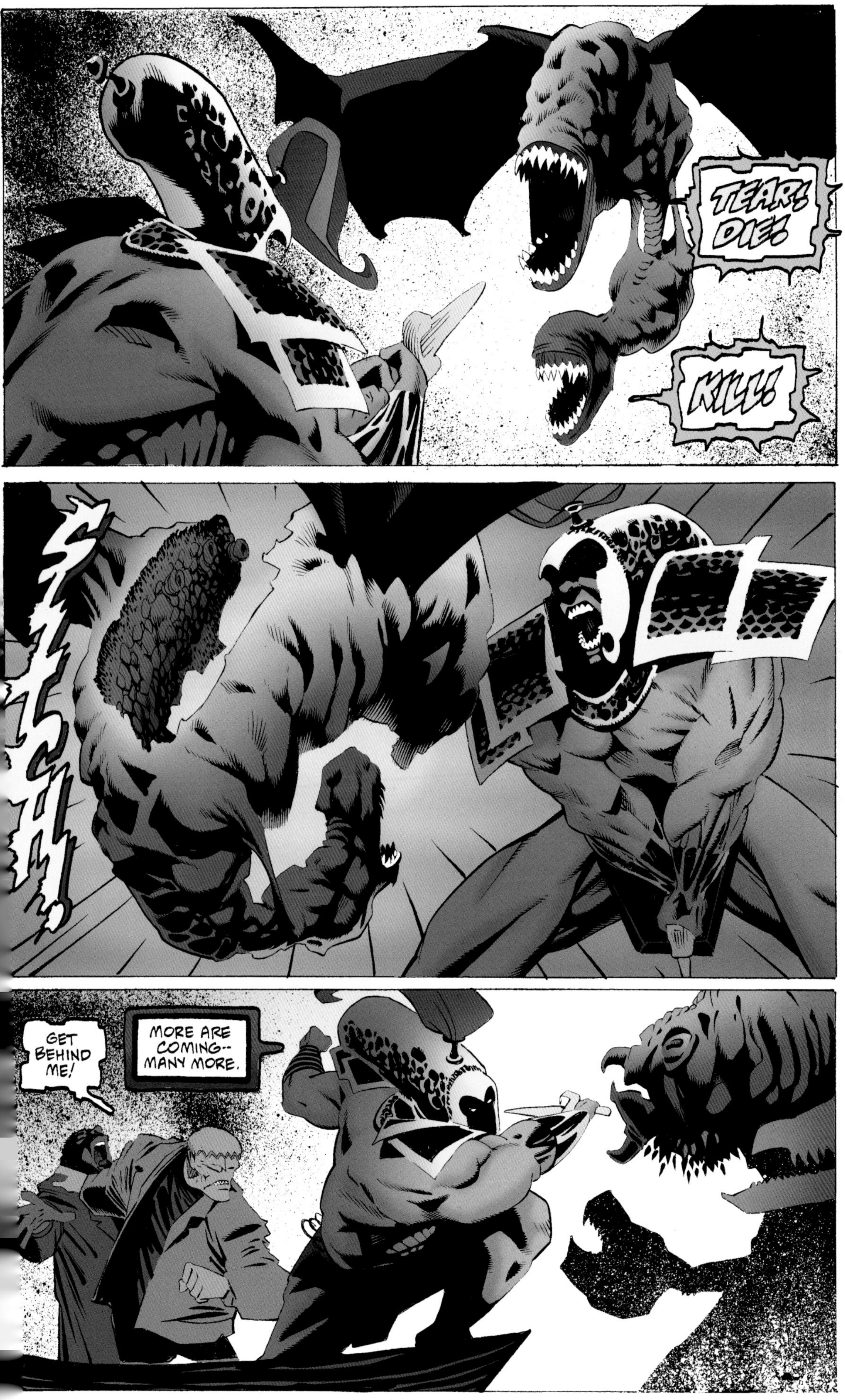

TEAR! DIE!
KILL!
GET BEHIND ME!
MORE ARE COMING-- MANY MORE.

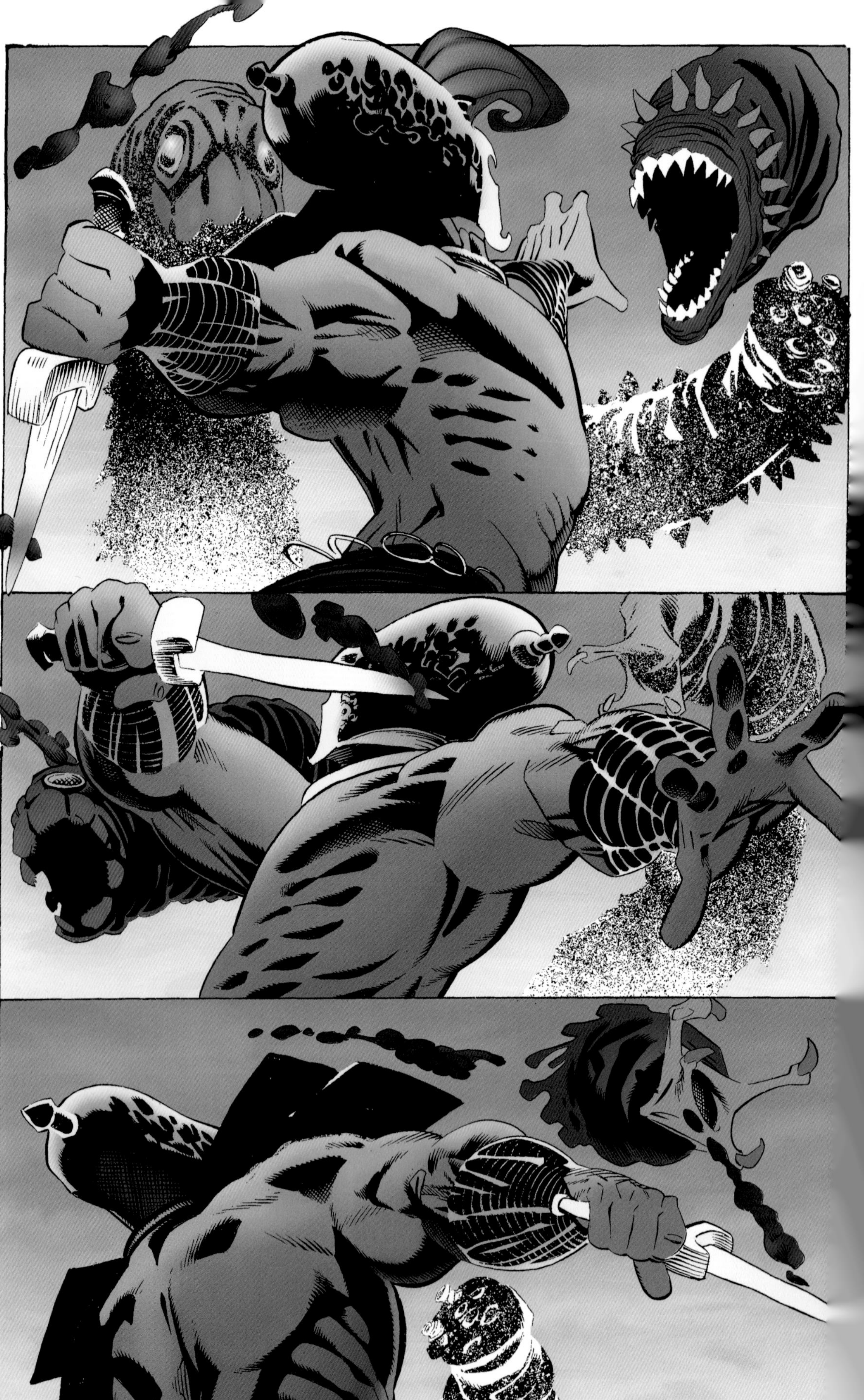

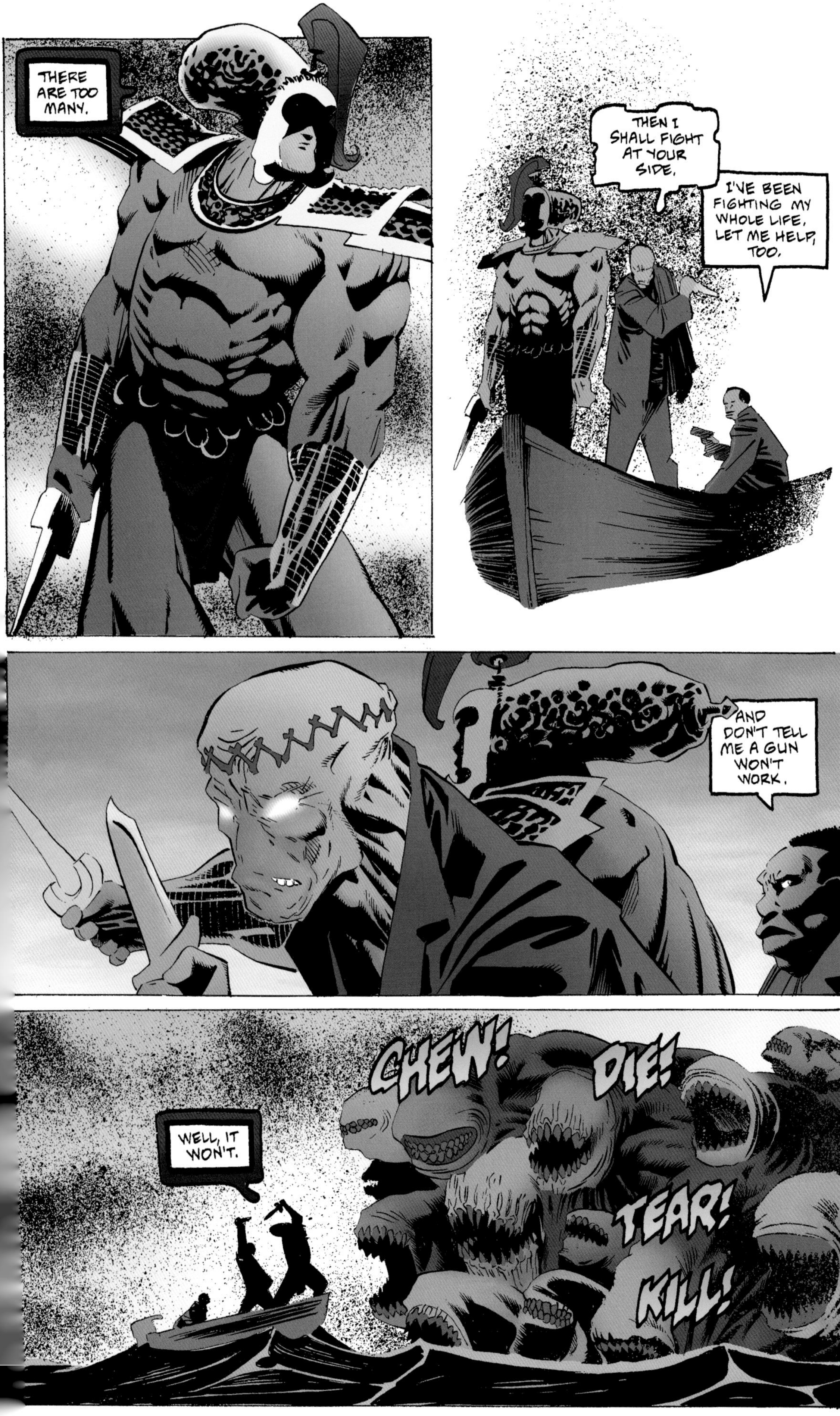
THERE ARE TOO MANY.
THEN I SHALL FIGHT AT YOUR SIDE.
I'VE BEEN FIGHTING MY WHOLE LIFE, LET ME HELP, TOO.
AND DON'T TELL ME A GUN WON'T WORK.
WELL, IT WON'T.
CHEW!
DIE!
TEAR!
KILL!

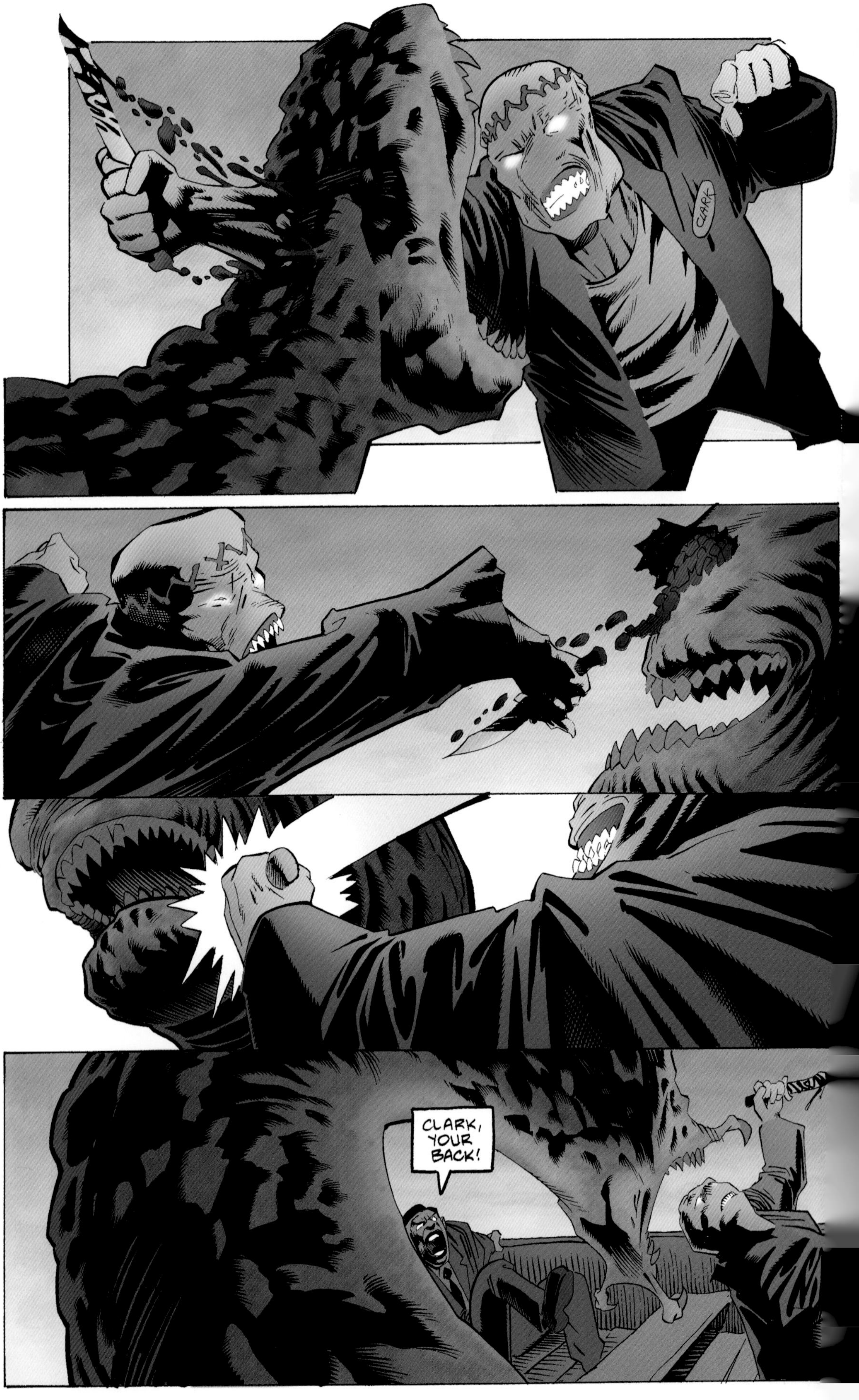
CLARK
CLARK, YOUR BACK!

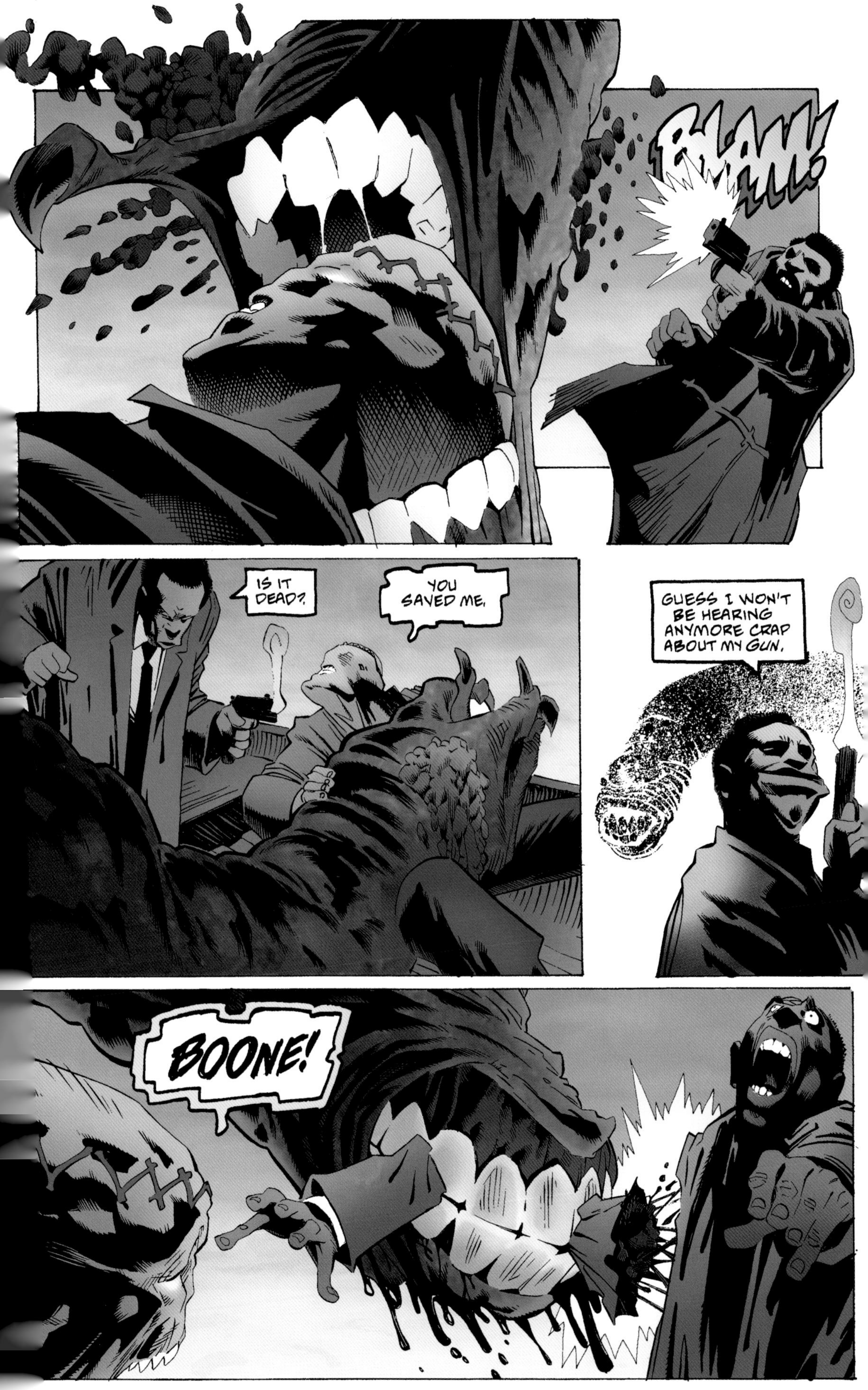
BLAM!
IS IT DEAD?
YOU SAVED ME.
GUESS I WON'T BE HEARING ANYMORE CRAP ABOUT MY GUN.
BOONE!

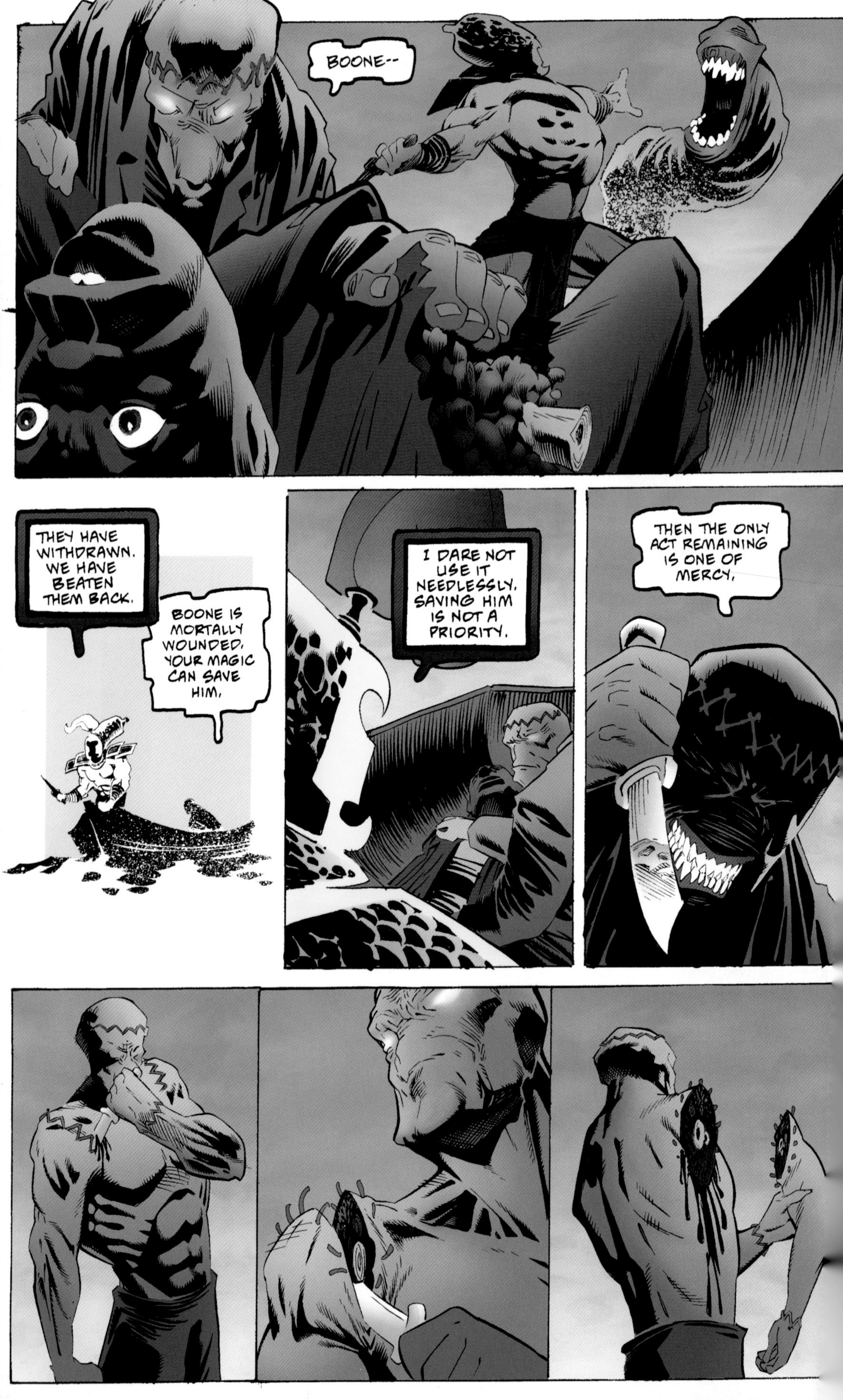
BOONE--
THEY HAVE WITHDRAWN. WE HAVE BEATEN THEM BACK.
BOONE IS MORTALLY WOUNDED. YOUR MAGIC CAN SAVE HIM.
I DARE NOT USE IT NEEDLESSLY. SAVING HIM IS NOT A PRIORITY.
THEN THE ONLY ACT REMAINING IS ONE OF MERCY.

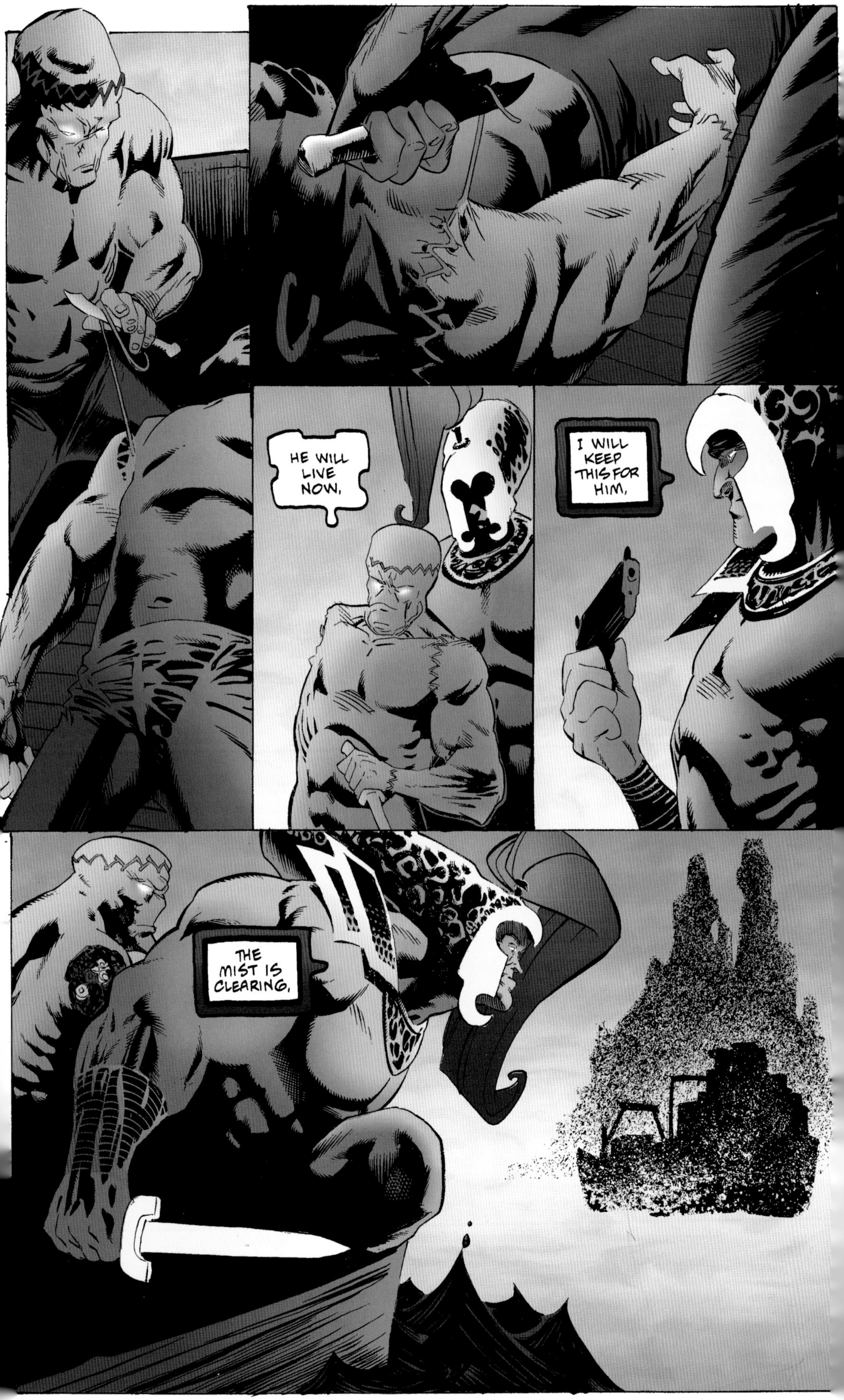
HE WILL LIVE NOW.
I WILL KEEP THIS FOR HIM.
THE MIST IS CLEARING.

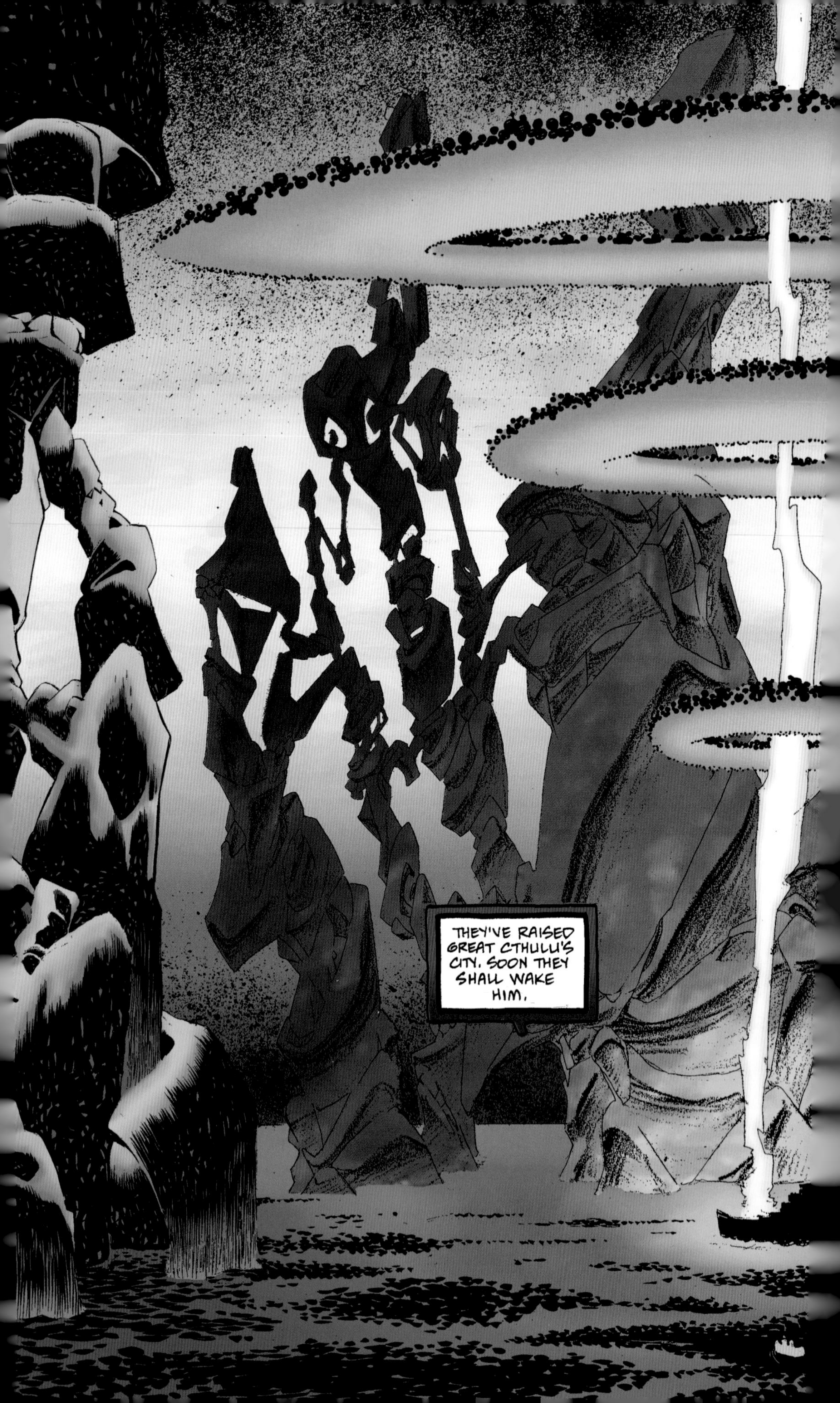
THEY'VE RAISED GREAT CTHULU'S CITY. SOON THEY SHALL WAKE HIM.

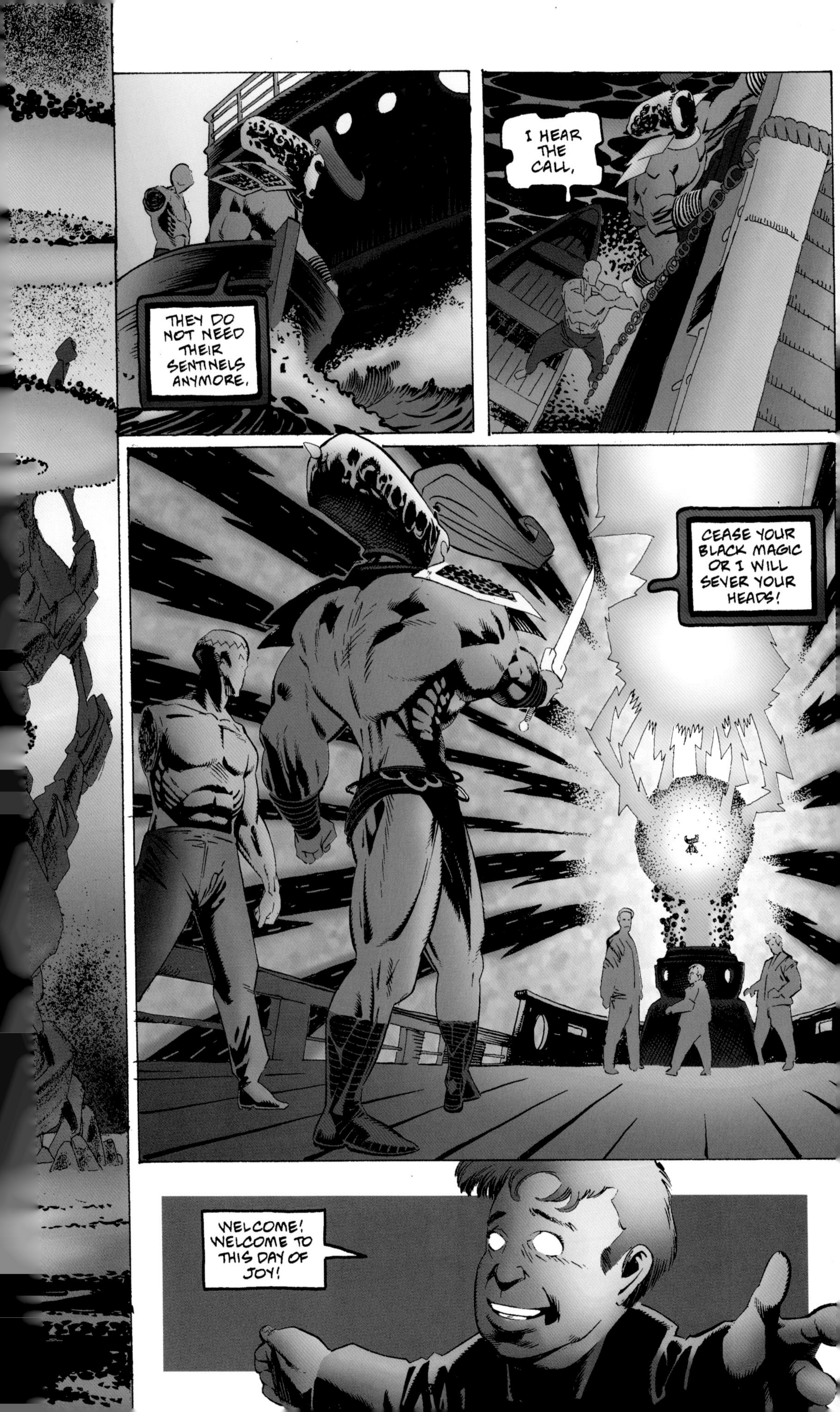

THEY DO NOT NEED THEIR SENTINELS ANYMORE.
I HEAR THE CALL.
CEASE YOUR BLACK MAGIC OR I WILL SEVER YOUR HEADS!
WELCOME! WELCOME TO THIS DAY OF JOY!

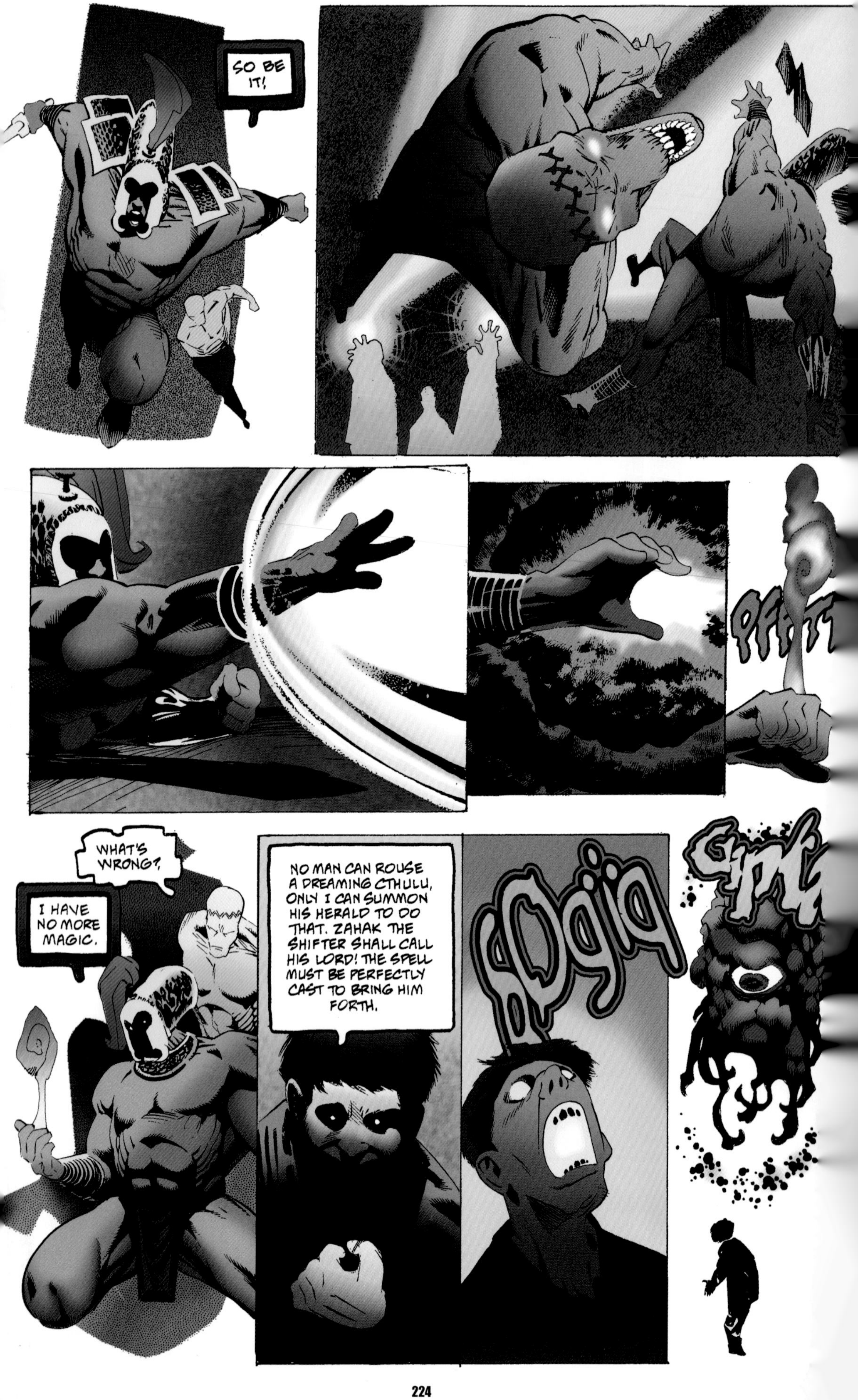
SO BE IT!
WHAT'S WRONG?
I HAVE NO MORE MAGIC.
NO MAN CAN ROUSE A DREAMING CTHULU, ONLY I CAN SUMMON HIS HERALD TO DO THAT. ZAHAK THE SHIFTER SHALL CALL HIS LORD! THE SPELL MUST BE PERFECTLY CAST TO BRING HIM FORTH.

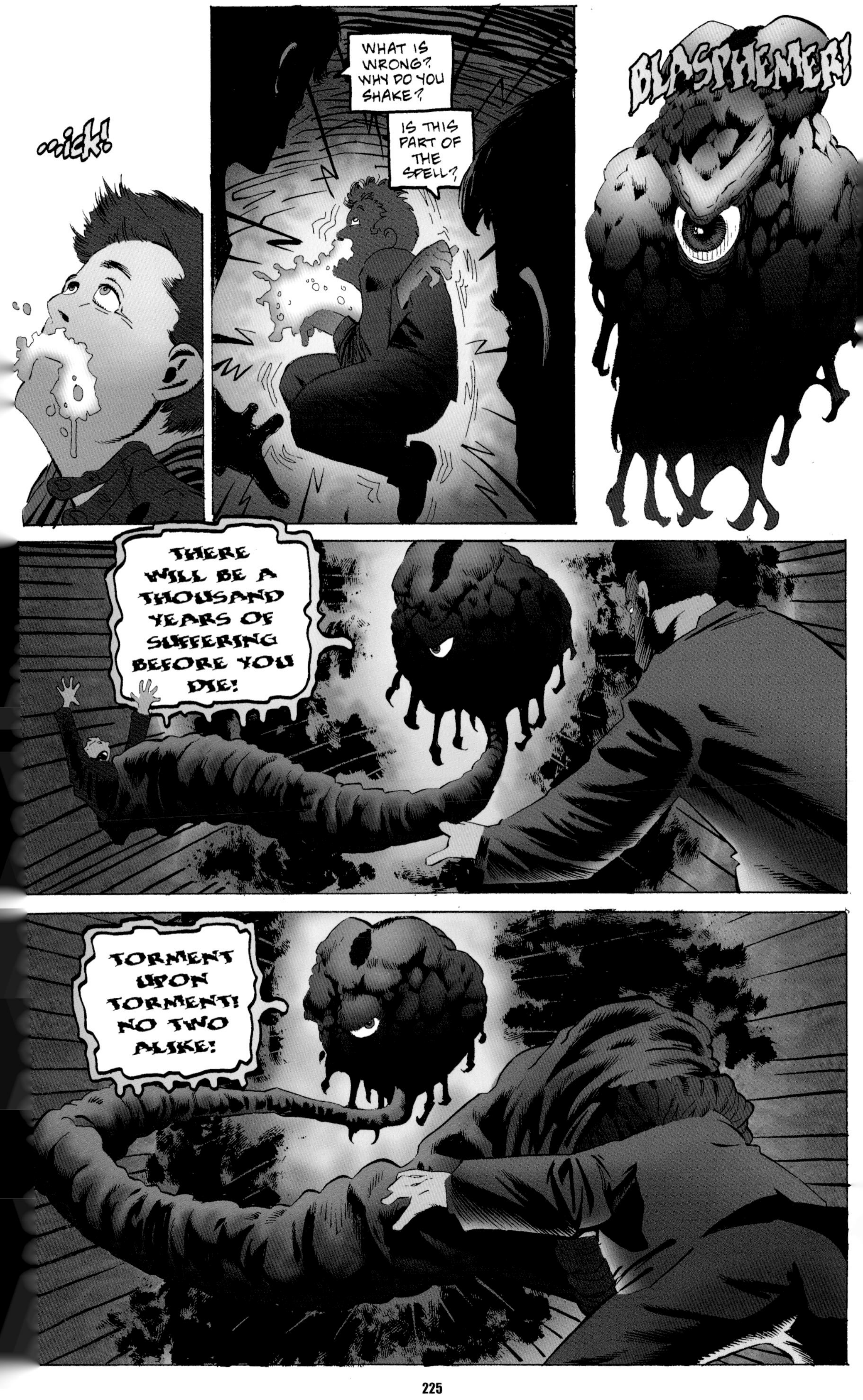
..ick!
WHAT IS WRONG? WHY DO YOU SHAKE?
IS THIS PART OF THE SPELL?
BLASPHEMER!
THERE WILL BE A THOUSAND YEARS OF SUFFERING BEFORE YOU DIE!
TORMENT UPON TORMENT! NO TWO ALIKE!

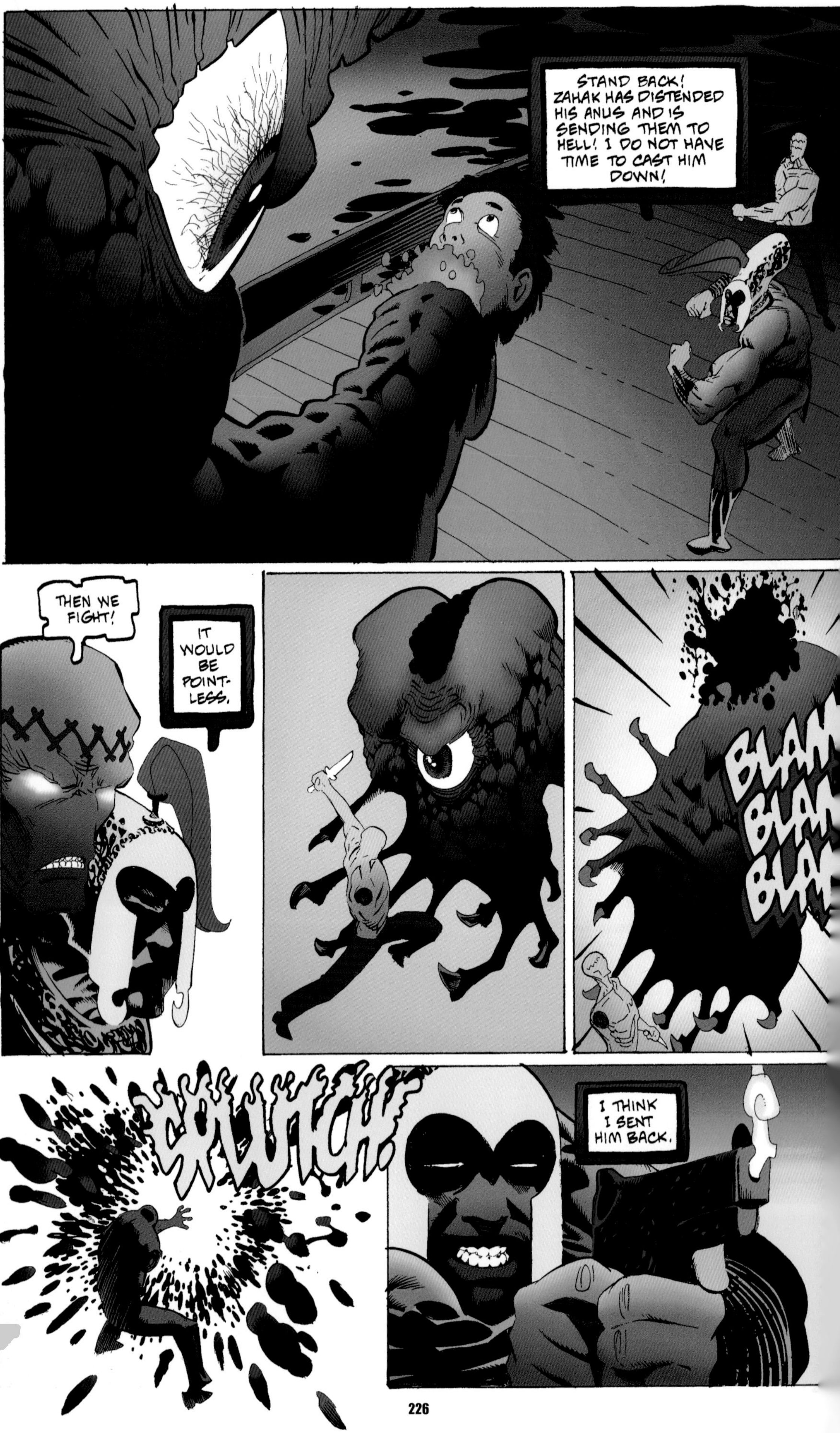
STAND BACK! ZAHAK HAS DISTENDED HIS ANUS AND IS SENDING THEM TO HELL! I DO NOT HAVE TIME TO CAST HIM DOWN!
THEN WE FIGHT!
IT WOULD BE POINTLESS.
BLAM BLAM BLAM
SQUTCH!
I THINK I SENT HIM BACK.

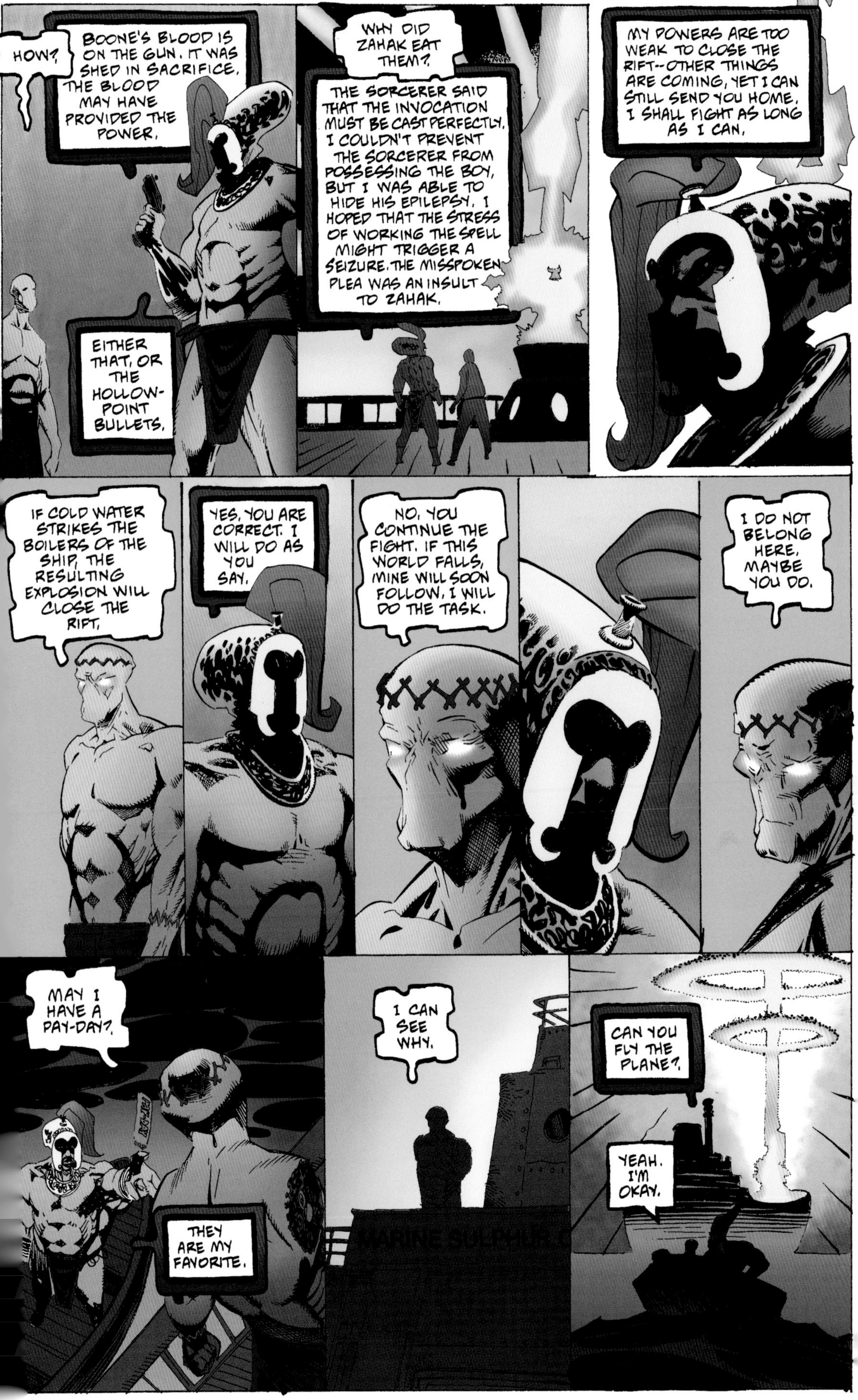
HOW?
BOONE'S BLOOD IS ON THE GUN. IT WAS SHED IN SACRIFICE. THE BLOOD MAY HAVE PROVIDED THE POWER.
EITHER THAT, OR THE HOLLOW-POINT BULLETS.
WHY DID ZAHAK EAT THEM?
THE SORCERER SAID THAT THE INVOCATION MUST BE CAST PERFECTLY. I COULDN'T PREVENT THE SORCERER FROM POSSESSING THE BOY, BUT I WAS ABLE TO HIDE HIS EPILEPSY. I HOPED THAT THE STRESS OF WORKING THE SPELL MIGHT TRIGGER A SEIZURE. THE MISSPOKEN PLEA WAS AN INSULT TO ZAHAK.
MY POWERS ARE TOO WEAK TO CLOSE THE RIFT--OTHER THINGS ARE COMING, YET I CAN STILL SEND YOU HOME. I SHALL FIGHT AS LONG AS I CAN.
IF COLD WATER STRIKES THE BOILERS OF THE SHIP, THE RESULTING EXPLOSION WILL CLOSE THE RIFT.
YES, YOU ARE CORRECT. I WILL DO AS YOU SAY.
NO, YOU CONTINUE THE FIGHT. IF THIS WORLD FALLS, MINE WILL SOON FOLLOW. I WILL DO THE TASK.
I DO NOT BELONG HERE. MAYBE YOU DO.
MAY I HAVE A PAY-DAY?
THEY ARE MY FAVORITE.
I CAN SEE WHY.
MARINE SULPHUR
CAN YOU FLY THE PLANE?
YEAH. I'M OKAY.

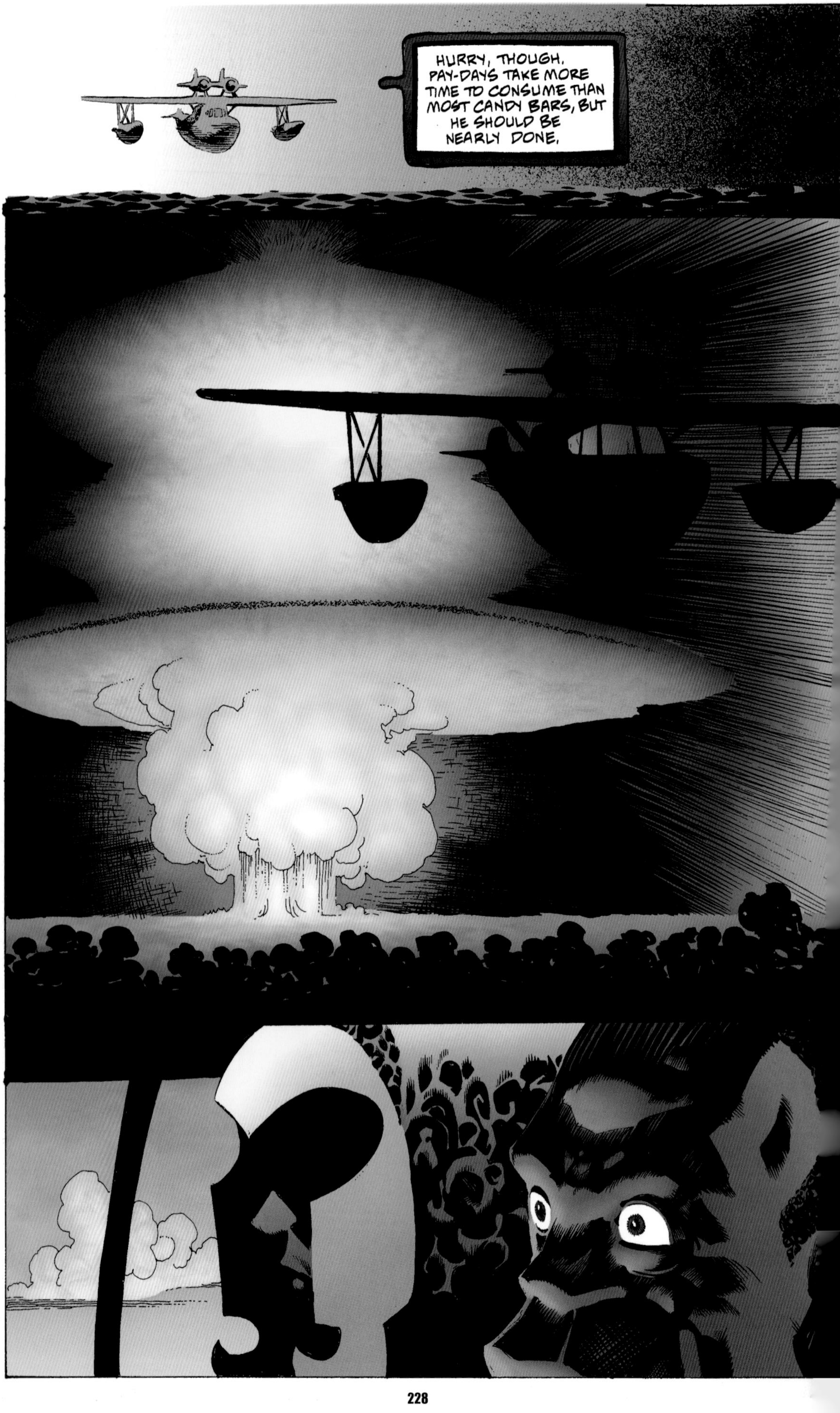
HURRY, THOUGH. PAY-DAYS TAKE MORE TIME TO CONSUME THAN MOST CANDY BARS, BUT HE SHOULD BE NEARLY DONE.

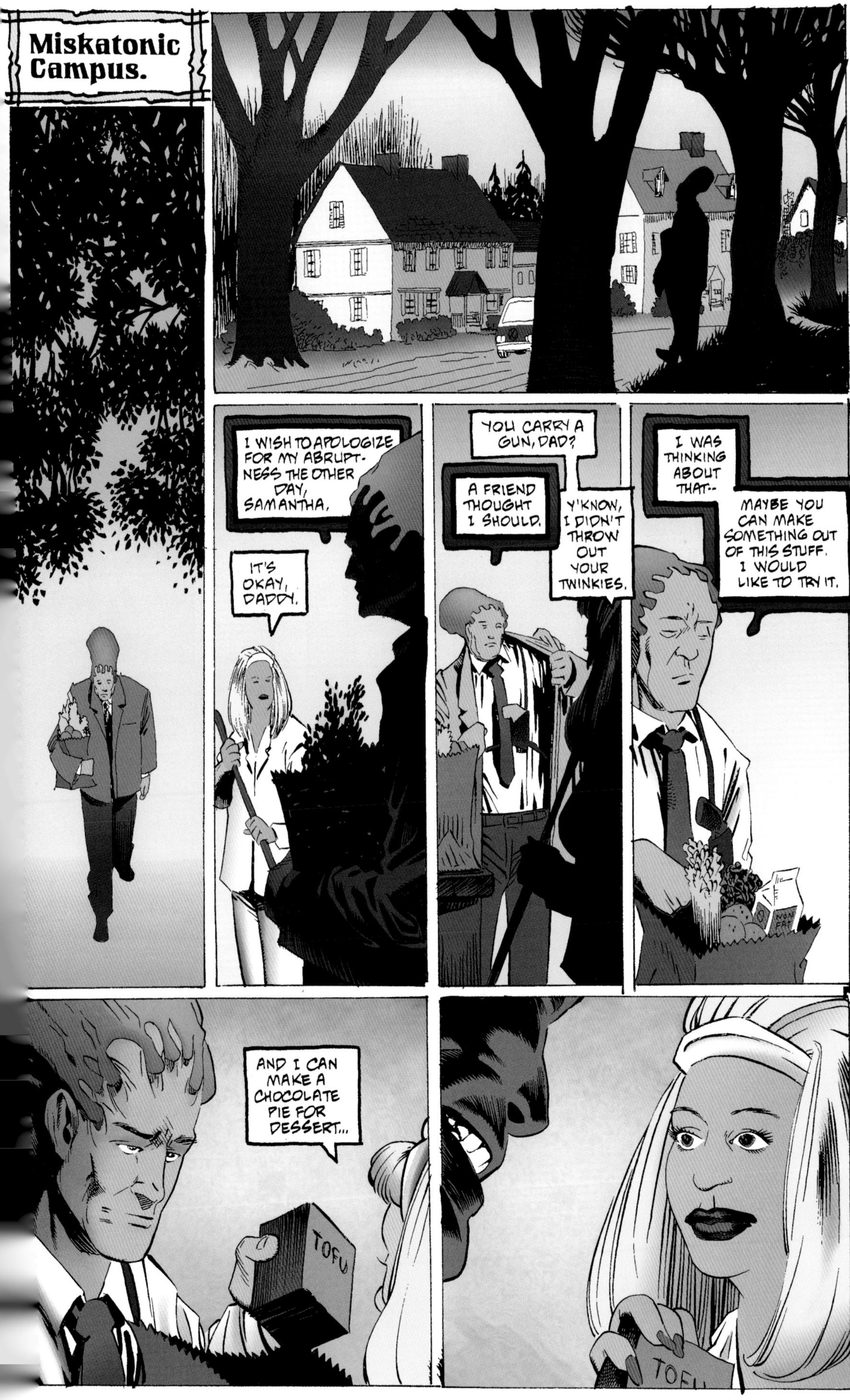
Miskatonic Campus.
I WISH TO APOLOGIZE FOR MY ABRUPTNESS THE OTHER DAY, SAMANTHA.
IT'S OKAY, DADDY.
YOU CARRY A GUN, DAD?
A FRIEND THOUGHT I SHOULD.
Y'KNOW, I DIDN'T THROW OUT YOUR TWINKIES.
I WAS THINKING ABOUT THAT--
MAYBE YOU CAN MAKE SOMETHING OUT OF THIS STUFF. I WOULD LIKE TO TRY IT.
NON FAT
AND I CAN MAKE A CHOCOLATE PIE FOR DESSERT...
TOFU
TOFU

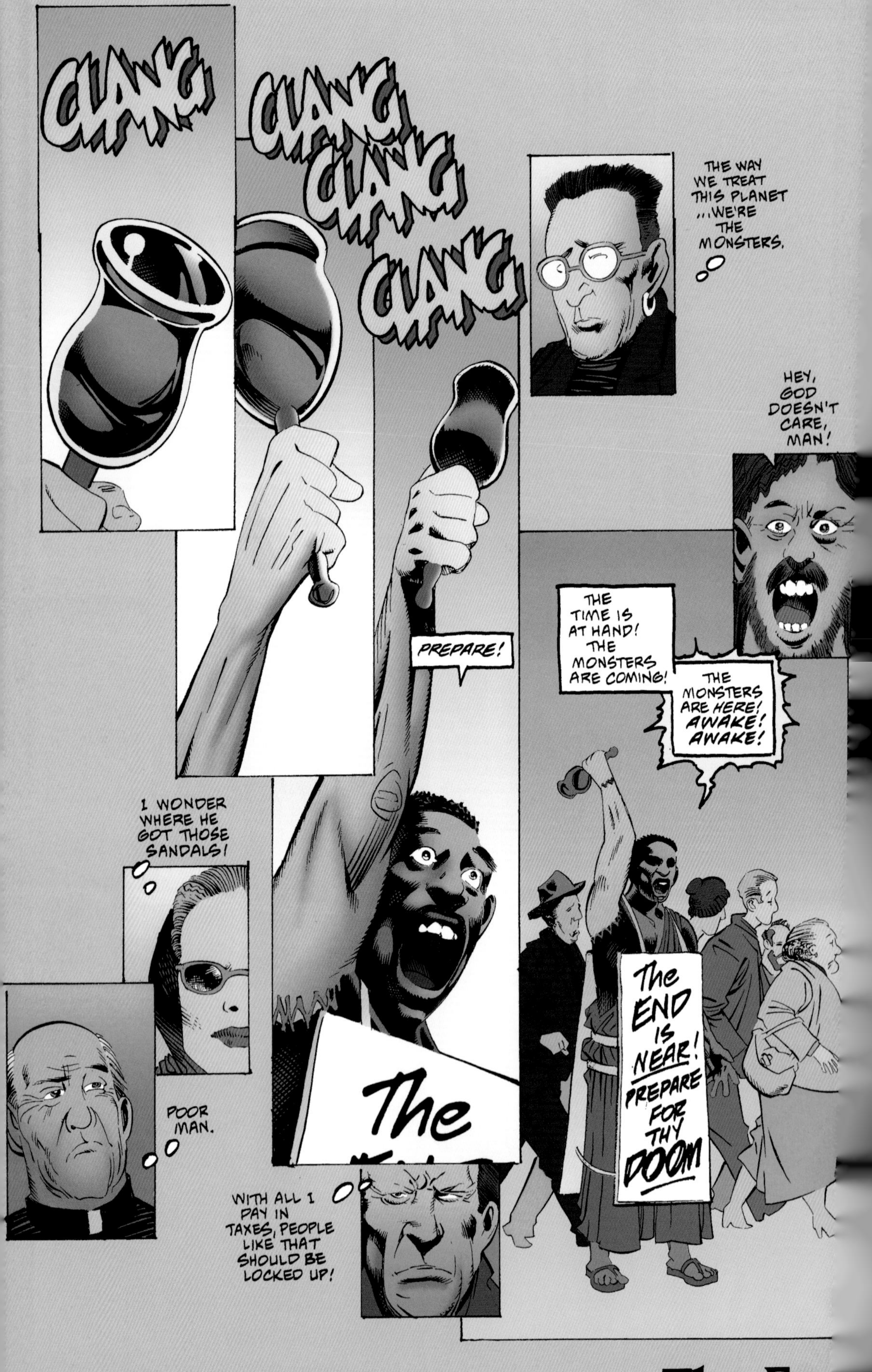

CLANG
CLANG
CLANG
CLANG
THE WAY WE TREAT THIS PLANET ...WE'RE THE MONSTERS.
HEY, GOD DOESN'T CARE, MAN!
PREPARE!
THE TIME IS AT HAND! THE MONSTERS ARE COMING!
THE MONSTERS ARE HERE! AWAKE! AWAKE!
I WONDER WHERE HE GOT THOSE SANDALS!
The
The END is NEAR! PREPARE FOR THY DOOM
POOR MAN.
WITH ALL I PAY IN TAXES, PEOPLE LIKE THAT SHOULD BE LOCKED UP!

The En

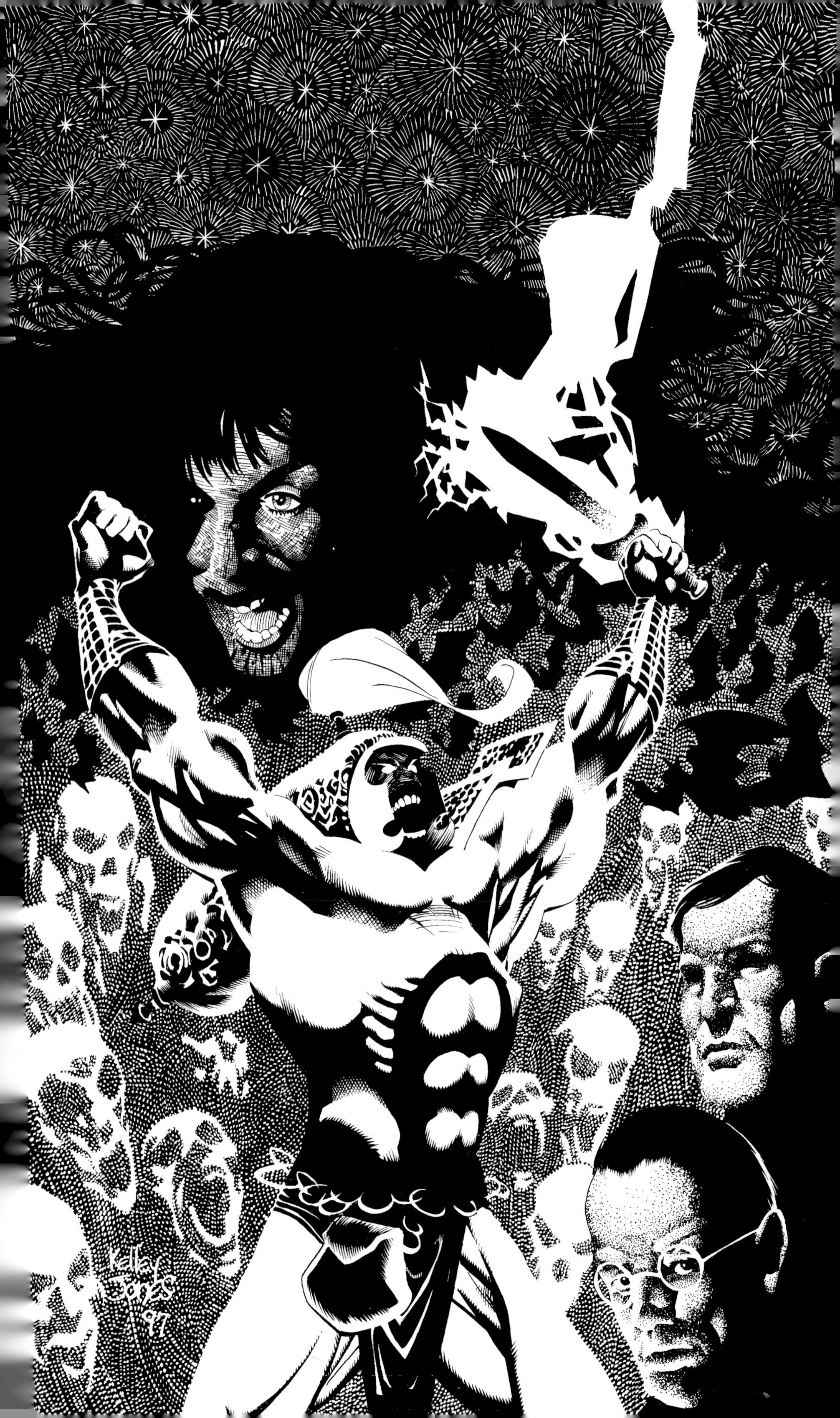
Kelley Jones '97

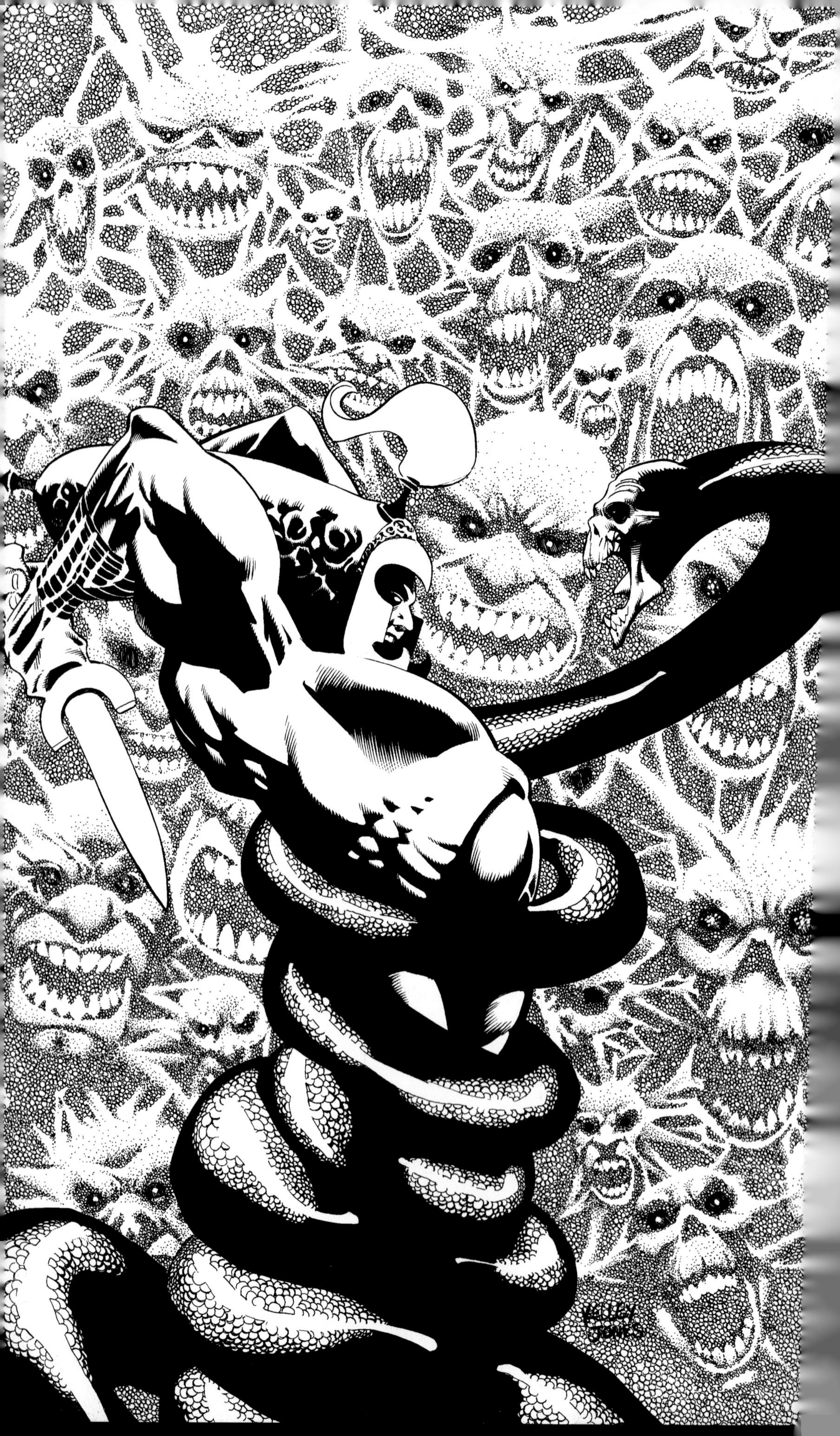

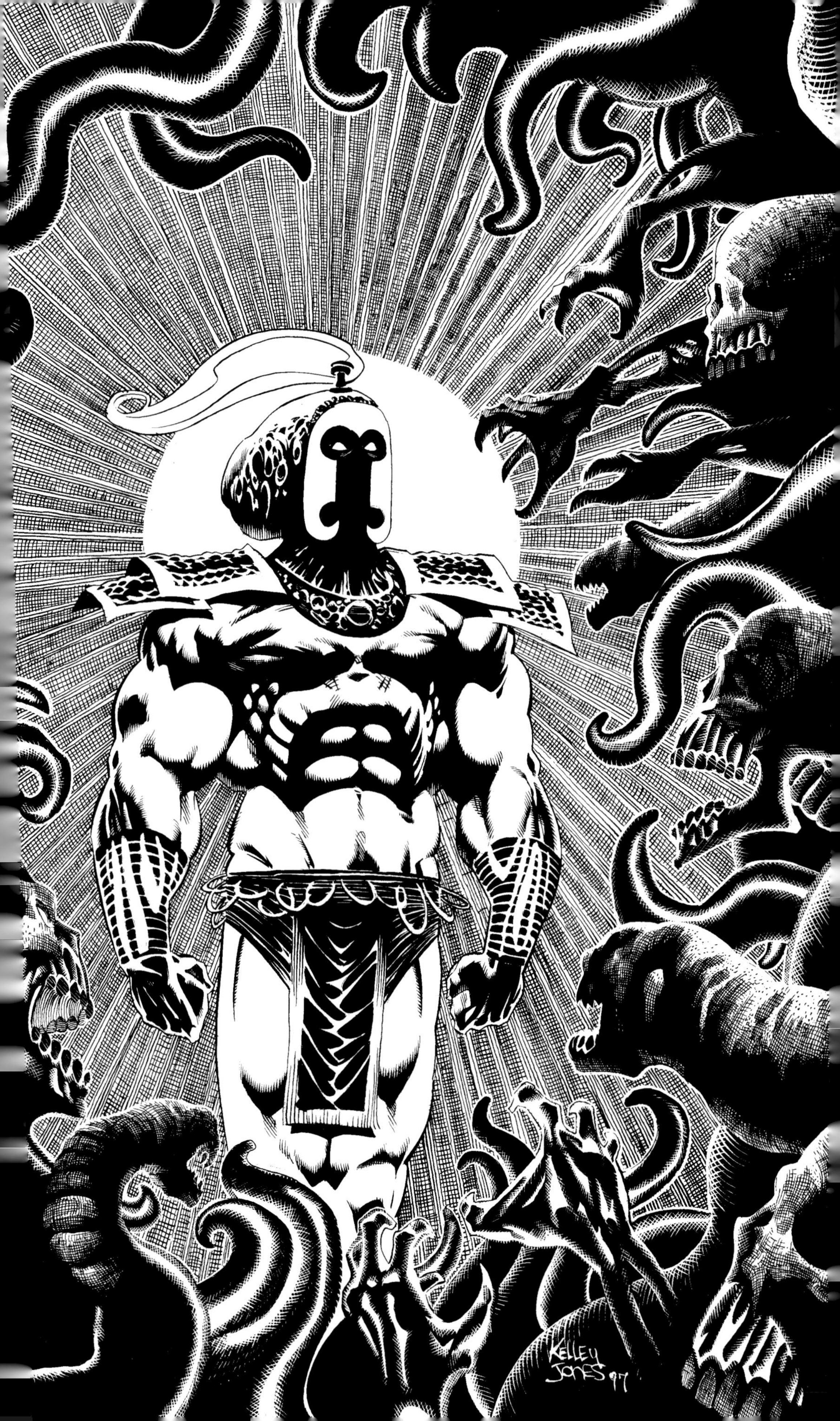
KELLEY JONES '97

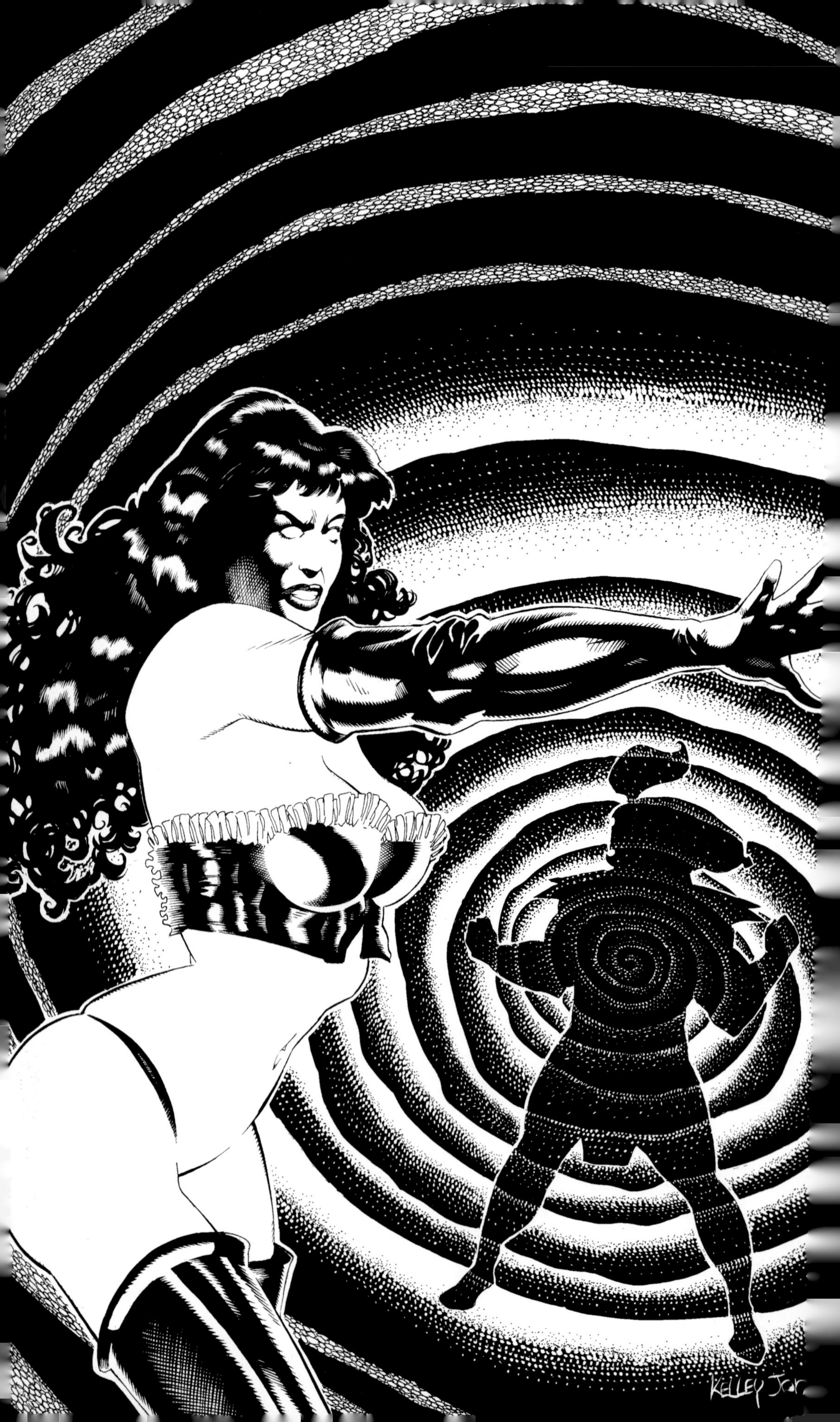
KELLEY Jon

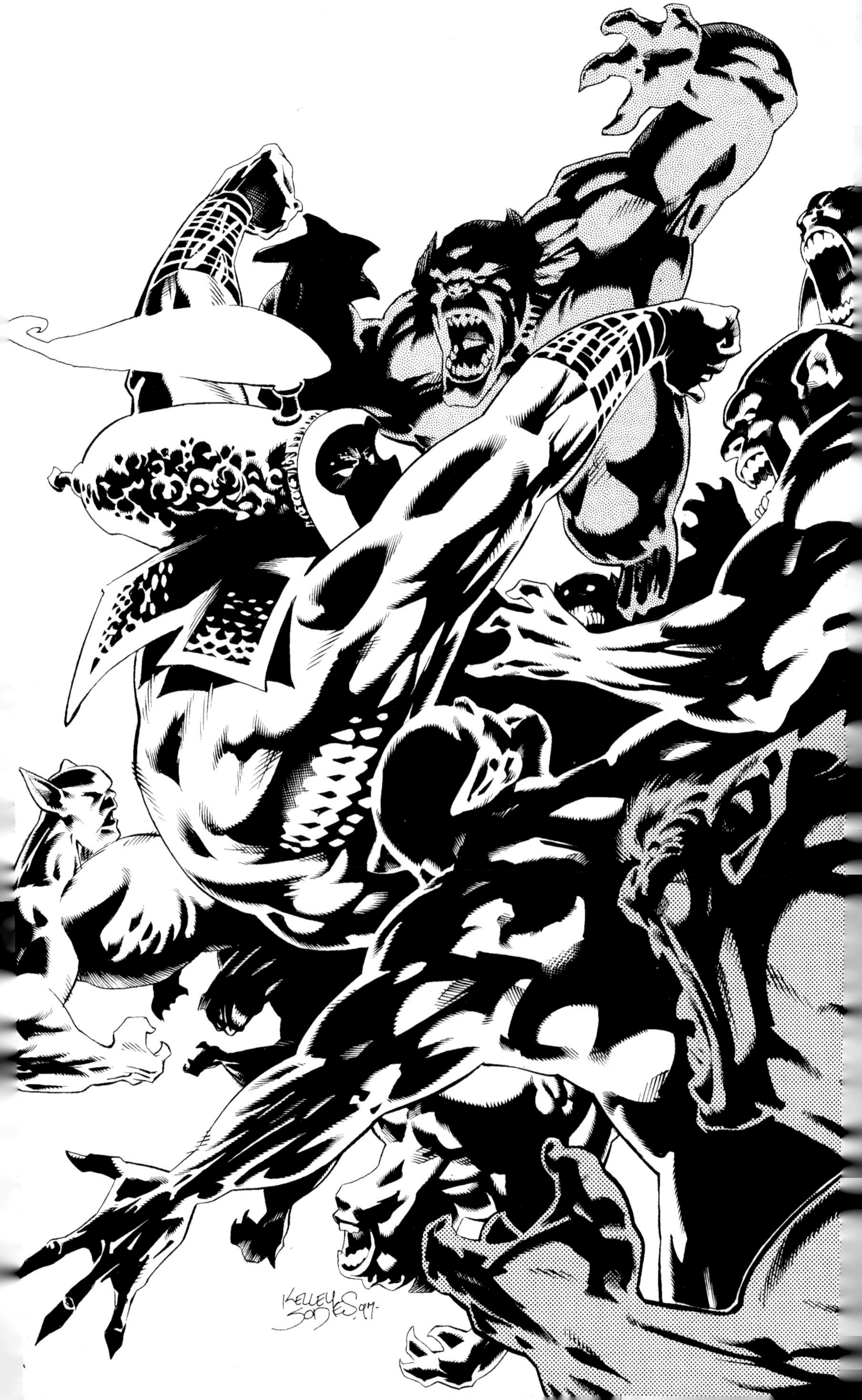

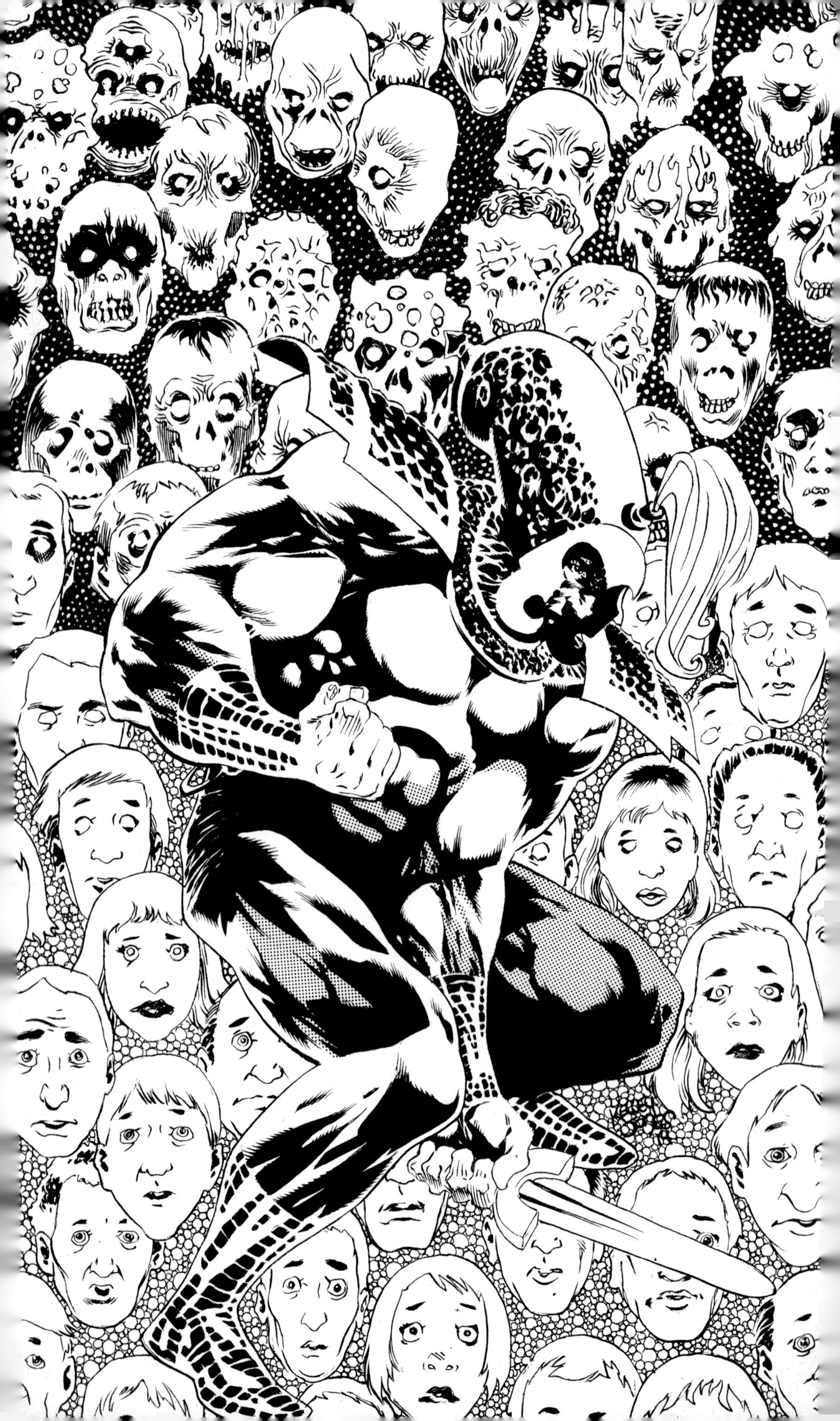